God in AIDS?

God in AIDS?

A Theological Enquiry

Ronald Nicolson

SCM PRESS LTD

Copyright © Ronald Nicolson 1996

0 334 02641 5

First published 1996 by
SCM Press Ltd
9–17 St Albans Place, London N1 0NX

Typeset at The Spartan Press Ltd, Lymington, Hants

Printed in Great Britain by
Biddles Ltd, Guildford and King's Lynn

Contents

Preface

My wife Gail is really responsible for this book. She prodded me out of my comfortable assumptions that the AIDS crisis was exaggerated and had nothing to do with me and insisted that I think about it seriously. This book is dedicated to her with my love.

Thinking about AIDS seriously took me to other parts of Africa where AIDS has cast its shadow, and to the United States and England where AIDS care is more advanced. A number of people made this journey possible. The University of Natal allowed me generous study leave. The Centre for Science Development (Human Sciences Research Council, South Africa) provided a financial grant. Opinions expressed in this book and conclusions arrived at are, of course, mine and are not necessarily to be attributed to the Centre for Science Development. The Centre for South South Relations invited me to join a group visiting Uganda and Tanzania to see church work with AIDS there. This was a paradigm-shifting experience for me. Bishop Hays Rockwell made it possible for me to spend time in the United States, opening many doors for me. He and his wife Linda made us comfortable in their home for several months, adding to their long list of generous acts to us and to the church in South Africa. Dean Michael Allen of Christ Church Cathedral in St Louis and members of the Cathedral community made us feel part of the Cathedral and made it possible for me to spend time with a number of men with AIDS and to be part of AIDS support groups and healing ministries. The University of St Louis generously provided an office in which I could study and have access to their library and very considerable periodical collection. I am grateful to Professors William Shea and Richard Valantasis for the warmth of their welcome there. I also thank my daughter Monica who gave us the use of her flat in London.

In London people in a number of organizations like ACET,

CARA, Caritas, Catholic AIDS Link, London Lighthouse, the London Ecumenical AIDS Trust, the Terrence Higgins Trust and several others all found time to talk to me when I turned up, unknown and from a far country, on their doorstep. The Revd Dr Anne Bayley was particularly helpful to me. All of these people, like the medical missionaries in Africa and the counsellors from TASO, who give their lives working for people with AIDS rather than merely writing about them, put me to humble shame.

Most especially, though, the book was made possible by the many people living with the virus or with full-blown AIDS and by their families and partners who were so generously willing to see me not as a voyeur but as someone wanting to learn from them. Some of them meet their situation with gallant gaiety (in the old and new sense of the word), some with quiet acceptance, some – especially those whom I met in Africa in the last stages of AIDS receiving minimal medical assistance – with uncomplaining faith. I am sure there are also some who are bitter and who react in ways destructive of themselves and those around them, but I never met any. I have tried to say in the book that people living with AIDS are the prophets and pioneers of a new way of understanding the human life and spirit. I have used the experiences of many of them in this book but in every case names and identifying details have been altered.

Things change fast. It is just possible, though not, I think, very likely, that an affordable cure for AIDS and vaccine against the virus may have been found by the time this book is published. Even if that is so, however, the insights which we get from AIDS are insights for all people in all situations. AIDS brings us back from the self-centred, self-confident views of human life which grew in the late second millennium, to a new humility and interdependence which hopefully may mark the beginning of the third.

Introduction

Every now and then something comes along which changes the way we think about everything. In January 1995 a major earthquake occurred in Kobe, Japan. Earthquakes are to be expected in Japan; but Japanese seismologists were confident that they could predict them in time to give warning. Japanese architects were confident that they had designed reasonably safe buildings should an earthquake occur. Nevertheless, the earthquake occurred where it was not expected, and much more structural damage took place than had been believed possible. More than 4000 people were killed, and a quarter of a million lost their homes.

Perhaps we could draw the conclusion that the Japanese were being taught a lesson in humility. An overconfident twentieth-century humanity reaching the end of the millennium, overweening in its pride about technological mastery of the universe, had to be taught that after all only God is really in control, that our powers are as nothing before the mysterious omnipotence of the divinity. After all, the theories of the Deists, an English theological school of the seventeenth and eighteenth centuries which preferred to trust in human reason rather than the mysteries of supernatural revelation, were largely abandoned after another earthquake, the one in Lisbon in 1755 in which 60,000 people died. The earthquake in Kobe might be seen to be God's way of recalling our own generation to faith.

I hope, though, that we should draw no such conclusion. It is not altogether true that twentieth-century *fin de siècle* humans are over-confident about human reason and human technocracy. We are no longer like the Victorians. We no longer think that industry, science and Western civilization can save the world, or that we have all the answers. A century of terrible wars and genocide, post-colonial guilt, post-modernism in the arts, and chaos theory in science,[1] have brought an end to all of that. Many modern people live in a period of profound uncertainty and lack of confidence. They do not expect technology or human wisdom to bring contentment.

In any case, a God who brought low our *hybris* by killing thousands of perfectly ordinary Japanese people is not a God whom we would choose to love. We might fear him. We would probably try to propitiate his wrath. But we would not adore such a God. The victims of the Kobe earthquake did not need to be humbled. They were not the politicians or scientists, sociologists or philosophers who might be held responsible for the sin of pride. They were, as usual, mostly the poorest part of the population. A triumphalist theology which emphasized the power of God rather than the love of God would be a very inappropriate theology.

So instead, the earthquake in Japan might drive us to a number of different responses.

• We might abandon belief in providence and divinity altogether on the grounds that a God who loved people would not permit earthquakes. But then we should also be abandoning much from our tradition that is rich in potency of hope in troubled times.

• Since for most of us who are not Japanese it happened to a far-away people with whom we have few ties of kith and kin, we might quite probably not respond at all. But that would be a diminishment of our true humanity.

• Or we might see it as an event which binds us together in some degree of common human concern but which also causes us to think again about all the assumptions we have made in the past, not only about earthquakes but about God. We would then not necessarily abandon all of our past assumptions, but after such a cataclysmic event we would need to see them from a new point of view.

This is a process which happens all the time. Our theological constructs change over the ages as our situation and context changes. We have become aware that in the Bible itself there are different strands or layers of theology. Early Jewish belief that

[1]Chaos theory holds that sometimes things behave unpredictably even though they obey well-understood physical laws. This is because a very tiny variable may have enormous consequences.

Yahweh loved only the descendants of Abraham and had chosen them to inhabit the promised land, thus enabling them with good conscience to invade and colonize the land of Israel (e.g. Joshua 1. 2–6), gave way to the universalism of the later prophets and their vision that all nations would be brought to share in the peace and the blessings of God (e.g. Isaiah 60.3). In this newer vision, Israel's role was not to be specially blessed with prosperity but to be specially privileged with carrying God's word to the Gentiles.

There are many other examples of changing theological convictions even in the New Testament. The early Christians believed that Jesus would return to earth almost immediately (Romans 13. 11–12). When this did not happen, the evangelists recast Jesus' stories, to teach that the church should be faithful in waiting for the bridegroom no matter how long he tarried (Luke 12. 35–40). Long after the biblical canon was finally accepted, the long and fruitful tension between Bible and 'tradition' ensured that Christianity continued to develop and change, all the while retaining some thread linking it with what had been handed down from the past, yet evolving as the context and the needs changed.

Though the battles between orthodox and revisionary 'heretics' could sometimes be bitter, changes continued to take place slowly and inevitably. In the twelfth century, Hugh of St Victor could seriously assert that God ordained that there should be evil in the world. Thus Christians, predestined to salvation, should know how fortunate they were to have received God's choice as they contemplated the sufferings of the damned. Such views did not seem scandalous then, but no theologian would even entertain such an idea now. It is not just a matter of different generations. Even those living in the same period of time do not always come to the same conclusions. In any era, people have different needs and live in different contexts. The theories of Hugh of St Victor have been universally cast aside, but we are not universally agreed on any one view of salvation in our own time.

Sometimes, like the Deists with the Lisbon earthquake, people witness something so big happening that a universal 'paradigm shift' or way of seeing things must take place. Things which were taken for granted cannot be taken for granted any longer. Long-held concepts, often held unconsciously, must be looked at again from a new perspective. The Flood, the Slavery in Egypt, the Captivity in Babylon, were all events of this kind. So was the period of persecution in the church. Above all for the first Christians, the death of Jesus and the unexpected experience of his presence after his death was an event which reshaped their Jewish theology.

For modern Jews the holocaust is a paradigm-changing event like this. Richard Rubenstein has suggested that for Jews the experience of the holocaust has made it impossible to go on believing in the same old ways.

'The destruction of the European Jews . . . has yet to be apprehended fully by the men and women whose values have been shaped by the religious and cultural heritage of Western civilization. Such comprehension may never be achieved . . . One of the most constant questions elicited by the holocaust has been whether the event could in any way be consistent with the Judeao-Christian faith' (Rubenstein 1992:81).

I suggest that in the present time the Human Immunodeficiency Virus and the consequent AIDS Related Complex and full-blown AIDS[2] are another such event. A columnist in a respected Roman Catholic journal writes:

'It is entirely possible that we members of the church are facing the greatest challenge to mature discipleship since Jesus walked among us' (Ryan 1988).

A columnist in another journal says

'A new page of church history will be written about AIDS' (Gamble 1989:3).

[2]Use of the term AIDS Related Complex to indicate a mid-way point between HIV infection when there is still no experience of illness, and full-blown AIDS when the person is seriously ill and will soon die, is debateable (Sontag 1989:31, Landau-Stanton and Clements 1993). Some medical experts now prefer to avoid the term, since they wish us to realize quite clearly that ARC is merely a stage on the inevitable path to full-blown AIDS. Other medical experts object, saying that it is still not proven that all those with AIDS-related complexes will inevitably get sicker and die. In this book, in order to keep things simple, we shall use the term AIDS to mean any experience of sickness as a result of the virus.

Or to quote the Catholic bishops of Uganda, we must see the AIDS epidemic as:

' . . . a phenomenon which constitutes a special time in salvation history' (Catholic Bishops of Uganda 1989:291).

If they are right, AIDS is an event which projects us into a *kairos*, a time of decision, testing and change after which nothing will be the same any more. *Kairos* is understood in the Bible as a critical time in human history, a time when God's purposes and the human response to God's purposes are brought into sharp focus.

But why make AIDS so important? Many more people die of motor accidents in the United States than of AIDS. More women die of breast cancer. In the Third World, widely though AIDS has spread, it is still not the greatest killer. More children die of tuberculosis than of AIDS (*The Economist* 1991:32).

In fact it is very important not to exaggerate the scale of AIDS or to 'privilege' AIDS above other diseases. AIDS is only an intense focus for theological issues that are universally with us. The death from AIDS of Rock Hudson as a famous star of the screen, or of Arthur Ashe as a well-known sports person is not more horrible than the death of an unknown woman whose breast cancer remained undiagnosed until too late because of inadequate health care facilities. The fame of many of those who have died of AIDS, and the fact that, in the West at least, so many of them have been artists, sportsmen and writers, may have helped publicize AIDS, but it does not mean that AIDS matters more. There is some truth in Ian Hislop's allegation (the editor of *Private Eye*) that AIDS receives so much publicity because it gave ' . . . the first experience of death to a generation of thirty something' (*The Independent on Sunday*, 11 June 1995).

AIDS death is a very terrible death, often involving blindness and dementia, and is nearly always the death of someone who should still be in the prime of his or her life; but it is no more tragic than any other young death. People with AIDS deserve as much, but not more, love and support as people with any terminal illness.

Betty is a Zimbabwean who has recently come to live in Britain. She has now been diagnosed as HIV positive, although she is not yet seriously ill.

Nevertheless, her T-cell count is now low enough for her to qualify for a
housing allowance, which has enabled her to leave her lodgings. She is
also eligible for assistance towards a car, which has enabled her to trade
in her old car and buy a newer model. She has no intention of returning
to Zimbabwe, where her benefits would be less.

Betty's case is both sad and worrying. It is sad that she has
contracted AIDS. It is worrisome because the fact that she has AIDS
opens up for her a range of benefits that she would not receive for
another illness. AIDS is for her simultaneously a tragedy and a way
of access to some financial benefit. Jesse Jackson, addressing a
gathering of American homosexual persons, said

> 'Gay health issues, such as a cure for AIDS, *are* important. But I
> suggest to you . . . that when you give life you gain life. If there is a
> commitment to health care for *whatever* the disease, based upon
> need and not upon wealth or class – then within health care is
> encompassed the issue of AIDS. AIDS is not the only disease in
> the nation tonight. Be concerned about AIDS, but also sickle-cell.
> Never let it be said that you are a one-agenda, self-centred,
> narcissistic movement' (quoted Fumento 1990:331).

It is important to say this because AIDS has been well documented. Moving books about AIDS win literary awards (Verghese 1994,
Monette 1988, Shilts 1987). The books are the more moving
because Monette and Shilts are now dead from AIDS-related
illnesses. The cinema too has given us powerful films on AIDS –
Shilts' book, and *Philadelphia*. The artistic emphasis on AIDS arises
partly because so many from that community have died from it.
People in the Third World often have no access to books or films.
Those who die of tuberculosis or malaria or just from starvation
do not have talented and well-known lovers to write their stories;
but their stories are important just the same. If we do not acknowledge this, we imply that the suffering of ordinary people does not
matter.

It is also important to keep AIDS in proper perspective because
the issue can get misrepresented for political propagandist purposes.
There are many dread diseases in our world. The decision to focus
on AIDS, the definition of AIDS as an epidemic or pandemic, is a
decision made by persons in authority for political reasons, perhaps

reflecting their disapproval of what they see as aberrant life-styles and their agenda of reinforcing a more traditional sexual ethic (Singer 1989:53), or perhaps conversely reflecting that men count for more than women.

The response to corrections of the Shearson Lehman report in 1990 illustrates how political agendas can affect AIDS forecasts. This report estimated that up to 67 million people in Europe and America would die of AIDS. But this estimate is now conceded to be far too high and can probably be halved (Cohen 1994:1374). It was based on the obviously incorrect assumption that all homosexual men are sexually active. It was also assumed that AIDS would soon spread in the heterosexual community as quickly as in the homosexual. Alarmist future projections were made. Almost everyone, we were led to believe, was at risk for AIDS. But this has not proved true.

'Significant inroads [of heterosexual AIDS] into more prosperous areas have been slow' (Rothenburg 1993).

Michael Fumento suggests that the risk of contracting AIDS through heterosexual sex has been overplayed,[3] considering the very small number of cases of this kind in the United States (Fumento 1990:32, see also Young 1993). Among the general population,

' . . . that section the media and the public health authorities has tried desperately to terrify, there is no epidemic. Most heterosexuals will continue to have more to fear from bathtub drowning than from AIDS' (Fumento 1990:32).

When it became clear that the projections were not coming true, and that AIDS was not in fact spreading in the heterosexual

[3]Although it is true that in Europe and North America not many people contract AIDS heterosexuallly, and that it is unlikely that a person who does not have many partners will contract the virus, this does not mean that a heterosexual person who is not very active sexually and does not use intravenous drugs cannot contract AIDS. It must also be remembered that a number of homosexual men also have sexual intercourse with women (Dixon 1990:26). Anyone who has sexual intercourse with a partner who has HIV can contract the virus.

community except in certain specific groups, those who pointed this out were accused of homophobia. They were accused of implying that only homosexuals were promiscuous. Or they were accused of irresponsibility in undermining attempts at AIDS education. Stephen Joseph, Commissioner of Health for New York in 1987, tells of how difficult it was to get people to listen to the revised estimates.

'The state was suggesting that every American was equally vulnerable to AIDS. In fact, precisely the opposite is true' (Joseph 1992:162).

For various reasons AIDS forecasts are influenced by politics. Fumento alleges that homosexual pressure groups were anxious that the authorities should perceive AIDS as a problem which affected the whole American population and not just homosexuals. These groups were thus resistant to findings which suggested that the issue in America was primarily a homosexual one. They feared that any such perception would reduce the amount of money which federal and state authorities would invest in AIDS cure and AIDS care.

But it is possible that Fumento's own views are coloured by his dislike of homosexuality. Perhaps the same bias against homosexuality lies behind other claims that women are less likely than men to contract AIDS. 'The fear of AIDS transmission through vaginal intercourse has been greatly exaggerated', says Robert Gould, who believes that the AIDS epidemic is not likely to spread in this way (Gould in Cozec 1991:59). But this raises the ire not only of homosexuals but of women's groups, who fear that if this view is accepted little help will be available for women with AIDS (Halpern in Hopkins 1991, Novello in Bishop 1992:33).

Neither Gould nor Fumento have any sensible answer about why AIDS in Africa is spread through heterosexual rather than homosexual intercourse or why women in Africa are proving to be so vulnerable if AIDS is not easily transmitted through heterosexual sex. Figures from South Africa, for example, show that virtually all AIDS cases amongst black people are in the heterosexual group and 48% of AIDS cases amongst black people are women (*Epidemiological Comments* 1994). Fumento suggests that AIDS in Africa is more homosexual than the authorities think. He says that African homosexuals do not openly declare themselves, and here he is probably right. But the size of the epidemic in Africa makes it extremely unlikely that even hidden homosexuality is the main cause of its spread. Fumento suggests that alternatively needles in African hospitals are not properly sterilized (Fumento 1990:107). But this is exceedingly unlikely in the still-efficient South African hospitals, yet HIV is spreading as fast in South Africa as elsewhere in Africa. He suggests that clitoridectomy is a cause; but clitoridectomy is not practised in South Africa or in Zimbabwe. He correctly observes that promiscuous sex is quite widespread in parts of Africa – but that flies in the face of his own argument that heterosexual sex is not a major cause of AIDS transmisison. Fumento is not being logical, which suggests that he has another axe to grind. He is allowing his own prejudices about not only homosexuals but Africans to colour his analysis.

All AIDS forecasts are therefore subject to the bias of the forecaster. AIDS tends to show up the prejudices in a community.

'In significant ways, AIDS care and services continue to reflect the prejudices and social values of the particular communities, states and regions in which an individual is affected by the disease' (Doubleday and Ports 1992:277).

It is therefore important that we at least try to be as open-minded and as free from preconceptions as is possible. Some people suggest that the size of the AIDS problem in Africa and Asia has been overestimated, just as it was in America (*World Press Review* 1994:40). We do need to be realistic and honest in our assessment of the AIDS crisis. If we overestimate the size of the problem in order to catch public attention, or in order to be politically correct in not singling out 'at risk' groups, in the end nobody will believe anything we say. It will also mean that we misdirect our attempts to deal with the problem. We need to shape our educational approach about AIDS appropriately for different target audiences (*The Grail* 1989). It is in fact very troublesome that AIDS does not affect all sections of the population equally, and we need to know that this is so, since otherwise we will be educating the wrong people about the wrong things. For example, the sections of society which are relatively unaffected by AIDS may well be indifferent to the needs of other sectors.

'If HIV does not spread to affluent suburban neighbourhoods, are we relieved of the burden of reconstituting the inner cities?' (Rothenberg 1993:575).

If it is true that affluent suburban people are less likely to experience an AIDS epidemic, then instead of putting all our emphasis in these groups on educating them about 'safer' sex, we need to educate them instead about unselfishness and our responsibility for the welfare of society as a whole.

If we are to respond theologically to AIDS, then it is very important the theologians also try to be as honest and objective about it as possible, for otherwise our theology is merely reflecting biases which already exist in the community. We cannot avoid unconscious bias, but we can do our best to be as well informed as possible.

But the talk about AIDS bringing us to a time of *kairos* is not misguided. Despite all that I have said about not seeing AIDS as more tragic than any other illness, there are particular aspects about AIDS which set it apart and which will, or should, change the way we think about God, about Jesus, about the church, about life and death and sexuality. We may find that some of our past beliefs which we had put aside as antiquated in fact take on a new significance. We may feel that we have to reconstruct some of our beliefs altogether. Professor Bonginjalo Goba of South Africa has commented that AIDS forces us to deconstruct our theology.

'For the AIDS epidemic deconstructs, challenges all our philosophical or theological presuppositions. To encounter those who have openly come to terms with the challenge of AIDS is to participate in a deep spiritual pilgrimage which attempts to redefine the ultimate meaning of human existence' (Goba 1995).

By deconstruction is usually meant the idea that the confident assertions of Western philosophy and theology have within them the seeds of their own unravelling, so that grand theories of meaning and metaphysics are no longer possible (Raschke 1982:x). Goba suggests that AIDS in Africa has the effect also of making grand theories untenable, so that we are left with more questions than answers.

All suffering matters. But AIDS is different. AIDS threatens to change our whole society. First of all there is the sheer scale of the illness, justifying calling it a pandemic. Stephen Joseph, Commissioner of Health in New York, whom I referred to above as saying that the future estimates for AIDS in New York had been exaggerated, does not mean that the revised figures are not alarming. By his estimate, by the late 1990s 10–15% of people of reproductive age in poor communities in New York will be HIV positive. There will be ten to twenty thousand AIDS orphans[4] in New York. AIDS will wipe out the gains made in public health and overwhelm attempts to provide adequate social services – all of this in a wealthy United States (Joseph 1992:47). The Centers for Disease Control concede that the rate by which AIDS spread in the US has slowed down since 1992 (*Wall Street Journal*, 11 March 1994). But people are still becoming infected, and AIDS is now the leading cause of death for Americans aged 25–44 (*Washington Post*, 29 June 1994).

This is alarming enough. But the AIDS numbers in America are as nothing compared to those in Africa, and increasingly in parts of Asia. In Africa it also affects a much wider cross-section of the community than in North America or Europe, where although the number of heterosexuals with AIDS is growing, most of those with AIDS are still homosexual. AIDS does indeed force us to rethink our ideas about homosexuality, and we will try to do that later. But the homosexual group, however important, is a relatively small group in any society,[5] and we might be tempted to say that something that only affects a small part of the population is a tragedy but need not upset the world-view of the heterosexual majority.

AIDS is not, however, a disease of male homosexuals only. It is no longer true, even in Europe and North America, that all people with AIDS are male and homosexual. By the end of 1987, blacks and

[4]'Orphan' means different things in different cultures. It may mean a child who has lost both parents. The term is better used, however, to mean a child who has lost his or her effective parent. It is not clear exactly what 'orphans' means in the above reference; but in many African statistics, the term means a child who has lost the one parent who provides care and support.

[5]We will not enter here the controversy as to just how small a proportion. Some now suggest that the proportion may be smaller than the research of Kinsey, for example, suggested.

hispanics accounted for 37% of non-paediatric AIDS cases reported in the United States (Alonso and Koreck 1989:103), and by 1994 AIDS was the leading cause of death for black or hispanic men aged 25–44 in the United States (*New York Times*, 13 September 1994). Although few of these were reported as homosexual, it is possible that in fact homosexuality may still be a factor, since in these communities a man who has sexual relations with a woman, even if he also has sexual relations with men, is not regarded as homosexual (Alonso and Koreck 1989). However, a growing number of cases in these population groups are women. By 1994 AIDS was the second highest cause of death for young black or hispanic women in the United States. Whether they contract the virus mostly through sexual intercourse or mostly through intravenous drug usage is disputed. The Centers for Disease Control suggest that most of these women were intravenous drug users (*New York Times*, 9 September 1994). But clearly AIDS is not a purely male homosexual disease in the United States. In Britain, the number of cases of heterosexually transmitted AIDS rose from 20 in 1986 to 300 in 1993, thus more than doubling every two years (*Catholic AIDS Link Newsletter* 1994).

Whatever may be true in Europe and America, in the Third World homosexuality is not a major factor. Once one reaches the point where 30% of women attending ante-natal clinics are HIV positive, as is the case in some areas of Africa, and once there are as many women affected as men, or more, we cannot think that most of those with AIDS are homosexuals. In these parts of the world statistics are harder to come by and estimates of AIDS change all the time (*The Economist* 1991). Testing for HIV positivity is expensive, and often people are only tested if they already show symptoms. In 1995, the World Health Organization estimated that the total number of HIV positive individuals in the world was 19.5 million (*ACET Newsletter* 1995). Caritas suggests that by the end of the decade this number will at least have doubled (Kelly 1995:598). The World Health Organization estimates that some three million women and children in Africa will die of AIDS in the 1990s (Hamblin and Reid 1994:16). 67% of those with AIDS live in Africa, but the World Health Organization estimated that in Asia in 1993 AIDS had increased over one year by a staggering 800% (*St Louis Post Dispatch*, 3 July 1994).

These figures may be too modest. Given the chaotic state of many health services in Africa, and the shortage of clinics in rural areas, it is likely that the number of AIDS cases in Africa are under-reported.

'A detailed and reliable quantitative account of the present and future demographic impacts of AIDS in Africa is not possible at present' (Barnett and Blaikie 1992:18).

In many African cities, 25% of women presenting themselves at ante-natal clinics are found to be HIV positive. Thus a major part of the young adult population is liable to die of AIDS. AIDS has disastrous effects on health and on economy. People do die in even larger numbers in Africa from tuberculosis or malaria. But AIDS is different. Tuberculosis and malaria flourish because of inadequate food, poor hygiene and inadequate spraying of mosquito breeding places. But both can be cured. AIDS cannot (yet) be cured. Perhaps it never will be curable, just as we have not yet discovered a cure for a cold. There are no vaccines or prophylactics. Because of AIDS, tuberculosis and other diseases take an even greater toll. Those who are HIV positive have no hope of resisting these other killer diseases of the Third World, when without AIDS they might have recovered. AIDS has reversed any gains in life expectancy in Africa (*New York Times*, 1 May 1994).

Other sicknesses continue to plague poor countries; typhoid or bubonic plague are still deadly. But AIDS is not exactly like the plagues of old. HIV infected persons cannot easily be recognized. They have no symptoms, so we cannot know who may infect us. Those who are infected are not the very old and the very young whose deaths have less economic impact, but those who earn the family's bread. Those who become ill do not die quickly as in bubonic plague, but may be chronically sick for many months before death, swallowing up their own savings and those of their family.

AIDS kills off those who are economically productive, the people whom a developing country most needs, and on whose training and education precious resources have been spent. Ironically, although AIDS is a disease which hits poorest countries hardest, within those countries it is often the newly rich men, the commercially successful, who fall ill first, because it is they who can afford money for prostitutes. Thus AIDS has created a developmental nightmare in

Africa. Yet the effect of AIDS is not confined to the cities and the (relatively) wealthy, but spreads from them back into the rural areas. Patterns of subsistence farming, where the women tend the smallholdings which provide the food for poor families, are crumbling. However faint, there were hopes that African economies might slowly improve in the 1990s from the disasters of earlier years. This will probably not happen now (*The Economist* 1991:32). Money has been invested in training workers who die before those costs are recouped. Those who are uninfected but bereaved cannot put their full energies into their work. Since in Africa funerals are lengthy, relatively expensive, and are attended by the whole community, the number of funerals is in itself a significant cost to the economy. And as part of this spiral, outside investors, seeing all this, are increasingly reluctant to invest in Africa (Dixon 1990:22).

AIDS is a disease which primarily affects young persons who are sexually active. Many Western populations are aging, and the proportion of young people is relatively low. The proportion of persons exposed to AIDS-linked behaviour in the West is also therefore relatively low. I am not implying that older people do not have sexual relationships or are not at any risk for AIDS, but their sexual activity is less and the risk is less. In Third World countries, by contrast, the proportion of the population who are under fifteen years of age is often very high. Soon they will come into that period in their lives of most frequent sexual activity. Thus we may expect, as these children come into sexual maturity, that AIDS will continue to spread ever more widely.

Many Third World countries already have severe economic and social problems. Poverty, civil war, refugees, all affect the health and economic well-being of the population. Already faltering health services in under-resourced countries are crumbling because of AIDS. It kills off people in their twenties and thirties, people who have just had children. In Third World countries the number of children born to a woman is likely to be double that in Western countries. Already there are millions of AIDS orphans; 1.5 million in Uganda alone (Uganda Aids Commission 1994). About one in three babies born to mothers with AIDS will themselves die of AIDS unless they have already predeceased their mother. Those who do not contract AIDS are more likely to suffer from malnutrition and thus from other diseases. The explosion of numbers of orphans is having a serious impact upon the tradition of the wider family in African culture as extended families reach a point of saturation, and will have a great effect on African social structures. As far as economy is concerned, Africa may be doomed to an endemic spiral of poverty which has no foreseeable end. AIDS confounds our economic plans.

These dry statistics confuse our minds. We cannot take in the scale of it all, nor the staggering quantity of human misery that they encompass. This is a real problem. The sheer weight of numbers makes it impossible for us to grieve for all those involved. We are presented daily with such a catalogue of pain in the world, from war, natural disasters, and mishap that we cannot emotionally engage with it. Writing of AIDS in South Africa, a scholar of law says:

'The figures create the same risk of devaluation that is affecting the rest of our national life. Our people are afflicted by massacres and atrocities whose perpetrators seem untraceable, whose causes seem impenetrable . . . We risk a failure of words, of concepts, of sympathetic insight in the face of AIDS. We need to respond with imagination and compassion to what is happening around us' (Cameron 1993:29).

Often it is only when someone close to us becomes ill with AIDS that we first begin to understand the sheer scale of suffering involved.

Its emergence in the West amongst white homosexuals masked the fact that AIDS is primarily a disease of the poor. This prompts us to ask why AIDS is so much more prevalent in poor countries than in richer ones. AIDS is spread by people having sexual relationships with a number of people, and no one seriously thinks that only poor people have sexual relationships outside monogamous relationships.

There are perhaps two answers. Poor people are less nourished, live in less hygienic circumstances, are often already ill with tuberculosis or malaria, and therefore have less resistance to the virus.

'AIDS is probably not caused only by the HIVirus but by other factors too . . . Co-factors have a major, if often overlooked, role in the progression of the disease' (Root–Bernstein 1993:259, also 301).

Research in Malawi suggests a link between AIDS, malnutrition and vitamin A deficiency (*New York Times*, 3 February 1995).

But also, in richer countries, there is less migrant labour, and in any local community men and women are in more equal numbers. This is not so in developing countries. Throughout Africa and Asia, men leave their families in the village in order to seek work in the growing towns and cities. In artificial city communities the number of men far outstrips the number of women. Prostitution and promiscuity are therefore more common as one woman services many men. Prostitution seems to be at the heart of the problem in Uganda, for example, or Thailand, where prostitution plays a large part in the country's economy (*The Economist* 1991:24). As Thailand's economy improves, however, Thai girls are less willing to be prostitutes, and other girls come from Laos, or South China, or India. Thus AIDS is spreading to those countries also (*The Economist* 1991:32, Katoppo in King 1994).

AIDS hits poorest countries hardest. Yet the resources to combat AIDS and to care for those with AIDS are not equally distributed. The quality of care for people with AIDS in North America and Europe is very different indeed from that in Africa. At a World AIDS Day conference in France in 1994, the Zimbabwean Minister of Health alleged that 90% of the funds spent on ministering to those with AIDS are spent on 8% of AIDS patients. Western AIDS treatment can involve regular blood transfusions, treatment with drugs like AZT, and all the medical technology which the West has at its disposal. An American with AIDS can expect levels of care and treatment that are inconceivable in Africa. Through the provisions of the Ryan White act, he or she can expect extensive help with medication, hospitalization and even accommodation. In most clinics in Africa, treatment in the clinics involves aspirin, skin ointments, rehydration after diarrhoea and nothing else.

It is reported that drug companies in the West are withdrawing funds for the development of an AIDS vaccine (Cohen 1994; Green 1995). This is partly because there are problems with testing vaccines; ethically those who are at risk must be told about 'safer sex'; if they do use condoms they will probably not be at risk for infection and the vaccine has nothing to fight. Alternatively, those using the experimental vaccine may be tempted to trust the vaccine and thus risk infection. But it is also because estimates of the number of people in Europe and America who will contract AIDS in the future have been halved. Any vaccine would therefore primarily be used in poor countries who cannot pay for it. There would be little economic return for the drug companies.

'For many drug companies the risk of failure is considered too great to justify a search for an AIDS vaccine' (Dixon 1990:60).

Cohen alleges that in fact no work is being done on a vaccine for the AIDS-type B virus found in Africa. Resources are not shared equally. AIDS shows up the unfairness of our world.

The Bible, and much modern theological literature, has encouraged us to believe that the poor are especially loved and blessed by God. AIDS must therefore receive our special attention; yet because of AIDS the poor, far from having good news preached to them (Luke 5.18), are even further burdened.

'For most of the [AIDS] patients we see, AIDS is just one among a host of survival issues they face: homelessness, drug addiction, imprisonment' (Edman 1992:292).

God may have a preferential option for the poor, but AIDS makes it clearer than ever that God's preferential option does not seem to involve actively intervening to assist them. Because of AIDS they have even less prospect of their situation changing for the better.

AIDS destroys our sense of order and control. However uncertain we may have become about our theology and metaphysics, we have grown accustomed at a more practical level to medical science being able to solve or at least alleviate physical illness. Polio has been eliminated, smallpox has vanished, measles can be (but in Africa is not) prevented. The last remaining major illnesses of our time were cancer and cardiovascular problems. With early diagnosis even these can often be checked, cut out, or surgically overcome. Dr Abraham Verghese, in his award-winning story of AIDS coming to a Tennessee town, writes of the days just before AIDS came into prominence.

'To say this was a time of unreal and unparalleled confidence, bordering on conceit, in the Western medical world is to understate things. Only cancer was truly feared, and even that was often curable . . . There seemed no reason to believe when AIDS arrived on the scene that we would not transfix it with our divining needles, lyse it with our potions, swallow it and digest it in the great vats of eighties technology' (Verghese 1994:24)

Yet since we first knew about AIDS from the early 1980s, we seem to be no further towards a vaccine or a cure. Better drainage, better hygiene, earlier diagnosis, all of our usual weapons against epidemics, are of no effect. Other sicknesses may at present take an even greater toll in Africa, but in principle they can be checked if not cured. With AIDS only a radical change in human behaviour can make a difference. Medical scientists, so far so invincible, have now failed us.

Helen, visiting Tanzania to learn about AIDS ministry, accompanies a home visitor on her cases. They visit a group of young women, some still healthy, but all infected with HIV. The young women have joined forces in order together to farm their shambas (smallholdings of banana and coffee plants), so that those who are too ill to continue manual work can still get some income. One of the women, herself obviously ill, has a baby, wizened like a small monkey, eyes deeply sunk into sockets, too weak to cry, dying of AIDS. Nothing can be done to stop the women falling ill. One by one they become too weak to work in the shamba. The load on the others grows heavier each month. The baby will soon be dead. Helen weeps, in rage at her powerlessness to change things for them.

Theologians are, usually, a literary people. We like books with a beginning and an end, and by the end we expect to know what the point of the book was. AIDS does not fit into these categories. It represents the frightening world of chaos, disorder and non-meaning from which we hoped our faith had delivered us. AIDS is a plague in a modern era when plagues should have no power. The AIDS pandemic recreates for us the frightening world of the earlier church where we do not control the elements and are in a place between creation and redemption in what the old *Salve Regina* prayer used to call a 'vale of misery'.

'Before this plague has run its course we will confront sobering and shocking reality' (Vaux 1989:278).

AIDS raises for modern theology, just as for modern science, the fear that there are no answers, only silence. Surprisingly little has been written about a theology of AIDS. Perhaps this is because AIDS forces us to face three issues with which the modern church feels profoundly uncomfortable: death, sexuality and otherness.

'Nobody wants to face questions about death, disease and sexuality except perhaps those involved in care and those working through these particular issues for themselves' (Woodward 1990:1).

Those who threaten to make us face these questions and disturb our fragile peace raise our hostility. We are disgusted by sexual offenders. We often avoid the sick and dying as a sort of pariah, as already dead. But, of course, although we do not think about them, death and sexuality touch us all, for we are all mortal and all sexual beings.

Death frightens us. We do not mention it or think of it even in church – but there is no cure for AIDS, and those who are HIV positive will almost all certainly die. How then can we believe in God the healer?

We are uncomfortable with our own sexuality; we find it hard to admit in church that we are sexual persons. We are even more uncomfortable with the sexuality of young people. AIDS makes us face the universality of our own sexuality. Some of those with AIDS have stepped over what we regard as boundaries for acceptable (if unmentionable) sexuality in the church. Some are homosexual, and many of our churches find that hard to accept.

Increasingly, many people with AIDS now are poor, black, hispanic, Asian – different from the white middle-class milieu that still dominates our theology, at least in the West (Davies in Russell 1990:95). Although gradually the church in America and elsewhere has begun to come to grips with the pastoral demands which AIDS makes upon us, the response was slow and sometimes judgmental and unhelpful.

'AIDS came along. Caring broke down. Families sometimes fled; committees were often idle or indifferent: churches and clergy frequently stood in judgment: and the once idealized medical establishment initially had little to offer and in some places even less inclination to provide it' (Doubleday and Porter 1992:275).

The church, as so often, has a mixed record as far as AIDS is concerned.

'Where AIDS is concerned, the religious community in America has been a major part of the problem as well as the solution' (South 1992:297).

There are some dedicated individuals, and some important projects. But because we are theologically embarrassed by the rise of an epidemic in a world where God is meant to rule, and morally embarrassed by the fact that many people with AIDS are homosexual or have contracted the disease from what we regard as immoral sexual activity, and because often the church is a predominantly middle-class institution amongst whom people with AIDS, either homosexual, promiscuous, drug-addicted or poor, do not easily belong, we have often done and said the wrong things, or done and said nothing. AIDS has come as a test or a judgment on the church.

There are, of course, good reasons for the church's slow response. We cannot easily abandon our teaching on sexuality; we are genuinely perplexed about how to reconcile the existence of AIDS with the existence of God; and the enormity of the problem has understandably rendered us dumb. In Third World countries the church has also had other major problems to deal with: poverty, warfare, refugee problems, ruthless dictatorships. It is not surprising that AIDS has only recently reached their agenda. But the church of Christ who is the Word of God cannot remain silent. We may have no explanations to offer, but we should at least be thinking and talking about philosophy and its implications.

AIDS is not only a medical problem, nor only a social problem. It affects the whole person in every aspect of personality. Part of the problem in Western society is that we often divide life into compartments, each to be dealt with by its own panel of experts.

Medical people want to treat AIDS by medical means: vaccines, prophylactics, condoms. Social workers want to concentrate on housing and financial care for people with AIDS. Lay people want to leave it all to the experts. But AIDS is part of an overall system in which we live which includes family, housing, economics, health, and everything else. We cannot separate off the biological from the psychological or from the social. AIDS has been primarily re-searched as a medical problem. But AIDS requires:

' . . . the sharing of research concerns between medical and social scientists . . . If this is not done, then only one arm of the pincer movement, that of the physical nature of the hazard, or the socio-economic characteristics of the population at risk, receives attention' (Barnett and Blaikie 1992:8).

We might add that this wholeness includes religion and spirituality. Barnett and Blaikie comment that the number of social scientists working on AIDS are few. There are also few theologians working on AIDS. We cannot deal with AIDS without taking the spiritual dimension of life into account, and we cannot continue in a spirituality which leaves AIDS off the agenda. Spirituality and theology can help to bridge the gap between the mind and the body. Religious belief is part of the healing of relationships, the provision of community, the forgiveness of self and others, the regaining of a sense of hope and purpose, and the ability to face the prospect of death, which are all such important parts of care for people affected by AIDS.

In this book we will not be dealing with AIDS pastoralia except in passing. That is not because pastoralia is unimportant. On the contrary, pastoral care is the key issue. But a good deal has been written about Christian pastoral care for those with AIDS and their families, complementing the work of other social agencies. Admitt-edly, most of what has been written on AIDS pastoralia is about the situation in Europe and North America. A great deal of that literature reflects the fact that at first in that part of the world almost all the cases of AIDS were found amongst homosexual men. Most of those with AIDS live in Africa, and increasingly in other Third World countries. The conditions under which they endure Aids are in many ways very different from those of people with AIDS in First

World countries. The church does a good deal of pastoral work in Africa, without much specifically African or Third World pastoral theology to support it.

AIDS also raises in a sharp way some crucial issues about human rights and legal ethics. Nevertheless, important though they may be, pastoral responses and human rights issues should go hand in hand with theological reflection if they are to be integral to the church's life and mission and not merely duplications of secular social work and legal ethics, and it is this theological reflection in which this book attempts to engage. Much less work has been done on this, and much of what has been written has been about the theological challenge which the AIDS pandemic raises for traditional Christian attitudes towards homosexuality. Important though this is, it is not the only, nor even the major, issue for a theology about AIDS. What we need to consider is the challenge which AIDS raises about our very understanding of God, and Jesus, and salvation, and eschatology, and resurrection. Too little attention has been given to this by those who write about systematic theology. Woodward suggests that we need a theology which attempts

'. . . to provide a map or framework that can make sense of HIV and the rich ambiguities that surround morality, sex and death. AIDS is a crisis and an opportunity for us to deepen our understanding so that we can support and care: to create communities where exclusiveness, interdependence, creativity and change are shared for the salvation of all. Theology must open itself to AIDS so that it can transform tragedy and despair' (Woodward 1990:7).

I am not so confident myself that we will be able to provide a map to make sense of AIDS, nor that we can transform tragedy. The title of Woodward's book suggests that he, too, really thinks that all we can do is to 'embrace the chaos'. But unless theology opens itself to the questions which AIDS raises, it cannot be a theology which undergirds the work of a church which must minister in this time of AIDS. This is especially true in parts of Africa where AIDS has changed almost every part of life. The agendas for theologians and for those directly concerned with AIDS need to converge. This has not happened to any great extent.

Theology, as we noted earlier, reflects our context and our life situation. There is a great need for people with AIDS themselves to reflect upon how their understanding of God is changed and affected by their situation. I will try, when appropriate, to draw on some of these reflections which people with AIDS have made public. I do not have AIDS, in the sense that I am not infected with the Human Immunodeficiency Virus. I cannot talk from my own experience about reconciling belief in God with experience of imminent, painful and disfiguring death; and I cannot presume to tell people with AIDS how they should think. We shall occasionally read small vignettes about people with AIDS or people caring for people with AIDS in order to try to keep our reflections in line with their experience.

Yet although I do not have AIDS, I am affected by AIDS, as are we all. In my country, many people will soon be dying of the illness. Even larger numbers of children will be orphaned. I cannot pretend that this makes no difference to how I see God and the doings of God. AIDS is a world-wide problem. It is true that it affects Africa far more than it affects people in Europe or North America. But if we are one church, AIDS is the business of us all, whether where we live 20% or only 1% of the population has AIDS. The theology of the whole church needs to take AIDS into account. That is what this book tries to address. Perhaps those of us who do not have AIDS may be able to make a contribution just because we are a little removed from the pain. It is hard to theologize when one is very close to the pain, and a little distance may be helpful.

I

AIDS and Our Picture of God

Bernard has AIDS. He is not yet confined to bed, but suffers from yeast infections and joint pains. He tires easily. He has had to give up his hairdressing salon. Each month he grows more tired. From childhood he has been a devout Episcopalian. He still is. I do not ask him how he squares this with the fact that he has a man as his lover. He serves in his congregation as Master of the Acolytes.

He is active in AIDS ministry, visiting people with AIDS in hospital as a lay chaplain, to pray with them and, if requested, to lay hands upon them and administer Holy Communion.

He addresses a study group in his parish. 'I realize,' he says, 'that God has given me AIDS.' Later on in his talk he says 'God has sent this illness amongst us'. He does not explain how he can believe this and continue still to love God.

The problem of theodicy, reconciling belief in a God who is all-powerful and belief in a God who is all-loving, in the light of our experience of various kinds of evil in the world, has been discussed over and over. But occasionally, as with the holocaust for Judaism, an event of such horrendous evil occurs that we are forced to face the question again and to retest our previous answers or solutions. Many people endure pain, or die while they are still young, from illness, accident or human crimes. Normally our theology takes that in its stride, especially when we are not personally involved. We are able to justify our continuing belief in God by saying that God's purposes are often too mysterious to understand, or by faith that in the end it will all work out for the best, or by suggesting that people's sufferings are caused by their own fault or, if not their fault directly, then by the consequence of some other human beings who, exercising free will against God's will, involve others in the consequences of their actions.

J. Michael Clark says, for example, that there are four responses we often make to justify God in the face of evil; and that in his view none of them fit in a time of AIDS (Clark 1989).

• We may see God as a cosmic judge who only gives us what we deserve. Therefore if we suffer, it is because of something we have done for which we must, in justice, be punished.

• We may say that God sends us suffering so that we may learn and be spiritually strengthened. Suffering is a kind of test, and when we have learned enough we pass the test.

• We may say that, whatever the appearances to the contrary, God does have a plan, and the suffering is all part of God's redemptive purpose. What we endure is all really to the good.

• We may say that however terrible the sufferings, they are only short-lived *sub specie aeternitatis*, seen through God's eternal eyes. Our eventual eternal bliss with God renders the suffering of no account.

The Book of Job long ago addressed the same problems. Job's comforters tell him that he must have sinned, even if unwittingly, and that his sufferings are a form of punishment. Job cannot accept this, and refuses to believe in a guilt he cannot honestly own. Job's situation is set in the context of a test, the consequence of God's whimsical wager with Satan to test how faithful a servant Job will be. Job refuses to accept the justice of such a God. He refuses to be the subject of a test. In the book God remonstrates with Job: 'Was Job present at the dawn of creation?' God asks. 'Does Job know what he is talking about?' Job humbly concedes that he does not.

> 'I have spoken of things which I do not understand, things too wonderful for me to know' (Job 42.3).

Usually this device by the author is taken as an example of an appeal to the mystery and paradox of God to which theologians frequently revert in tight corners. We are being told that Job's sufferings are terrible, but that they are short-lived; with our limited knowledge we cannot understand the eternal ways of God; all will be well in the end, if we can but persevere in faith.

But Clark suggests that this is not what the author means. He has another interpretation of the meaning of the book. The author of Job means that what God is really saying to Job is: 'I did the best I could.

You could not have done any better if you were the creator.' The author is admitting the divine weakness and vulnerability; this may not be a perfect universe, but it is the best possible universe, given the limitations of an intractable creation with which God must work.

Whether Clark has really explained to us the intention of the book's author is not really at issue. What matters is whether the idea of God as vulnerable and 'doing the best God can' is helpful, or even viable, in a time of AIDS, and whether Clark is right in rejecting the other four responses, especially the idea that suffering is sent either as punishment or learning experience.

Hypothesis: AIDS is a punishment for sin

Abraham Verghese in his book about AIDS in an American country town quotes a nurse who boiled over with frustration and anger about caring for an AIDS patient who died.

> 'I don't think we should have bothered in the first place. He deserved what he got. It's no one's fault but his. And I don't see why *we* should have to take care of him' (Verghese 1994:131).

Her feelings are not uncommon. If AIDS is brought on by sex, often homosexual sex, often very promiscuous sex, why should we tear ourselves up with pity and fruitless attempts to help people with AIDS?

In fact the nurse's need to express her anger at how much this man's 'sin' had cost her is perfectly legitimate. We shall discuss whether AIDS can indeed be seen as a consequence of, or a punishment for, sin; but our care to be theologically and ideologically correct in not ascribing blame to anyone should not take away from those who are hurt or endangered by sexual promiscuity the right to feel and to say that they feel angry.

Should we reject the notion that our sufferings are the consequence of human sin and an expression of divine punishment? The two halves of this proposition do not, of course, necessarily hang together. We may say that pain is a consequence of sin without necessarily implying that it is a punishment inflicted by God.

Pain and evil, said Augustine, are the consequence of human beings and angels exercising their free will and putting the wrong things first, so that the universe becomes disordered.

'St Augustine has probably done more than any other writer after St Paul to shape the structure of orthodox Christian belief' (Hick 1966:43).

Augustine's complex theory about evil is rooted in the idea that while God did not create evil, God did allow to humans and angels the freedom to choose.

'The cause of evil is the defection of the will of a being who is mutably good from the Good which is immutable' (St Augustine, quoted Hick 1966:65).

The theory is complex because although Augustine believed that humans chose evil of their own accord, he also believed that God knew from the outset that they would do so, so that really evil is after all part of God's plan.

All Christians believe in the idea of free will. God does not wish us to do evil. God wishes us to love and serve God voluntarily – for love and goodness which are involuntary, forced, or inevitable, are not what we mean by love and goodness. Goodness must be freely chosen. In their freedom humans chose instead to disobey God, and what could have been a wonderful balance of God, humans and nature was thrown off balance, bringing in its train not only human sin but human and animal pain and suffering.

In the end, however, while God will not overturn human freedom, God's power is such that even the worst of sins, the killing of the incarnate God, can be turned around into a saving event, so that in the end good and God will triumph. With this theory Christians have been able to hold together a belief in a God of power and love despite human suffering.

In this theory, not all pain is precisely a punishment for sin. In traditional theology, animals, who have no souls, cannot sin, but they still bear pain as a consequence of human sin. Augustine is quite insensitive to the moral issue of animal pain (Hick 1966:63). Sometimes humans also bear pain as a consequence of the sin of others, and this does seem unfair even to Augustine. But in

Augustine's view all human beings (except Jesus) have inherited Adam's fatal flaw of 'concupiscence' or love of self and sexual self-indulgence. All human beings are therefore sinful. Jesus alone is free of inherited sinful bias. Jesus was the innocent sufferer bearing the consequence of our sin and sharing undeservedly in our punishment. Augustine, like almost all Christians of his period, believed that God punishes evil. The Christian tradition continued that belief. Houlden suggests (in Woodward 1990) that Augustine did not mean that God punishes individuals. The punishment is sent upon the whole human race corporately. But, of course, we experience the punishment as individuals, and this is the problem with Augustinianism. Individuals experience the punishment unequally and unfairly. Later on, Anselm would teach that human beings have inherited not only Adam's fatal weakness, but also Adam's guilt, and that therefore we all deserve to share in Adam's punishment. Calvin would develop this belief into his penal theory of atonement.

'The theodicy-tradition, which has descended from Augustine through Aquinas to the more tradition-governed Catholic theologians of today, and equally as we find it in the Reformers and in Protestant orthodoxy, teaches that all the evil that indwells or affects mankind is, in Augustine's phrase, "either sin or punishment for sin"' (Hick 1965:179).

When AIDS came along, associated as it was in North America with homosexuality, it was inevitable that some would draw the conclusion that AIDS is God's punishment on homosexuals for their sin. If we believe AIDS is a punishment from God, then logically we ought not to try to intervene with healing. The Moral Majority movement in the United States has explicitly said that homosexual persons with AIDS get what they deserve and do not merit our sympathy or help. Rejecting the spending of federal dollars on AIDS research, Ronald Godwin, an executive of Moral Majority, said:

'What I see is a commitment to spend our tax dollars on research to allow these diseased homosexuals to go back to their perverted practices without any standards of accountability' (quoted Shelp and Sunderland 1987:19).

Churches sometimes responded negatively to people with AIDS out of self-righteousness kindled by fear. A pastor whose family contracted AIDS through blood transfusions was forced to resign (Giles 1992). Children with AIDS were sometimes forced to leave Sunday School.

'With a sweet smile on his face, a minister informed one of my female AIDS patients that she was no longer able to attend Sunday services as her presence would empty the church rapidly and he did not like preaching to empty pews' (Kübler-Ross 1987:7).

However, it would not be fair to say that this response is typical. Very few theologians have agreed that people with AIDS should be cast out of the church or abandoned to their fate. The evangelical theologian Ronald Sider argues vigorously that far from regarding people with AIDS as deserving of all they get,

' . . . our Christian understanding of both creation and redemption tells us that people with AIDS are of inestimable worth, persons so important and precious in the sight of their creator and redeemer that God declares them indelibly stamped with the divine image' (Sider 1988:11).

Similarly, the Catholic Cardinal Joseph Bernardin says:

' . . . [Jesus] never ceased to reach out to the lonely, to the outcasts of his time, even if they did not live up to the full demands of his teaching . . . When some objected to his compassion he responded "Let the one amongst you who is guiltless be the first to throw the stone"' (quoted *The Grail* 1989:16).

So even the guilty are not rejected by God. God loves them and seeks to recall and rescue and redeem them. But does God not chastize and punish them too? The existence of AIDS makes many want to say that God is punishing people with AIDS. There are several reasons. In North America and Europe many people who presented with AIDS were male homosexuals. Although new HIV infections in North America are increasingly amongst heterosexuals, even now most of those in North America with full-blown AIDS are homosexual. Many of the heterosexual cases have contracted AIDS from sharing needles in their drug usage. Admittedly in Africa the picture is very different. Neither homosexuality nor intravenous drug usage are important factors in the spread of AIDS there. But many of those in Africa who present with AIDS have been involved in sexual promiscuity. We do not approve of homosexual sex, we do not approve of promiscuity, nor of drug taking. Christians fear, with justification, that the fabric of society and family life is being undermined by such activities. AIDS provides a powerful weapon with which to reinforce conventional morality. We shall return to examine these questions later.

But perhaps the real reason why we are so eager to assign blame to homosexuals is that otherwise we *must blame God*! Rabbi Richard Rubenstein, in his revised edition of *After Auschwitz*, recalls his conversation with the German Christian Dean Grüber who, although a Jewish sympathizer and one who tried to help Jews even during the Third Reich, was nevertheless convinced that Hitler acted as 'the rod of God'. Dean Grüber had in mind Isaiah 10.5, where Assyria is called the rod of God's anger, used to chastize the people of Israel. Thus the Holocaust happened because Jews, God's chosen people, had failed to keep God's law and therefore had to be chastized (Rubenstein 1992:13).

Rubenstein, in his first version of the book, was understandably outraged by what he took to be an antisemitic attitude. But, as Rubenstein later recounts, he became aware of the astonishing phenomenon that Jewish theologians also, after the Holocaust, preached that their sufferings were the consequence of their faithlessness which God had to punish. Rabbi Elchonon Wasserman said it was because Jews had flirted with modernism (Rubenstein 1992:160). Our astonishment is lessened when we remember that this was the consistent teaching of the Jewish prophets. Jeremiah taught that the destruction of Jerusalem and the exile of the people was in punishment for disobedience.

> 'They did not obey your voice or follow your law: of all you commanded them to do they did nothing. Therefore you have made all these disasters [i.e. the Chaldaean invasion] come upon them' (Jeremiah 32.23).

Isaiah taught the same about the earlier invasion of the Assyrians.

'They have rejected the instruction of the Lord of hosts, and have despised the word of the Holy One of Israel. Therefore . . . he will raise the signal for a nation far away and whistle for a people at the ends of the earth' (Isaiah 5.24b–26).

Amos promises poverty, drought and pestilence because of the oppression of the poor and the crushing of the needy (Amos 4.1–10). Belief that we bring disaster upon our own head is a consistent prophetic theme.

In the Old Testament, God is often thought of as sending affliction, sometimes in punishment, sometimes in warning. Even in the New Testament, the evangelists appear to attribute the destruction of Jerusalem in 70 CE not so much to Roman cruelty or to misguided Jewish nationalism as to the fact that the people of Jerusalem had closed their ears to Jesus.

When disasters happen to us, we must either say that God intended this to happen to us, that Nebuchadnezzar or Hitler is a 'rod of God'; or we must say that God could not help what happened to us. But we do not want to believe that God is helpless. Therefore we must say that God intends or allows the disaster as the consequence of our own behaviour.

'Self accusation and introjected guilt can permit a group to retain a belief in the existence and goodness of a deity' (Rubenstein 1992:85).

Groups will often accuse themselves rather than give up their beliefs or live with an unresolved inconsistency between belief and reality. Thus, Jewish people took upon themselves the blame for the Holocaust.

Perhaps this explains why Bernard, in the vignette with which we started this chapter, is able to say 'God sent AIDS upon me'. Perhaps he, like Rabbi Wasserman, would rather say 'God is punishing me', than change his central image of God. For if I have sinned I can repent and turn aside the punishment or at least be forgiven and reconciled to God. If God is helpless, then I have no grounds for hope for any help.

When the disaster happens to other people it is even easier for us to say that it was all their own fault. For those of us who are not homosexual, it is easy to say that the calamity of AIDS which has killed so many homosexual men is their own fault for their 'unnatural' behaviour and God's way of warning against the sin of sodomy.

But Rubenstein points out that the Jews who died in the concentration camps were not themselves all guilty of modernism. Faithful, conservative rabbis died; little children who could not for a moment be held responsible for modernist theology died. So with AIDS: some who die are certainly homosexual, some are promiscuous. But people also die who have contracted AIDS from blood transfusions. Increasingly in Africa the greater number of those who die are women, faithful wives whose only 'sin' is to have married a man who has not always been faithful. Increasingly, too, the number of babies who die of AIDS is growing. A punishment which hits the innocent as well as, and even more than, the 'guilty' is a very strange justice.

If God has sent AIDS as a punishment for promiscuity, why has God waited for so long, since promiscuity is hardly new? If God is punishing homosexuals, why not lesbians, amongst whom, unless they are also intravenous drug users, AIDS is virtually unknown?

Anna lives in Zululand, South Africa. She is married to Jabulani, with whom she has three children. Jabulani is fond of his wife and children; but he works in Empangeni, 100 miles away, and only visits home one weekend a month. He believes that a healthy man needs sexual intercourse. He therefore uses prostitutes. Because Empangeni is on the lorry route from Mozambique to Durban, the prostitutes in Empangeni are also often used by truck drivers. Anna has discovered that she is HIV positive. She has never had sexual intercourse with anyone except Jabulani; but he refuses to believe that he can have given the sickness to her and refuses to go for testing. Soon she will fall ill. She and Jabulani will die. Their children will be orphans.

If we accept the idea that God punishes homosexuals or promiscuous persons by sending them AIDS, we have to explain why many people with AIDS are not guilty of these 'sins' but have been caught up in the consequences of the sins of others. If we decide that AIDS is God's punishment, we are declaring that God is unjust, punishing the good along with the wrongdoers.

'The tendency to find someone to blame for the things we fear is easily indulged in without regard for the morality of love, justice and truth' (*Pastoral Statement* 1990).

Clearly the matter is much more complex. God does not run this world on a basis of reward and moral recompense. The sun and rain shine and fall alike on the just and the unjust (Matthew 5.45, see Luke 13.1–5). In any case, as Paul pointed out, all of us have sinned, all have fallen short (Romans 3.23), none of us can be said to be truly innocent.

'The differences in human merit, if they exist at all, are so slight in God's eyes as to be of no use in governing the world' (Countryman 1987:126).

Perhaps if we are all sinners we may say that AIDS is a punishment sent upon all of us and not just upon homosexual persons? But we are still faced with the difficult truth that the punishment is not equally distributed. Why are some of us, sinners though we are, spared like Noah without Noah's claim to righteousness? It is not justice as we understand it. Despite this, some will still claim that we may not obscure the clear biblical teaching that God sends natural disasters, sickness and pain upon earth to punish evil. John Piper suggests that AIDS is merely a foretaste of ' . . . the penalties that God will impose in the age to come' (Piper 1987:16). John White reminds us (White 1990) that whole families share in the guilt of their leaders. When Korah rebelled against Moses and thus against the Lord (Numbers 16), the Lord in stern justice killed not only Korah, Dathan and Abiram but all their wives and children.

Lest we should think that this is merely Old Testament savagery, White refers us to Acts 5, where Ananias and Saphira, having lied to God, are struck dead. Perhaps, therefore, says White, God has indeed, as of old, sent AIDS amongst us as a plague, a punishment, and a terror to recall us, when all else has failed, to God's law concerning sexuality. In a world which is becoming increasingly permissive about sexual 'vices', God must warn and punish.

It is true that the Bible, Old and New Testaments, does sometimes explain plagues and disasters natural and political as a warning and a punishment from God. But the Bible is ambiguous on this point. After the Noahide flood, the editor of Genesis has God saying, in effect, that this was the wrong way to deal with sin and would not be repeated (Genesis 8.21). To legitimate suffering on the grounds that terror may bring us to our senses is a very dangerous view indeed. Even if our whole society is guilty of sexually permissive attitudes, many of those who die of AIDS can hardly be held responsible for those attitudes, especially the AIDS widows and orphans of Africa. To speak of God visiting terror on innocent and guilty alike in order to establish a moral point is to justify the deeds of human terrorists who use just the same argument. Terrorists justify the deaths caused by their indiscriminate bombs on the basis that through general terror the authorities may be persuaded to redress whatever political injustices the terrorists are concerned about. God, we may hope, is not a terrorist thug. We surely cannot continue to believe that the wives of Korah, Dathan and Abiram were justly killed for their husbands' offences. We cannot share the view of the editor of the Book of Numbers.

In the end not even John White is saying that sinners who have AIDS are to be rejected, or that we must accept AIDS as punishment and leave it at that. Sickness and AIDS entered their world by God's decision, says White, just as at Adam and Eve's disobedience Satan entered the world by God's decision. Satan is therefore an agent of God's judgment, but Satan must still be resisted and fought against now just as Jesus resisted and fought him. AIDS is Satanic, and must be combatted. God's final word, says White, is never judgment but blessing (White 1990:63). White would agree with Paul: 'For God has consigned all men to disobedience, so that he may have mercy upon all' (Romans 11.32). God's intention is mercy, not punishment.

Yet even with this more generous conclusion, this view still leaves us with a painful dissonance between what we believe is fair and just, and how we believe God has acted. If God sends AIDS as a punishment for sin, even if in the end God blesses those who are chastized, then in many cases, even most cases, the wrong people are chastized. Many promiscuous people, perhaps because they use condoms, do not fall ill. Many innocent people do.

And despite White's more generous conclusion, it is very important that we say loudly and clearly that AIDS is not a punishment for sin. Few theologians think that it is; but churches do not say this very loudly, perhaps out of fear that they will be seen to be compromising sexual standards.

'While a minority of religious responses have simply seen AIDS as a divine punishment, the majority of responses from American religious groups have called for compassion for the sick. Yet many of these groups uphold the traditional condemnation of homosexuality' (Kowalewski 1994:27).

Kowalewski is talking of American churches, hence the emphasis on homosexuality. But the same has been true of the churches in Africa. They mostly do not believe that AIDS is sent as a punishment. But they do believe that AIDS is a consequence of heterosexual promiscuity, and they are reluctant to appear to condone or to understate their resistance to such promiscuity. So on the whole they have said very little, and what they do say, being cautiously phrased, does not catch the attention of the media. Only the vocal extremists, the Moral Majority spokespersons, are heard in the media. Since the rest of the church remains silent, the world assumes that these views are the views of the churches.

Of course there is a tension here. It is quite right that we should be reluctant to compromise on sexual standards. Later in the book we shall explore a theology of sexuality. I shall be saying that it is very important that the church should positively embrace our sexuality as a gift from God, and that at the same time it should uphold responsible standards of sexual behaviour. The immediate major cause of AIDS is promiscuity. Present indications are that AIDS will not be checked until promiscuity is checked. In considering sexuality we shall also give some attention to homosexuality. Obviously this will mean taking the biblical injunctions against homosexuality seriously.

'Avoidance of illicit use of drugs, sexual abstinence before marriage, and monogamous fidelity within marriage, recommend themselves as being medically necessary as well as morally responsible. The recovery of the virtue of chastity may be one of the most urgent needs of contemporary society' (Pastoral letter of California Catholic bishops, quoted Kowalewski 1994:53).

It is right that the churches should proclaim that AIDS can only be checked by a change in life-style, since nobody else seems to be doing so. But churches need to take care not to use AIDS merely as a way of re-imposing traditional sexual ethics. In our chapter on sexual ethics we shall explore this further. As long as we do teach that homosexuals are all sinners, it is hard for homosexual persons to come to the church for help with AIDS. As long as our primary message is seen to be that sex outside marriage is always sinful, then ordinary people, very many of whom have had sexual experience outside marriage, feel embarrassed to approach the church. If people with AIDS believe that the church also teaches that AIDS has been sent as a punishment for homosexuality and promiscuity, it is almost impossible for them to come for help.

'I believe that the church should do good to people, learn from them and build them up, not make people who are already having a bad time feel worse' (Pattison in Woodward 1990:9).

As Grace Jantzen puts it,

'One thing Jesus did not do was to reinforce internalized shame: what he did was to set people free to see their worth in his eyes and in God's eyes' (in Woodward 1990:28).

Ron Russell-Coons quotes a homosexual person as saying that many homosexuals are convinced that their parents would rather they were dead than gay; and indeed that many homosexuals with AIDS, overcome with guilt which their parents and society place upon them, wish that too.

'As a Christian I believe that the story of Jesus could offer narrative substance to the meaning we have already discovered – because Jesus is crucified as we are, because Jesus dies as we do, and because Jesus rises again into newness of life, as we will . . . Unfortunately, the history of the gay community with the church makes it nearly impossible for us to claim the promise' (in Russell 1990:64).

If White is correct – and of course he is – about God's final word being blessing and not judgment; if Bernardin and Sider are right that our message should be one of love and not of judgment, then it is important that church leaders and spokespersons say so very loudly. For this is not the perception of the media, who think the religious 'right' speak for us all.

In an episode in the British television serial *Eastenders*, the young man who is HIV positive and his fiancée go to meet her Scottish minister father. The father reacts with stereotypical prejudice, judgment and Calvinist wrath. Viewers protested that the programme gave an unfair picture of the Scottish churches. So it did; there is no reason to think that Scots ministers are any more ignorant about AIDS than the rest of us. But the point is that the programme scripters, the media, think that the minister's response was stereotypical. Unless we speak up much more audibly with a different message, those who are ill with AIDS and are not close to the church will not easily trust us.

> 'Those who had no close relationship with the institutional churches in adult life seemed to feel they had nothing to offer except reinforcement of guilt, shame and rejection' (Pattison in Woodward 1990:12).

It is not only people with AIDS who need to know that God's message is blessing and not bane. Susan Sontag suggests that we are living in a time of cultural distress. In the Western world, at least, we no longer have a confident belief in ourselves or our culture. With some justification, we feel we are living in a time of moral uncertainty. We all feel corporately guilty about so many things: rising crime rates, rising marriage breakdown rates and illegitimacy rates; ecological destruction. We almost hope that God is going to send another flood to drown everything so that humans can make a fresh start.

> 'The sense of cultural distress or failure gives rise to the desire for a clean sweep, a *tabula rasa*. No-one wants a plague, of course. But, yes, it would be a chance to begin again' (Sontag 1989:87).

But we don't want to be swept away personally. So we believe that God is doing it with other people – homosexuals for their perversity; black people because their population expands too fast.

Neither extreme relativism nor extreme moralism really helps.

'To offer unconditional love and acceptance of persons is not to imply moral agreement or to licence sin' (Christensen 1991:14).

The church needs to be in a middle place. It needs to reconsider carefully its own ethics of sexuality, and to uphold standards of care and responsiblity in sexuality. It also needs to offer love and acceptance without exception to everybody. Jesus acknowledged the sin and did not pass it over, but he did not see sin as a reason for not loving; indeed, he is reported to have said that sinners were closer to the kingdom of heaven, and that those who had been forgiven most also loved the most (Matthew 21.31; Luke 7.47). We may not intend it so, but the general perception of many both inside and outside of the church is that the church is the enemy of sinners. The opposite should be the truth. Like Jesus, the church should be the friend of sinners. Unlike Jesus, members of the church are themselves all sinners. Yet we claim Jesus as our friend, and must wish to bring others to the same realization.

Hypothesis: AIDS is not a punishment but a consequence of free will

We cannot say that AIDS is a punishment for sin. But if we say that AIDS is a consequence of sin, we say something rather different. AIDS clearly is, in part, a consequence of humans disobeying God's life-giving laws. In this view AIDS became a killer disease because some human beings live such irresponsible lives. Ronald Sider, while saying that persons with AIDS are precious in God's eyes, and denying that God has sent AIDS as a punishment for homosexuality, still maintains that since God is a just God, there must be consequences if God's laws are broken.

Thus we may want to say that AIDS is not a punishment but is nevertheless something that God permits because human beings, if they are free, must bear the consequences of their actions. Richard Swinburne has said that in order to grow, human beings must learn from their mistakes (Swinburne 1979:200ff). In order to learn from our mistakes, the consequences of our mistakes must be real. To the extent that God cushions us from these consequences, we will not truly learn to be responsible. Does this view enable us better to reconcile our dissonance between our experience of AIDS and our belief in God as both all-capable and all-loving?

But what about the fact that with AIDS, as with so much suffering, the people who endure the pain are often bearing the consequences of the sins of others? In his authoritative study of evil and belief in a God of love, John Hick made clear his preference for the so-called 'Irenaean' theodicy (Hick 1966:289). Building on the ideas of the second-century Irenaeus and the eighteenth-century Schleiermacher, Hick suggests that in our own time we can understand that God wishes above all that human beings should learn to live in love and harmony and with responsibility to one another, to creation and to God. God does not primarily desire that we should be happy; rather God desires that we should be good and holy. Goodness and holiness have to be learned through adversity, through making mistakes and learning from them. Pain and the possibility of sin are therefore necessary as part of the growing into goodness.

Both sinner and sinned against suffer in the AIDS pandemic; but perhaps all of them will be made stronger for the challenge which faces them? God does not wish us to endure AIDS. But because we must learn to be strong, God will not interfere to rescue us. If we do contract it, innocent or not, God is able to work within us to make us more holy, more perfect. AIDS is a consequence of human misuse of free will. Yet, *o felix culpa*, o happy sin, even the misuse of free will may lead to grace. A person with AIDS writes that 'I feel that I am a stronger, better and more spiritual person for having to deal with AIDS' (Adams 1989:259).

To see AIDS as a consequence of sin which unfortunately often falls upon the victim rather than the evildoer, but which may still be a source of grace for all, does surely provide a better fit between belief and experience. What, after all, is the origin of AIDS? No one really knows. Theories often reflect the prejudice of the holder. Western people commonly believe the virus to have started amongst Africans, perhaps caught from monkeys. This theory originated in the discovery that AIDS already existed in Zaire in the 1960s and that a similar virus is found there amongst green monkeys. How the disease spread from monkeys to humans was never clear; some people darkly suspected that Africans made sexual use of monkeys. The theory has distinctly racial overtones and confirms Western prejudices about African hygiene and sexuality.

'The subliminal connection made to notions about a primitive past and the many hypotheses that have been fielded about possible transmisson from animals . . . cannot help but activate a familiar set of stereotypes about animality, sexual licence and blacks' (Sontag 1989:52).

The theory about the African origin of AIDS may or may not have scientific basis, but it is easily accepted because of Western prejudice. Too often, the Western world continues to see all of Africa as the heart of darkness. In this view Africans are licentious, disease-ridden, corrupt and violent. Those in the West who contract AIDS are seen to have succumbed to these primitive instincts.

'The construction of African AIDS tells us little or nothing about AIDS in Africa but a very great deal about the changing organization of sexual and racial boundaries in the West, where AIDS has been widely harnessed to the interests of a new hygienic politics of intense moral purity' (Watney 1989:97).

The theory of an African origin of AIDS fails to explain why a supposedly African disease amongst heterosexuals would re-emerge in New York and Los Angeles amongst white homosexual men when the main trading links between Africa are with Europe and not the United States. The Russian weekly *Literaturnaya Gazeta* put forward a rival theory that the virus was engineered by Americans experimenting with DNA genes (Sontag 1989:52), a theory which Africans have sometimes shared with enthusiasm (Agadzi 1989:37).

But AIDS has probably been around for a long time. Before either the DNA experiments or the outbreak of AIDS in Zaire,

' . . . hundreds of AIDS-like cases were documented in medical journals for decades prior to the recognition of AIDS' (Root-Bernstein 1993:2),

with cases in America, England and Norway. Probably the virus in various forms has existed for a long time, but only became noticeable once social conditions led to frequent and widespread changes of sexual partners, thus encouraging the rapid spread of the virus.

These social conditions were present in the homosexual communities in North America and elsewhere. They were also present in the chaotic conditions of modern sub-Saharan Africa. AIDS is not sent by God, but is an opportunistic virus like any other which normally does little harm but became epidemic when conditions encouraged its spread.

However, it would be much too simplistic to say that sexual promiscuity is the cause of AIDS. In America and Europe, intravenous drug usage with shared needles is another factor. And although sexual intercourse with many partners is still the major immediate cause of the epidemic, certainly in Africa, we must consider social circumstances as a proximate cause. Post-colonialist developments, the unpredictable demands of the world market and the breakdown of rural economies force men into towns to seek work, leaving their families at home in the villages. Men away from home have recourse to prostitutes. Young women have no way open to them to earn money outside the sex trade. If we would speak of guilt, the guilt is difficult to determine.

'Those whose usurious and avaricious deals lead to the hunger and death of their brethren in the human family indirectly commit homicide, which is imputable to them',

says the new Catholic Catechism (*Catechism* 1994: no. 2269) – but whose avariciousness is being referred to? All of us, buying at the cheapest prices, investing at the best returns, help drive the merciless wheels of economy which fuel Third World poverty.

There are social factors underlying homosexual promiscuity as well. Perhaps part of the reason for multi-partner homosexual activity is the refusal of non-homosexual society to recognize and encourage stable same-sex relationships, thus forcing homosexuality into the shadows and into secretive anonymous relationships. Those who use intravenous drugs often do so as an escape from hopelessness about their life circumstances: drug usage thrives on poverty. Drug usage and promiscuity are often symptoms of a despair which is not discussed or dealt with in our society.

'Both are ways, generally unsatisfying, for people to ease the pain, often perceived to be unique, that they experience living in the overwhelming disconnectedness of modern society' (Sabatino 1992:99).

The spread of AIDS has a great deal to do with a swing to a more competitive, less caring, political and economic ideology. Jan Grover points out that the AIDS epidemic coincided with the move away from centralized health and social care in the United States (Grover 1989). In the Third World the poverty which is such an important factor in AIDS is linked with the insistence by the World Bank that African countries adopt less socialistic, more market-related economic policies. The World Bank and the International Monetary Fund in recent years have been insisting that Third World countries must pay back at least the interest owing on outstanding debts. There are good reasons for this at a macro-economic level. Endless handouts of money with no strings attached led to a growth of bureaucracy, rampant inflation, inefficient use of that money, lack of accountability, nepotism, a culture of dependency and the many other political problems of Third World countries. Now that they must pay back interest, countries are having to trim the number of government jobs, control inflation, cut spending, and insist that land is used for cash crops in order to generate money. But at a micro level this has meant that there is much less money for health care.

'Among the poorest 37 nations of the world spending on health care has decreased by 25% over the past decade' (O'Donahue undated:6).

Thus the conditions in which AIDS runs rampant are created. The spread of AIDS is hastened by harsh financial discipline imposed upon countries who cannot afford it. What seems like good economic policy becomes in fact, partly because of AIDS, very bad policy.

The more AIDS spreads, the greater is the cost to the economy in terms of health care, lost personnel, lost time, the cost of orphans and in many other ways. The structural adjustment programme insisted on by the International Monetary Fund and the World Bank as a condition of lending to developing countries has meant that in order to repay their debts and earn further loans, countries have had to export their agricultural products rather than consume them themselves. Subsistence economies are therefore weakened. People grow cash crops, not food crops. When the cash crop fails or is not fashionable, they starve. Transport infrastructures are developed. There is much migration to towns where jobs can be found in industries. Countries must use their income to repay debts, and thus have less money for welfare and health programmes (Lurie et al. 1995:541).

'In the early years of the AIDS pandemic the link between AIDS and development was not made. AIDS was regarded as a health problem' (O'Donahue, undated:6).

We now see that AIDS is not only a medical problem, and does not only result from sexual promiscuity and drug abuse, but is closely linked to poverty. Agricultural poverty leads to the increase of urbanization and the development of urban slums; poverty is closely linked with selling children into prostitution, and to women entering the sex trade since they have no other way to earn money. Long-distance lorry drivers make use of prostitutes, and AIDS spreads along transport routes. Poverty leads to the collapse of national health services, and people who are already malnourished or infected with sexually transmitted diseases are more vulnerable to AIDS. Prejudice, poverty and social disruption are all factors underlying promiscuity, homosexuality and drug abuse.

'World-wide efforts to stem the HIV epidemic have to date emphasized inducing behaviour change in individuals at high risk for HIV infection . . . we argue that social and economic forces have also played a critical role in promoting the spread of HIV, and that these have been largely overlooked in favour of factors that operate at the individual level' (Lurie et al. 1995:539).

Thus Cardinal Basil Hume is both right and wrong when he says that AIDS is ' . . . one of the many disastrous consequences of promiscuous sexual behaviour' (quoted *The Grail* 1989:65). Blaming AIDS on sexual promiscuity narrows the blame to only part of society. Christian people do need to be honest and to continue to say that promiscuity causes AIDS. Some have accused the churches of being afraid to speak out against promiscuity for fear of appearing negative, judgmental, out-of-date and prudish.

'Orthodox and traditional Jews and Christians and other persons with a high regard for the monogamous, married, heterosexual family unit have no need to apologize for attempting to inject a healthy dose of moral rectitude into the AIDS crisis. They should not be cowed by the supercilious derision of homosexual activists and their sympathizers crying foul for "using" AIDS to promote traditional sexual morality' (Antonio 1986:198).

But those who speak in this way mislead us in two ways. AIDS, in a world-wide perspective, is not primarily a sickness of homosexual persons. And promiscuity, hetero- or homosexual, must be seen against the wider background of the social factors which cause it, which are not merely human lustfulness but loneliness, poverty and the resulting pressures on family life, alienation and unjust social structures for which we all bear some responsibility.

People in Africa, where AIDS has spread so widely, and Asia, where AIDS is spreading now, are not by nature more promiscuous than anyone else. Patterns of sexuality are responses to structures of cultural alienation and economic devastation (Saayman and Kriel 1992:24). The primary reason for the high incidence of AIDS in Africa is not aberrant sexuality but aberrant economy (Saayman 1991:21).

Some Christians have taken offence at the slogan 'Our Church has AIDS', since in their view people who get AIDS are sexual sinners, and sexual sinners by definition do not belong in the Christian church. Leaving aside the dubious assumption that real Christians don't sin sexually, the truth is that all Christians are part of the sinful structures of a selfish society which we all help shape – through our investments on the stock exchange, through our looking for cheap bargains in the supermarket – in which poverty still thrives and in which therefore AIDS multiplies. We all have AIDS because we all share in creating an environment for AIDS even though we may not ourselves be involved in sexual promiscuity.

We also all have AIDS in the sense that those who do have AIDS have to be our concern.

'Jesus places no conditions on his expression of concern for the wounded of his world and society' (Diocese of Southwark 1992).

Nor should we impose conditions, for we are in no position to judge who is the worse sinner (Matthew 7.1). AIDS is the result of human sin, but human sin of many kinds, including sinful social structures for which we all bear some degree of responsibility. In this way we see new relevance in Paul's message to the Romans which I mentioned earlier: we have all sinned and fallen short. In traditional theological language, AIDS is a consequence of the fallen state of humans. AIDS is not a punishment but a consequence of that sinful state with its many ramifications, and none of us except children can be held entirely innocent.

The sufferings are very real and tragic. Human freedom means that God cannot intervene to soften the consequences of what we do (for then we are not truly free but have only an apparent freedom with limits beyond which God steps in to resume control). The consequences do not necessarily fall on those who most deserve them, but nevertheless none of us is entirely free of blame. God does not wish the pain upon us, but we cannot avoid it as a necessary part of our freedom. Ultimately, though, God's grace is mightier than the tragedy, and the lives of those affected by AIDS can be turned into lives of triumph and holiness as they are strengthened by their pain.

So might go a response to AIDS along the lines of the theodicies of Hick or Swinburne. Does God then stand innocent of the charges we have levelled against the deity, charges of cruelty at worst or indifference at best? It is surely true that some people with AIDS are strengthened by their pain. They stand as an example to us all. Those who minister to people with AIDS also seem to develop great spiritual strength and are often witnesses to God's grace.

Sister Monica is a Catholic nun and medical doctor working in and around an African city, far from the cool hills of her native Ireland. Day by day she tends the long lines who come to the clinics in various centres around the city. In addition she also organizes clubs for young people where they may meet, socialize and support one another in affirming higher standards of sexual morality. There is no financial reward and, one might think, not much emotional reward when the lines continue to grow daily, and when members of her teenage clubs fall away because they are pregnant, or, worse, become HIV positive.

Dr Lars is an American of Swedish origin. He trained as a doctor and *specialist in infectious diseases. He was offered a prestigious research position in a prestigious American medical school. But he and his paediatrician wife Helga read an account of Lutheran church work in Tanzania, and offered their services as medical missionaries. They live in a simple bungalow in the mission compound, on a joint salary of $1000 per month. Their children must go away to boarding school in Kenya for education. Through their dedication the treatment of AIDS in their hospital is informed by the most up-to-date medical knowledge. Their patients experience the love of God through them.*

AIDS may, and does, crush and destroy both 'innocent' and 'guilty' alike. But it also enables a few to develop those qualities of courage, goodness and selflessness which show human nature at its redeemed best. Without disaster there could be no heroism, and we would never have our best and bravest qualities called forth. Could this not be the reason why God allows AIDS and major disasters?

Richard Rubenstein looks at similar Jewish responses to the Holocaust. He describes the views of Ignaz Maybaum, who sees the Holocaust as a necessary sacrifice which God required in order to wean Jews from superstitious medievalism. Medievalism had to be destroyed, even though that meant destroying millions of morally innocent, if medievally minded, Jews at the same time. Maybaum parallels this with the Christian belief that Jesus, the just one, had to die in order to destroy an old religion and build a new one. If we were to apply this line of thinking to AIDS, we might with justification say that the church in the West has grown stale and complacent for lack of spiritual challenge, and the missionary church in newly evangel-ized countries has lost its zeal and spirit of heroic self-sacrifice and adventure. AIDS may change all of that.

But Rubenstein points out that the Christian view of the sacrifice of Jesus is not a true parallel, for in this context God is understood to be sacrificing himself, not millions of innocent others. The affront to our sense of justice is too great for Maybaum's theory to help us reconcile belief with experience (Rubenstein 1992:166).

Or, says Rubenstein, there is Emil Fackenheim, who sees the death camps as a kind of test. God was in the camps all the time, says Fackenheim. A voice speaks from Auschwitz, and there are Jews who hear that voice, and Jews who deliberately shut their ears so as not to hear that voice (Rubenstein 1992:181). Those who heard the voice had sparks of resistance kindled within them, and even if they died, they died knowing and asserting their own personhood and worth before God. So we might say that in this time of AIDS, too, the voice of God may be calling, and those who hear the voice, even if they die, may die reconciled to him.

We cannot deny that this is often true. Just as there were Jews in the concentration camps who we might say heard the voice, and in whom sparks of resistance and affirmation of self were kindled, so too AIDS has called forth heroic qualities. AIDS has brought lost and alienated people back into new faith and a relationship with God.

But would it really be fair or just that those terrified lines of men and women, some old and frail, some mothers with children, were herded off the transport trains straight into the gas ovens so that in that brief interval of time they might hear a commanding voice and become renewed in faith and obedience? Does this really help us reconcile belief with experience? What of those who failed to respond to the voice? If this is God's intention, are we not morally outraged? Would it be fair or just to say that those who went to their deaths in cowed fear, or those who were kept alive as slave labour and who failed to assert themselves but became collaborators in their own destruction, had denied the voice of God? Did they deserve their fate because of their failure to hear the voice? For many Jews it was only possible to bear the pain and the fear by a numb, withdrawn acceptance which shut out the reality. Some people were brought closer to God. Others were reduced to subhuman beings. Can we honestly blame them?

William Countryman has suggested that in much the same way AIDS is a temptation, a *peirasmos* which will test our response to God (Countryman 1987:128). In some ways this statement must be true. AIDS is a test: for the church, for the general community, as well as for the individual who contracts it. Certainly some will respond bravely and selflessly, some will not. What we must not say, however, is that God sent the test. Since AIDS, at least in Africa, hurts mostly the poor, who have already faced 'tests' of malnutrition, of sickness, malaria and tuberculosis, can we really believe that God would test people with AIDS even further? Surely such a view is no less morally outrageous than that of Fackenheim concerning the Jews. For many people, AIDS will not strengthen them but will be the final straw which destroys them.

If God knew that the exercise of our free will would lead to such terrible consequences, should God have permitted freedom? Yes, says Swinburne: for otherwise we would not be free nor fully human. But there is an unexamined paradox in this very orthodox claim. Traditionally, Christians regard Jesus as being fully human and fully God. Since he is God, although Jesus has free will it is presumably ontologically impossible for him to sin. We will wish to say, with the writer of the letter to the Hebrews, that he was tempted like us (Hebrews 2.18), that he battled with the devil and felt the pain of temptation; but it is not conceivable, for traditional Christianity, that Jesus might have lost the battle.

Thomas Morris (1986:146) provides a philosophical explanation for how Jesus might have been truly tempted even though he could not ever have chosen sin. But if Jesus had free will, was truly tempted, yet by his very nature could not possibly have succumbed to the temptation, why could God not have similarly arranged that in the end we would never actually sin or do harm to others?

And if, in the interests of free will, God does not intervene in history, does not have a concrete historical role, does this God then not become functionally irrelevant? Many questions are raised by this kind of theodicy. In the face of actual suffering it sounds rather like the proverbial question about the number of angels dancing on a pin point. Kenneth Surin brings us down to earth. Suffering cannot be reduced to an intellectual theory. Suffering cannot ever be justified, and any attempts to explain it by an elegant theodicy in fact legitimate what cannot be legitimated (Surin 1986). It is improper to argue, as do Swinburne and Hick, that the pain is justified because of the moral improvement it may potentially bring to human capabilities.

Samson is thirty-four. He lives in Kagera, Tanzania. He has a wife and children, but when he became sick with AIDS he left them and returned home to his parents. His mother has now died. His father is in his seventies and is blind. Samson is now too weak to cook for himself or wash himself when (as frequently happens) he has diarrhoea. His blind father must do that for him. They both fear that the father will die before Samson, for who then will care for Samson? There are no hospices in Kagera; he must rely instead on the visits of the home visitor from the hospital every few days. Only when he is finally near death, will the overcrowded hospital try to find him a bed.

AIDS may bring opportunities for heroism and renewed faith, but in many cases it leads to degradation and despair. An AIDS death is not dignified. There is often severe and long-term incontinence and diarrhoea. Some die with words of faith and courage; but many people with AIDS suffer from dementia at the end.

'Many patients die terrible deaths. Gasping as much as sixty breaths a minute, they often drown in their own fluids. They die of fever, respiratory diseases, cancers and dementia. AIDS is the ugliest death I have seen' (a nurse, quoted Christensen 1991:122).

For many people with AIDS the outcome, as far as we can see, is not renewed commitment to God or to the service of other people, but well-founded despair and eventual disintegration. Can the free-will or natural-law or Irenaean theodicies help bridge the gap between our belief in a loving and powerful God and our experience (albeit at second hand for many of us) of the AIDS epidemic?

This is especially problematic when we consider the children.

Mwira is fourteen years old. She has now left school, as she must earn her living, since she is the sole supporter of her two younger brothers. Her parents are both dead from AIDS, having died within six months of each other more than a year ago. Following local custom, their father is buried outside on one side of the hut, their mother on the other side. Mwira's local church has seen to it that she was able to inherit her father's shamba or allotment plot. The church also pays the cost of her brothers' school fees and school uniforms. Mwira must give up her youth for her brothers; but she is comparatively lucky. The Lutheran diocese where she lives cares for some 10,000 orphans in this way; there are another 40,000 orphans in the same district who are not helped by any outside agency, and no one really knows what is happening to them.

Dostoevsky's dialogue between the monk Alyosha and his agnostic-but-wanting-to-believe brother Ivan is well known. Ivan wonders whether, perhaps, the existence of evil can be explained through God's intention to bring about some better future good and harmony.

> 'Is it possible that I've suffered so that I . . . should be the manure for someone else's harmony?' (Dostoevsky 1990:244).

Is someone else's harmony a fair bargain for my present suffering?

> 'I want to be there when everyone suddenly finds out what it was all for. All the religions in the world are based on this desire, and I am a believer. But then there are the children . . . ' (Dostoevsky 1990:244).

We might echo this as we consider AIDS. Suffering may be the ground on which future harmony is built; but then there are the children, innocent of any evil themselves, who are the main sufferers in the AIDS pandemic. Thousands are orphaned, with no prospect of education or improvement. Increasingly they can no longer be absorbed into the traditional African extended family. A retired Anglican bishop in Uganda tells me in an informal conversation that he and his elderly wife have adopted their son's five children, and three other children, all AIDS orphans; but now they can take in no more. This situation is being duplicated in many places.

Does it make sense to justify AIDS on the basis that it leads eventually to greater human wisdom and maturity, when so many children are sacrificed in that cause? Ivan Karamazov tells the story, which Dostoevsky took from actual contemporary court cases in Russia, of the little girl molested by her parents, smeared with excrement, locked in midwinter in an outside lavatory, beating her breast and calling on her 'Dear Lord' for help. But there is no help, for that would contravene the necessity to allow her parents free will. God insists that humans in general must bear the consequences of their own actions and also the actions of their fellow humans. Ivan asks:

> '"Imagine that you yourself are building the edifice of human destiny with the object of making people happy in the finale, of

giving them peace and rest at the last, but that you must inevitably and unavoidably torture just one tiny creature, that same child who was beating her breast with her little fist, and raise your edifice on the foundation of her unrequited tears –would you agree to be the architect on such conditions?" "No I would not", said Alyosha softly' (Dostoevsky 1990:245).

Does God send AIDS to punish us? Or does God permit AIDS in order to wean us from sin and strengthen us in enduring pain? Does God permit it in order to teach us to use our freedom responsibly? Is God not building the edifice of divine creation on the foundation of the unrequited tears of the AIDS orphans? Is such a God believable, or worth serving? Ivan could not bring himself to deny that God exists. But he chose to 'give his ticket back', to refuse to co-operate with God.

Surin's response is helpful. A theodicy which seeks to explain why God permits evil can never work, he says, because all such attempts end up justifying the unjustifiable. Such a theodicy is asking the wrong questions. The right question is not 'Why?' but 'What now?' What is God doing about AIDS? What does God want us to do about AIDS? Although Surin himself does not put it in this way, we may borrow from the liberation theologians and say that a good theodicy does not aim at orthodoxy but at orthopraxy. We are not called to explain AIDS; we are called to do something about it.

'Surely the task for the church is to cease labouring so much over the construction of elaborate theodicies and clever "moral responses" for AIDS, to cease all of that and simply to cherish who we are as persons: lonely, hurting, frightened, loving, healing, encouraging human beings who need each other desperately' (Pryce in Woodward 1990:55).

There is a point in exploring theodicies, if only to avoid false theodicies like seeing AIDS as a punishment. But in the end it is action, not intellectualization, which counts. Michael Clark makes the same point. 'The issue becomes not "why?" but rather "what do I do now, and who is there to help me do it?"' (Clark 1989:46).

There is, however, a postscript to our invocation of Dostoevsky. If we feel, with Ivan, that God should not allow human free will such

untrammelled power to hurt the innocent little ones, then we must
concede that humans ought not to allow that freedom to one another
either. We must concede the right and duty of the community to
check and, if possible, to prevent the sort of human behaviour which
leads to AIDS, especially sexual promiscuity. The ethical question
of balancing individual human rights with community needs is raised
sharply. Many church leaders in Africa believe that these rights must
be curtailed. We shall return to this point later. It does, however,
throw some light on the problems involved.

Hypothesis: God neither sends AIDS nor permits AIDS but is powerless to prevent it

> *Mathilda first discovered that she was HIV positive when she went to the ante-natal clinic. The counsellor broke the news to her, explaining the implications of the virus, and told her that it was possible that her baby, too, would be born with the virus and would die. Mathilda was able to accept the prospect of her own illness, but was adamant that God would not let her baby die. 'Surely he is a mighty God,' she said. 'He can do anything. I will pray to him each day that my baby will not get this sickness.'*

I ended the last section suggesting that what we should be asking
is not why God permits AIDS, but what God is doing about AIDS. Is
God doing anything? Perhaps after all God neither sends nor
permits AIDS but is unable to prevent it. How are we to understand
the nature of God in the light of the AIDS pandemic? Does AIDS
make us change our conception of God?

Traditional theology sees God and the world, creator and
creation, as separate entities. It says that God makes the world, God
ordains what happens in the world, but God is not of the world. God
is utterly independent of the world. God exists entire unto God's
self, totally other, of his own essence. Although God loves the
created world, God is not changed by what happens in it; God is not
really affected. Usually God acts through secondary causes in the
world, amongst which we are most keenly aware of human causes.
But God remains the primary cause of all that is and all that occurs.
By giving creatures free will God opens the way to some temporary

deviance from the divine will – temporary in the context of eternity, that is, for the deviance has lasted for millennia. In the end God's will shall be done and God's original intention shall be enacted. Since God has (for good reason) given free will to humans and perhaps to angels, in some sense God must be held accountable for what happens because of that gift. Nevertheless, in God's eyes and therefore in ours, free will is worth the cost and the risk. It is part of God's plan.

If we think of God as being in control, and as ruling over everything, then we must say that God has some purpose in permitting suffering. We must see suffering as being God's will, even if it is God's secondary will and not what God would ideally have wanted had we not misused free will.

Some have suggested that this traditional idea of God with its essential divisions between God and the world is not the most appropriate in this age of AIDS, and have suggested that process theology offers a better model for conceiving of God (Shelp and Sunderland 1987, Clark 1989). If all the power lies in God's hands, then AIDS is God's fault, and we will tend to think that only God can do anything about it. But if we see God and creation in a more interdependent relationship, if we see that suffering is not by God's will nor even by God's permission, but happens because God has no power to prevent it, perhaps we shall better understand how AIDS can have come about; and perhaps too we shall see more clearly that we have a shared responsibility with God to try to overcome AIDS. In the end, however initially dismaying, a concept of a limited God perhaps fits our experience of AIDS better.

Process theologians see God and creation as being in some sense co-eternal and co-dependent. God, they say, did not create *ex nihilo*, from nothing, for creation in some sense was there from the beginning with God. Our present physical world is therefore the consequence of an eternal interaction between God and creation. God does not exist independently of creation, because the nature of all existence, even God's, is to belong, to be in relationship. God depends upon creation, and always has.

Process theology is based on the philosophy of Alfred North Whitehead. His philosophy is too complex to summarize adequately here. For our purposes it is enough to understand that he said that reality is best conceived of not as a system of tiny atoms or particles all revolving around one another following some set of physical rules. We would do better, he said, to see reality as a series of 'becomings' rather than as a sort of cosmic machine. 'For Whitehead, . . . reality is composed of moments of experience and not bits of matter' (Mellert 1975:28). What we have in the past thought of as individual entities are in fact societies of 'moments of experience' (Cobb and Griffin 1976:15) temporarily combining into a system.

Whitehead does, of course, accept the idea that there may be minute particles of being. He has not entirely written off Newtonian physics. His emphasis, however, is not on the particles themselves but on the constant flux of interrelationships between the particles as they form a momentary system of mutual connectedness, and as these momentary systems enter into interrelationship with other systems.

> 'Each occasion of experience begins as a reception of a multitude of influences from the past . . . However, precisely how the present subject responds to the past, this is not determined by the past . . . this is determined by each present actuality' (Cobb and Griffin 1976:25).

Thus everything is in a state of flux, of becoming or process, in a network of relationships. Free will in creation extends beyond humans into every part of the process, into every momentary system or what Whitehead calls parcels of energy. All being is, in a sense, capable of making 'decisions' and interrelating with other 'decisions' made by other parcels of energy. Free will is therefore not so much a gift from God, which the traditional view held, but a necessary condition of being.

Within this flux Whitehead believes that there is still a thread of purpose. First of all, as we saw in the quotation above, each new event is built on the foundation of what went before. Past decisions do not determine, but they do affect what will be decided in the present and in the future. Secondly, God does have a vision of what God wants creation to become. God seeks to persuade, or 'lure', entities in creation to share in the accomplishment of that vision; God tries to influence us with that vision of the future. God is inextricably bound with creation. God is in everything, which is what process theologians call *panentheism*; God shares in the flux. God is dependent upon the decisions and movements made by the other existents. But God is not the same as the other existents. They, without exception, are transitory. They come into existence and they cease to exist. God alone is immortal. God both holds the past in memory in order to feed the past back into the present and is the one who lures creation into patterns for the future. God is the one who gives purposeful direction to creation for what God longs creation to be. This is what process theologians call the *superjective* aspect of God.

'Because of his vision, and because of his concern and care for what is happening in reality, he is constantly luring reality on to newer and greater things' (Mellert 1975:46).

However, and this is important for our discussion about God and AIDS, God's vision and longing cannot be imposed on the world. God can only persuade, not force.

'God is not an all-powerful, arbitrary ruler of the earth. In fact he is powerless before the freedom of each individual moment. In this sense he is no different from every other actual entity' (Mellert 1975:47).

'God is not in complete control of the events of the world' (Cobb and Griffin 1976:53).

God exists in a co-operative universe in which God is, to be sure, the senior partner, but God cannot force the outcome.

'In a world of genuinely self-creative beings, the possibility of no evil or suffering occurring is, quite simply, unrealistic. God's role is not to enforce a maximal ratio of good to evil but a maximal ratio of chances of good to chances of evil. That chances of evil remain is not because evil is good or useful after all but because the chances of evil overlap with the chances of good' (Hartshorne 1953:107).

Is this view really any different from that of, say, Swinburne that God must allow free will and that therefore suffering is virtually inevitable? I think it is. In Swinburne's view and those like him, God (doubtless for our good) prefers a free will universe to one in which goodness is enforced and thus not real goodness. The emphasis is on the free will which humans are permitted so that they may be free moral agents. God therefore makes the decision to allow free will. This view opens itself to the criticism that the cost of free will is too high to be morally acceptable.

In a process theodicy, God does not *allow* free will. It just is part of reality. Free will extends beyond humans into all levels of being. Austin Farrer paints a somewhat similar picture in his view of a physical universe which exists in a tension and balance between all sorts of life forms from particles to animals to humans, each striving for its own place, and in which therefore conflict is inevitable. This, says Ferrer, is what physical life means; to wish for something different is to wish ourselves out of life.

'Because we take the physical creation to be good, we are outraged by the presence of certain distressing features in it; but once they are proved inseparable from its general nature, there is no further question we can rationally ask. To regret the [physical] universe is either morbidity or affectation' (Farrer 1962:61).

In that case there is no point arguing about the moral acceptability of the price of free will.

In some ways the process account of reality fits with our experience of AIDS. It also excuses God from the moral responsibility of sending or permitting the disease. It accords with how viruses seem to behave. Viruses seem to behave like sentient beings. They seem to strategize, to plan, to have malicious intent, to outsmart us. This is anthropomorphic, to say the least, and we cannot take it literally. Susan Sontag warns us of the dangers of using metaphors drawn from military campaigns when we speak about AIDS and which make us paranoid (Sontag 1989:18). But one of the difficulties with the AIDS virus is that it mutates constantly. Drugs like AZT (zidovudine) or more recently 3TC (lamivudine) or other protease drugs work for a while in combatting the virus, but at least at the time of writing the effect is not permanent because sooner or later a mutated form of the virus becomes resistant to the drugs.

'The worrying thing about this virus is its ability to alter its shape . . . We are currently seeing new HIV-like viruses emerging every year or two somewhere in the world' (Dixon 1990:54).

'There is no evidence yet that any of the new drugs, combined or alone, show long term effectiveness' (*Wall Street Journal*, 2 February 1995).

What process theodicy says about parcels of energy making their own decisions and not obeying set rules therefore seems to be at least analogous to our experience of AIDS. Woodward asks:

'Has AIDS got some profound, hidden meaning that reveals truth about life? Or is it simply an opportunistic infection that serves to reinforce our sense of the randomness of life and our powerlessness?' (Woodward 1990:1).

AIDS seems to be the latter: a virus that does its own thing in a random way which we cannot, and God cannot, control. The process theologians say that life is just like this. 'The inbreaking of randomness, chaos, humanly experienced as tragedy, simply happens' (Clark 1989:45). Edward Norman, while acknowledging that we cannot altogether escape the idea of God and judgment, says that it is 'ludicrous' to think that God sends suffering upon particular individuals. 'Illness has, for the individual, no moral qualities, and carries no human message' (Norman in Woodward 1990:85). Illness is part of being physical, it is neither punishment nor blessing, it is not sent upon us, it simply is. The moral issue is what we do about it.

Process theodicy also seems to accord with our experience of people and AIDS. People do not follow rules or behave predictably any more than viruses do. At first in North America, once AIDS was finally acknowledged and the causes of AIDS better understood, it seemed as if the spread of the disease could be limited. Many homosexuals changed their sexual behaviour, and either limited sexual activity within a closed circle or used condoms. But the disease began to spread amongst other groups, especially black people and hispanic people, perhaps through heterosexual activity or perhaps through intravenous drug usage. Now to everyone's surprise, the disease is beginning to spread again amongst young homosexual men once more. They know the danger of unprotected promiscuous sex, but don't seem to care.

'Data from the Columbia School of Public Health shows an increase in sexual partners and episodes among young gay men in New York City' (The Director, AIDS Research Unit, Columbia School of Public Health, *New York Times*, 7 February 1995).

In Africa the existence of AIDS was initially not acknowledged, but once the official silence ended, it was thought that if people were taught how AIDS spread they would naturally avoid behaviour which could lead to AIDS. Education would ensure that future infection diminished. Experience has shown this to be a false hope in many cases. Statistics provided by the Uganda AIDS Commission (Uganda AIDS Commission 1994)[6] suggest that while around 90% of young people of both sexes in Uganda have accurate knowledge about how AIDS is contracted, around 50% of young men in that age group and 20–25% of young women also report engagement in sex with casual partners. This scenario is repeated in many other parts of Africa. In America, ' . . . a recent survey showed that homosexuals in New York had reduced risky behaviour, but there was no increase in total abstinence' (Dixon 1990:25).

Humans would like to be in control. We would like to make rules about people and predict the rules that govern diseases. We wish we could eradicate AIDS through technology. But AIDS cannot be prevented by spraying, or better drainage, or even by better health care, although some experts believe that better health conditions might make us more resistant to the virus, or at least delay the onset of full-blown AIDS (Root-Bernstein 1993:311). AIDS can only be prevented by behaviour change. As long as persons who are infected with the virus infect even just one other person in their lifetime, AIDS will not be checked. Yet behaviour change is precisely the thing we wish we could achieve but cannot. 'People have to be persuaded to alter their sexual behaviour. That is not easy' (*Economist* 1991:32).

[5]The Ugandan government, having initially tried to ignore or minimize the extent of AIDS in that country, has now become a model of frankness and openness, and tries to provide information as accurately as possible.

Thus the process understanding of God seems to fit. We understand a model which says that creaturely beings, human or sub-human, do what they choose to do and that neither God nor we ourselves are able to prevent them. We understand very well what is meant when process theologians speak of God luring or persuading, not being just unwilling (as in traditional theology) but unable to force obedience. This is precisely our own experience with AIDS. We have no option except to continue to try to educate, just as God must continue to persuade. Yet there is no way we can force people to conform to the required behaviour. Even public policy makers recognize this.

'Public efforts at controlling the spread of HIV, whether it be national or international, are more likely to succeed if the focus is on education for behaviour change rather than on official actions [i.e. official sanctions, etc.]' (Chunn in Fleming et al. 1988:65).

But if God is powerless to force change, how then can God be said to have any relevance in the struggle against AIDS? Process theologians, as well as wishing to modify our concept of God's omnipotence, also wish to abandon that understanding of God which sees God as immutable, impassible and invulnerable. Traditional theism, they say, envisages God as of-his-own-essence. That is, traditional theism sees God as entirely self-sufficient, dependent upon nothing outside of the Godhead. To put it crudely, process theologians allege that in traditional theology God governs, but God does not feel. They suggest that we need to conceive of God as one who shares our pain with us. God is not a judge, but a fellow sufferer.

Allan was diagnosed as HIV positive some years ago. Now he is starting to feel sick. He has recurrent yeast infections. He takes seventy-five medications daily. He fears that his sight is beginning to be affected. Allan's parents are also worried because their apartment is too small to accommodate Allan and if he is blind they do not know how he will cope.

Neither Allan nor his parents need judging. They do need someone to understand and identify with their pain. Traditional models of God did, of course, find some place for speaking of God's sorrow and God's love, not least because these are clearly biblical concepts. But, as the debate over patripassianism makes clear, it is

true that traditional models of God did find it difficult to accommodate such concepts. Patripassianism was a third-century theory,
rejected by the orthodox tradition. It maintained that because the
three persons in the Trinity are one, and because Jesus, the Son,
suffered on the cross, the Father must have suffered too. A large part
of the reason why the orthodox theologians rejected this theory had
to do with the church at that time having great difficulty with
the notion that the deity, perfect and self-sufficient, could suffer
or indeed feel at all. Feelings imply vulnerability and emotional
need.

Process theologians, on the other hand, want to say without any
reserve that God does suffer. Because God does not force but only
lures, God suffers frustration and disappointment, God suffers
uncertainty as to what 'decisions' will be made by creaturely beings,
and is deeply hurt when part of creation is in pain.

> 'He knows more, because he envisages more. He suffers more,
> because he knows more. He is, says Whitehead, "the great
> companion, the fellow sufferer who understands"' (Mellert
> 1975:47).

Therefore, say process theologians, God's righteousness and justice
are not compromised by the existence of evil, for God cannot prevent
the evil, and endures infinitely greater pain than we do because of it.
God is a co-sufferer with the world, and therefore, we may assume, a
co-sufferer with a world with AIDS.

> '. . . if God is the co-sufferer of each and every victim, then quite
> clearly the justice of his ways with men and women cannot be in
> dispute: what is meted out to them is no less than God must
> endure' (Surin 1986:90).

We hurt, but God hurts even more.

But is this enough? Surin points out that a vulnerable God who
cannot change our situation but shares our pain is not what sufferers
are really looking for.

> 'God too powerless to overcome evil will not conceivably be able
> to occupy the "logical space" which circumscribes the afflicted
> individual, who will in all probability be more interested in the

essentially practical matter of waiting and hoping for the conquest of evil and the cessation of pain' (Surin 1986:91).

Surin has a point. People in pain want the pain to stop more than they want sympathy. Process theology may satisfy the intellectual concerns of the theologian trying to reconcile God and the existence of evil. But that intellectual exercise runs into the danger of passively accepting suffering as an inevitable part of the scheme of things. Process theologians may be less vulnerable on this point than an Augustinian kind of theodicy. But some process theologians do, like Augustine, even talk about the aesthetic need for evil to exist.

'Human beings require experiences which maintain the "aesthetic mean" between too much order and too much disorder . . . An ordered, utopic paradise is not a suitable environment for significant human life' (Whitney 1985:38).

This kind of rationalism is unlikely to be of immediate help to the person in desperate anxiety because he fears encroaching death, or is in pain because his lover is dead, or is sitting in agony at the side of her demented and dying son, or is having to deal with increasing disability caused by encroaching AIDS symptoms. What that person looks for, we might suppose, is relief from the pain, not assurance that it hurts God even more than it hurts them! Austin Farrer made the same point about his own theodicy. 'What we have written is, we know, quite useless to those who rear imbeciles or lose infants' (Farrer 1962:191).

Even if people with AIDS want miraculous cures, however, they do not seem to get them. Is it fair for Surin to raise this objection? Does the God whom sufferers want actually exist? Is there a different kind of God from the process God? Is there a God who does display his omnipotence in AIDS-healing miracles? A poster in Kampala, Uganda, advertising a healing service to be conducted by a visiting tent evangelist, promises: 'Hear Prophecies. See miracles. The blind see again. The lame walk. AIDS is cured.' But does the evangelist keep his promise? Quite probably there may be a temporary cure of immediate symptoms; but does the AIDS go away?

Abraham Verghese tells the story of the young man who, perhaps in his dementia, saw a vision of Christ by his bedside. The effect on him was to make him calmer. The effect on the boy's father was to make the father certain that the boy would now get well, a belief he maintained vehemently until the day, shortly afterwards, when the young man died. The truth is that although there may be rare cases where HIV positive persons mysteriously do not become ill with AIDS, such cases are rare indeed, and healing miracles of the kind expected by the father do not happen. The process concept of God may seem inadequate to people with AIDS, but the God such people are alleged to want does not exist.

Perhaps, although as far as I know none of the theological literature on AIDS has suggested this, the only intellectually honest theological position is to go further than the process theologians. Perhaps we should join Don Cupitt and the Sea of Faith group and say that there is no God out there to rescue us or help us. Our concept of God, say these 'non-realists', is one that humans have created for themselves, which does not relate to an actual Being but is an expression of our human hopes and ideals (Cupitt 1980). We may wish to contest that such a view can be called a theology at all, since it has no *theos*. But Cupitt and those like him do not wish to cut themselves off from the Christian tradition or Christian worship and liturgy. They see themselves as faithful followers of Christ. They do not believe that a 'real' God exists, but they do believe that the tradition and the imagery of theism which humans have created can be helpful to us as we seek to live our lives with meaning and with concern for the common human good.

The position of Cupitt and his 'Sea of Faith' supporters is in fact very similar to the position which Rabbi Richard Rubenstein in the end adopts for himself. He also does not wish to cut himself off from the Jewish tradition which is part of who he is, or to cease to be a Jew. He cannot say that he believes in an actual God: the reality of the Holocaust has made that impossible for him. In the second edition to *After Auschwitz* he is, he says, more understanding than he was of those who cannot share his agnosticism. But he remains, not defiant or resistant, but silent before the mystery. He will neither affirm nor deny. 'All that we can affirm is our reverent and attentive silence before the Divine' (Rubenstein 1992:200).

Does it matter whether or not we believe in a 'real' God? Albert Camus in his famous novel about an outbreak of plague in an Algerian town looks at many of the same issues that we have addresssed here (Camus 1972). '[*The Plague*] is a book that has a tremendous amount of meaning for those working with AIDS' (Mann in Fleming *et al.* 1988:5). People deny that the plague has come. The town officials will not admit that there is a problem. Once the existence of the plague is undeniable, people withdraw into themselves. The priest, Fr Paneloux, assumes that God is punishing the city for its sins. Then in the face of suffering children Paneloux changes his mind. He concedes that we cannot understand the suffering, that it is not a punishment. But rather than deny the existence of God we must accept the terrible mystery and just go on. The doctor, Rieux, rejects this. Like Ivan Karamazov, he says

'No, father. I've a very different idea of love. And until my dying day I shall refuse to love a scheme of things in which children can be put to torture' (Camus 1972:203).

Rieux does not believe in God. He has a good reason to leave the city – his wife is gravely ill elsewhere. He has no logical nor theological reason to stay in the city, or to continue with his ministry at great risk to himself. But he does choose to stay, out of sheer self-chosen goodness. He needed no God to help him make that decision. Do we need God to face AIDS?

John Hick says that Cupitt's position – and thus by implication Camus' position – is too bleak to provide hope for humans facing the harshness of life. Theological non-realists ' . . . abandon hope for humankind as a whole' (Hick 1993:13). For all the courage, rigour and virtue of Cupitt's position, it does not seem likely to be a theological model that will have much power to motivate people with AIDS or for those who care for them. Camus is, perhaps, more influenced by his Christian background than he thinks. Nor will non-realism help the church to take on its own ministry to people with AIDS. Cupitt concedes that the church is unlikely to agree with him (Cupitt 1989:71). In the same way Rubenstein admits that his beliefs will not be widely accepted in Judaism.

'Of necessity [most] Jews will reject the interpretation of Divinity I have set forth in these pages. That is to be accepted. It is by no means certain that Judaism can survive without faith in the God of Israel as traditionally understood' (Rubenstein 1990:200).

Perhaps we are forced back on to a process model after all. Surin may be right that this model is too insubstantial to offer to a suffering person what he or she is seeking. He thinks that suffering people want a God whose presence and actions as first cause is to be seen more clearly. I have suggested that God does not, in our experience, become manifest in this way. In fact, once the initial period of denial or bargaining is over, none of the people with AIDS with whom I have spoken has ever expressed any expectation of miracles of physical healing. Without exception they have all accepted the medical opinion that, sooner rather than later, they will get sick and die.

'I believed that I could pray for strength to accept my illness, but I thought the goal should be to attain peace with myself by the time I died. A goal of not dying always seemed vain, not worthy of prayer' (Sabatino 1992:96).

The miracle that they seek is not to be delivered from AIDS but to be delivered from fear, to be enabled to forgive and to be forgiven. They seek personal transformation, and power to take charge of their lives. They often claim to have found it. In the process model, where God is not primarily seen as King and as Judge, guilt-laden self-deprecation is no longer necessary. We focus our anger, not on God but on the situation. We are more able to regain our self-respect and self-motivation.

Rich and his partner are at an AIDS support group Bible Study. They are discussing Luke 4, where Jesus says he has come to fulfil Isaiah's prophecy concerning setting prisoners free. His partner mentions a recent incident when an uninformed relative said that he was glad about AIDS because it got rid of faggots and drug addicts. Rich says, 'Well, I'm glad about AIDS too. Before I got AIDS my life was nothing. Now my life has taken on meaning; I have learned to tell my father that I love him; I have learned to hug people; I know how to be joyful. Jesus sure set me free.'

One critic has said that a God who can only persuade or 'lure' does not meet our need for a God who transforms human beings as Rich described his own transformation.

'Process theologians will have to explain the apparently large number of people who remain unpersuaded before they can claim meaningful application for the theory' (Peterson in Nash 1987:129).

This criticism is misplaced. Rich was transformed because he wished to be. He was open to be persuaded and lured. A 'luring' God can certainly transform those who wish to be transformed. The people with AIDS whom I have met do not expect their illness to be taken away. Some of them have given in to lethargic despair. But some, like Rich, have indeed found a source of transforming power.

Process theologians lay great stress on God suffering with creation. Surin is right: this may be of no great comfort to the sufferer. The people with AIDS do not seem to lay much stress on the notion that God is suffering in agony with them. What comforts them is the belief that God *loves* them, that they are not forgotten or pushed to the margins of God's love. And again and again people with AIDS say that they have come to believe God loves them because they have experienced people loving them in God's name.

Bryan used to belong to a conservative evangelical congregation in the mid-West United States. When he was diagnosed as HIV positive he was reluctant to tell his pastor. He assumed his pastor would condemn him as a homosexual. He was brought by a friend to an Episcopal cathedral. There he felt welcomed, and became a very active member. He tells the Dean that in him and in the cathedral congregation he experienced God loving him, and came to believe that he mattered to God.

Those who give love to people with AIDS are not necessarily church people, nor consciously loving their friends in the name of God. On the contrary, sometimes people with AIDS find more love and acceptance outside the church than within (Pattison in Woodward 1990:12). God's love, God's luring, God's transformative power does not begin nor end with the church. That is not what I am claiming. But if we say that all love, within and without the church, is a response, conscious or unconscious, to God, are we not making our concept of God so wide that in fact it becomes meaningless? People inside the church show love, and we say 'It is by God's grace'. People outside, non-Christians even, show love, and we say still, 'It is by God's grace'. Have we not made God so vague, so generalized, that we have lost any real God altogether? Anthony Flew long ago criticized a theology which clung to a God made meaningless through a thousand qualifications (Flew and Macintyre 1955:98).

That objection would be valid if we were trying to use the AIDS crisis as a way of proving God's existence. That, however, is not what we are trying to do. We cannot use the tragedy of AIDS in this way for propagandist purposes of our own. Our intention is a more humble one: to ask how our existing faith and our existing commitment to the God of church faith can be reconciled with and be useful for our experience of AIDS. Therefore we can gladly say that love, wherever it is found, is for us an example of people responding to God, so that we may commit ourselves more fully to that same response of love.

It is in this that the process model has great power. People with AIDS may not be much comforted by believing that God is suffering too. But those of us who are not infected and are not sick need to be reminded that we need to love and care for those who are. If we believe that it is not only the sick who are in pain, but that God is also in pain with them, then the words of Jesus really make sense to us:

> 'As you did it to one of the least of these my brethren, you did it to me' (Matt. 25.40).

> 'We must then relinquish our notions of God's all-powerfulness, either as the source of tragedy or as the rescuer from tragedy. As we come to accept the unitary balance of God and chaotic randomness, we discover in our experience of God-forsakenness God's real compassion and empowerment on behalf of the victims of oppression and tragedy' (Clark 1989:53).

It is not my concern here to defend process theodicy as the most appropriate model. Substantial criticisms have been offered; in turn process theologians offer substantial criticisms of the traditional paradigm. In an age of AIDS, which is also an age of pluralism and contesting philosophies, we are not likely to be able to fix on any one concept of God, but will have to switch and juggle between models, sometimes contradictory models. That is the nature of a post-modern situation. But process theology offers some important pointers:

• God neither sends AIDS as a punishment nor permits AIDS as a test;

• There is an element of chaotic free will operating at every level of life;

• AIDS and other physical illnesses are sheer accident, part of a physical universe filled with diverse and competing entities;

• AIDS is, however, turned into pandemic because of various kinds of human sin;

• God cannot provide a quick fix. What God offers is a deep concern and compassion to support us, and, if we will receive it, grace and strength to transform our own outlook and spiritual resources;

• Because of God's compassion we are encouraged and called to be compassionate in turn. God's compassion motivates and strengthens our own. Because of God's compassion, people with AIDS can know that they do indeed matter and are not merely the unnoticed casualties of a cruel brute force universe. People with AIDS have a right to respect themselves and to expect respect from others;

• God's compassion is not merely an example but is an enablement for those who will receive it;

• Despite the random cruelty there is an emerging purpose in life of which we can be a part;

• Despite the isolation of fear and pain, God's love provides a community centred upon God where we can feel we belong;

• Despite the sin of all of us which has led to AIDS there is forgiveness, and therefore there is also the possibility and the challenge to forgive one another.

Nevertheless, process theology, with its talk of suffering being an inevitable consequence of the free will of natural entities, its emphasis on the gently luring love of a God who cares and who suffers with us, is in danger of ending up in the same place as the other theodicies we have looked at. By implying that AIDS is an inevitable consequence of free will, at whatever level that free will is

perceived to operate, we run the risk of a passive acceptance of
AIDS.

Brave acceptance is morally admirable, even desirable in some
individual cases. But there is a place, too, for rage.

> 'Do not go gentle into that good night.
> Rage, rage against the dying of the light,'

said Dylan Thomas in his famous poem on death (Thomas
1971:298). Death may be inevitable, but we should still rage and
fight against the wastefulness and cruelty and pain of it just the same.
Susan Sontag warns us against using imagery drawn from the battle
field in our discourse about AIDS (see p. 56 above). She is right to
warn us. The AIDS virus is not a sentient enemy whom we may
outwit. It has no malignancy, no evil will. But there is a sense in
which AIDS is a mortal enemy of humanity in our time. We may lose
the battle, because at present our weapons are inadequate: 'You fight
tough, you fight dirty, but you cannot fight dirtier than it' (Monette
1988:2).

Nevertheless we cannot give up the war. Military imagery may
help the person with AIDS to think of himself or herself as a brave
soldier rather than a passive victim; it may make all of us feel that, as
in any war, personal and petty differences have to be laid aside in
order to put our combined talents and energies into the battle in
hand. 'If everyone doesn't stop and face the calamity, hand in hand
with the sick, until it cannot break through any more, then it will
claim the millennium as its own' (Monette 1988:45).

There is no tidy solution. Rage and acceptance do not go together;
yet each has its place and each response may correct what is missing
in the other. Dostoevsky's Karamazov was unable to co-operate with
a God who, for whatever reason, permitted evil in the world. He did
not have before him the process model as an alternative. But he did
not wish to abandon belief in God; and there was his dilemma. As
well as accepting the fact that AIDS exists and that at present AIDS
is incurable; as well as accepting that God either permits or cannot
prevent AIDS, there is a psychological need to rage against God as
well as AIDS. The rage is theologically legitimate. Belden Lane
reminds us of the Jewish tradition of arguing, Job-like, with God,
rather than meekly lying down under what seem to be divine

injustices. As we argue thus with God and tell God of our hurt and pain, says Lane, so our concept of God becomes less remote and more personal.

> 'This tradition of boldness in prayer, extending even to the hurling of accusations at heaven, exhibits . . . a robust faith' (Lane 1986:568).

The idea of entering into a contest with God is at the same time absurd and pastorally helpful, for the contest leads to our expressing to God our innermost fears. God becomes a person standing beside us in our torment rather than an outsider who has sent the pain.

> 'God's role becomes less of an antagonist, and more that of an affiliate, sharing in the pathos out of which redemption finally comes' (Lane 1986:584).

This has implications for those who minister to people with AIDS. Often the hurt and bewilderment drives persons with AIDS to make the pastor or the carer the target of the anger within them. Perhaps this anger, too, has a therapeutic quality.

AIDS and the Bible

Although we would not expect to find specific mention of HIV or AIDS in the Bible, we may at least hope to find help in knowing how God regards sickness in general. We may hope also to find guidance about sexuality, or about broken human relationships. The Bible may have been written in a different time and culture from our own, but there will surely be inferences to be drawn from parallel contexts. On the other hand we will expect that scriptural guidance will be complemented or modified by experience, by the cumulative tradition, and by the discoveries of modern science.

The Bible is an open-ended text

AIDS raises many issues which are deeply religious: that is, which are part of our search for ultimate, deep and lasting truths. Alan Cadwallader (1992), aware that popular attitudes to people with AIDS often combine compassion and disapproval, sympathy and revulsion, looks for some biblical guidance on the question of clean versus unclean. Specifically he looks at Mark's Gospel. But, as he observes, the issues of clean and unclean were not precisely the same for Mark as they are for us. So Mark's Gospel, argues Cadwallader, is open-ended, requiring thought and interpretation in the light of our own experience, before we can expect to know what it might mean for us today. In his study he provides a model which is useful for others coming to the Bible with their own questions about AIDS. Mark can only be sacred text for us, text which reveals to us God's word, if we establish a dialogue between the text and our own experience. Mark himself, says Cadwallader, expected his Gospel to be approached in this way; not as a closed and final text, for then

God's word would be trapped in a past context and dead for us, but as a text which could kindle an ever new and living encounter with God's word.

'Within Mark's gospel, the possibility is established of coming to the gospel as sacred text with our present experiences, both to find and to make sacred text. To press this further, I believe that Mark confers on "us" the responsibility to do so, if we, like the women, are to move from terror, flight and silence; if we are to discover by a return to Jesus, understanding and meaning for our puzzles, in short, if we are to have anything to offer' (Cadwallader 1992:159).

Others have made the same point about how to approach the Bible for guidance about AIDS. Theological reflection is

' . . . the process of critical conversation and interrogation between contemporary situations or experience, aspects of the Christian theological tradition, and insights from sources of contemporary knowledge such as the social sciences' (Pattison in Woodward 1990:8).

So following this model, we shall attempt to look at the Bible passages to be considered in the light of our own experience, often forged in a different context from that of the Bible authors and their community. In this way we hope to discover deeper and more lasting significances in our own issues. There will be no easy congruence, not only because our context is in many ways different from that of those in the various books of the Bible, but even more because psychology and sociology have changed our understanding of the human condition.

John 9: sickness and sin

We immediately consider the importance of this as we consider John 9. 1–12, the story of the blind man concerning whom the disciples ask 'Rabbi, who sinned, this man or his parents?' The disciples were still set in the way of thinking which believes that everything that happens to us is sent by God, and that therefore the blindness must signify that God has some reason to punish the man for his own sin or that of his parents. The relevance of their question to our own question about AIDS is very clear.

I mentioned in an earlier chapter that it is not surprising that some Jewish post-Holocaust theologians attributed Jewish suffering to Jewish sin, since this was consistently taught by the Old Testament prophets. So we can hardly blame the disciples for their assumption. But the Old Testament prophets, except perhaps for the writer of Job, were not primarily interested in explaining the origin of suffering. Their business was to convince the Jews and the Israelites to change their ways, to help them see the political realities around them in a new light. They were concerned for behavioural change rather than philosophy.

> 'The task of the prophetic ministry is to nurture, nourish and evoke a consciousness and perception alternative to the consciousness and perception of the dominant culture around us' (Brueggeman 1978:13).

The prophets speak out because they love the land and its people. Despite their righteous anger they speak not merely to condemn, but to warn. The suffering they foretell is nearly always endured by themselves also. They experience rejection and mockery; and then when what they foretell comes to pass, they share in the pains of the national defeat. Their warning comes from within the experience, and is spoken to those who will be fellow sufferers.

This is as true of John the Baptist as it was of the earlier Old Testament prophets. He warns the people, not as an outsider but as one who shares in the dangers that confront them, and is ultimately consumed by those dangers. To turn momentarily to Mark's Gospel before commenting on the Johannine text, it is clear that Mark sees Jesus carrying on where John left off (Mark 1.14). And in that Gospel, as we shall comment below, the crucial, 'hinge', passage is in Mark 8, where Jesus declares that his prophetic and messianic destiny leads to the cross, and the disciples find that so hard to accept.

To comment, then, upon John 9.1–12: we are perplexed by John's report of Jesus' reply: 'It was not that this man sinned, or his parents, but that the works of God might be made manifest in him.' On one level Jesus' reply is helpful, for Jesus makes it quite clear that punishment has nothing to do with the man's blindness. Sickness is not punishment. It is true that sickness and sin are often connected together in John's Gospel: the man healed of paralysis in John 5.14 was forgiven and healed simultaneously and told to sin no more lest worse befall him. Yet though by implication sin may cause sickness, Jesus never sends sickness upon humans (we cannot say the same for pigs or fig trees!). Sickness is an enemy, and he heals sickness by forgiveness.

We cannot be surprised at the disciples' question, since very often in the Old Testament sickness and plague are seen as punishment. Part of the difficulty of referring to AIDS as a plague is the echo that it creates in our mind of the plagues in Egypt, sent to punish and persuade a reluctant Pharaoh to free the people of Israel. We recall Fr Paneloux in Camus' novel *The Plague*. But that is not John's view. Sickness, says Jesus in this passage, is not punishment. This is the view, too, of the Synoptic evangelists. Matthew makes the same point in a different way in Matthew 5.45. Since God gives gifts to everyone regardless of their moral worth, says Matthew, good fortune or ill is clearly not sent in reward or punishment. The Jesus of Matthew does not support Ecclesiasticus 39.25 and 39.28, where God creates good things for good people and pestilence for vengeance. Luke has his own parallel story. Referring to the Galileans who had been executed, and to some people who had been killed in a fall of masonry, Jesus denies that these unfortunate people were in any way more culpable than other people. Luke does not deny the consequences of sin. We are all sinners, and unless we change we shall all perish. This will not be because God makes a wall fall upon us but because suffering is the natural consequence of irresponsible behaviour.

Thus far the correlation between New Testament teaching about sickness or affliction and our own observations about AIDS accord very well. AIDS is not a punishment for sin, although sinful human actions and attitudes are major contributing factors. We are called to love and bless those with AIDS even though on some occasions they may be in part responsible for their own situation. But what Jesus says in John's Gospel about the blind man is: 'It was not that this man sinned nor his parents but that the works of God might be made manifest in him.' In other words, it would seem, God allowed him to be blind so that Jesus could cure him and show God's power working through him. This is problematical on a number of levels. It seems morally unacceptable; we much prefer the Jesus of the Synoptic Gospels who is reluctant to draw public attention to his miracles. It takes no account of blind people in the world who were and are not healed. Above all it does not fit our experience of AIDS, where Jesus does not heal in any literal physical way.

But perhaps we mistake John's purpose here. Just as the Old Testament prophets were trying to get people to change their ways, rather than trying to explain the existence of sickness and sadness, John here is not dealing with questions of theodicy, but using a healing story about Jesus to make a theological point. Jesus enables the blind man to see again. Jesus is the light of the world whom the Pharisees, though they are not ignorant or blind, refuse to acknowledge. John is disclosing to us the identity of Jesus, not the spiritual cause of blindness. When we think in this way about the story, perhaps we can say that AIDS does indeed bring an opportunity through which Jesus enables those with AIDS to see themselves and him in a new light, changing their vision of life. Jesus heals the blind man by touch and by saliva – a challenge to those of us who are so afraid of AIDS that we keep ourselves at a sterile distance; and the Pharisees, the religious leaders, resent his ministry to the blind man, for they do not wish to be shown the light of God shining where they do not expect to find it. Does this have some bearing on the difficulty which the church has in recognizing God at work in the lives of homosexual persons with AIDS?

John wants us to understand that, in healing the blind man, Jesus confronts those who believe that sickness is punishment, and who accept suffering with fatalistic resignation. This is all part of the prophetic ministry of Jesus.

> 'Compassion constitutes a radical form of criticism, for it announces that the hurt is to be taken seriously, that the hurt is not to be accepted as normal and natural but is an abnormal and unacceptable condition for humanness' (Brueggeman 1978:85).

Yet still, how can we say that the works of God are made manifest in the blind man? As we think about people with AIDS, we cannot say that the works of God are made manifest by healing them, for they are not physically healed. However, for John, the works of God in Jesus are made manifest not just in the resurrection but on the cross. For John, the cross is the throne upon which Jesus reigns in glory. It is his highest accomplishment; it is his time of triumph.

> 'Now is the judgment of this earth, now shall the ruler of this world be cast out; and I, when I am lifted up from the earth [and he means, lifted on the cross], will draw all men to myself' (John 12.31–32).

On the cross at the moment of death, he cries 'It is accomplished' (John 19.30).

Thus we are left holding two deep but apparently contradictory truths: suffering is abnormal and to be overcome and defeated, yet suffering may also be a time of triumph and glory. This would not have seemed contradictory to John, who in his rather Platonic view of reality always saw two levels of truth operating simultaneously, a 'worldly' truth and a 'spiritual' truth.

Jesus disturbs conventionality

Thus we interact with the Gospels, sometimes finding points of resonance, sometimes finding concepts which do not seem to fit until we look at them in another way. All the time our own creative and lovingly responsive thinking about AIDS is drawn into more depth. Take, for example, the story of the Samaritan woman with whom Jesus speaks at the well (John 4.6–30, 39). If the blind man in the earlier story could have stood for people with AIDS in the way that the Pharisees and even the disciples of Jesus condemned him as the victim of his own sin, the Samaritan woman can also reflect those with AIDS. She is a Samaritan, holding heretical views, she does not keep proper Jewish religious observances, she is a woman, and she is involved in an irregular sexual relationship. Some people with AIDS have been involved in what we might regard as irregular sexual practices. Many people with AIDS are women. They do not all hold orthodox Christian beliefs or come to church. They are all, in one way or another, marginalized.

On the face of it the story has nothing to do with AIDS since the woman is not sick. But if we look deeper, there are parallels. Although her spirituality may have seemed alien to Jewish observers, the woman is quick to respond to Jesus' lead, and generous in her eventual recognition of who he is. Jesus defies proper convention in speaking to a Samaritan and to a woman, and clearly enjoys the encounter. John is making a point here about people who do not fit into what we regard as a 'proper' mould. In a later chapter we will be looking at the way in which people with AIDS, even though some of them have religious beliefs which differ from orthodox Christianity, and live in a way of which many Christians disapprove, may still have a relationship with God which is real and which is instructive for us. Perhaps we need to see in them persons whom Jesus not only loves but even enjoys.

In John 5 we are told the story of the paralysed man by the pool of Bethzatha or Bethesda. The details in the story make it more than just a healing miracle for those of us who come to it with questions about AIDS on our minds. Letty Russell (Russell 1990) points out that before the pool can be an effective place of healing, the water must first be 'troubled' (John 5.7). Secondly, the paralysed man is without friends to bring him to the water in time. Here are two themes of thought. As long as we wish to avoid turbulence and preserve the calm, healing does not happen. Healing involves changes in relationships, which is disturbing. In a later chapter we shall look at church attitudes to different forms of sexuality. That subject is one which causes turbulence very quickly! It would be easier to let it stand. After all, we can be compassionate to people with AIDS without asking questions about our attitudes to homo-sexuality or prostitution or discussing what constitutes promiscuity. In this way we could take the church along with us in AIDS ministry without controversy. But perhaps, by fearing to trouble the waters, we block the way for healing to happen. By our remaining silent, the voice of more extreme 'right-wing' elements in the church dominate.

We see, too, that the man is friendless. No one brings him to the water. Unless we befriend people with AIDS, they have no one to encourage them to come for the help that is available. The fear and rejection that they evoke causes them to hide their problem rather than openly ask for assistance. Jesus becomes the man's friend (John

5.7–8), the friend of the friendless. He encourages the man to seek
healing. He thus incurs the wrath of the authorities. The point of the
story as it is editorially placed in John's Gospel is certainly to imply
that by healing this man, Jesus troubled the waters. 'This was why
the Jews sought all the more to kill him' (John 5.18). Surely again this
means that we have a duty, regardless of how unpopular it may make
us, to side with and care for those with AIDS.

The Good Samaritan: unconditional compassion

The story of the good Samaritan is one we all know well (Luke
10.30–37). Katherine Sakenfield, looking at the story from the
perspective of the AIDS epidemic, helps us to see several helpful
points. The Samaritan does not ask why the man is on the road. We
know that Jericho was a place of brothels and low life. It is quite likely
that anyone going to Jericho would be seeking dubious delights like
this. That point, however, is not important for Luke. He does not tell
his Gentile readers, ignorant of the local background, anything
about Jericho. The important point is not what the man was doing on
his way to Jericho, but how he could be helped in his circumstances.
We have no idea who robbed him and put him in the ditch. The
circumstances of how he got into his predicament are not important.

We know that AIDS spreads because many people are sexually
irresponsible, and that often people are irresponsible because of the
state of our society. But the circumstances of how a person contracts
AIDS are not as important as the fact that they are ill and need help.

In the story the Samaritan man does not ask whether the injured
man could pay him back, or how long the period of care would be.
His generosity to the man is shown as being open-ended. Since he
was a Samaritan, the rescuer was himself a despised and rejected
person.

With whom in the story do we associate people with AIDS?
Probably we think of the victim; but people with AIDS are not just
victims. Helpers do not necessarily have to be unwounded themselves. Luke implies that the Samaritan was able and willing to help
precisely because he was himself despised and rejected. People with
AIDS are often the Samaritan, the person who cares and offers help.
'You must love your neighbour', said Jesus. 'Who is my neighbour?',

asked a lawyer. And Jesus' answer is, if we look carefully, not 'The victim' but 'The Samaritan who cared'. We are, perhaps, willing to love the needy; but Jesus is asking us to love the unpopular helper.

There is some tension to be discerned in Britain and America between some 'Christian' AIDS service groups and the wide network of support groups that have been established by the homosexual community, some Christian and church-based, some not. The 'Christian' AIDS groups do not want to be seen as legitimizing homosexuality; we hate the sin but love the sinner, they say. The homosexual groups resent what they see as a rejection. The Samaritan would certainly have been perceived by orthodox Jews as falling short of God's commandments. Jesus' parable implies that whoever is the helper is our neighbour whom we must love.

AIDS, leprosy of our time?

The analogy between AIDS and leprosy has been noticed by a number of people (Gilkes 1991, Christensen 1991, Saayman and Kriel 1992, Jantzen in Woodward 1990). Leprosy in the Bible was a disease for which there was then no cure, though sometimes people could spontaneously recover. It caused fear and revulsion. The disfigurement is analogous to Kaposi's sarcoma, the skin lesions which appear with AIDS. People did not necessarily think that lepers were being punished by God. There are only three Old Testament references to leprosy being sent as a punishment for sin (Numbers 12.10; II Kings 5.27; and II Kings 15.5, which is paralleled in II Chronicles 26.20). Rather than as a punishment, leprosy was seen as a mystery which only the mind of God could explain. King Azariah was struck with leprosy, says the editor of II Kings, for his tolerance of idolatry (II Kings 15.5). But in the same book leprous people are sometimes seen in a very favourable light, like Naaman (II Kings 5.1) or the lepers who brought news that the Syrians had departed (II Kings 7.9). Naaman is portrayed as a brave yet humble man and there is no hint that his leprosy is the result of any sin on his part. Four lepers discover that the Syrian army besieging Jerusalem have mysteriously left, abandoning all their food and belongings. The lepers start to loot, but then remember the needs of the community, and go to the city to tell about the good news.

So leprosy was not always seen as punishment, and lepers were not necessarily sinful people. But before Jesus there was no suggestion that lepers should be cared for. Instead, because they were a danger to the community, they were banished until a priest certified that their skin was clear of active leprosy. Lepers could not mix with society, just as Jews were not to mix with Gentiles, for in both cases pollution would follow. This recalls for us the isolation of people with AIDS. There are many ways to divide humans into different camps, 'them' and 'us', 'clean' and 'unclean'. AIDS is just one more thing in our modern world which threatens to keep us apart, 'non-infected' from 'infected', sexually orthodox from sexually unorthodox. In the South African prison system, for example, persons with AIDS are kept in cells apart from other prisoners for fear that they might pass on the infection – but also for their own protection, since if the other prisoners knew they were HIV positive their lives would be in danger.

Jews believed that when the Messiah came, leprosy would come to an end. In Luke's Gospel Jesus replies to John the Baptist's query concerning whether he is the Messiah, 'Go and tell John what you have seen and heard: the blind receive their sight, the lame walk, lepers are cleansed' (Luke 7.22). Mark for his part also tells us about Jesus healing a leper at the beginning of his ministry (Mark 1.40–45, paralleled by Matthew 8.1–37). Even more important for our purposes, Mark tells us that, seeing the leper, Jesus was 'moved with pity', or, perhaps more accurately, moved with anger against the poor man's plight. And then, in the story, he goes against all the religious regulations and all the community prejudices, and touches the leper.

Much later St Francis of Assisi would follow Jesus' example. People were afraid to touch or even look at lepers because the condition was contagious, but also, perhaps, because the lepers reminded them of their own mortality. Leprosy was a very disfiguring illness; to see them was to be reminded about the frail flesh and bone under our own skin. To open ourselves to lepers, or to people with AIDS, is to embrace our own humanity in all its frailty, contingency and vulnerability.

There are other stories about Jesus healing lepers. Matthew tells us that Jesus cured many lepers (Matthew 11.5). Luke tells a story about Jesus healing ten lepers (Luke 17.12–19) and in this case only one of the lepers is grateful. Those who are healed are not necessarily converted!

We must be careful not to push the parallel between leprosy and AIDS too far. Whatever Jews may have believed about the healing when Messiah comes, AIDS is not being cured yet. But in his compassion for the suffering, despite their physical disfigurement, and despite, too, the inward ingratitude of some, Jesus is surely a model for us in reaching out to people with AIDS. Above all, in the simple act of touching them, which most people of his day would have considered to be extremely dangerous, he shows us the importance of human care and physical contact.

Jesus and the marginalized

Cheryl Gilkes (1991) points out that Jesus, having announced to John the Baptist his credentials as the Messiah, chooses to dine with one Simon the Pharisee (Luke 7.36). But Simon the Pharisee in Matthew and Mark is called Simon the leper (Mark 14.3). At the meal Jesus is anointed by a sinful woman (Luke 7.37–38). This is surely meant to be analogous to the messianic banquet, where all are welcome and those whom society rejects are restored to the community. Lepers and prostitutes, the sick and the sinners, are all welcome at Jesus' table. So are tax collectors, justly hated by the people for their collaboration with the Roman authorities for their own personal enrichment (Luke 19.2–5).

Jesus makes very great ethical demands on every part of our lives. We are to love our enemies and do good to those who hate us (Luke 6.27). His demands with regard to sexual ethics were equally radical; we are to avoid all lascivious thought (Matthew 5.28), to be in permanent monogamous relationships (Mark 10.9), and some of us are even to renounce sexual love altogether (Matthew 9.12). But that has nothing to do with who will be welcome at the Messianic banquet, the image often used by the evangelists to describe the joy of the community of heaven. As Cardinal Bernardin says, '[Jesus] never ceased to reach out to the lowly, to the outcasts of his time, even if they did not live up to the full demands of his teaching' (*The Grail* 1989:16). Jews and Gentiles, males and females, sinners and the righteous, all gather around Jesus' table. Jesus lives out what Paul describes in Galatians 3.27–28. Cardinal Bernardin is by implication referring to homosexual persons. He means that persons who engage in homosexual sex are not living up to the demands of Jesus' teaching, but that they are not excluded from his love, and therefore should not be excluded from the love of the church and its members.

But can we include people while refusing to accept their life-style? Kowalewski suggests that the American Catholic church, simultaneously condemning homosexual behaviour while including homosexuals in the church's concern, is trying to accomplish two contradictory aims. It wants to retain the authoritative traditional ethical teaching of the church while at the same time it wants to appear sympathetic, appealing and relevant to the American people (Kowalewski 1994). It is very difficult for homosexuals to feel that the church is concerned for them when the church is at the same time condemning their deepest relationships as inherently sinful.

> 'Pastoral care badly needs to be delivered from the double standards which decree that people . . . can be condemned from the pulpit while as individuals in private they are treated with understanding and compassion. The lack of integrity here undermines the credibility and accessibility of the church . . . People do not want to be loved despite what they are but because of what they are' (Pattison in Woodward 1990:19 n.21).

We shall discuss the issue of homosexuality in a later chapter. Because AIDS first presented in America as a homosexual sickness, much of the ethical reflection about AIDS centres upon homosexuality, and thus we have it fixed in our minds that people with AIDS have mostly been involved in what we have been taught to regard as sin. But we have observed that in countries where AIDS is most prevalent, homosexuality is not a major contributory factor. We have observed, too, that in many cases the women and children who are sick with AIDS or widowed or orphaned have not been involved in any sin. AIDS is not typically a sickness of homosexuals. It is a sickness of the poor. It is a sickness of the Third World. It is a sickness of women and children.

Jesus' ministry was to the marginalized and the poor. It is they whom the evangelists believe are invited to Jesus' banquet. Those who live in the Third World, especially women and children, are certainly marginalized. In the Old Testament, again and again, it is emphasized that the needs of the poor are to be recognized and addressed. Those who oppress the poor are rebuked. In Exodus 22.22 it is said that those who oppress strangers or widows or orphans will be punished. People with AIDS are the alien strangers among us, kept at arm's length. Their widows and orphans are left in distress. Deuteronomy 14.29 enjoins us to feed the stranger, the orphan and the widow. The prophets sound this theme continuously. 'I do not want your worship', says Isaiah's voice of God, 'unless you seek justice, defend the orphan, care for the widow. Woe to those who fail to do this' (Isaiah 10.2). We look at the situation with AIDS and cannot fail to see the parallels.

> 'At present, in the United States, AIDS is largely a disease of oppressed groups: gay men, black and white hispanic women and men, prostitutes and intravenous drug users . . . These groups of people are oppressed because they do not fit into the defined norm of personhood for our society, and because they are the victims of institutional and economic power and both institutional and individual violence' (Susan Davies in Russell 1990:93).

Susan Davies, who wrote this, believes that people with AIDS, because they are oppressed, deserve our support. Yet perhaps the Bible does not teach that the poor or oppressed should always be supported. The South African black theologian Itumeleng Mosala has suggested that, indeed, some parts of the Old Testament were written from the perspective of a privileged landed class propagating justification for their rights to the land against the class of those whom they had disempowered (Mosala 1989). As Cadwallader reminded us, we need to interrogate the Bible from within our own context in order to make sacred text.

Liberation theologians have taught us a lot about the need to interrogate the text, and a lot about Jesus showing us that God has a 'preferential option for the poor'. One difficulty with liberation theology, however, as McCann points out (McCann 1981:214), is that it tends to 'unchurch' those who are not poor; or, in the context from which this book is written, to make those who are not HIV positive feel that the Bible is not really meant for them.

Thus we could take issue with Susan Davies in the quotation above. We could argue that God's preferential option for the poor is one thing, and that God's preferential option for those who by their own sinful and self-destructive behaviour – anal sex, intravenous drug usage, prostitution – bring AIDS upon themselves is another. God may love and care for them in their sufferings, but, we may ask, why are they to be singled out for special treatment?

It is because we all share in their 'sin'. At least to some extent poor people in American cities are driven to intravenous drugs through their own despair about ever having a place in American society. To a very large extent prostitutes in Africa are driven to their trade by the need to feed themselves and their children. White gay men may not all be poor, but they are traditionally regarded with distaste and scorn by a large section of the community. Perhaps, again, the legendary promiscuity of the San Francisco bathhouses was in part because the 'straight' community was unwilling to recognize and encourage the caring, committed love that can exist between persons of the same sex.

AIDS spread not only because of the sins of gays or drug abusers or promiscuous people. AIDS spread because all of us, in one way or another, have shared in building a society in which the structures do not allow fair distribution of security and self-determination to everybody.

Clean and unclean: who is excluded?

In the New Testament the commitment of Jesus to the poor has to be winkled out of the text. It is undoubtedly there, but it is not very openly reflected in Paul, or Mark, or Matthew (Luke does make the commitment to the poor much more overt). What is overt through-out the New Testament is Jesus' commitment to sinners. And so we are all of us, after all, involved. All of us share to some extent in the sin which has created the AIDS pandemic. All of us ought to share, to some extent, in the pain. All of us are caught up into the cleansing, redeeming love of Jesus. If AIDS is to be defeated, all of us have to be involved. All of us, and not just people with AIDS, need forgiveness and grace.

Cadwallader, addressing the issue of clean and unclean, points out that the first healing in Mark is of a man with an unclean spirit (Mark 1.23). Jesus cleanses the young man. The man cries with a loud voice, and is cleansed. But what, or whom, does Mark think Jesus is really cleansing? For the possessed man is in the synagogue, the place of righteousness and conventional religion. Thus the 'unclean' is not to be found only outside religion but within. By chapter 3 of Mark's Gospel the authorities of the same synagogue are planning to kill him. In Mark 11.15, Jesus enters the temple to cleanse it. The temple itself is unclean.

In Mark's chronology, as Jesus enters Gentile territory for the first time, again his first miracle is cleansing a man with an unclean spirit. Again the man cried with a loud voice (Mark 5.7), and is cleansed. Uncleanness exists in the heart of Israel, and uncleanness exists also in the world outside.

Therefore Jerusalem and Rome, Jewish and Gentile authorities, sacred and secular, combine to kill Jesus. Jesus hangs on the cross, representing, for Mark, all of humankind, hanging there because of Gentile and Jewish sin. Are we meant to understand that all humans have been cleansed of their uncleanness? Jesus cries with a loud voice (Mark 15.34), and the veil of the temple, barrier between the holy of holies and the sinful, unclean world, was immediately torn following the loud cry (Mark 15.38).

Cardinal Bernardin is right that sin is no barrier to God's loving care. But the barrier of sin which is breached is the barrier thrown up by the corporate sin of all of us. AIDS does indeed lay bare the wounds of our world: our judgmentalism towards those who are different, our inability to give our young people a sense of hope and purpose, the disparity between rich and poor, or North and South, the indifference of Europe and America to the sufferings of the millions of poor in the rest of the world. But all of us are called to the banquet, the messianic feast. All of us belong there, if not by right then by invitation.

Yet Matthew talks of the guest who was thrown out of the banquet because he had no wedding garment (Matthew 22.11). What might this mean? That although sinners are welcome they must be penitent sinners? That is a possible interpretation. But elsewhere Matthew describes the selection of those who are ultimately invited to the kingdom of God, which is what the messianic banquet really signifies. There is only one criterion: did they feed the hungry, give drink to the thirsty, welcome the stranger and clothe the naked (Matthew 25.31ff.)? The only people to be excluded from the feast are those who neglect the needs of the poor. Could the man without a wedding garment be a man without compassion?

Jesus is not ashamed to befriend people who are poor or people who are sinners. There is only one instance where Jesus is reported to have expressed shame. He was ashamed of Peter, when Peter opposed the idea that a Messiah must share in the people's suffering. The context of Mark 8 is that of Jesus' first announcement of his coming passion. In Mark's chronology, Jesus' ministry in Galilee has now ended, and the next phase of ministry begins. In this moment of commitment, he asks the disciples who they think he is; and Peter correctly answers that he is the Messiah. But then Jesus begins to explain what that means; that he must go up to Jerusalem to be mocked and to be killed. Peter is outraged, for that is not what he thinks is meant to happen to the Messiah. And Jesus rebukes him, 'For whoever is ashamed of me and of my words . . . of them will the Son of man also be ashamed' (Mark 8.38). Compassion means to share in the pain. All of us are part of the sin which leads to AIDS. All of us must share in the pain. That is a hard thing for those of us who are only tangentially affected.

The church as a body: interdependence

We may not want to embrace the sufferings of those with AIDS. Those of us who are relatively rich and relatively healthy may not wish to be bothered with the complicated and hopeless sufferings of those with AIDS, especially those who have AIDS in Africa, that bottomless pit of misery into which so much money and effort has been poured with so little apparent result. But unless we want Jesus to be 'ashamed' of us we really have no choice.

David Smith is Dean of an Episcopal cathedral in mid-Western America. An important part of his ministry for many years has been to homosexuals. Now an important part of his ministry is to those with AIDS. One day somebody asked him 'Why did you choose this ministry?' His answer is that he did not choose it; once the need was clear to him, there was no choice. As a Christian his duty was clear.

We have no choice about ministry to those with AIDS. All of us are part of the problem. We share in a world which has created the conditions for AIDS. We are committed, as the people of God, to those who suffer with it. We cannot be God's people and not minister to people with AIDS. And since we are all hurting with AIDS even though we may not know it, we all need ministry too. Paul's teaching about the church as a body (I Corinthians 12), in which there are varieties of gifts but all with the same honour, varieties of backgrounds but all are one in Christ, and all interdependent so that the suffering of one or the joy of one is really the suffering or joy of all, fits exactly. We cannot marginalize people with AIDS, because we too are part of the disorder in society which has led to the spread of AIDS. The evil which must be cleansed is in all of us.

'The way the order approaches those who are living with AIDS or the virus will ultimately be the judgment on that order' (Cadwallader 1992:168).

Failure to minister to them will be to bring judgment upon ourselves.

But just as the New Testament took the prophetic teaching about caring for the widows of Israel further to include Gentiles within the concern of the church, so we must extend the New Testament concern for the church and Paul's vision of the church as body, to include the whole human community. Michael Christensen tells a Hasidic tale. A rabbi asked his students, 'How can we determine the dawn when night ends and day begins?' The students answered, 'When from a distance one can tell a dog from a sheep.' The rabbi asked again. The students answered, 'When we can tell the difference between a fig tree and a grape vine.' 'No,' said the rabbi, 'it is when you can look into the face of human beings and you have enough light to recognize them as your brothers and sisters. Until then the night and the darkness are still with us' (Christensen 1991:77).

Jesus cares about the marginalized. Jesus also cares about those who are sinful. Even when the people of Jerusalem turn against him and turn instead to hatred, Matthew and Luke both suggest that Jesus longed to comfort them.

> 'O Jerusalem, Jerusalem, killing the prophets and stoning those who are sent to you. How often would I have gathered your children together as a hen gathers her brood under her wings, and you would not' (Matthew 23.27; Luke 13.34–35).

Jesus wants to gather them in to his peace. We recall the promise of Third Isaiah, that those whom the sin of Jerusalem had sent into the harshness of exile will return.

> 'Behold I will extend prosperity to her like a river, and the wealth of the nations like an overflowing stream; and you shall suck, you shall be carried upon her hip and dandled upon her knees' (Isaiah 66.12).

Jerusalem, the community of God's people, will welcome back the exiles and give them prosperity and motherly love. Then as Isaiah continues, the imagery subtly changes and God himself becomes the mother.

> 'As one whom his mother comforts, so I will comfort you; you shall be comforted in Jerusalem' (Isaiah 66.13).

God is our mother; Israel, or the church, is our mother. The love of God and the love of the community of God's people seem here to be interchangeable. Either way, that mother longs to bring back all her people and gather them in peace. Thus all humankind are our brothers and sisters, one family held within the love of that mother. Again, to apply this to our own issue, we are to recognize those who suffer with AIDS as our brothers and sisters. They belong within our family. God longs to comfort them through us.

What is our hope?

Yet can we be comforted in a time of AIDS? Modern theologians have taught us that liberation means liberation *now*, not just liberation after death. We are keenly aware of the well-worn Marxist adage that religion provides comfort for the masses, the 'opium of the people', by promising them that everything will be better in the heavenly life to come. We want to give people with AIDS hope and comfort now. We want to help them to live victoriously with AIDS, not merely comfort them as they die with AIDS. But in truth they will die. Do we have no hope to offer but the opiate of heavenly bliss?

> 'Though our outer nature is wasting away, our inner nature is being renewed every day. For this slight momentary affliction is preparing for us an eternal weight of glory beyond all comparison, because we look not to the things that are seen but to the things that are unseen; for the things that are seen are transient, but the things that are unseen are eternal' (II Cor. 4.17–18).

Life after death is a mystery, and we cannot limit our response to AIDS to saying that in heaven it will all be put right. Yet Paul is not only talking about heaven in this passage. He puts it in the present, not the future, tense. Our inner nature *now* is being renewed every day. Ron Russell-Coons, a pastor and a person with AIDS, used Paul's text to talk about his own experience with AIDS.

> 'Occasionally I am tempted to view my faith as akin to "wishing on a star". If I wish upon a star it might happen . . . I wish upon a star that there was no such thing as HIV . . . But the reality is, *we have AIDS*. And the reality is that my faith enables me to journey through AIDS' (Russell-Coons in Russell 1990:36).

> 'I find a new revelation of God in our experience of AIDS. We are beginning to understand God in new and inspired ways . . . Possibly the persons with AIDS among us are the learned rabbis of this age. We have AIDS, and we are learning new lessons about both God and ourselves' (Russell-Coons in Russell 1990:41).

No search of the Bible for a sacred word about AIDS can sidestep the resurrection. But resurrection must be understood as a present reality. Whatever the resurrection means about life after death, it has a great deal of meaning about life after AIDS, life with AIDS, and a transformation now.

> *Jennifer is a pastor to a group of homosexual and bisexual persons. She is herself openly lesbian, and thus, although a pastor in a Presbyterian church, somewhat on the outskirts of that church and her continuing ministry within it is somewhat uncertain. Inevitably in her pastoring of this particular group, she must care for many who are sick and dying of AIDS. One day she preaches on the transfiguration of Jesus. She describes being called to the bed of a young man with AIDS in his hour of death. She and some friends watch as the young man's chest rises, falls, rises, falls . . . and does not rise again. 'But Jennifer, look at his face,' cries one of the friends. And, says Jennifer in her sermon, his face was shining, radiant, beautiful. We knew he had seen God. We knew we had seen God in him.*

Despite her unconventional circumstances, in her theology Jennifer is really an old-fashioned evangelical believer. For her, the young man had literally seen God's face at his hour of death. But all of us who have spent time with people who are seriously sick with AIDS can recognize the experience. Sometimes God does shine through them. 'First, I thank my God through Jesus Christ for all of you, because your faith is proclaimed in all the world' (Romans 1.8). People with AIDS and those who work with AIDS sometimes discover and demonstrate great courage and faith. They are doing what Paul is talking about, proclaiming faith and the power of the good news of God's grace to the world. They are testifying to resurrection now.

Yet that good news is heard in pain. Before the resurrection, there is crucifixion. In our attempts to speak positively about transformation and hope with AIDS, there can be no soft-pedalling about the pain. The author of the First Letter of Peter speaks of the coming pain for those to whom he writes: in this case the pain of persecution.

'Since therefore Christ suffered in the flesh, arm yourselves with the same thought' (I Peter 4.1).

'Beloved, do not be surprised at the fiery ordeal which comes upon you to prove you, as though something strange were happening to you. But rejoice in so far as you share Christ's sufferings, that you may also rejoice and be glad when his glory is revealed' (I Peter 4.12).

Paul, too, speaks boldly about having been crucified with Christ (Galatians 3.20).

We must be very careful about suggesting that people with AIDS are being crucified with Christ. There is sometimes a language of predestination about the cross in Christian discourse. This is a theological debate into which we will not enter now; but we must not suggest that just as God sent Jesus to endure the cross, so God has sent people with AIDS to endure their sufferings for the redemption of the world. God's ways may be mysterious, but we must not allow a theology which encourages fatalism about other people's pain.

Yet there are parallels which we may draw, albeit with care and with reverence. People with AIDS do suffer because of the world's sin; I have made this point a number of times. Like Jesus, the world's sin has put them on a cross. And people with AIDS in their encounter with suffering are sometimes transformed and do become ministers of grace to us all. Like Jesus – or perhaps we should say, through Jesus – their pain becomes redemptive for us all.

AIDS is a kind of crucifixion, but within the crucifixion is also resurrection. Like all those with a prophetic ministry, Paul endured crucifixion, not only in the sense that he was, according to tradition, martyred, but in his daily life after his conversion. He speaks about his sufferings and persecution.

'We are afflicted in every way, but not crushed; perplexed, but not driven to despair; persecuted, but not forsaken; struck down, but not destroyed; always carrying in the body the death of Jesus, so that the life of Jesus also may be manifested in our bodies' (II Corinthians 4.8–10).

He shared in human suffering, just as all of us must share in some way in the pain of AIDS. But through it all, he also believed he was experiencing resurrection, not just in a promised future but within the sufferings themselves.

It is this kind of resurrection to which Ron Russell-Coons points us. People with AIDS often show us how to live with joy and newness of life in the shadow of death. We must not trivialize this. AIDS is painful and humiliating. As well as the illness, those with AIDS often face painful situations with their families, especially when families must face for the first time that their son is homosexual. As the illness progresses, they often lose their jobs. Soaring medical costs absorb their income. Homes must be given up. But sometimes they triumph over it nevertheless. As they experience the love of God (perhaps through the love of others), they may come to realize their own worth before God, and that nothing can take away their sense of God-given personal worth and dignity. The resurrection is here and now.

Albert and Joan felt called to start a Christian mission to black people in KwaZulu-Natal, South Africa, who had AIDS. Because AIDS has come more recently to South Africa than to other parts of Africa, they had no experience of AIDS, but they knew that people died of it. They dedicated their farmhouse as a refuge where people with AIDS could come to be cared for as they died. Their first inmate was HIV positive but not yet very sick. He was given a comfortable room, and allowed to watch television – but only the Christian programmes. He was given a diet of holy books to read. Albert and Joan believed that their mission was to help those who came to them to die knowing the Lord and thus to go to heaven.

Albert and Joan in their well-meaning efforts missed the point. Our ministry to people with AIDS is not only to prepare them for life after AIDS, but to help them find new life within AIDS.

But Paul did not mean that resurrection was only about an existential here-and-now experience. He certainly believed in a literal resurrection after death. We cannot ignore this.

'If there is no resurrection of the dead, then Christ has not been raised; if Christ has not been raised then our preaching is in vain and your faith is in vain' (I Corinthians 15.13–14).

Resurrection is an embarrassing concept for many liberal theologians. We prefer to interpret it existentially rather than literally. AIDS forces us to think again about that. Any death is sad. But the death of young people, many of them talented, makes us see more clearly the wastefulness of an incomplete life; and most people who die of AIDS are young and in the prime of life. Bereavement affects us all, but the parting of husbands and wives, or of homosexual lovers, through AIDS, makes the one left behind hope and long for reunion beyond the grave. Not everybody with AIDS expects life beyond the grave, but AIDS does raise again, in a sharp and poignant way, all of the feelings that unless there is life beyond the grave, it is hard to find purpose and meaning in lives cut so short. Both AIDS and the New Testament make us think again about resurrection. Yet resurrection is both now and then, both present reality and future hope. We shall return to this in a later chapter.

Albert and Joan were also misguided in their attempts to use AIDS as a context for evangelization. The evangelists suggest that Jesus healed people whether or not they converted to being his disciples. Twelve lepers were healed, even though only one returned to give thanks. Yet evangelism was certainly central to Jesus' ministry, not in the sense of seeking for conversions so much as seeking to bring everyone to the knowledge that God loved them. Thus the author of I Peter can say, 'Once you were no people but now you are God's people' (I Peter 2.10). This is the difference between the church as the new people of Israel and the old Israel. Where the Old Testament taught love within the community, Jesus taught love beyond the community, bringing people into the community not in order to convert them but to love them.

Conclusion: living with uncertainty

Although AIDS and HIV were quite unknown in Bible times, and although our context is so different, we do find in all sorts of ways that reflection on the Bible helps us see AIDS and people with AIDS in a new and different way from before. The dialogue between text and present context bring new light to both the text and the situation in which we find ourselves.

But the Bible does not provide us with a basis for insisting that our view of God and AIDS is the only correct view. We live, so we are constantly told, in a post-modern era when confidence that we can ever understand the whole truth about life has disappeared. There are no 'grand theories' any more, no world views which claim universal acceptance in any one culture. Ideologies and ethics, metaphysics and theology, are all seen to be merely arbitrary patterns built upon selected and limited perceptions.

The title of Woodward's book about theology and AIDS, *Embracing the Chaos*, captures well the situation in which we constantly find ourselves, and in this time of AIDS perhaps more than ever. We are slowly coming to realize that a neatly systematic theology never quite fits the facts, never really squares with our experience. Chaos lurks beneath the surface of the order we have tried to impose upon our perception of life. Ideologies always oversimplify. We can either deny the chaos, forcing our ideology upon the facts and misinterpreting the facts, or embrace it and live within the tension of ambiguity. The mystics always realized this. Our experience of all life, but especially of that which we call God, ultimately defies and deconstructs our human thought systems. Systematic theology can never have the final words about God, because humanly speaking there is never a final word.

Thus Meister Eckhart could say,

> '[God's] nature is causeless, therefore it is unfathomable except to causeless understanding. Creaturely intelligence is finite, so it has a cause, hence it cannot fathom causeless mind . . . Where God is beholding his own nature, which is groundless, it is incomprehensible except to groundless understanding' (quoted Fleming 1988:28).

The mystics warn us that we cannot hope to fathom the deity. The author of *The Cloud of Unknowing* tells us that we may be able to understand the created world, but never God nor the ways of God, who can be reached not by reason but only by love.

> 'A man, through grace, may have full knowledge of all other created things and all their world – yes, and of the works of God too – and be well able to think about them. But of God himself no one can think . . . by love He can be reached and held, but by thought never' (Way 1986:19).

Theology begins with experience, not with dogma. The intention of theology is not to control our experience of God to make sure it is consistent with what the church says it should be. Instead it is to help us make what sense we can of our diverse, different and ever-changing experience of God in life, whatever that experience may be. If we are Christian, we shall wish to find continuity in our experience with that of the biblical authors and the Christian tradition. But we have come to see that there is no one theology of the Bible, of the New Testament, or of the historical tradition. There are a range of theologies developed out of different backgrounds to fit different contexts.

Of course there are common themes. All the writers of the New Testament, says Leslie Houlden, are convinced that Jesus is the Lord, Jesus is the answer to the questions which they pose. But they all pose different questions (Houlden 1986:133).

All of the theology of our tradition, of the Bible and the Councils, is based initially upon experience. The Chalcedonian Definition of the nature of Jesus is not really logical. There are gaping holes in the Definition – for example how it is conceivable or possible for Jesus to be simultaneously perfect and yet tempted, almighty and yet victim, divine and yet human. These questions are left unanswered; but Athanasius and the fathers of Chalcedon would reply: 'We do not know how this can be. But our experience of Jesus is that he recreates us as only God can, he renews us as only God can. In order to do that he must also be human; the recreation of human nature requires that God take human nature. We therefore experience Jesus as divine yet human, and the logic will have to catch up later.'

All theology begins as pastoral theology, or it ought to; all theology is aimed at helping us respond more constructively to our life situation. Anthony Dyson says that pastoral theology is the central theological discipline, rather than dogmatic or biblical theology (Dyson 1994). But perhaps this is a misleading statement, for in fact dogmatic and biblical theology start out as pastoral theology.

Pastoral theology seeks to respond to experience rather than impose upon experience. The primary questions will always be: What am I meant to do? How am I meant to respond to the present situation in which I find myself? A theology must be true for me, consistent with my experience, and cannot be subservient to dogma, canon law or all the other theologies which the church seeks to impose upon us. My experience will not be totally new, and I will need to build upon and learn from the experience of others. There will need to be an interplay between how I make sense of my life and how the church in the past has perceived things. But the fit will never be perfect, because my experience and that of everyone else will always be somewhat new and different. Thus, past and present, the mapped-out tradition and the unmapped existentialist now, will be held in creative tension.

Often it will be easier to express and interpret what we experience through stories rather than creeds, in images and poetry and music. Here we can learn a great deal from other less literate religions where the importance of story and imagination in communicating religious truth is much more clearly recognized than in Christianity, where we are more inclined to think that truth is expressed through philosophical formulae. But life stories, unlike novels, never finish. They are always open-ended and developing. So too with our theology there will always be change and open-endedness. We may end up in a differrent place from where we thought we would at the start. A personal theology will always be fragmentary rather than complete, changing rather than static, open-ended rather than closed (Dyson 1994:170).

So we are thrown back into chaos, into the as yet uncontrolled and formless void of which Genesis 1 speaks. The world is a changing chimera, in constant need of reinterpretation, and theology does not capture timeless truths which will hold forever. This is particularly true of a time of AIDS. As yet incurable, AIDS challenges the control which modern humans thought they had imposed upon creation; it challenges our medical and economic and political theories and throws them into some disarray. Of course in time we shall probably learn how to tame the AIDS virus, and we shall reformulate our economic and political theories yet again. But new challenges – perhaps the Ebola virus – will erupt to overthrow our control yet again.

Theologically AIDS forces us all to consider areas of life where our theological control over human nature is most fragile: sex, alternative kinds of sex, death, the treatment of the poor and marginalized, drugs, rebellious youth (Dyson 1994:171). The confident missionary expansion of the church, the evolution into full maturity of the church in previously colonial lands, are seriously undermined.

'I want to characterize my own personal experience of visiting Uganda and Tanzania in terms of what I prefer to call the Logic of Disintegration. For what I heard and saw in our encounter with various institutions and individuals working with AIDS shattered all preconceived notions about every aspect of our understanding of human nature' (Goba 1995).

But this is nothing new. The story of theology is a story of constant disintegration and, hopefully, of reintegration. Jesus came, and the first Christian believers' experience of Jesus shattered many of their traditional Jewish predispositions. The church took the gospel to the Greeks – and theology was reformulated once more. Francis of Assisi came and upset the neat balance in the medieval church of religion, wealth and power. Martin Luther came; John Wesley came . . . and the story goes on. In hindsight we can see that the reformulation of the gospel each time was in continuity with what had gone before. But that is rarely clear to those facing the challenges at the time. Each new wave is met by strong church resistance. Each time it is as if chaos is enveloping the church once more. The church must either resist the chaos – which is never possible – or embrace the chaos. This is profoundly uncomfortable. Now with AIDS having such an enormous effect on the human race, theology must again face the discomfort of ' . . . the dialectic of the Christian narrative and the narrative of HIV/AIDS in mutual abrasion and reinterpretation' (Dyson 1994:174).

If we will embrace the chaos, AIDS may prove to be something which helps Christians find new freshness and strength in their faith. Kierkegaard made a distinction between what he called 'religionness A' or religion A, and 'religionness B' or religion B (Kierkegaard 1941). He was drawing a distinction between the conventional piety of churchgoers who accept religious dogma and ritual without serious thought, whose concerns are for a short-term sense of contentment and comfort, and the earnest seeker after truth like himself who could never be content with such inauthentic religion.

True religion, religion B, focuses not on superficial needs but upon absolute ends. No one in search of absolute truth can ever be satisfied with easy religious answers (Kierkegaard 1941:355). But absolute truth can only be sought after, never captured. Religion B is always aware of the polemical, ambiguous nature of truth, deeply conscious of personal shortcomings and sin. There are no guarantees that we shall ever find it. True religion is not a matter of proof or of certainty but of faith (Kierkegaard 1941:516).

We might not wish to identify wholly with Kierkegaard's views, which were coloured by his own unhappy life and neurosis. I am not suggesting that we should become ridden with self-doubt like Kierkegaard, nor with the paradoxical sense of 'holier than thou' with which Kierkegaard looked upon followers of religion A. Nevertheless Kierkegaard did not dismiss religion A altogether. He saw it as a stage through which those following religion B must go. AIDS does push us, like it or not, into leaving behind our comfortable and secure religiosity and going forward in faith rather than in certainty, where there are no easy answers, and where we are deeply conscious of our own shortcomings, our own responsibilities for having helped create the circumstances in which the virus spreads, and our own inability to deal with the virus. To some extent at least, AIDS does bring us into the 'dread' which Kierkegaard said characterized true religion. AIDS brings us into a more authentic and more faithful response to reality.

So embracing the chaos does not mean becoming less religious, but becoming religious in a different way. Embracing chaos is not less consistent with the gospel experience but more. There is an energy, a power, in the disorder. Religion seeks to tame disorder and chaos by discovering God's will within it. In order to do this, we select out of the chaos those elements which seem to us to be significant. This is how human consciousness works, by selecting and ordering relevant elements and learning to ignore the rest. This process is always necessary, for we cannot cope with all of reality at once. It is also always incomplete, for our patterns of order always exclude some parts of reality. Therefore they must always be broken down and renewed as freshly recognized truths are integrated into our patterned order. It is precisely in the previously unnoticed and unintegrated truths that fresh energy is to be found.

'Christianity depends for its very existence on keeping in touch with the energy and power of chaos at the margins' (Pattison in Woodward 1990:13).

The church often seeks to maintain its authority by resisting this process of disintegration. It often values the past rather than the present, looking nostalgically back to past certainties rather than embracing present uncertainties; it values structures rather than people. Above all it values its own unity and is resistant to those who make waves or threaten to upset the balance of power. People with AIDS, as they face their own situation and work out their own answers, may challenge and upset our neat conventions. Instead of fearing and resisting this, the church needs to see it as a source of renewal. Chaos is frightening and destructive; it is also filled with energy and new possibilities. The time of AIDS may be a time of renewal for the church in its search for a religion which is authentic for our own time, like Kierkegaard's religion B.

In this time the task of the church is not merely to reimpose patterns from the past, patterns made by other people and other authorities, but to enable individuals to find authenticity and congruence in their own path. We may offer such individuals insights from our own personal or corporate experience, but since no two experiences are identical, we may not impose these insights. The church will therefore not be a community of uniform belief – though certainly we shall find many common points of reference in our journeys. It is called to be a community which seeks to be mutually supportive in its diversity, mutually encouraging, mutually challenging and testing as we all find what are going to be our own individual responses to our own unique circumstances. Anything else would be inauthentic.

This concept of the church may seem dangerously loose and individualistic. But this is the reality of modern life and the modern church. The church no longer reflects one single culture and world-view, if it ever did. Local congregations will include people of differing philosophies and ideologies. People no longer accept the authority of the church hierarchy in decisions that affect their lives, if they ever did. There are wide differences of value within the church, about contraception, about abortion, about homosexuality and sexuality in general, about socialism, about pacifism, about animal rights, to name but a few. This tension of competing ideas need not be a weakness but a strength for the church, a basis for true authenticity. Seeking to suppress these differences will only lead to pretended complicity or to exclusion.

Yet although we may hold different and conflicting ideas there is, perhaps, one grand theory which Christians can offer that can still hold us together: quite simply, the recognition of human solidarity, and the belief that it is in that very solidarity that God is to be found.

'For where two or three meet in my name, I shall be there with them' (Matthew 18.20).

'He is the peace between us, and has made the two into one and broken down the barrier which used to keep them apart' (Ephesians 2.14).

For people with AIDS, the church can offer a community where they can explore their own experience, make their own pilgrimage, in common with others who are similarly seeking to make sense of the chaos of their own experience. It will be a community of faith – that is, a community which continues to hope that there is indeed meaning and purpose to be found in the chaotic pain, though we cannot quite capture that meaning. Each person will be free to be true to himself or herself. Yet each person will expect and hope to find God, both in the search, and, even more, in the community which supports us in that search. We will be company for each other on the pilgrim journey.

'The church, like so many individuals . . . is being called on a pilgrimage into the mysterious gift of sexuality and of its co-creative and/or co-destructive potential' (Kirkpatrick 1988:19).

So writes Bill Kirkpatrick, companion for many on their AIDS journey. However, it is to a pilgrimage not only into sexuality that we are called, but into death and political unpopularity and all else that subverts our neatly ordered world.

At least, this would be our ideal. In reality the church will often be less tolerant, more uniform, making God a prisoner of dogma and tradition. In that case, we cannot be surprised if people with AIDS look for their support elsewhere – and find God elsewhere.

3

AIDS and Sexual Ethics

Marilyn is unmarried. She has not been a churchgoer since reaching adulthood. She has AIDS, contracted against statistical probability through a one-night fling after too much wine at supper. Now that she is beginning to feel ill and afraid, she would like to go back to the Methodist church where she was raised, where she once belonged to the youth group, and where her parents are still active members. But she feels she cannot. In counselling she concedes that her pastor will probably be loving and supportive. But she feels if she goes back the congregation will soon know that she has AIDS, and that she has therefore been sexually involved. She fears that her parents will be embarrassed by the congregation's disapproval and will feel rejected in the church which is part of their lives.

'AIDS should not be the first thing young people hear from the church about sexuality' (Phillips 1988:548).

The writer is quite right. It is very important indeed that the church should provide reliable information about sexual practices which may lead to AIDS. This is especially important in Africa where in many areas church and mosque have more access to more people than any other institutions in the continent. But our sex education should go beyond merely warning against AIDS, or against pre-marital pregnancy or any other dangers. Sex education needs to be about more than what we must avoid. Children need to be brought up with healthy sexual attitudes from the beginning. They need to learn a positive attitude towards their bodies and themselves, and not merely be warned against the dangers of sex in their teens. This is not only because children are often targets of paedophiles and child abusers and thus need to know what sex is all about, but because they are already, in their own way, thoroughly sexual beings.

If sex education aims to create a sense of fear in young people it can, like drug education, be counterproductive. Fear does not prevent premarital sex. In the many places in the world where violence is common there is no reason to renounce sex for fear of a disease which may kill you in ten years, when you stand a good statistical chance of being murdered before then anyway. Some teenagers may be drawn even more towards sexual activity because fear gives them excitement. 'A person drawn to high-risk behaviour by compulsivity does not respond to education alone' (Jones 1989:212).

In many parts of the world, sexual attitudes and ethics are in such a morass of uncertainty and self-indulgence that a major task of rethinking and re-education is necessary. This was true even before AIDS came along. It is very important therefore that the church should talk about sexual ethics and sexual values.

Now that AIDS has come along, many secular AIDS agencies try to adopt a 'value-free' attitude towards sexual practices. They do not moralize about sex. Their only concern is to advise against sexual practices which put one at risk for AIDS, and their only advice is to use condoms. The impression given in many educational leaflets about AIDS is that casual sexual relationships, hetero- or homosexual, are normal, and quite harmless as long as a condom is used. This is because the agencies do not feel it is their place to prescribe particular mores, but also because they believe that preaching to people about sex will mean that no one listens to them about AIDS. Although the World Health Organization has said that sexual abstinence is the only way to control the spread of AIDS, AIDS education programmes do not usually mention this (Lucas 1993:11).

'This basic sexual theory [the liberal sexual ethic] which has underpinned Western societies since the 1960's, is also assumed in nearly all AIDS education programmes' (Saayman and Kriel 1992:57).

The apparent permissiveness of many AIDS programmes, and the adoption of a value-free approach, is partly because AIDS agencies need to get information from clients about sexual activity in which they may have been involved, and those who are afraid their answers will offend either lie or do not come for treatment. It may also be because in many cases these agencies are involved in counselling people with AIDS. A Rogerian non-judgmental, unconditional client-centred relationship is entirely appropriate in many counselling situations.[7] As a counselling technique, an apparently value-free approach, allowing the client to make up his or her own mind without pressure or interference from the counsellor, is probably best. But of course there is really no such thing as a value-free approach. Counsellors are assuming, at the very least, such important values as the need to give attention, time and care to those who suffer. 'Value-free' counselling often only means that pre-existent values are allowed to remain unexamined and taken for granted.

A positive sexual ethic

Christians also cannot pretend to enter into the debate without bringing to it some pre-existent values, some of which may be shared with our contemporaries in the secular world, some of which will be drawn from our specific Christian tradition and orientation. We cannot compartmentalize sexuality. Our concern is for the whole human person, body and soul, *soma* and *psyche*, and every part of a person's life and being. We cannot separate Christian faith and spirituality from sexuality, for they are all part of the same person. We cannot leave behind our Christian convictions.

Our Christian responsibilities include, but go beyond, one-to-one counselling. All over the world traditional sexual ethical norms have broken down. This has many social consequences, as well as enabling AIDS to spread. Promiscuity is not new, of course, and Christian people have never universally observed Christian sexual ethics. But sexual intercourse with a variety of partners with no serious emotional commitment has become even more widespread

---

[7]Carl Rogers has been very influential in promoting a kind of counselling which assumes that the client often knows best what the matter is and how to resolve it; the counsellor's job is not to advise but to help clients discover and consciously adopt the course of action which in their subconscious they always knew was best.

than before. We cannot pretend as Christians that this does not matter to us. As well as AIDS, the growing numbers of single mothers, of broken families and other social problems are often consequences of this breakdown of sexual standards. While the breakdown is itself the product of other social causes – people have not suddenly just become more sexually abandoned or more selfish – Christians have a responsibility to provide reasoned, sensible, achievable standards of sexual behaviour which may help the various societies and cultures of the world to provide the basis for personal and family stability which we have lost.

But to be honest, this is not an easy task for the church to undertake, for a number of reasons. People do not think that the church has anything helpful to offer. They think that the church will be prudish and priggish about sex. Therefore they do not take church pronouncements on the matter very seriously. To quite a large extent they are justified in their attitude. Throughout much of the church's history, human nature has been seen in a dualistic way, as divided between body and soul, with the soul by far the most important part. Instead of promoting the view that sexual desire is a gift from God to help us be more loving, Christians have seen this desire as a dangerous force likely to hold the soul back from its spiritual longing for God. We have taught that the body in its weakness craves sexual release, that we are conceived as a result of our parents' sexual lust, and inherit their lust. In this case the soul must be rescued from this prison of physical desire by denying the body. Desire or concupiscence might with reluctance be permitted expression within matrimony, but even then primarily for the propagation of the species. The main, and often the only, value of sex was seen to be procreation. The higher course, many Christians have believed, was to renounce marriage and sexuality altogether.

The modern church would not wish to sound purely negative about sex. The view of sex which I have outlined was never absolute or universal, but it was strong enough to be seen in the public eye as the church's teaching on sex. Even now the church in the main disapproves of premarital sex, which many people in the rest of our society accept as perfectly normal. It disapproves of homosexuality, which makes the church an uncomfortable ally of the ugly homophobia of very conservative politicians. When President Mugabe of

Zimbabwe denounced homosexuals and lesbians as perverts who have no human rights and whose behaviour is lower than that of pigs, a delegation of the Anglican Mother's Union visited him to congratulate him (*The Natal Witness*, 17 August 1995). And the largest part of the world-wide church, the Roman Catholic church, still officially disapproves of the contraceptive pill which is part of the life of most modern women. So the church is seen to be prudish and out of touch with reality.

This does not mean that the church must go along with popular sexual values; but it must overcome, and be seen to have overcome, the remnants of an attitude which says that all sexual activity is shameful. The seeds for this attitude lie partly in the New Testament. While the Old Testament took a robustly positive view of marriage, Jesus remained unmarried. The stories of his virginal conception, while originally testifying to his divinity, were soon seen to testify to his purity. Mary came to be seen as 'ever virgin', Joseph as her 'spouse most chaste'. Jesus' brothers and sisters were merely his cousins. The Jesus of the Gospels speaks about some who have made themselves eunuchs for the kingdom of heaven's sake (Matthew 19.12).

Paul takes this further; in his view it is preferable to remain unmarried, but those who cannot suppress their sexual longings had better marry than burn (I Corinthians 7.9). To set our eyes on the flesh (*sarx*) is death; those who set their mind on spiritual things (*pneuma*) have life and peace.

There is nothing wrong with the idea that some are called to renounce marriage for other responsibilities. Paul was not as negative about sex and the body as might appear. He does not say that the body is evil, for the body is the temple of the Holy Spirit and must therefore be treated with reverence (I Corinthians 6.19). By being 'fleshly minded' he probably did not simply mean being mindful of the body, but rather being obsessed with what is merely physical. It is likely that Paul's views about marriage were coloured by his expectation that the second coming of Jesus was imminent and that marriage was therefore irrelevant.

Nevertheless, his langugage was to lay the foundations for the later church fathers, who leave us in no doubt that sex and marriage are distractions for the soul which has set its sights on heaven, where there is neither giving nor receiving in marriage, but where we are like angels in heaven (Mark 12.25).

Augustine is a major influence in this regard, though his views were shared by almost all Christians of the period. To do him credit, he did not take the view that bodies are sinful. He tried to soften the views of ascetics like Jerome who saw all sexuality as evil. Augustine was too aware of the dangers of Manicheism to fall into that trap. But as a neo-Platonist, convinced that the soul's destiny is to escape from the prison of bodiliness, he could not help but believe that sexual passion was a distraction. 'You delivered me from the chains of my desire for sex by which I was so closely bound', he writes (Augustine in Clark (ed.): 1984:88). Augustine did not see sexual intercourse as sinful. Sex for the purpose of begetting children is what God has commanded. But sexual desire distracts the soul from seeking God who should be our only desire. 'Yet this affection itself the Christian mind, having thoughts of heavenly things, in a more praiseworthy manner surpasses and overcomes' (Augustine, quoted Battenhouse 1995:382).

He imagines that Adam and Eve might well have had sexual intercourse before the fall. That would not have been sinful. But the necessary erection of the penis would have been accomplished by will, not by spontaneous physiological and therefore uncontrollable sexual desire, which Augustine sees as sinful and concupiscent. It is the desire that is sinful, not the act in itself. What concerned him was that sexual intercourse is accompanied by passion.

> 'Augustine's belief in the proportioning of love to reason made him distrust the spontaneity of sexual emotion as a sign of irrational passion' (Childress and Macquarrie 1986:47).

Thus, despite his wish to avoid Manicheism, Augustine does end up distrusting sexuality. In theory sexual intercourse is not sinful; in practice, because it is always accompanied by desire, it is regrettable. All of us are born as a result of our parents' sinful concupiscence. Jesus alone is born free of that stain, since he was born of a virgin. Virginity is a higher state.

> 'Christ did not will that his flesh should come into existence through this kind of encounter between male and female, but in

his conception of the virgin, without any such human passion'
(Augustine in Clark 1984:419).

Christians, therefore, must be reborn in baptism to be cleansed of
this stain.

Here lie the seeds of the attitudes which plague us still. Sexual
intercourse in marriage is permissible, in Augustine's view and in the
view of the church for centuries after, but there is a better way. 'With
reference to marriage you [i.e. God] have advised something better'
(Augustine in Clark 1986:145). As Henry Chadwick remarks,

> 'Augustine injected a powerful and toxic theme into medieval
> theology, namely that the Virgin Birth presupposes that even
> within marriage the sexual act cannot be done without some taint
> of cupidity' (Chadwick 1986:112).

Yet sexuality and the flesh cannot be denied or willed away; they
are part of who we are. By promoting a sense of guilt about sexual
desire the church has been responsible for a great deal of harm in the
world for many centuries and ruined many lives. Almost all of us are
aware of sexual desires. The church has made us feel that this is
sinful. The church has created the impression that it disapproves of
all sexual behaviour. It still often talks about sex in dry moralistic
tones as something of which to beware. A recent document on AIDS
from the World Council of Churches admits that:

> 'For many churches, though sexuality is tolerated as a means of
> perpetuating the human race, the subject remains taboo. In many
> Christian communities to talk about it is to risk being regarded
> askance, as someone of doubtful morals. This theology and this
> attitude pose a problem when it comes to the preventative
> measures necessary in the fight against AIDS . . . It is in fact
> extremely difficult for churches having a purely spiritual theology
> to be fully involved in the fight against this deadly pandemic'
> (Adam 1994:2).

We find it hard to throw off this mentality. We are still
embarrassed to speak about our sexual needs and experiences. We
punish sexual sins but not other sins. Marriage after divorce is still

grounds for excommunication in the Catholic and parts of the Anglican church; in many congregations in Africa premarital pregnancy means that the mother is excluded from Communion until after the birth and suitable penitence; but greed, violence, unkindness are not similarly punished. We still see sex as something dangerous which must be hemmed around.

This negativity about sex is disastrous in a time of AIDS. Other AIDS agencies are sometimes unwilling to work with us because of it.

'This thinking has led to attempts to deny Catholic leaders positions on secular AIDS panels, ignoring the role the church has played in AIDS care . . . As detestable as some church policies may be, political battles should not be fought in the AIDS arena where lives are at stake' (Adam 1989).

Since, apart from rare exceptions, AIDS is almost always contracted through sexual activity, the very statement that one has AIDS is seen as a confession that one has been involved, or one's partner has been involved, in illicit sex. To get AIDS reveals your secret behaviour and forces into the open sexual behaviour that might otherwise have remained hidden. AIDS is seen as a disease of sexual excess and perversity (Sontag 1989:26). In these circumstances the last person in whom many people with AIDS wish to confide is their minister or priest, and the last place where they feel free to search for support is the church, where they are sure they will meet disapproval.

The negative view about sexuality is based on a wrong understanding of human nature and a wrong understanding of sexuality. We do not have two natures, a higher and a lower, but one nature, a human nature, a psychosomatic nature in which the human spirit exists in a human body. Since we believe that God created the physical universe, we must see sexuality as God's gift of love to us. Since Jesus took upon himself a human body, true incarnationalism will involve believing that God's nature in Jesus is expressed through a human body. The body is a fit and proper temple in which divinity and the highest human ideals can be embedded. Our sexuality cannot be divided off from our spirituality.

Sexuality is not confined to the genital. It is part of who we are and thus part of our whole personality. All of us are sexual beings. Sex is the physical and psychological basis of all our human relationships and human love. Clearly that does not mean that we have a genital relationship with everybody. But because whatever we do we are men and women, driven by our male and female genes and hormones, because we are embedded in our bodies, our relationships all include physicality and sexuality to some extent.

I do not mean to imply here that our friendships are all disguised sexual relationships or that subconsciously we desire intercourse with everyone we meet. I mean that we cannot separate out the sexual part of who we are. We relate to everyone as a woman or as a man. Our relationships involve the whole person, which includes sexuality. A distinction is sometimes made between 'gender' and 'sex', but I do not mean only that we are conditioned by our upbringing as a man or woman and by the social roles ascribed to gender. I mean that the genetic, hormonal, instinctive aspects that are part of being a man or woman cannot be corralled off and excised from relationships.

Because we are all different, our sexuality will be expressed in different ways. There is no one, single norm of sexuality which can be imposed on everybody.

'Much Christian discussion of sexuality starts from an idealistic approach about what should be, rather than a realist and historical materialist analysis of what is' (Leech in Woodward 1990:62).

Because we are all sexual, sexuality is not confined to marriage. Married people, single people, priests, nuns, virgins, we are all sexual beings through and through. To be chaste does not mean merely to avoid sexual intercourse or to confine sexual intercourse to marriage, but to integrate in a healthy and holistic way the sexual longings which are part of who we are, and the sexual awareness of our own body and the bodies of others, with our spirituality, our ideals, our values, our whole person. Henri Nouwen says:

'Healthy sexual activity . . . includes an integration of the sexual and the spiritual . . . Sex can vitalize, concretize and incarnate love, and love can deepen, transcend and spiritualize sex' (quoted Renouf in Woodward 1990:78).

Chastity involves recognizing and enjoying our sexuality and integrating that enjoyment with other human and Christian concerns. When our passions are thus integrated, we are able to direct and determine our own sexual behaviour. But directing our sexuality in a chaste way does not mean denying our sexuality. Our sexuality will not be suppressed or denied. When we seek to do so, it bursts out in other unrecognized and therefore perhaps unwelcome and unhealthy ways. True chastity, says Cardinal Bernardin, seeks to invoke reason and order and passion as a whole (*The Grail* 1989).

It is therefore nonsense to say that sex is something that only concerns us if we are married and then for the primary purposes of procreation. At many times in its history the church has tried to impose this view of sex. It has never been successful. On the whole people have never been able to live as the church wanted them to live. All that has happened is that the church has made them feel guilty or alienated from God for their inevitable failures. It is a ' . . .grave pastoral mistake to use the Christian view of marriage as a means of alienating couples from the life of the church' (Thatcher 1993:109). This has helped neither the people nor the church. When people have found that Christian teaching on sex was impractical and not congruent with their experience, they stopped listening to what the church says about sex. Despite the Popes having forbidden contraception, we know that many Catholics use 'artificial' methods of birth control. By 1974 only 12% of North American Catholics accepted their church's teaching about birth control (Greely 1990:23). Despite Christian teaching about confining sexual intercourse to marriage, many Christians of all denominations do not see anything wrong with sexual activity between unmarried persons. By 1986 only 22% of North American Catholics and 34% of Protestants thought that premarital sex was always wrong (Greely 1990:97). 'In sexual matters the Church has lost its ability to demand effectively different attitudes and behaviour from its members' (Greely 1990:98).

This does not mean that popular ethics are necessarily correct ethics, but unless people understand the reason for a particular ethical stance and participate in shaping that stance, they will not be committed to it. The church is inhibited from making any useful contribution to the debate because what we have to say is seen as without ground, even by our own members.

'What is needed today on a broader scale is a theology of sexuality, not only on the question of AIDS. What we are teaching and holding on to simply is not what the people are accepting' (Kowalewski 1994:71).

If all of our relationships include sexuality as part of ourselves, we cannot draw hard lines between married and unmarried, between homosexual and heterosexual sex. Christian attempts to put sexuality into rigidly defined boxes cannot work. I am a heterosexual person with no interest whatever in a genital relationship with other men. I love my wife and have no intention of having a genital relationship with other women. But of course I am aware of both men and women in their masculinity and femininity, of their bodies, of their male and female personalities, and I relate to them as a man to other men or as a man to women. My sexuality, my awareness of gender and of my own physicality, is part of these interrelationships. Even in our most spiritual moments, even in the peaks of religious ecstasy, sexuality permeates the experience, as a study of Christian mysticism soon shows.

Teresa of Avila describes her experience of union with God.

'In his hands I saw a long golden spear and at the end of the iron tip I seemed to see a point of fire. With this he seemed to pierce my heart several times so that it penetrated to my entrails' (Teresa of Avila in Peers 1946a:192–3).

Deirdre Green denies that Teresa's imagery is necessarily sexual or phallic (Green 1989:46). But we cannot deny that the writing is filled with abandonment and passion.

'The soul was conscious of having been most delectably wounded . . . It complains to its Spouse with words of love, and even cries aloud, being unable to help itself' (Teresa of Avila in Peers 1946b:276).

This is not surprising. Sexuality is at one and the same time a rejoicing in the other who is different from me, and a longing for union with that different other. We have learned to see the trinitarian nature of God as a model on which to base our ideas of human social relationships (Hodgson 1943). If we can see our concept of God as Trinity as the basis for our need as humans to live in community, we can also see the Trinity as a basis for our sexuality. A Catholic document on homosexuality says that: 'All human love is a reflection of the love of God which is the life of the Trinity' (*Created Design* 1994:4). In marriage we experience in an especially deep way the unity at the heart of God; but then we must grant that everyone, in his or her own way, married or not, has the same need for union with the one who is other than one's self. Thus love of God, love of fellow humans, and sexual love are all facets of the same thing. A life without love is not what human life is meant to be like. The love which we discover has its origins in how we are made, and in the love which God has for us.

Love does not always have to be expressed in an overtly sexual, let alone genital, way, and the Catholic document quoted above is certainly not approving genital homosexual relationships. But we do need to say clearly that love, wherever it exists, including love between persons of the same sex, is in itself good and godly. Our rules about sex ought to encourage the expression of love, while warning against ways of living which are merely selfish or manipulative of others.

> 'For people who are not married, whether they are homosexual or heterosexual, love and affection can be given some form of expression. But there is the need to be aware that perfectly legitimate expressions of affection can lead to genital activity which could not only be wrong, but destructive of a worthwhile and supportive relationship' (*Created Design* 1994:10).

Genital relationships between, for example, adult and child, teacher and pupil, doctor and patient, are wrong and destroy the proper relationship that should exist in these cases. However, our fear of uncontrollable sexual urges is such that we have often been afraid to permit any expression of affection, for example in what were termed 'special friendships'. The same document insists therefore that such friendships, even between persons of the same sex, are not in themselves wrong (*Created Design* 1994:5). All love is a reflection of the image of God in us. Jesus, we are told, loved Mary, Martha and Lazarus (John 11.5).

Perhaps what we are afraid of when we cling to rigid sexual codes is a loss of control. Older people fear that the young, in whom sexual desires are supposed to flow more strongly, will not live as older people think they should live and that the familiar patterns of social life will change. The sheer force of the sexual urge threatens our sense of order and authority. People who attend church regularly are often traditionalists who believe that stability and unchanging moral standards are necessary in a confusing and changing modernity. They find any relaxation of sexual control painful and dangerous. We fear that if we give way to passion we shall lose control even of ourselves. We are suspicious of passion; and passion and sexuality run hand in hand. But without passion, our lives and relationships, even our relationship with God, become cold. 'Without a sense of the "living flame of passion" religion becomes dry, cold and repressive' (Leech in Woodward 1990:65).

That does not mean that we must spend our lives in search of emotional, sexual and spiritual 'highs', becoming seekers after orgiastic sensation. Both religious and secular life in the West have fallen into this trap. The secular world sometimes seems to have abandoned all rules in order to pursue instant gratification of every sexual urge. It sees sexuality as self-gratification rather than as an urge to give and to receive love. Faithfulness, modesty, self-denial are all abandoned in what is defended as non-judgmentalism but is really short-term self-indulgence. A director of popular romantic soft-pornographic movies, asked how he would feel if one of his daughters wanted an acting role in one of his movies, replies: 'I've never never never never never made a value judgment about what my children do' (Zalman King, in *The Independent*, 11 May 1995).

Mr King seems to have confused two issues. Being non-judgmental in the sense of never excluding our children from our love, and loving them unconditionally, is one thing. Having no opinion about their behaviour is another.

In the religious life, the same desire for instant gratification that we find in secular life re-emerges as religious sensationalism and emotional revivalism. The kind of religious fundamentalism which is growing today is not that of sober conservative Calvinism; it is a world of religious ecstasy, of speaking in tongues, of laughing in the spirit. A good deal can be said in defence of neo-Pentecostalism; no doubt it is popular because it gives people a sense of warm community, of joy, of expectant faith, all of which are hard to find in main-line churches. But it is nevertheless a disguised expression of the eros, the sexual energy, within us all.

Secular hedonists are often deeply suspicious of the religious Right. Similarly, those within the more fervent forms of religious revivalism are usually opposed to what they regard as the sexual licence of the secular world. But each side is perhaps guilty of losing the wholeness which, as said earlier, is what chastity really means. Thus we get what Leech calls the 'creeping fanaticism' of some Christian fundamentalists (in Woodward 1990:61) as they fanatically and fearfully deny the sexuality inherent within us all, and the mindless sexual obsession of secular hedonists who have forgotten that we have other spiritual and emotional needs, too.

The Christian mystic saints, despite the overt sexuality so close to the surface of their experience, were not seekers after sensation. They often said that spiritual joy is a mark of a somewhat immature spiritual life.

'The soul which begins to walk resolutely in this way of mental prayer and can persuade itself to set little store by consolations and tenderness in devotion, and neither to be elated when the Lord gives them nor disconsolate when he withholds them, has already travelled a great part of the journey' (Teresa of Avila in Peers 1946a:68).

They were well aware of the long periods of dryness, *accidie*, that had to be endured. Their search for union with God was a highly disciplined one. A Christian holism demands that passion and reason belong together.

'Both mysticism and prophecy depend on passion, on self-giving, on the integral union of heart and head, on a profound liberation of the personality . . . A failure to take our sexual nature seriously results in the mysticism of deranged religiosity and the politics of fanaticism' (Leech in Woodward 1990:66).

I am therefore certainly not saying that in a search for a more positive attitude towards sexuality the church must abandon all calls for discipline and restraint. The AIDS pandemic forces upon our attention the desperate need in our various societies for a sexuality balanced with love and with reasoned social concern. Selfish hedonism has led, to put it bluntly, to massive deaths. That is why Christians really cannot go along with a non-judgmental counselling approach and leave it at that.

I have said enough in previous chapters to make it clear that people with AIDS are not to be despised and rejected as sinners, for we are all, in one way or another, part of the sin which has led to AIDS. One-to-one counselling will still require non-judgmental-ism. One-to-one counselling does not work well if we impose our moral opinions upon others. Counselling is intended to help people take responsibility for their own decisions, to decide for themselves what is the best and most responsible thing to do. The one being counselled is the only one who can make this decision; the counsellor in many cases will not even know what is the best decision to be made. But our Christian concern is not only with individuals but with all of society; it is not only with counselling but with shaping social values. A Christianity which opted out of any search for sexual guidelines, which pretended that anything goes, would be faithless to the Bible and the Christian tradition and would also be of little relevance to the modern world faced with AIDS.

'Traditional liberalism proves inadequate to an epidemic situation which lacks the fundamentally rational teleology that liberalism assumes to characterize most social phenomena' (Singer 1989:53).

A liberalism which assumes that everybody will choose responsibly if left to themselves; that nobody therefore needs guidance because they will be able to figure out for themselves what is best, and that all will be well in the end, does not work in the face of AIDS. The sexual freedom and adventurism that was so fashionable in the West in the

1960s proved to be fatal for many. It is no longer fashionable or desirable.

Searching for sexual guidelines will not be easy. Just as with theology, so too with ethics, we need to embrace the chaos. The Bible will not provide ready-made blueprints for action. Even the clearest of biblical texts – for example about homosexuality – cannot be applied without thought and without re-interpretation to our own very different context. This is not new. Norman points out (in Woodward 1990:87) that new issues such as contraception and new medical knowledge continually force the church to adapt its sexual ethics. It is quite widely thought now that a homosexual orientation may be genetic; it is generally thought that such an orientation in an adult person is unchangeable. Paul could not possibly have known this. His view that homosexuality is deliberate perversity is simply wrong, and we cannot base an ethic about homosexuality on it.

Each person is different, and each context is different. Rigid and universal rules have not worked in the past and will not work now. Nevertheless, Paul reminds us that our bodies and our sexuality are a gift from God and are therefore to be regarded with reverence and not trivialized (I Corinthians 6.15). There is every reason to insist as the basis for a sexual ethic that our sexual activity, like any activity, must include consideration for others, avoidance of hurt, making other people's needs at least as important as our own – in short, for recognizing that our sexuality too must bring us to the cross as well as to resurrection, to self denial as well as to self fulfilment. Sexuality is ' . . .the raw material of holiness and creativity' (Leech in Woodward 1990:66).

The views of C. S. Lewis represent a sensible modern Christianity for many people. He suggested that there are different kinds of love (Lewis 1960). He distinguished between affection, friendship, *eros* and charity. In some ways this is a useful distinction. It might well be said that in the Western world we place too much emphasis on *eros* and not enough upon friendship. We concern ourselves with our lover of the moment, or with our family, or with our business colleagues, but have no time for friends with whom we can talk, explore common interests and be ourselves. In all of his ethics, Aristotle wrote two volumes on friendship but nothing on sexual relationships (Aristotle 1980). Lewis was not a prude. He was not at all opposed to *eros*. His definition of *eros* excluded the kind of relationship where the object of our lust is merely that, an object. By *eros* he meant a love which included but transcended sex. But Lewis was wrong, in my view, to separate out these four loves. They are different, they are directed at different people, but since I am only one person I bring all of me, including my sexuality, to all my loves, including friendship.

Lewis is horrified by the suggestion that friendship between men may have homosexual elements. His horror betrays him into language which must even then have been offensive, where he calls homosexual men 'pansies' (Lewis 1960:75). But however deeply we suppress it, we are all aware of others, whether of the same sex or the opposite, in a sexual way. Mostly that awareness is only an undercurrent which does not involve us in any explicit or conscious physical sexual contact. But in fact there is only one love, expressed in different ways, experienced in different contexts, always undergirded with our sexual being. Rather than suppressing the erotic, we need to suggest ways in which it can be combined with reason and with concern for others.

If everybody in the world was utterly celibate before committing themselves to a permanent relationship, and utterly faithful within that relationship, AIDS would not exist. A number of Christian commentators have taken this to mean that we must enforce with new vigour and strictness the traditional Christian teaching that bans premarital sex, post-marital adultery and all homosexuality alike (Antonio 1986:198, etc.). If people will not be sexually monogamous out of piety, perhaps AIDS will mean that they do so out of prudence (Coleman 1991:172). But it is not constructive to use the fear of AIDS as a way of re-imposing rigid rules. Before contraception came along, the fear of pregnancy and venereal disease did not prevent extra-marital sex. One day a cure or prophylactic may be found for AIDS, and fear-based morality will collapse again.

AIDS does remind us, rather forcefully, that we need to think hard about guidelines for sex; but it cannot be the sole reason for such guidelines. Jack Dominian says:

'When sexual integrity is observed, it becomes not only an answer to AIDS but goes beyond it as the predominant basis for sexual ethics in the twenty-first century' (Dominian 1987:149).

Dominian is clear that it is important for Christianity in today's world that it should not try to regain control by the negation and inhibition of sexuality. Rather, it needs to combine a positive and welcoming attitude towards sexuality with a code of discipline based upon theories of human development (Dominian 1987:65).

Amanda first entered into a sexual relationship at university where she and her boyfriend shared a flat for three years. However, after graduation their interests diverged, and when John moved away to a job elsewhere the relationship ended. Subsequently she met Robert, also on his own after a previous relationship ended. After a period of dating they moved in together. They feel they are now ready to marry. They went to see their local vicar. When he discovered they lived at the same address he lectured them about the evils of living together, mentioning AIDS as one of the possible consequences.

If sexuality is at the heart of all relationships, and if we all need relationships of one kind or another where we find love and trust, then our emphasis should be on the quality of relationships, not upon whether they are heterosexual and post-marital. Sex based primarily upon selfish lust is not part of a bonding and growing trustfulness and can therefore only be harmful. Yet an unmarried but loving couple already involved in a sexual relationship may well be bonded by that sexual relationship into a more caring, giving, trusting relationship with each other. As Dominian remarks, since marriage is (at least in the ideal) the ultimate expression of commitment to another person, sexual relationships reach their most meaningful context within marriage. But there are gradations of commitment. 'Living together' may well be a kind of commitment; a couple living together are not necessarily having merely casual sex (Dominian 1987:74), and the church needs to recognize this. Some people living together will go on to be married in due course. A Church of England report says that such couples should not be described as 'living in sin' (*Something to Celebrate* 1995:117). Some people may be involved in what they hope will prove to be a committed relationship but find in due course that in fact it is not possible to remain committed to one another. Many people, like Amanda and Robert, move through a series of sexual relationships before eventually finding someone with whom the commitment can grow and become lifelong.

The church continues to advocate the family as the ideal Christian relationship. Either we must be virgins or we must be fathers and mothers with children, the church seems to say. Of course family life is important for children to grow up in a stable context, but increasingly the nuclear family is becoming a myth. A majority of children in the townships of Africa are born to unmarried mothers. Unmarried mothers in the white group in the United States are becoming almost as common; the number of white unmarried mothers has risen there by 94% since 1980 (Centers for Disease Control 1995). Perhaps we need to find ways to enable the many people who are not in neat family units, and who are not being offered one, to find constructive ways to find and express love. We need to broaden our model of what it means to be family.

> 'I find it interesting that the centralized Church is always pushing the family as the ideal Christian relationship. I find it interesting because try as I might I can find no basis for it in Jesus' teaching. He seems to have had an endearingly ambivalent attitude to his family',

writes Catholic theologian Elizabeth Stuart (*Catholic AIDS Link Newsletter* 1994). Jesus was ambivalent not only towards his own family (Mark 3.33–35) but also towards the families of those whom he called (Mark 10.29). It seems that he took a far less rigid view about the need for a conventional family than we do.

That does not mean that we must accept with no qualms single parenthood or successive children born to a series of different fathers. It does mean that when we think about family life we must be more flexible than we have been. Since churches have reluctantly had to come to terms with the reality of divorce and remarriage, there is really no new principle at stake here. Of course divorce is always deeply to be regretted. All marriages go through periods of difficulty and readjustment, and our counsel ought to be that people need to work at their marriages rather than allow them to disintegrate. Divorce is always harmful for children. But sometimes the initial marriage, often entered into youthfully with poor understanding of self or the other, sometimes entered into because the couple have begun a sexual relationship and feel pressurized by traditional morality into regularizing the relationship by a belated marriage, is even more to be regretted than the divorce. Sometimes a relationship cannot be sustained, perhaps because of severe personality defects, alcoholism, violence, or merely because one partner is no longer willing to try. Sexuality is most fully expressed in absolutely trusting deep relationships. The reality, however, is that deep relationships, like ordinary friendships, do not always work out. Since almost all churches now have a more flexible attitude to these situations, permitting marriage after divorce or annulment in a much wider range of situations than previously, it is clear that they accept this.

Because so many babies are born to single mothers, and so many marriages end in divorce, the nuclear family is no longer the norm and the idea of 'family' has become much more complex and extended. For all sorts of economic and educational reasons, and because of our expectation that marriage means having a house and financial independence, young people come to sexual maturity many years before they regard themselves as being in a position to marry. During those years they do form sexual relationships, sometimes with the person whom they will eventually marry, sometimes with several people before finding that person.

The church gives the impression that it assumes that all couples will be celibate until married, and when no longer married will revert to celibate status. Clergy are often disapproving of couples who ask to be married having lived together for some time previously. They disapprove of unmarried people having sexual relationships. In consequence people feel that the church is out of touch with real life.

'To many singles, who consider themselves Christian, the church's position is inadequate and irrelevant to their actual experience of life' (Renouf in Woodward 1990:76).

It is very important that the church distinguish between people living together, perhaps in a series of two or three relationships before marriage, and the sort of promiscuity where casual one-night stands with a variety of partners is the norm.

By rejecting as sinners couples who live together, we oversimplify the moral issues involved. The couple may well love each other faithfully and unselfishly. If the relationship is a good one, our role ought to be to commend and support that love, and to encourage them to become even more committed and stable in the relationship, rather than rejecting the love they have. If the relationship is likely to become destructive, our role ought to be to help them to recognize that they are not suited, to break up and to move on. Whether or not they have had sexual intercourse is really irrelevant.

Young people come early to sexual maturity, long before they are ready to know their future career path or be in a position of economic independence. It is simply unrealistic to expect that they will have no sexual relationships over the ten or fifteen years between reaching sexual maturity and finishing tertiary education or post-school training and settling to a job, a town, and family life. The church, if it wishes to be taken seriously, will have to find a middle line between recognizing that many people will have several sexual relationships before marriage, and accepting that widespread promiscuity is a norm. We cannot make rules about this. To say that, for example, two relationships before marriage is acceptable, ten is promiscuity, is tempting but artificial. In fact this is our problem: we want to give helpful advice about sexual ethics, we do not want to abandon all constraints, but there are no hard and fast rules, and as the world changes so the right course of action changes too. Popes have found it hard to change their minds about contraception though even their own theologians and scientific advisers have urged them to do so; because to change our mind invites mockery, invites the forces of *anomie*. The Lambeth Conference had to do a U-turn on the issue of contraception between 1920 and 1930.

'For the church honestly and realistically to explore issues of sexuality requires a willingness to be vulnerable, a willingness to be exposed, suffer, and lose control over a dynamic it cannot fully understand or direct' (Renouf in Woodward 1990:78).

Sexual ethics are part of, but go beyond, a theology of AIDS. The sufferings caused by AIDS make us realize rather acutely how badly in need we are of a new and more realistic, constructive, positive view of sexuality as part of love and being. From an AIDS perspective, these points seem to be important.

• The church needs to be able to communicate with ordinary, mostly non-church-going people about sex if it is to make a useful contribution to a new shared sexual ethic.

• The need to communicate requires that the church does not assume a rigid, authoritarian stance.

• Because of its historical negativity about sex, and because of the widespread perception that the church sees sexuality as something to be ashamed of, the church needs to discover and vigorously to promote a healthy, positive, unembarrassed attitude towards sexuality which recognizes it as part of what God has made us.

• AIDS makes all of us in society re-examine our sexual ethics. But Christians must be careful that the fear of AIDS does not make us revert to seeing sexual sins as worse than other sins. AIDS comes about through economic greed even more than through sexual promiscuity.

'We must not be led into using HIV/AIDS as the excuse to pass judgment on people's sexual preferences or behaviour on moral grounds. HIV/AIDS and the threat to public health has brought to our attention many "social problems" which society has tended to ignore' (Thomas 1992:37).

If we concentrate only on sexual morality in our AIDS education, we shall miss the point that unfair economic systems, traditional tribal practices, wrong social policies, the exploitation of the poor, of the peasantry, and of women, are all part of what has caused AIDS.

• The teaching that sexual lovemaking helps to create, and belongs best in the context of, a loving, trusting, committed relationship which finds its fullest expression in marriage, goes beyond the immediate concerns of AIDS but is not irrelevant to it, since a person with AIDS needs a loving and committed partner to share in the pain.

• Yet the need to be constructive requires that the church make a stand against a superficial or selfish view of sexuality which divorces sexuality from love, from social responsibility, from higher human aspirations. This is the hard part. The church needs to become more flexible in its sexual ethics; yet it needs to teach quite clearly that selfish sex and promiscuous sex is damaging and, in the face of AIDS, likely to be fatal. If the church merely mirrors general views about sex to be found in modern society, it has no contribution to make.

• In many parts of the world the church needs to provide information about sex, about how AIDS is transmitted, and about contraception, to both adults and children, since no other agency exists to do this.

• AIDS becomes epidemic when many people are having sexual relationships with many partners. Promiscuity creates a serious risk that AIDS will spread. Promiscuity is impossible to define. Having one or two partners before marriage is not necessarily promiscuity. Nor is it a major factor in creating the conditions for AIDS. Having many sexual partners is. It is, of course, possible to contract AIDS when one has only had a few sexual partners, or even one partner if that partner is HIV positive. We all know the mathematics. If each person has sex with only two others in their life, then since each of their partners has also had sex with two others each has been exposed to an almost infinite number of sexual relationships. But we need to be honest: the chances of contracting AIDS in such circumstances are very small. In those heterosexual societies where there is not much prostitution nor drug usage nor frequent partner changes, AIDS has not spread to any extent. We have good reasons for saying that living together before marriage is problematic, but we cannot truthfully invoke AIDS as a major reason.

• It is extremely important that the church should encourage sexual faithfulness. Celibacy, monogamy, or even faithful polygamy would end AIDS. Saayman and Kriel, writing in the context of Africa, and anxious not to exclude traditional African people or homosexual people from a sexual ethic which will combat AIDS, suggest that instead of polygamy we use the term 'open sexual relationships' to describe relationships with a number of changing partners, and 'closed sexual relationships' to describe relationships, which may be heterosexual or homosexual, within marriage or outside, monogamous or polygamous (Saayman and Kriel 1992:21). It is open sexual relationships, not homosexuality nor polygamy, which create the risk of AIDS.

Perhaps this concept of 'closed sexual relationships' needs to be widened beyond polygamy to include the small number of serial relationships before marriage that are part of many people's life story. It is extremely important that the church become involved in education about sex and education, and the church needs to contribute towards a sexual ethic which encourages closed sexual relationships and discourages open ones. But we need to do this in an open, non-judgmental way which recognizes that because sexuality is universal, single people often do enter into sexual relationships. We need to share in ways which help them to express and enjoy that sexuality responsibly, rather than merely denying its existence.

> 'To affirm their Christian faith, they [i.e. single people] feel that they must repress and deny their sexuality and lead a life devoid of any sexual intimacy' (Renouf in Woodward 1990:76, quoting John Mitchell).

As long as people feel like this, the church is not going to be able to make a real contribution in education about sexuality and AIDS.

This is not an easy situation for the church to be in. Honesty, realism and love require that we be less legalistic about sexual relationships. Yet AIDS requires that we shift opinion throughout the whole world towards confining sexual intercourse within responsible, caring, committed relationships. It is, quite literally, a matter of life and death that we succeed in this. We shall return to this theme at the end of this chapter.

Homosexuality

AIDS demands that the church take up with renewed commitment its search for a viable ethic about heterosexual relationships. It also demands that the church think again about its traditional total rejection of homosexual acts.

> 'The appearance of AIDS in the world gives the churches the opportunity which so far they show few signs of taking, to re-examine the theology of human sexuality or . . . to ask whether homosexual orientation and conduct should be revalued' (Edward Norman in Woodward 1990:86).

The very term homosexual is problematic. Although attraction between members of the same sex seems to be culturally universal, not all cultures would see homosexuality as being a distinct and separate category. Some men and women are drawn exclusively to members of the same sex, some exclusively to the opposite sex, but some seem to be drawn in both directions to some degree. Thus determining just what homosexuality means is not easy. Also, some in the homosexual community dislike the term 'homosexual' because of its negative association and the medicalization of the concept, and prefer to call themselves gay and lesbian (Stuart 1993:3). However, the term 'gay' also seems to me to carry associations of meaning, for example that homosexual sexuality is always happy and carefree; and especially when used against its colloquial antonym 'straight' seems to imply that homosexual sex is bent. So here we will continue to use the terms homo- and heterosexual and try to reduce the negative associations of either.

I have said that homosexuality is not a major factor in the AIDS epidemic outside America and Europe and therefore should not dominate our thoughts about AIDS and sexuality. It is nevertheless true that male homosexuality has been, and still is, the major factor in AIDS in Europe and America and therefore the church cannot ignore the issue. Homosexual anal sex is particularly risky behaviour for contracting AIDS. Nobody knows for sure just what proportion of any population is homosexual, and therefore what proportion of homosexual persons have contracted AIDS, but anecdotally almost everyone in the homosexual community has a friend or several friends who have died of AIDS. It seems likely that a rather high proportion of the homosexual community have contracted AIDS. AIDS and homosexuality in the West are so linked that to state publicly that one has AIDS is more or less equivalent to stating publicly that one is homosexual.

In itself this does not mean that homosexuality is wrong, nor even that anal sex, between heterosexual or homosexual persons, is wrong. Anal sex is risky because it causes minute tears in the lining of the anus through which the virus may pass, but, although not so frequently, the vagina may also be torn in heterosexual intercourse. Anal sex is not the only kind of risky sex. And if it is true that one in ten women in Britain and America also have anal sex (Dixon

1990:78), then it is not anal sex alone which causes AIDS, since relatively few women there are HIV positive. The issue is not just anal sex, but the number of partners. Again, if a homosexual couple are entirely faithful to each other they cannot contract AIDS. Despite all appearances to the contrary, the primary sexual ethical question facing the church which has relevance to AIDS is not homosexuality but promiscuity.

'If you are an active homosexual, a major predictor of whether you are infected or not has less to do with whether you have anal sex, passive or active, but has to do with the number of different men you have had intercourse with over the last few years' (Dixon 1990:78).

Yet it is still important for the church to rethink its attitude towards homosexual love. It is important for a number of reasons.
• Since so many of those with AIDS in Europe or America are in fact homosexual men, we cannot minister to the AIDS crisis there as long as our attitude is one of judgment.
• As long as we continue to say that homosexual love is sinful, we put a large barrier between ourselves and people with AIDS who are homosexual. Because many of the mainline churches were embarrassed about homosexuality, they were slow to begin AIDS ministry to the homosexual community, and homosexual persons found it difficult to come to them for help. In many places in America non-denominational 'community' churches sprang up where homosexuals could be sure of a welcome for themselves, places where they could be ministered to if they were sick and offer ministry if they were not. The lines between giving and receiving ministry were quickly blurred, and these churches became examples to the mainline churches of Christian community and interdependence. If we reject the love for their partner which sustains homosexual people who have AIDS as something sinful and disgusting, we are in fact rejecting the person for whom that love is so central. We cannot really claim to accept them 'despite' their homosexuality. They do not want to be accepted despite who they are but because of who they are. They wish to celebrate, not mourn, their sexual condition. 'We understand ourselves as graced and our sexuality as a gift', says a document produced by Dignity, a Christian homosexual group (quoted Kelly 1990:368).

• We must recognize that society's refusal, and the church's refusal, to recognize and to affirm stable homosexual relationships has
been a major cause of homosexual promiscuity. For bonding to take
place it is important that people should be able openly to affirm, and
be affirmed in, their bondedness. This has been denied to homosexual couples. We have made them feel ashamed of their love, and
have therefore driven it into secrecy. Secrecy and shame are not
conducive to stable ongoing relationships. Unstable relationships
lead to promiscuity, which leads to AIDS.

• We must recognize the quality of love given by many homosexual
persons to their partners who are suffering and dying from AIDS.
That love transcends but includes sexual orientation. To be blind to
that love is to be blind to God who is love. We must also recognize
the grace and courage with which many homosexual persons have
died. We must recognize the way in which the homosexual
community has given caring ministry in a time of AIDS. Many self-
supporting AIDS groups which have sprung up in the homosexual
community are filled with love and concern to a degree that often
puts the church to shame. Unless we wish to be Pelagian,[8] we must
acknowledge that God's grace has worked in them. This must give
us cause to doubt whether the traditional refusal to see anything
good or holy in homosexual relationships can be theologically
defended.

> 'People with AIDS offer examples of quiet nobility in suffering –
> which at times seems to suggest, even to those unable to recognize
> it, the divine presence' (Norman in Woodward 1990:89).

The grace of God works through homosexual persons and through
their relationships with each other. We cannot therefore dismiss
them as people sunk in disobedience and sin.

• Many homosexual persons, having faced and triumphed over
their fears of death and darkness, have become prophetic witnesses
to God and to the risen Christ.

• Homosexual persons are amongst those who are 'despised and
rejected' (Isaiah 53.3), and the church must therefore be very careful

---

[8]Pelagianism was a fifth-century heresy which taught that human beings are
able to chose to do good in their own strength.

about refusing to minister to them on their own terms. Our rejection of them often makes them reject themselves. They often feel very guilty and of no worth. This is a kind of oppression.

'I have stood up in church groups as a priest, as a gay man, and as an HIV positive, and talked about living with the virus, and discovered that people have got very angry with me. I think they would have been much happier if I had been in a hospital bed, if I had gone away to die' (Randall in Woodward 1990:70).

'My religion's discomfort with discussing sexuality, coupled with my own homosexuality, led me, inaccurately, to believe that I was not a spiritual person' (Sabatino 1992).

'Though gay men have begun to understand it is something in themselves these upright men so fear, too many of us have internalized their self-hatred and shame' (Monette 1988:124).

Verghese talks about his experience as an Asian doctor working in Virginia. Aliens in a new country try to blend, try to learn the accent, try to be something different from who they are, to pretend to be like everyone else. Homosexuals, he says, are in the same way turned into aliens in their own land.

'Gay men, in order to avoid conflict, had also become experts at blending, camouflaging themselves but at great cost to their spirit' (Verghese 1994:51).

Any rethinking about homosexuality and Christian belief cannot be done without taking into account what homosexual persons themselves think about this. If theology is based on experience, we must listen to those who have had the experience. The church is very divided on the issue of homosexuality, and church leaders, under pressure from their vociferous right-wing members and from the moralistic gutter press, are often reluctant to appear to condone it. Usually the arguments in the church against accepting that homosexual sex may be a legitimate part of human sexual expression are that the Bible so clearly condemns it. Sometimes arguments from natural law are used to back this up – that is, the argument that nature and therefore God has clearly equipped us to be heterosexual and not homosexual. The fact that many homosexual men have contracted AIDS is then interpreted as a sign either that God is punishing this wicked behaviour, or that AIDS confirms that homosexual sex is against what our bodies are made for. We have discussed the notion of punishment in earlier chapters. The latter allegation – that homosexual sex must be wrong because it leads to AIDS – is clearly nonsense, in view of the fact that most people with AIDS, if we look at a world-wide perspective, are not homosexual. Clearly vaginal intercourse also puts us at some risk, even if not quite so great, as anal intercourse.

What would change our minds about the suggestion that homosexuality is unnatural and therefore wrong, would be any evidence that a homosexual orientation is caused by genetic factors. Whether or not this is the case is still debated. It is not yet possible to decide on the issue of heredity versus environment, nature or nurture, whether homosexual persons are born with that orientation or become homosexual for psychological or social reasons. Indeed, whether we can even give a kind of medical ontology to the status of homosexuality is debateable. In some societies men who mostly have relationships with other men but who still engage occasionally in intercourse with their wives would not be regarded as homosexual. The concept of homosexuality is a human social construction rather than a medical condition.

But since it is clear that some men in many different cultures, covering a variety of social systems, are erotically drawn exclusively, or almost exclusively, to other men, it is stretching the point to say that there is no such thing as homosexuality.

'It is also clear that homosexuality exists in many different cultures across many centuries, and it is therefore hard to agree that the state is purely one of social construction' (Herdt 1987:445).

There are men in all societies whose sexual orientation is towards other men rather than towards women. Not all societies think this is important; not all societies therefore see this as an unusual or noteworthy condition. What we must say is that there are no fixed boundaries which define exactly when a person is to be regarded as homosexual, and that the causes of this orientation are probably complex rather than simple, many rather than few.

'Probably no single factor alone is present in all instances [of homosexuality], and possibly no single factor alone is exclusively responsible in one individual; but to a greater or lesser extent, many of the causes outlined above are found, as a thread of continuity, in most instances of exclusive or overwhelming homosexual development' (Cory 1961:488).

We cannot say, therefore, whether God or 'nature' made them homosexual or whether 'unfortunate' circumstances in their upbringing are the cause, or a combination of these things. We note, however, that by already labelling the causes as unfortunate, we are implying that homosexuality is to be regretted. It is this negative attitude towards homosexuality that is a social artefact, not the condition itself; and it is this negative attitude which the church must reconsider.

Whatever the causes of homosexuality, most scholars now agree that a homosexual orientation is rarely reversible.

'General consensus is that the changes from homo- to heterosexuality are few and far between. Most counselling is now directed towards making people accept their sexual orientation' (Ruse 1988:62).

What is also clear is that persons with a homosexual orientation do not show more signs of psychopathology than persons with a heterosexual orientation.

'Homosexuality *per se* implies no impairment in judgment, stability, reliability, or general social or vocational capabilities and should not be regarded as a psychiatric disorder, but simply is one form of sexual behaviour' (Macourt 1977:30).

The American Psychiatric Association with the publication of DSMIII therefore deleted homosexuality from its list of mental disorders.

This brief summary of medical and psychiatric opinion, while incomplete, strongly suggests that we have no basis in natural law for claiming that homosexuality is a disorder. Just because psychiatrists say so, does not mean that the church must agree that homosexuality is an acceptable human condition. But because homosexuality is widespread over all cultures and historical periods, we cannot say that it is against human nature. On the contrary, it seems to be part of human nature everywhere at all times. Homosexuals are not more perverse, more selfish, more depraved than other human beings in any way. Therefore we cannot say that they are sunk in sin. We must concede that whatever the cause, a homosexual orientation is not usually changeable, and that homosexual persons are often admirable human beings. If all this is the case, can we really believe that God hates their state?

Many Christians today say that we should not condemn the homosexual state. That is, persons who through no fault of their own are attracted solely or primarily to people of the same sex should not be condemned because of that attraction (e.g. *Created Design* 1994:9); but, they say, they should be expected never to act on that attraction. They should live their lives in chastity just as a person with heterosexual leanings but who is unmarried must live in chastity. The 1986 letter from the Catholic Congregation for the Doctrine of Faith certainly says this (Stuart 1993:8). The English Catholic bishops reaffirm this (*Created Design* 1994:9,10). 'Being a homosexual person is, then, neither morally good nor morally bad', says Cardinal Hume (Hume 1995) in his welcome statement that homosexuals are entitled to the same dignity as anyone else; but he adds that ' . . .it is homosexual genital acts that are morally wrong'.

Why does Hume, and the Catholic church, say that such acts are wrong? Hume gives two reasons, neither of them very convincing. The church has always taught that the genital expression of love should take place exclusively within marriage between a man and a woman; thus it is so because the tradition of the church says it is so. That argument has been used to defend slavery, to oppose socialism and many other views which the Catholic church now wishes had never been its official teaching. But also, says Hume, genital homosexual love is wrong because the genital expression of love must be open to the possible transmission of new life. This is patently nonsense. The Catholic church does not oppose married sexual love between a couple when the woman is past menopause. Of course we know that Sarah bore a child in her old age; but the church also does not oppose married sexual love when the woman has had a hysterectomy and there is no possibility whatever that she could conceive. I believe that a major part of married sexual love, babies or no babies, is to give deeper expression to that love and to provide a physical, sacramental-like foundation to the love.

Some are called to, and some choose, celibacy. But since I have already said that sexuality is part of all of us, and that sexual intercourse is a physical basis for intimate love and companionship, can we really say that God intends all homosexual persons never to find that intimacy?

> 'What sort of God is envisaged who sends his children into the world with compulsive instincts, which they did not choose, and who then denies them the affection and consolation of shared sexual experience?' (Edward Norman in Woodward 1990:81)

In their very carefully worded document, the English Catholic bishops say, therefore, that each person must make his or her own decision in good conscience about this:

> 'A specially delicate situation arises when the homosexual persons are convinced that, although they accept that homosexual acts in themselves cannot be justified, it is found impossible in practice to lead a celibate life. They might then claim that the choice remains between a stable union, in which there is a necessary and inevitable physical relationship, and an obviously distasteful promiscuous way of life' (*Created Design* 1994:11).

Voluntarily renouncing sexual love for one reason or another is one thing, but if sexual chastity is imposed, the result is often that sexual activity still takes place 'illicitly', or that the sexual longings re-emerge in hidden and unhelpful ways. The person may become preoccupied with sex, or may be stunted through the lack of the intimate love of another human being.

Most Christians have long ago abandoned Augustine's idea that married sex is permissible only because it leads to children. We do not oppose marriage between persons known to be sterile, or for women beyond the menopause. We see sex as part of, and as contributing to, the 'mutual society, help and comfort that the one ought to have of the other' (Solemnization of Matrimony, Book of Common Prayer). But if love and companionship in marriage are strengthened and grounded in sex, then why should we wish to deny to people with a homosexual orientation the same love and companionship?

A Church of England report on family life, in a brief reference to lesbian and homosexual family groups, says that 'gay and lesbian partnerships are built on the desire for commitment and interdependence' (*Something to Celebrate* 1995:120). Similarly, Thielicke, while unable to accept that homosexual love is compatible with Christianity, was still able to observe:

'It is true that homosexual relationship is not a Christian form of encounter with our fellow man: it is nevertheless very certainly a search for the totality of the other human being. He who says otherwise has not yet observed the possible human depth of a homo-erotic-coloured relationship' (Thielicke 1964:272).

Why then does Thielicke still think homosexual relationships cannot square with Christianity? And why do the Church of England bishops say:

'Heterosexuality and homosexuality are not equally congruous with the observed order of creation or with the insights of revelation' (quoted Thatcher 1993:148).

or the English Catholic bishops:

'There has been an attempt to reestablish parity between a normal marriage and the on-going homosexual relationship. This is a false and unacceptable analogy' (*Created Design* 1994:10)?

They take this stand because of Bible teaching. We are still left with the fact that the Bible forbids homosexuality as being contrary to the will of God. Must we ignore the Bible? A number of efforts have been made to show that the Bible does not really forbid homosexuality. The story in Genesis 19.1–29 from which we derive the name of sodomy, telling of the men of Sodom who wish to sodomize the guests of Lot and upon whom fire and brimstone were poured down, can convincingly be shown to be a story about inhospitality rather than homosexuality. We cannot seriously believe anyway that God intends to punish modern homosexuals by burning them to death. But the author of the story, who does believe God acts in this way, does not suggest that it is because of sodomy that they are thus punished. It is because they mistreat aliens and strangers within their gates. If we understand the story correctly, the real sodomists are not those who indulge in anal sex but those who bully vulnerable people within the community. In view of the way that some members of the modern church have bullied the homosexual minority in their own ranks, perhaps it is they who might more biblically be called the sodomists. Ezekiel 16.49–50 commenting on the story is much more concerned about the pride and greed of the Sodomites than about whatever is meant by the 'abominable things'. Wisdom 19.13–14 confirms the view that the sin of the Sodomites was 'bitter hatred of strangers' and gluttony. Jeremiah 23.14 seems to associate Sodom with adultery, but the context is one of religious adultery, that is, worshipping false gods.

A similar story is told in Judges 19.22–30. But again it is not homosexuality *per se* which is being condemned here, but mistreatment of the vulnerable. Denied access to the alien man, the men of the city rape the concubine instead. The story is about cruelty and oppression of the weak, not about homosexuality. Sadly, of course, the author of the story seems oblivious to the oppression of the concubine by both the men of the city and her master.

Leviticus 18.22 and 20.13 are texts which do seem clearly to forbid male homosexuality. With somewhat less conviction, it might be suggested that what is being forbidden here is not homosexuality in itself but homosexuality which is associated with pagan temple rituals; in other words, that what is being forbidden here is not homosexuality but religious syncretism. The context is one in which various Canaanite customs are forbidden. But since the prohibition comes within a list of other sexual prohibitions, it is not merely syncretism that is the issue. The author of Leviticus sees homosexual sex as something which confuses what ought to be clear boundaries between men and women, just as there ought to be clear boundaries between humans and animals (Leviticus 18.23). But before we concede that this text means that homosexual sex is evil, we must note that the text is just as opposed to adultery (Leviticus 18.20) and incest (Leviticus 18.6). Homosexuality is no more abhorrent than these sins. More to the point, the text also forbids sex with a menstruating woman (Leviticus 18.19), and eating black pudding (Leviticus 17.14), eating pork (Leviticus 11.3) or lobster

(Leviticus 11.10). There is no textual reason to think that rules about purity of food should be taken less seriously than rules about purity of sexual acts. If rules about kosher food are not taken as binding upon Christians, then it is hard to see why Leviticus' rules about sex are any more binding. In fact, Leviticus takes us into a mind-set that is quite foreign to us, a mind-set about what is 'natural' and 'unnatural', and is not really any help in guiding us about homosexuality today.

However, the New Testament also forbids homosexuality. The Gospels do not record any sayings of Jesus about homosexuality. Indeed, although it would be going much too far to suggest homosexuality, Jesus' relationships with his disciples were physical to a degree that would be uncomfortable to many men in a modern Anglo-Saxon society. Judas kisses Jesus (Mark 14.44). John leans on his breast (John 21.20). But Paul makes his opposition to homosexuality clear.

In Romans 1.26–27 he says:

> 'For this reason God gave them up to dishonourable passions, for their women exchanged natural relations for the unnatural, and the men likewise gave up natural relations with women and were consumed with passion for one another, men committing shameless acts with men and receiving in their own persons the due penalty for their error.'

It is clear that Paul disapproves of homosexuality. But in this text he is not actually saying that homosexuals are sinners because they perform homosexual acts. Rather, they perform homosexual acts because they are sinners. They have not chosen a homosexual condition; God has sent the condition upon them because they have not listened to God. Paul does not tell us why homosexuality is sinful; he assumes that we will all know that this is the case. He assumes the Leviticus standpoint that it is against nature. His point is about the consequences of religious belief.

> 'Since they did not see fit to acknowledge God, God gave them up to a base mind and to improper conduct' (Romans 1.28).

This surely is not something we can now accept literally. It is not conceivable that God, angry because people are spiritually disobedient, then makes people homosexual – and then condemns them even more because they are homosexual. It also implies that Paul thinks that homosexual persons change from being previously heterosexual. We now know that, whatever the cause, a homosexual orientation emerges in early teens, long before a person could be held responsible for any spiritual disobedience or refusing to hear the word of God. We have to say, quite simply, that Paul was wrong.

While Paul certainly sees homosexuality as sinful, he does not see it as more sinful than many other vices. He mentions evil, avarice, envy, murder, a spirit of strife. We cannot assume that Paul would have sided with those in the Church of England General Synod calling for a ban on homosexual clergy; he might just as likely have called for a ban on quarrelsome clergy or unloving clergy. Those loudest in their condemnation of homosexuals might have found that Paul thought they were unworthy of their priesthood. Nevertheless it is clear that Paul does see homosexuality as a sinful state.

Robin Scroggs has been at pains to show that in this and other Pauline texts Paul is not really against homosexuality at all but against pederasty and homosexual prostitution (Scroggs 1983). In I Corinthians 6.9–10 we are told about *malakoi* and *arsenokoitai*:

> 'Do you not know that the unrighteous will not inherit the kingdom of God? Do not be deceived: neither the immoral, nor idolaters, nor adulterers, nor sexual perverts (*malakoi oute arsenokoitai*) nor thieves, nor the greedy, nor drunkards, nor revilers, nor robbers, will inherit the kingdom of God.'

I have quoted from the Revised Standard Version to be consistent, where, as also in the Revised English Bible, 'sexual perverts' covers both terms, elsewhere translated as homosexuals and male prostitutes (New International Version), catamites and sodomites (Jerusalem Bible), or just 'homosexual perverts' (Good News Bible). The varied translations show that we do not know really what Paul meant. *Malakoi* means a soft and gentle person: by implication, when used of men, an effeminate person. Paul was the first known person to have used the word *arsenokoitai* in the Greek sources available to us. So we don't really know what he meant. Scroggs suggests that Paul is referring to male prostitutes who dress and act in effeminate ways (*malakoi*) and to men who use such women (*arsenokoitai*). He is not referring to loving sex between two equal male partners (Scroggs 1983:118–19).

However, although Scroggs shows us that the exact meaning of the words is uncertain, we cannot doubt that Paul is opposed to homosexuality. The same is true of 1 Timothy 1.9–10. Paul gives a list of vices which includes *pornoi, arsenokoitai* and *andrapodistai.* Scroggs argues that these words do not apply necessarily to homosexuals but to male temple prostitutes and those who use them (Scroggs 1983:120). Rather than try to work our way around Paul and suggest that he was not really talking about male homosexuality, it is surely more faithful to the text to concede that Paul was opposed to homosexual acts, but that he did not know as much about the origins and status of homosexuality as we do two thousand years later, and that had he lived now, Paul might have taken a different view. We cannot take Paul merely at his word; we have to set his word against our own knowledge and experience. The Bible does not give us as much clarity on the matter as some people think.

'Although the scripture texts carry authority with them, they are nowhere near as precise as they are made out to be' (Dominian 1987:24).

In the light of that knowledge and experience, the church may well come to the opinion that it is not homosexuality as such that we should label as sinful, but homosexual (or any sexual) acts which treat other people as objects, which diminish the link between sex and love. We cannot say too clearly that it is not homosexuality which causes AIDS but promiscuity. Because anal sex is more risky than vaginal sex, homosexual promiscuity is even more likely to spread AIDS than heterosexual promiscuity. If the church can move towards a position which encourages homosexually orientated persons towards loving, stable, faithful relationships, it will be helping homosexual persons find fulfilment and joy in their lives, and will be helping to reduce the circumstances which lead to the spread of AIDS. If we persist in denying homosexuals the right to express their sexuality in mutually loving acts, then we continue to make them feel guilty, rejected, and less likely to find stable love. We drive homosexuality underground into an ethos of shamefulness. We make it difficult for homosexuals with AIDS, or homosexuals who have lost a partner to AIDS, to come to us for help. We contribute towards the pool of human unhappiness; and we contribute towards the AIDS pandemic.

Anthony Harvey, acknowledging that for some people it is impossible to form heterosexual relationships, nevertheless believes that we must do all in our power to help people for whom it may be possible to form heterosexual relationships.

> 'So long as it remains possible that they may happily marry and have a family, there is a responsibility laid on all of us to help them find their sexual identity in this way' (Harvey 1994:119).

But this means that 'incurable' homosexuals are to be regarded as unfortunate persons deprived, for some reason known only to God, of normal human fulfilment. Will this help homosexual persons, in a time of AIDS, to turn to the church for acceptance and support? If the best we can say for homosexual relationships is that they are unfortunate, but that the poor victims of nature's cruelty cannot help themselves, we are surely humiliating them. Do not homosexuals have the right to choose their identity rather than merely being the victims of circumstances (Thatcher 1995:151)?

Kevin Kelly points out that as long as we reject all homosexual activity, we do not have a Christian ethic which is able to distinguish between permanent, faithful homosexual relationships and temporary casual stands.

> 'Put bluntly, is genital sexual expression appropriate as an expression of any kind of loving relationship (being good friends, for instance) or is there something about it which means that the only completely truthful context in which it can be used is that there is a deep level of personal commitment, which usually means a relationship which is permanent and exclusive?' (Kelly 1990:370).

If we reject all homosexual sex, then we have no basis for encouraging homosexual couples to be faithful.

AIDS provides the church with a new opportunity to reassess its hostility to homosexuality. It provides us with good reason to encourage a faithful, caring, committed love between two persons, even though they are of the same sex. The impact of AIDS upon the homosexual community has been very tragic, but it may also help that community to see that stable and committed relationships are more fulfilling than short-term, merely physical, uncommitted ones that use the other person only to satisfy lust. The pain suffered by homosexuals with AIDS has enabled many Christians to see homosexuals for the first time as persons who deserve and need to be loved rather than despised. AIDS has enabled many heterosexual persons to abandon their homophobia. The brave and gallant response of many in the homosexual community to AIDS has evoked our admiration.

AIDS has also brought out into the open just how many entertainers, sports stars, and also clergy and church workers are homosexual. Homosexuality has become something less hidden. Many homosexual clergy, religious and church workers who are not HIV positive have been able, because of AIDS, to own and even welcome their homosexual orientation as a way of standing with and understanding people with AIDS. If we can say that God brings good out of AIDS, a lessening of secrecy and hatred towards homosexuality is one such good.

Having said, however, that the church needs to abandon legalism about sexuality, positively to accept sexuality as part of our humanness, and to be less judgmental about premarital sex or homosexual sex, it is still true that sexual relationships, heterosexual and homosexual, are the major direct cause of the AIDS pandemic. AIDS must force all of us to reject sexual promiscuity. It is important that the church should fulfil its responsibility in making this clear. Casual sex is not the only kind of sin; it may not be the worst kind of sin; but it is a deadly kind of sin.

Condoms

But will not condoms protect us from these consequences, and enable us to indulge in casual sex just for fun without fear? A major emphasis in most secular AIDS educational programmes is that those who have sexual relationships with a new partner or with a variety of partners should use condoms. Condoms are their major defence against AIDS. Most church AIDS agencies, at least in

Africa, teach that abstinence is the major defence. There is often a dividing of the ways about promoting the use of condoms. This division of opinion is probably less marked in Europe and America where churches are not in the front line of AIDS education.

It is well known that the Roman Catholic church forbids the use of condoms or of any 'artificial' means of birth control within or outside of marriage. It forbids extramarital sex anyway, so that those who are involved in extramarital or homosexual sex and use condoms are seen to be doubly sinful. It is also well known that in the West, many otherwise faithful Roman Catholics take no notice of the prohibition of artificial contraception, and are encouraged by their priests to take no notice (see p. 109 above).

But while this may be true in the West, it is not necessarily true in Africa that lay-people feel free to disobey their church in this matter. This is not because African people are more gullible, but because condoms and contraception are not so well established in their culture anyway, and because the Catholic church plays a major part in African education. The Catholic church is very influential and very large in Africa. About 19% of the whole African population are Catholics, even more in sub-Saharan Africa (Barrett 1982:782). If the Catholic church refuses, as it mostly does, to promote condoms, this could be seen to be a major blow to preventing the spread of AIDS.

But the main-line Protestant churches in Africa, while presumably having no doctrinal objections to the use of condoms in marriage, are just as opposed to the promotion of condom usage among the young and the unmarried. In places like Uganda, where the Catholics and the Anglicans between them control a major part of the education and health resources of the country, or Tanzania, where the Lutheran church also plays a major role, it is very important for the issue whether the promotion and facilities of condom usage is compatible with Christian ethics to be explored.

As a result of the AIDS pandemic the Ugandan government, from having initially been opposed to sex education in state schools, now makes it mandatory. This sex education, while encouraging abstinence and 'zero-grazing', that is, faithfulness within the family, also actively promotes condoms amongst teenagers. This has led to some tension with the churches. In any case, since so many schools are mission schools and not state schools, the compulsory sex education does not spread to all children.

Some Catholics and Protestants even in the West are opposed to the promotion of condoms, not only because, in the eyes of traditional Catholics, condoms are a contravention of natural law and an obstacle should God wish an act of intercourse to result in pregnancy, but because to promote condoms amongst the unmarried is tantamount to condoning premarital sex. Jack Dominian, although encouraging his own Catholic church to be more realistic and open-minded about sexual acts outside of marriage, still says about condoms:

'An emphasis on condoms [in the AIDS campaign] is mistaken because it relies on means rather than principles and does nothing to remove the mistaken notion that sexual premarital intercourse has the same value and validity as within marriage' (Dominian 1987:66).

This is not entirely logical, for Dominian is saying that premarital sex, although not equal in value to married sex, is not always sinful or unloving, and he surely is not advocating premarital pregnancy. But what I assume Dominian means is that condoms are not associated with sex with a single partner – for who would wish, with a permanent and single partner, never to have sex except with a condom? – but with promiscuous multi-partner sex. He accuses the condom-culture of promoting sex without responsibility.

Others have put the case even more strongly from a Protestant point of view. John Piper says that advertising condoms amongst young people is encouraging promiscuity. Since promiscuity leads to AIDS, condom advertisements, far from preventing AIDS, encourage the spread of AIDS.

'Should we not cultivate nobler principles to govern our appetites and channel our desires in appropriate relationships of commitment and loyalty, trust and permanence?' (Piper 1987).

Ronald Sider suggests that an appropriate wording for condom advertisements might be:

'The only safe sex is within a lifelong monogamous relationship. I wish I had lived that way before I got AIDS. But if in spite of today's hard facts you want to play Russian roulette with your life, then please use condoms. They are not fail proof but they do improve your chances' (Sider 1988:14).

There can be no denying that Dominian, Piper, Sider and many others who share their opinions are right. However carefully we phrase it, when we tell young people that if they should have premarital sex they should use condoms to protect them against AIDS, we are implying that we expect that it is probable that they will have premarital sex. We contribute towards a climate which accepts premarital sex as normal.

But condom education is only one small part of what creates this climate.

'AIDS and the user of condoms are not the cause of human sexual behaviour in this century, but simply an indication of it' (Ada 1994:3).

Whether we like it or not, the fact is that premarital sex amongst young people in Europe, America and Africa, and probably many parts of the world, *is* normal. In most cases, these teenagers do not use condoms anyway. A survey in Scotland showed that 80–90% of young people there will have had sexual intercourse by the age of twenty, and that although they knew about AIDS, 82.5% of them were certain that they and their partners would never contract it, and consequently many did not use condoms (Aggleton et al. 1990). Over 50% of adolescents in the United States have had sexual intercourse, nearly a quarter of them anally receptive intercourse, by the age of eighteen, few of them using condoms (Gardner et al. 1990:5). Most pregnancies in my own country, South Africa, are to unmarried women; many schoolgirls have their first baby before completing schooling. This is not the consequence of condom education since they have not had such education.

Attitudes to premarital sex are formed by films, television soap operas, novels, peer behaviour. In all of these, it is taken for granted as a part of everyone's life. Even Mills and Boons novellas, where until fairly recently the heroine, however weak at the knees, never

went to bed with the handsome hero until after the wedding, now
have her in bed with him before she is even certain that he intends to
propose (although, of course, he always does). Condom advertisements are part of this scenario, but they do not create it.

Because premarital sex is common does not mean that it is good or
that the church should endorse it. I have already suggested that to
make a constructive contribution towards building up more responsible attitudes towards sexual behaviour, the church will have to make
a distinction between a few serial premarital relationships and
promiscuity, for it is promiscuity that really creates an environment
in which AIDS spreads. But even those who disagree with me will
surely agree that if we want to stem promiscuity, merely stopping
condom advertisements will not do that.

> *Thandi is at school; because of breaks in her schooling career she is now
> eighteen. Her mother finds it hard to pay for her schooling; there is
> nothing left for pocket money. But she gives Thandi money each day to
> pay for the minibus ride to school. The driver of the bus gives Thandi free
> rides, however, in return for sexual favours. He is aware of the danger of
> contracting AIDS from prostitutes, and therefore like many men uses
> young girls instead. Thandi, on the other hand, has never given a
> thought to AIDS.*
>
> *Her friend Vusi is also at high school; like many 'children' at high
> school in Africa she is in fact nearly twenty years old and sexually
> experienced.*

Some young people in all of our cultures are involved in
promiscuous relationships. In Africa, many girls like Thandi are
involved in relationships with 'sugar daddies' who pose a very serious
AIDS risk. At least if she knew about condoms she might be a little
safer. Do we want to withhold knowledge about and access to
condoms which might well save their lives? If no information about
condoms is given to them, it does not mean they will not have sex;
only that they do not protect themselves from AIDS.

Withholding condom education is more serious in Africa than in
the West, for, with or without the churches, most young people of the
West are hardly going to be ignorant about condoms even though
they may need encouragement actually to use them. This is not so in
many parts of Africa. The churches are so bound up with the

educational system, and with providing authoritative guidance which people take seriously, that withholding condom education is not unlike pronouncing a sentence of death.

Perhaps church people might think that if only we provide AIDS education which makes clear to people the risks they are running, they will renounce premarital sex without our having to raise the condom issue. Experience shows that this is naive. Unprotected sex has always carried the risk of venereal disease and pregnancy. That has not stopped people. In parts of Africa like Uganda where the HIV positivity rate is so high that there is a very good chance of contracting AIDS through casual sex, people continue to have casual sex. The Uganda AIDS Commission reports that although most Ugandans aged fifteen to twenty-four – 90% of them – have an accurate knowledge of how AIDS is spread, 50% of them have reported sexual engagement with casual partners in the past year (Uganda AIDS Commission 1994). One of the earliest and worst hit areas for AIDS in Uganda is the Rakai district. The Ugandan government has been promoting 'zero-grazing', i.e. not grazing in fields outside the marital home. But,

> 'Seroprevalence reported from the Rakai district indicates that while zero-grazing may have been accepted at the level of answering questionnaires, it is not actually practised' (Barrett and Blaikie 1992:46).

Clearly, and as Christians should know very well, human nature is such that knowledge does not necessarily lead to behaviour change. As Paul said, often in our fallen nature we behave in just the opposite way to what our better self tells us. In such a situation, to oppose condoms for the unmarried is to add to the risk of death.

In the light of AIDS, even some Roman Catholics have said that while condom usage is evil, it is less evil than risking life in unprotected sex (US Catholic bishops' statement, Bouchard and Pollock 1989). Perhaps, say some, the papal document *Humanae Vitae* does allow for the use of condoms in marriage by those who are HIV positive to prevent the spread of AIDS (Tuohey 1990:53–69). We live in a pluralistic age, and people have different understandings of morality. Not everyone is guided by church or Christian teaching. Some people will be involved in sexual and drug-usage behaviour which can lead to AIDS. Therefore, on the basis of permitting the lesser of two evils, the church should provide information about condoms.

> 'In the interests of public health . . . it may be licit to tolerate . . . the use of condoms and to counsel their use through advertising and educational programmes' (Bouchard and Pollock 1989).

But other Catholic authorities disagree (Smith 1991:122), and the publication of the encyclical *Veritatis Splendor* is likely to strengthen the negative view. Bishops in Africa have said:

> '[Condoms] only reduce the risk . . . Indeed, having recourse to this method ignores the real cause of the problem . . . namely, the permissiveness which corrodes the moral fibre of the people' (Ugandan Catholic Bishops conference, reported *African Ecclesial Review* 1989:295).

However, the issue is not confined to Catholics. In many parts of the world, Catholic and Protestant churches are reluctant to take education about condoms on board in their AIDS education. The issue is more stark than some Western theologians realize. It is really this: young people are already involved in permissive sex. Condom education, let us concede, will further endorse that permissiveness to some extent. But if they can be persuaded at least to use condoms, they will not die of AIDS. Do we think that it will be better for some 20% of our young people to die because we don't want an already permissive age to become more permissive?

The church has a responsibility to teach its young people about sexuality in a positive and constructive way which will enhance the probability that young people will enter into sexual relationships only in a context of love and stability and commitment. As Jennifer Phillips said in the opening quotation of this chapter, AIDS should not be the first thing young people learn from the church about sexuality. So far we have not done this task very well. Because the church, along with the rest of society, has been so backward in providing positive sex education, we are now experiencing an AIDS pandemic. But re-education and reforming of sexual attitudes is not something that can happen quickly. In the meantime people are dying.

In the short term, condom education as part of a wider package of sex education is certainly the lesser of two evils. Samuel Ada of the World Council of Churches suggests that sometimes we need a theology of crisis to complement the theology of normal life – like Jesus saying that to heal on the sabbath, or to eat the sacred 'shewbread', is better than allowing people to die (Ada 1994:4). Therefore of course the church needs to make information about condoms and access to condoms available without judgment or hindrance to its members. At the very least, churches should not prevent secular and state agencies from making condoms available to young people.

Ronald Sider says that 'I do not ask that public policy enforce biblical sexual norms, but I do ask that public policy not undermine them' (Sider 1988:11), and many Christians will agree with that. But at the same time we must ask the church not to undermine attempts by public policy to save the lives of young people. Educators in an Anglican youth AIDS education programme in Uganda, CHUSA, told me that they are not permitted by the church actually to promote condoms, but that in their talks they often mention condoms as a method of preventing AIDS which other less Christian people might use. They leave a packet or two lying around on the table. The packets invariably disappear. This kind of sidelong approach is weak and ambivalent. It implies that we really hope that young people who intend to disobey our advice and get involved in sex will use condoms, without our actually telling them. This is being less than honest.

With well-planned and well-run educational drives, it is possible to increase the use of condoms where their use has been uncommon. Condom use has increased greatly in Africa since knowledge about AIDS became more widespread. It is clear that where condom use becomes even somewhat more common, the rate for sexually transmitted diseases, a fairly good indicator for the prevalence of AIDS, drops. Between 1988–1990, the rate for STDs in Zambia dropped by 41% (Mouli 1992:45). State education drives and attempts within business and agriculture to increase condom usage in Zimbabwe have clearly been effective, with the same drop in STD rates (Williams and Ray 1993).

But nothing about sex is ever plain or simple. I have argued as strongly as I can that churches need to say to people, 'If you are going to have sex outside the closed circle of committed relationships, you must use condoms'. Churches need to say to governments that condoms should be made easily available to all who are likely to be involved in sexual activity, however young they may be. But in what might seem a contradictory move, the churches also need to say very strongly to governments and to AIDS agencies that condoms are not the solution to AIDS. Condoms may help to reduce the number of new HIV infections. They will not eradicate AIDS. This is something which Western agencies seem to find hard to grasp.

That is not only because condom usage does not entirely prevent AIDS, although this is true. Sex with condoms is not safe sex, only safer sex. A study of a number of couples who used condoms in which one partner was HIV positive showed that one in four non-positive partners became infected (Dixon 1990:109). But also, condoms are not the answer because they are not compatible with many non-Western cultures. In many African homes there are no private bedrooms, and sexual activity takes place furtively under blankets in the dark. Storing, finding and donning a condom in the dark without everyone else in the room knowing what is going on is very difficult.

Males have to be actively involved in a decision to use condoms. For this reason condoms have not been widely used as a contraceptive method in non-Western countries. The most prevalent form of contraception in Africa (if any contraception is used other than coitus interruptus) is a depa-provera injection, which requires a three-monthly visit to the clinic and no permission from partners. Men are therefore not accustomed to condoms. They do not find sex with condoms as pleasant or as stimulating as sex which allows direct flesh-to-flesh contact.

Most people who are HIV positive do not know they are infected until they actually feel ill. For condoms to eradicate AIDS it would be necessary for those who have sex outside marriage to use condoms all their life and in every sexual encounter, long before they feel ill. It is extremely unlikely that this will happen.

'HIV infection is lifelong and the temptation to experiment beyond the rubber straightjacket must occur in time' (Schoub 1989:34).

Even in Europe and America, women often do not feel free to discuss with their men what they prefer with regard to sexual activity. This is even more true in the Third World. It would be almost impossible for many African women even to raise the issue of condoms with their husbands. To do so would be to imply that he had been unfaithful; or, more likely, would be taken as an indication that she had been unfaithful. Most of our societies are still male-dominated. In such societies it is common to assume that women are the cause of adultery, since they tempt men; and that women are the carriers of sexual diseases. In these circumstances a man does not think he could cause AIDS, and if his wife asked him to wear a condom would be likely to assume that she had become HIV positive. Alonso and Koreck suggest that this is a problem not only for African women but for American Latino women too.

'For Latino women, to raise issues of sexuality is not only to challenge the male authority they are culturally enjoined to obey, but also to put their reputations as women on the line and to risk being perceived as "loose" or "immoral". Thus Latino women may be reluctant to ask their men to engage in safe sex practices or to use condoms' (Alonso and Koreck 1989:118).

A major cause of the spread of AIDS is prostitutes. Certainly efforts need to be made to persuade prostitutes to insist that their clients use condoms. But in countries where because of poverty there are more prostitutes than clients, prostitutes are in no position to insist on condom usage. Clients will turn elsewhere, offer to pay more, or turn to younger women, often virgin schoolgirls, in order to get sex without condoms.

But above all else, those who think that condoms are an effective answer to AIDS are simply ignorant about conditions in the rural Third World. Condoms in Africa are not universally available and are universally unpopular (*The Economist* 1991:32). In rural Africa there are no condom dispensing machines – and no money to put in the slot if there were; there are no chemists shops or supermarkets where condoms can be discreetly purchased. They are available virtually only from clinics or hospitals, which in many cases are an expensive bus ride or several days walk away, or from visiting health workers who might come once a quarter. There are no refrigerators in homes or even in rural clinics to keep stored condoms cool in the tropical heat. How would it be possible to fetch and store a whole three months' supply of condoms in an African hut which is shared by a whole family?

Speaking of Uganda, one report says condoms are:

' . . . rarely available outside Kampala and the largest provincial towns . . . the use of condoms in Rakai district is virtually zero' (Barnett and Blaikie 1992:45).

'It has to be recognized that recommendations to use condoms may fail [in Uganda, but for that matter anywhere in the Third World] because of practical difficulties of obtaining and using them in communities where there is little money or privacy, much sexual modesty, and perhaps, above all, because this is a method over which inevitably women have little control and which men dislike' (Barnett and Blaikie 1992:3).

'The AIDSCOM study in the Copperbelt and Northern Provinces [of Zambia] found that only 27% of people had ever used a condom, and only 8% had used one the last time they had sex' (Mouli 1992:44).

Partly, says the author, this is because they are simply unavailable.

This does not mean that the church should refuse to promote condoms. What it does mean is that AIDS will only be eradicated when society as a whole adopts a new attitude to sex and sexual relationships. This is where the church can make a very major contribution.

'AIDS in Africa [but everywhere else too] will not be successfully controlled by attempts aimed mainly at making open sexual relationships as safe as possible . . . A successful campaign against AIDS will have to hinge on the issue of closed sexual relationships' (Saayman 1991:24).

So: be flexible yet demanding!

This does not mean trying to reimpose old rules and old conventions. Many people will wish the church to do this. Attempts to redefine sexual attitudes will evoke fear and misunderstanding. Bishop Holloway of Edinburgh made the very moderate suggestion that we are not by nature monogamous. All of us, he said, are genetically driven to multiply the species, to have sex with as many people as possible. But all of us also need loving relationships, which cannot easily survive promiscuity or adultery.

'So a human dilemma has grown from the need to balance our natural instincts with our want for a loving relationship . . . The Church must accept that adultery is caused by our genetics and help people to control their instincts so that they can share loving, caring relationships' (quoted in *The Times*, 17 May 1995).

This is a very sensible beginning to a series of lectures on Christianity and sexuality. Holloway says that we must help people control their instincts, but understand that they will not always find this easy. As would be expected, his speech was greeted with horror from the Evangelical Alliance and other conservative church people, who all said they stood by the Ten Commandments (as if the bishop did not), and who presumably therefore believe that we should not show any understanding towards those driven to adultery. But Holloway was also roundly condemned by the tabloid press. Sounding as if adultery and extramarital sex were quite undreamt of amongst its journalists and editorial staff, *The Sun* scornfully named him 'Bishop Bonkers'.

Shortly afterwards there was another example of hypocritical tabloid prudery. The Church of England published a report on family life. The bulk of the report was about the status of family life, the stresses of poverty, the need for family care. However, in one paragraph of the report it was suggested that not everybody living with a partner to whom they were not yet married is involved in a temporary and uncommitted relationship. Cohabitation, said the report, should not be called 'living in sin', and the best pastoral response to such couples was not condemnation but encouragement to take the further step of commitment to marriage.

'The wisest way forward may be for Christians both to hold fast to the centrality of marriage and at the same time to accept that cohabitation is for many people a step along the way towards that fuller and more complete commitment' (*Something to Celebrate* 1995:115).

The only part of the report that the daily press commented on was this one paragraph suggesting that not all cohabitation is sinful. Again, on page 2 *The Sun* was loud in its protests. It is the church's duty to stand by traditional morals, it thundered. On the next page it published its regular picture of a young lady with no clothes on!

The views of the tabloid press might seem not worth bothering with. But the views expressed in *The Sun* are whatever views Mr Murdoch, its owner, thinks will boost circulation. What *The Sun* says is what it thinks its readers want to hear. And what readers want to hear, apparently, is that ordinary people should continue to indulge in sexual affairs and ogle naked girls while the church should continue to disapprove of all such things as a sort of moral balance to stop things getting out of hand.

To speak constructively about sexuality is not to surrender to pressures from society. On the contrary, it will probably lead to ridicule and criticism. Many people will not want the church to speak constructively about sex. They will want the church to continue to say that everybody should remain a virgin until marriage, and never have sex except with someone of the opposite sex to whom one is married. That is not to say that many people will live like that; only that they will want the church to be like a kind of pretty Victorian Christmas card, upholding charming sexual conventions which they personally will disregard. If the church does this, it would not be making a truly constructive contribution.

To be constructive the church will need to embrace the chaos of ethical uncertainties and relativities; to be realistic yet to point to better ideals; to be loving and forgiving yet to be firm about the harmfulness of irresponsible sexuality; to admit that we do not always have neat answers yet to show that we are not left without any sense of direction. Sometimes it will mean facing the ridicule of the religious right and the tabloids, and being fools for Christ's sake (1 Corinthians 1.20).

Yet within this ethical chaos, we must work very hard to change people's life-styles. There is some evidence that prepubescent girls and girls in early puberty are especially at risk for contracting the

HIV virus. There is a great deal of evidence that sexual encounters with multiple partners leads to AIDS, and to other sexually transmitted diseases.

'Our bodies were not designed for multiple sexual encounters. Such a lifestyle has consequences. It is physically unhealthy' (Dixon 1990:144).

So it is important that we move towards a situation where girls start sexual activity later; where people have fewer partners; where mutual faithfulness is the rule and not the exception. We can only do that if we have a positive attitude towards sexuality, and if we have abandoned a rigidly rule based sexual morality. But can we do it at all? Given all we have said previously about the difficulty of changing people's behaviour even when they know the risks, and about people taking no notice of church teaching on sex, is there any hope of succeeding?

There is no certain answer to that question. There are claims that educational programmes of the Copperbelt Health Education project in Zambia have changed patterns of sexual behaviour. 63% of respondents in one survey said that they were now staying with only one sexual partner (Mouli 1992:42). Respondents may not have answered absolutely truthfully, but the number of sexually transmitted diseases on the Copperbelt dropped by 42% between 1988 and 1990 (Mouli 1992:45). Much the same claims are made by health authorities in Mutare, Eastern Zimbabwe (Williams and Ray 1993:51). These projects, of course, are secular ones based within industry or commercial agriculture rather than church projects. But three years is not very long. The Zimbabwean authorities attribute the drop in sexually transmitted diseases to a more widespread use of condoms. The Zambian project claims that condom usage is still negligible, and attributes its success to people adopting more faithful sexual relationships. Either way, they show that behaviour change is not impossible to achieve, even if our efforts are only partly successful.

But such changes are only possible when the effort is aimed at changing community peer attitudes. This is why programmes amongst young people are particularly important. In Zambia there are the 'anti-AIDS clubs'; in Uganda the Catholic church runs the

'Youth Alive' programme and the Anglican church the SYFA (Safeguard Youth From AIDS) outreach. There are similar programmes in other places. The intention of the programmes is not just to educate about sex education and about how AIDS is contracted, but to provide community settings in which young people can meet to have fun with their age group without having sexual intercourse. Alternative ways are found to build self-esteem. Girls and boys need to feel that they do not have to prove their attractiveness or their manhood by having sex. It is not enough to give people guidance about sex or AIDS. As long as people believe that unless they have a sexual partner they are a failure as a man or a woman, and that the only proof that one is beautiful or attractive is to have sexual partners, they will be quite prepared to risk death rather than be branded a failure as a man or woman.

Thus we have to help create different criteria for measuring self-worth. This means working with the whole community. We have to help build up an alternative community support system for those who choose not to be involved in casual sexual relationships. Sex education cannot be divorced from education in human relationships generally. A sex education programme which merely passes on medical facts or demonstrates how to pull on a condom is unlikely to make a major impact.

4

AIDS and the Church

As with every aspect of our theology, AIDS also makes us rethink our theology of the church. Words we have used about the church for centuries, to which often we give a purely notional assent, take on new significance, especially those relating to the church as an interdependent community.

We have a rich set of metaphors to describe the nature of the church. It is one, holy, catholic and apostolic; it is the body of Christ in whom there is neither Jew nor Greek, male nor female, slave nor free (Galatians 3.28).; it is the community of love – 'behold how these Christians love one another'; it is the bride of Christ awaiting expectantly the coming of the bridegroom; it is the community of people living a new life which is an example to the world of the coming kingdom of God; it is the messenger of the good news and the announcer of truth.

And we know the reality is sometimes somewhat different. The church is not one but divided; there are thousands of separate denominations. It is not expectantly waiting for the future but often clings with some desperation to the past. Far from the church being an example to the world of the kingdom of God, class and race divisions have existed in it as in every other part of human society so that the church itself becomes a 'site of struggle'. Whatever we may say about the church being for Jew and Greek, people of different race groups have been discriminated against. Women in the church do not feel that they are seen as being of equal importance to men.

This should not surprise nor dismay us. The church has only ordinary human beings to call upon for its membership. That we fail to live up to our ideals does not mean that our ideals are necessarily wrong, just that we have to keep on trying to achieve them. The AIDS crisis shows where the church has failed, but also gives us reason and motivation to try all the harder.

People with AIDS therefore do not always find the support and the love which they seek in the church. Fear and prejudice have caused Christians, just like anyone else, to close their doors. In America, because of the homosexual link, mainline churches were often slow to respond to the AIDS crisis. African countries initially responded to AIDS with fear and denial, in which churches shared. Referring to Kenya when AIDS began there, a correspondent writes:

'In some churches . . . people who had died with AIDS were not permitted to be buried in church, nor were people with AIDS, if they were known, allowed to attend church. The stigma even affected their families in some cases' (Worsnip 1994).

Local congregations are often a rather closed community of like-minded and respectable people. They can be quite loving and caring to each other, but do not know how to respond to someone whose values and life-style threatens their own. In their closedness they may well exclude members of the community in which they are situated. But congregations which are actually exposed to people with AIDS learn to respond more positively. Some American city churches have quite large numbers of homosexual persons in the congregation whose sufferings and bereavements have touched the hearts of the congregation. Because of AIDS, some churches in California have become more caring towards homosexuals (Godges 1986:773). In those parts of Africa where AIDS has hit virtually every family, where even the children of the clergy or the clergy themselves have died of AIDS, the church has learned to accept and to care for people with AIDS.

But this is not universal, and even those congregations who do care for and welcome people with AIDS do not always realize how AIDS helps to highlight and make sense of aspects of our theology of the church which had become merely theoretical, nor how much people with AIDS can help us to rediscover our true identity as the church. For most Christian congregations, AIDS is something that happens to someone else, somewhere else, which does not change the way we think about anything. AIDS can help revitalize the church, but only when we rediscover a sense of the wider church beyond the local congregation, a church in which every member, even one of apparently least importance, counts.

'The parts of the body which seem to be weaker are indispensable' (I Corinthians 12.22).

'He who is least among you all is the one who is great' (Luke 9.48b).

AIDS brings judgment upon the church. If we are right in saying that AIDS brings a time of *kairos*, what we mean by that is that AIDS compels the church to make choices. AIDS, like the persecutions of the early church, like the Nazi period in Germany, like the situation in the apartheid era in South Africa, is a moment in time when the church must respond in a Christ-like way or compromise its essential nature. In some places and at some moments, parts of the church have indeed faced that challenge and made that response. But often, people with AIDS find more support and more understanding elsewhere, particularly in support groups with other people with AIDS. Often, the care, love and commitment to help shown by those in secular or non-church agencies is the sort of care which ought to be found in the church and is not. Often, too, the degree of unity with each other which people with AIDS find in combatting the effects of the virus is the sort of zeal which the church ought to have for God's kingdom and does not.

But we cannot leave it at that, and say that since the secular organizations are often more caring and more understanding the church can leave it all to them. For outside the West, these secular support and self-help groups are much less common. Unlike Europe and America, the church plays such an important social role in much of Africa that it *cannot* be allowed to evade its responsibilities.

AIDS is not the only issue that churches should care about. I have suggested previously that people with AIDS and their families deserve as much love and care as, but not more than, those who suffer and die for any reason. In Southwark cathedral in London or the cathedral of St John the Divine in New York, special chapels are set aside as a memorial to those who have died of AIDS. Since inevitably in those churches the list of names in the AIDS memorial

book are predominantly male, there is an unintended implication
that men's illnesses matter more, and we can understand why some
women's groups are now pushing for memorial chapels to be set
aside, and ribbons to be worn, for women who die of breast or
cervical cancer, still the major cause of women's deaths in the United
States.

Nevertheless, while all suffering deserves our care, the sheer size
of the AIDS pandemic in the Third World means that AIDS does
have particular significance, and we must give those cathedrals
credit for helping to bring AIDS to the awareness of Christians who
might otherwise ignore it. Since they have been conceived in a
context in which most of those who have died of AIDS are
homosexual, these memorial chapels, memorial books and memorial
quilts are also powerful statements to the rest of the church that
despite their homosexuality the dead are still accepted by God.

AIDS not only brings a challenge to the church to show
unconditional and caring love. It also enables facets of the church
which had grown dim to shine in a new way.

One

If we call the church 'one', then we stand in unity with all who suffer,
even if they live on another continent, belong to another race or class,
or have a different sexual orientation. If one suffers, we all suffer
(I Corinthians 12.26); if one has AIDS, we all have AIDS.

> 'AIDS is not only an affliction of individuals or of particular
> groups. AIDS is an affliction of the whole human family. Our
> religious vision proclaims that living with AIDS/HIV is a
> condition in which we must all participate actively' (The Atlanta
> Declaration of the AIDS Interfaith Network, *Ecumenical Trends*
> 1990:61).

So we can say, our church has AIDS. AIDS affects us all.

Churches need to re-examine the boundaries which divide us in
practice. The church, one in theological theory, is fragmented in
reality. The ecumenical movement to reunite separated denominations is one side of that search for unity. There are other boundaries

which divide us. The church, said Paul, transcends racial, class and gender localities. In practice it often does not. At a local level a congregation is likely to reflect the predominant race and economic group of the majority, making it hard for those of other races or classes to feel that they belong. They may be allowed to join, and even made welcome, for we want to be kind in Jesus' name – but the power and the vision of the local congregation is likely to be centred upon the core group.

If we are truly to be a united church, we need to see our unity not only from the perspective of the centre looking out, but from the perspective of the periphery, those who are the 'least important members' and who seek to belong and to make their contribution (Schneider in Russell 1990). This means going beyond allowing people with AIDS to belong to the church, and beyond being kind to them on our own terms. Being kind to people is a trap. We must beware of any kind of 'victim theology'. People with AIDS are victims, of course, in the sense that they suffer because of their sin or the sin of the world. It is not wrong to be kind to people who suffer; but it is wrong to see them merely as objects of our pity. This is a perspective which sees people with AIDS as weak and ourselves as strong.

We may like this perspective because it makes us feel both virtuous and powerful, but this is also why the perspective is false. For we are not virtuous; we all participate in the sin which leads to AIDS; and we are certainly not powerful. There is no room in the church for a 'victim' and 'benefactor' relationship. People with AIDS, and other marginalized groups, need to influence and direct how the church sees itself. People with AIDS are not just people to be cared for (though that is important). They are also people with something to offer. If we treat them as objects of our pity, if we care for them only on that basis, we humiliate them. Even worse, we deny ourselves the very great difference that people with AIDS can make to our own perspective about life. To see the church as one means seeing those parts of the church, for example the church in Africa, not merely as far-off places to send our missionary money to, or as younger children of the Western church who may be seen but not heard. We need to take the churches of Africa and their experience of AIDS seriously and be willing to learn from them.

It is very difficult to overcome an 'us' and 'them' mentality, even within the church. In theory, in a church which is one church, there is no 'us' and 'them', there is no 'other', for all are one in Christ. This has been difficult for the church to put into practice from the very beginning. The New Testament church battled to achieve true unity. Jewish Christians wanted to insist that Gentile Christians had to become Christians in a Jewish mould, to cease being 'the other' by being made just like 'us'. Openly in Paul's letters, and implicitly beneath the surface of the Gospels, we see the church going through a struggle as it changed the centre of its vision from a Jewish to a universal one. This struggle continues throughout the church's history as the newly integrated become the new 'us', only to confront immediately a new wave of 'thems'. In our own time poor people, people in developing countries, people with AIDS, people with different sexual orientations, people in different classes from our own, are the 'thems' needing to be taken into the centre of the church's being now. AIDS highlights the 'us' and 'them' divisions but may also help us to overcome them.

Letting people with AIDS into the centre means not deciding for them what needs to be done. It means looking into church structures, heeding the needs of the oppressed and weak within those structures and seeing where our structures make it hard for them to be heard. It means letting those who are oppressed and afflicted tell us in what ways they are being denied well-being, in what ways they are being excluded, in what ways we can help, rather than defining this for them.

> 'How does the church love God, and exhibit holiness, in these times [of AIDS]? We do so by standing with those who suffer, embracing them with inclusive love, and by questioning our institutional structures in openness and transformation according to the laws of love' (Suchocki in Russell 1990:121).

Persons with AIDS are not to be patronized. The African churches who bear most of the burden of AIDS are not to be patronized either. Although they need the love and support of the rest of the church, the rest of the church needs the new vision which they bring. We are interdependent.

'It is crucial that we should be able to hear what help the people we are concerned with require, not what we, with the bias of our needs, think is needed' (Kirkpatrick 1988:73).

What this would mean in practice would differ from congregation to congregation. We need to guard against any idea of the strong helping the weak. In some places, people with AIDS, finding the church inhospitable, have set up their own networks of care. They are often well able to help themselves. In many ways the rest of the church which is not HIV positive needs the new vision, the new discoveries, of those who are HIV positive more than they need us. Often we will find evidence of love and peace and courage, in other words evidence of God's Spirit, in AIDS support groups which operate outside official church groups and accepted religious norms (Pryce in Woodward 1990:52).

Ed, Bill and John are members of an AIDS support group that meets each month for home communion in one another's homes. Every member of the group is HIV positive, or is a partner of an HIV positive person – except the Rector! But it is, of course, the Rector who leads the service. One month the Rector is on holiday and does not attend. The group begins to discuss why membership of the group has been steadily dropping. The discussion becomes quite animated. Someone observes that it is a long time since discussions have been so animated. Bill says 'To be honest, I've almost decided to stop coming myself. When I first started to attend I was touched by Fr Tom's (the Rector's) concern. I needed his affection. But I've come to realize that whenever we reflect on the Bible at these meetings, it's only Fr Tom's reflections that we hear. I'm getting tired of always being encouraged by him and told not to lose hope and told not to be bitter. I'm not some poor miserable sinner to be preached at. I'm not a beggar waiting for some kind words.' It seems to the group that the discusison has become more animated tonight because for the first time they can express their ideas without being censored and corrected.

Clergy do not have the last word. Some people with AIDS, through their exposure to fear and death, through having been raised from fear to a life of courage and defiant hope, have become prophets for the rest of us. 'You have become sacred by virtue of

being in touch with what we cannot speak or understand' (Countryman 1987:130).

They have earned the right to rebuke and guide us, for they have
plunged to depths and been raised to heights which we who do not
face such challenges have not reached, and they see further than us.
In the days of the Jewish temple, only the high priest was permitted
to enter into the holy of holies, the inner part of the temple, for only
he could dare to be so close to holiness. In a way, those who are HIV
positive and know that they will die, those who stand by the bedside
of partners, sons or daughters as they die, are close to holiness too
and have become the high priests of our time. They have been part of
sacred and terrifying situations. They lead us into paths where we
must eventually follow. They are pioneers of faith. This means that
we need to listen carefully to what they have to say; it means that
often they can teach us, rather than the other way around.

They are not only prophets, but also priests. They touch holy
things. They offer sacrifice. AIDS deaths come about through the
sin of the world. People with AIDS, especially perhaps the widows
and the orphans of Africa, have become victims of other people's sin,
joined with Christ in his vicarious death on the cross. Just as he, the
sinless one, shared in the painful consequences of sin, so do they
(I Peter 4.13). In this sense too they are priests, sacrificing their lives
for the world. This is especially true for those with AIDS who are
victorious over bitterness and despair. They have risen from the
death of the human spirit in order that we may follow and have life
through them.

We need to phrase this carefully in order not to equate them with
Christ. Of course they are not without sin as Christians believe he
was; and of course their own victory over death is already part of the
fruits of Jesus' victory. Of course, too, not all those with AIDS are
victorious, courageous, free of bitterness. But to a degree, people
with AIDS, like people who face any death with courage, are priests
and prophets for our own age.

'We must learn to think of the individuals who live the sero-
positive life with grace and maturity . . . as heroes in this
encounter with disease, fighting at the barricades while others
move to safety. Many in this group will provide the leadership

both in prevention of the epidemic's spread and in care for the afflicted. Learning to value them in their difficult role is part of learning to live with AIDS' (Grover 1989:68–9).

Holy

If we call the church holy, we do not mean merely that the church sets its mind upon spiritual things. Nor do we mean that Christians are better than other human beings or closer to God. The holiness of the church does not come from itself nor belong to itself. It is understood to come from and belong to God. The church sees itself as relying on the grace of the Holy Spirit, and in this sense is holy.

But if indeed the church is filled with the grace of the Spirit, there ought to be a corresponding ethical quality in its life. A church filled with the Holy Spirit ought to be a loving church. For the church is doubly holy. It shares in the holiness of all humanity, made in the image of God, in the likeness of God. All humans are able to imagine, to dream of better things, to love, to reach out for the God whom we dimly resemble. But in Jesus, the church believes that its members have been twice born. The die of God's love, become worn and distorted, is restamped upon us. 'You have put on the new nature, which is being renewed in knowledge after the image of its creator' (Colossians 3.10). Therefore we ought to be doubly loving.

Some theologians have been urging the church to rediscover the significance for us of trinitarian faith (for example Gunton 1991:97), to think of the Trinity in a way more like that of the Eastern church as three distinct persons bonded into a unity of love and will. This kind of theology matches well what is demanded by the AIDS crisis. Margaret Suchocki (Russell 1990) ties it in with Wesley's doctrine of perfection. God, who is three distinct and separate persons united in one, created in the world distinct and separate creatures who are also called to live united in love. When humans failed in that love, God sent Moses and the prophets. But human beings who have lost love cannot be recalled to love by law or by commandment, but only by love. God sent Jesus to love the loveless, the lost, and the marginalized, but also to forgive his persecutors. In just the same way, Christians who are made one with Christ in baptism, who are thus taken into the reality of trinitarian unity, are called to be one with Christ in his love for the world. Just as Christ incarnated that love in the praxis of his life, the church is called to incarnate that love in its own practice and day-to-day organization.

'The church, called to holiness, is called to be transformatively present not only with interpersonal love but in the power of structures that mediate well-being, which is love' (Suchocki in Russell 1990:118).

Wesley in his doctrine of perfection believed that it was not only possible, but necessary, that Christians, born again in Christ, should actually live in love for others and for God. Perfection was not merely an ideal but a practical possibility. Wesley did not believe that Christian perfection meant sinlessness or a state of perfection achieved by human effort; rather, that since the believer is caught up into an unbroken fellowship with Christ, the believer is also caught up into Christ's love, a love which then overflows into all relationships. Wesley's emphasis was more on relationships than on ethics. So too the holiness of the church needs to have a relational, practical quality to it. Holiness is not otherworldliness, but also has to do with politics and power.

'[Wesley's] reform of personal and social morality resulted to a large degree from the spiritual renewal which accompanied his work' (Shelton 1984:83).

John is a Catholic priest. From minor seminary onwards he was trained to avoid intimacy with women. He avoided sexually explicit novels and averted his eyes from pictures which might create sexual desire. In younger days inevitable thoughts would occasionally come to mind. But he learned to banish them. Over the years these thoughts grew less and now in late middle age never trouble him. He is a virgin, and will always be one. At his mission in Zimbabwe he had to care for women with AIDS. He felt indignant on their behalf with their husbands who had given it to them – but the husbands were not in his congregation. Then in the confessional he began to hear from men who had AIDS. He gave them absolution, but in his counsel was stern and scolding. One day in the confessional a penitent interrupted the counsel John was giving. 'It is easy for you priests to talk,' he said, 'but you don't know what it is like to

be lonely in the town; you have no need to pay women to give you love.'
John was defensive; but came to see that loneliness had taken its toll on
him too. He came to recognize his own intolerance, his need for malicious
gossip with fellow clergy, his dependence upon whisky when the loneliness
was too acute.

The church is called to love those who are hurting. It is also called
to love those who have sinned. The church is holy because its
members are called by God to a holy vocation, a holy responsibility of
mutual love and service. But loving sinners does not mean merely
forgiving them. Our attitude towards people with AIDS, even those
whose promiscuity has led to them contracting AIDS, is not merely
one of forgiveness. It is one of fellowship. The church may be holy,
but its members are all sinners in need of forgiveness. We all are in
sin and despair. Pastoral ministry on any other basis to people with
AIDS would be patronizing, hypocritical and false.

'Pastoral care in the age of AIDS is a journey that begins with
personal awareness of where and when we . . . have fallen in the
ditch' (Wallace 1993:358).

This has important implications for church people who seek or are
called to minister to those with AIDS. Such a ministry must begin by
facing our own weaknesses with painful honesty and owning our own
past. It is important that with Wesley we understand the holiness of
the church to mean something practical, something that we are
expected actually to be and not just an unattainable spiritual ideal.
But then it is just as important that we recognize that very often we do
not attain that level of practical holiness. We need a sense of our own
sinfulness. We who offer any message to those who are in the ditch
do so with the mud of the ditch still staining our own faces.

We know in theory that we 'live in a ditch'. We invariably include
confession in our liturgies. In our healthy-minded modern age[9] we
have rejected the more intense language of earlier liturgies. Where
once we said that the burden of our sins was intolerable and we
begged for mercy, now we merely confess that we have sinned and

[9]When William James (James 1960:92ff) talks about healthy minded religion,
he means a religion of optimism without self-doubt, a religion where we are sure
God has forgiven any sins.

claim our forgiveness. We no longer warm to old-style preachers who whip up in us a sense of sin and dread.

Nor should we, since the sole purpose of the old-style preacher was to foster personal piety and self-deprecation. Our preaching should go beyond that. It is right that our emphasis now should be on forgiveness and not on damnation. But perhaps we do need to rediscover the awfulness of our own complicity with the world's sins. We middle-class Christians, as we watch the suffering of the world paraded before us on our colour television screens in our comfortable homes, have suppressed or lost any sense that the very life-style which has brought television and satellite networks within our reach is part of what has caused the suffering. We are part of the selfishness of the world. AIDS is yet one more hurt, a very serious one, that we have all shared in creating. A truly holy church will rediscover its own true sinfulness.

So we are united in love, but also in penitence. People with AIDS may help us to realize this. They may help recall the church to its true identity and vocation.

> 'Perhaps the AIDS crisis is God's way of challenging us to care for one another, to support the dying, and to appreciate the gift of life. AIDS need not merely be a crisis, it could also be a God-given opportunity for moral and spiritual growth' (*Pastoral Statement* 1990).

The Catholic bishops who authorized this statement might have worded it more carefully. AIDS cannot be God's way of doing anything. We may not say that God sent AIDS as an opportunity for the church to be made stronger. If God is a just and loving God, then AIDS is not sent or given by God. But AIDS may nevertheless be an opportunity for the church.

> 'We have failed to realize that people with AIDS are a gift to the church. In relationship to those who suffer, the church has an opportunity to experience new depths of love. If we are willing, people with AIDS will teach the church how to be a community of love which is pleasing to God' (Jones 1989:208).

The modern church in many parts of the world, but especially perhaps in Europe, has lost confidence in what it exists for. Its numbers decline steadily, partly because post-enlightenment human beings rely on themselves and not on God, and so see no need for church or Christian belief. Its clergy are caricatured in plays and television dramas and are regarded with half-mocking affection as charming but irrelevant anachronisms. Many of those with AIDS turn elsewhere for help. A young man with AIDS asks:

> 'How can the church help me? I don't trust the church – they fight too much. Actually I wonder if God isn't making me better because he wants *me* to start a church' (Hector's story in Russell 1990:153).

The church has come to believe in society's estimation of its place. Many clergy wonder whether their ministry does make any difference.

But it is also true that many people with AIDS have found support and care in their local congregation. In Africa the church plays a major role in AIDS ministry, and without the church, AIDS ministry would be non-existent in such places. If the church will grasp the opportunity, AIDS has created a need in which the world-wide church can play a vital and irreplaceable role, rediscovering its own identity and the practical truth of many of its half-forgotten doctrines about itself in the process. The church with all its weaknesses is very far from being an unnecessary anachronism.

Church leaders can help with AIDS by being a visible, vocal presence in caring for AIDS. The Princess of Wales, when she hugged a child with AIDS, was certainly acting out of a sincere motherly concern for a suffering child. But her action also served as a very important public relations gesture. Bishops and church leaders may not look as charming as the princess, but when they are seen in public sharing sacraments with people with AIDS, hugging them and taking their side, their actions help mould public opinion. 'At the end of the day, actions are the only things that really encourage others' (Dixon 1990:172).

Church people, clergy and lay, can offer practical support. Churches are often wary of being involved in AIDS ministry, feeling that they lack both the skills and the financial resources to make a significant contribution. Yet much of what is needed requires no special skills. Practical help with shopping, laundry, planting and reaping, is something anyone can offer. Emotional support for the person with AIDS and for family and carers also does not require that we are all certified psychotherapists or social workers. Often people just need a good friend.

Anywhere in the world where Christian missions have established themselves to any degree, there are networks of local congregations linked to the centre and through that to the international church. In places where there are no schools, no clinics, no other communal buildings, there is likely to be a church. In places which no teacher, social worker or health worker reaches there is likely to be a minister, catechist or lay preacher who is in regular contact with the people. Local congregations have their own rosters of visitors. Wherever the church has been established, there are in place both personnel (paid and unpaid, full-time and part-time) and plant which would be the envy of any other social institution, all of which can be used in ministry. Where the existence of AIDS is still a shameful secret to be kept hidden from the neighbours (still the case in many places), and a visit from an AIDS health worker would set neighbours' tongues wagging, a regular call from a parish visitor to make contact and to supply, perhaps, some basic necessities like sugar and cornmeal, attracts no surprise or attention.

In parts of the world this incredibly valuable network of support has been harnessed to help with AIDS. But this has not happened everywhere. Church indifference or resistance to involvement with a sickness caused by sex sometimes gets in the way. Sometimes it is because the church underestimates the difference that it can make. When the church becomes truly itself, it can make a contribution to AIDS education and AIDS ministry which in many places no other institution can match.

Catholic

The adjective 'catholic' in the creed, we were told, is an ambiguous word meaning both orthodox and universal. The church received from Jesus Christ ' . . . the correct and complete confession of faith, full sacramental life and ordained ministry in apostolic succession'; it is also meant for ' . . . the whole human race' (*Catechism* 1994:193).

We have learned from liberation theology, however, that orthodoxy cannot be separated from orthopraxy, right belief from right action. Beliefs which do not contribute towards building the kingdom of God on earth are irrelevant, if not actually false. Orthodox belief which does not lead to caring for God's universal family is a self-contradiction.

This is partly the reason why AIDS must impact upon theology. If it does not, if the sheer scale and horror of the pandemic does not make us rethink how we conceive of God, of Jesus, of the Holy Spirit, of the church, then our theology is on the way to extinction.

'Catholic' also means universal. In fact AIDS may not impact directly upon a small Norfolk parish or a Baptist church in Idaho. It is quite probable that in many congregations nobody has AIDS or personally knows anyone with AIDS. But the situation in many other congregations will be quite different – in an American city congregation with a high proportion of homosexual men, for example, or a congregation in a run-down inner city where drug usage is high, or a congregation in Central Africa. Because we are one church with universal interests, we need to find out what it means to open our hearts to be concerned for humans everywhere, and for Christians wherever in the world they try to meet human needs.

'Now the time has come for the church to climb off the fence, to stop taking pot-shots at the tip of the iceberg, the bit they see (erroneously) as consisting entirely of promiscuous homosexual men and drug addicts, and to start considering the whole picture; the millions of men, women and children dying world-wide' (Dixon 1990:172).

If we are a universal church, then, as Paul said, we are a church for all cultures, all classes and both genders. But Paul did not know about sexual orientation. It was not possible for Paul to conceive of human beings born with a different sexual orientation. A universal church will surely find room for people whose sexual orientation is towards their own gender.

A universal church will also find a place for sinners. The Samaritan woman with her irregular personal relationships, the tax gatherer with his questionable public ethics, were not excluded from

Jesus' love and friendship. 'Ah, but,' people may say, 'they were penitent; they left their sinful ways behind them before Jesus welcomed them.' But this does not seem to have been the case. Jesus entered into conversation with the Samaritan woman before he challenged her. He invited himself to Zacchaeus' house before Zacchaeus promised to share half his goods with the poor. We do not know whether all those whom Jesus healed or helped subsequently repented or changed. We do know that the disciples who abandoned Jesus on the cross were still included in the Easter experience, even though they hid away (John 20.19). There is a place for tough love in the church (Christensen 1991); with regard to AIDS in particular, sexual irresponsibility cannot be condoned. But those who are guilty of it are still not excluded from our love and our concern. The love of a universal, catholic church is unconditional.

Apostolic

Letty Russell reminds us that alongside the credal description of the church as apostolic, we also need to rethink the reformed insistence that the true church must be a church in which ' . . . the word is truly preached and the sacraments rightly administered' (Russell 1990:142).

An apostolic church is a church which is in continuity with the apostles' mission. It will be a church in which the apostles' ministry of baptism and eucharist, but also of preaching, healing and forgiving, is maintained. The right administration of the sacraments is not just a matter of making sure that minister and liturgical form conform with traditional church discipline. We need, says Russell, to make communion a 'welcome table', and a sacrament rightly administered will be one where people feel welcome. We could extend rightly administering the sacraments to comment that the sacramental rites of anointing, reconciliation and unction also take on renewed significance in an effective AIDS ministry. Like the apostles, the church is sent by God into the world with the good news that God has come into the world to restore us into fellowship, to love us, to help us help ourselves. It is a church which is in continuity of message and in continuity of service. A church which has lost its message, or no longer has a sense of being sent, or is no longer in service, is no longer truly apostolic.

The word which is truly preached is not just a matter of correctly interpreting scripture along orthodox lines, nor just a question of avoiding historical heresy, but must be a word consistent with Jesus' preaching, a word preached from the perspective of the poor. As liberation theologians have reminded us, it is the poor who in some ways best understand what God is doing in the world, because what God is doing, God does primarily for the poor. Thus the existence of AIDS means that we cannot continue to preach as if AIDS were not there. Alongside other perspectives, the gospel must be seen from the perspective of people with AIDS.

Healing

Some churches hold regular services of prayer for healing. In most cases they have learned that the prayer has to be for all manner of illness – mental, physical, spiritual and relational – and not just for people with AIDS. When the prayer service is only for those with AIDS it becomes too introspective. People with AIDS need to remember that there are others who suffer also. They want to be able to pray for and share in ministry to others so that they are not always merely recipients of other people's prayer and concern.

The prayer service, often accompanied by the laying on of hands and anointing, acts as a powerful catharsis for those who grieve. The regular prayer service also becomes a service of remembrance for those who have died. It becomes a service of unity amongst those who survive. The physical touch, the laying on of hands and anointing, is itself healing for those who, because they have AIDS, are kept at physical arms' length by society. 'Touching is one of the most important ingredients in all AIDS counselling' (Cherry and Mitulski 1988:86).

Churches in the West can learn a great deal about healing services from the independent Third World churches that are found particularly in Africa and the Caribbean. In the West, religion is often one compartment among many. Our lives are divided into different fields, each field with its own set of experts. Western religion is just one field, a diminishing one at that, with often very little overlap with the fields of work or of health and healing. Western medicine is often primarily concerned with the individual and his or her body. The Western medical model is often rather mechanistic, fixing whatever is wrong with the body. Thus the Western medical approach to AIDS is to find a vaccine to neutralize the virus, or to recommend a condom to trap the virus. The social causes of AIDS receive rather less attention.

African traditional religion is utterly holistic. Religious well-being, physical well-being and general prosperity are all one. Bodily health cannot be separated from spiritual health nor individual health from community health. If one person in the family or community is ill, the illness makes the whole community less whole. If one individual is alienated from the community, the community and the individual are ill. 'Sickness in Africa is thus understood completely in terms of community. It is not strictly speaking an individual who falls sick' (Saayman 1991:25).

Therefore inevitably in the independent African churches influenced by this traditional culture, healing is given major emphasis. It is not too much to say that healing is the major part of the ministry of these churches, and no service would take place without prayer and laying on of hands for those who are ill. The concept of illness is not confined to physical illness. It is well recognized that family quarrels, jealousies, loneliness, are all part and parcel of illness and therefore part of what must be healed.

The laying on of hands is not gentle, but often more like a thumping on the back. As Ronald Eyre says of a Zulu Zionist healing service observed in a television documentary, one could not undergo that kind of laying on of hands and feel that one had not been noticed (Eyre 1977)! Making people feel noticed and part of the community is an integral part of the healing.

AIDS occurs because of the disruption of the 'macrocosm'. Society is disordered, leading to widespread exchange of sexual partners. To have any effect on the AIDS crisis, we shall have to give attention to that macrocosm. But the individual is even more affected by the microcosm, the network of immediate friends and family. The first requisite for health in the African model is to belong to a healthy microcosm or extended family setting. In African culture, ' . . . healing pertains to a person's microcosmic social structure; that is to say, his or her day-to-day relationships with neighbours and kinsmen' (Schofeleers 1989:119). This is something we can learn about from the independent churches. The church, to be effective in AIDS ministry, needs to be this kind of community in which individuals count.

We need to be realistic, though, about healing services and sacraments. We must not create false hopes. There are cases where people who are HIV positive have not yet developed AIDS many years after being diagnosed, and cases where people who do have full-blown AIDS still do not die. But these are rare exceptions which we do not understand. In almost every case the sickness follows the predicted pattern. Sometimes those who attend prayer services are disappointed at not getting the miracle for which they hoped. The healing for which we pray is often received as a healing of the spirit, as renewed courage, perhaps, or as power to forgive those with whom we are bitterly estranged. There are many forms of healing, but not always the form that we desire. Then again, many who attend the service when first diagnosed as HIV positive do not feel ill for many years, and are able in time either to deny or to ignore the fact that they have the virus. It is depressing and boring to be constantly involved in prayer for healing when you do not feel sick. Many churches, therefore, have begun healing services, only to drop them when attendances fall away. This is partly why it is important that such services are not only for those with AIDS.

Reconciliation

A ministry of reconciliation with God and with estranged others is important in a time of AIDS. Those with AIDS often blame themselves and condemn themselves; they feel guilty about partners whom they have infected. They feel bitter towards those who infect them. They feel angry with themselves, with others and especially angry with God. Yet since we cannot live comfortably with anger, they also long for peace and reconciliation. They need, like everybody else, to know that they are loved and forgiven; they often need to be given an opportunity to forgive and be reconciled with others. This kind of ministry needs pastors who understand the issues involved which are often hidden beneath brash and defiant words. There is a fine line which we must walk. We must not make people with AIDS feel more guilty than they already do; it is not our role to place guilt upon them, but paradoxically we must also allow them their need to own and confess their sinfulness.

Reconciliation is not only a matter between the person with AIDS and God, but between individuals and families. Wives discover for the first time that their husband has been unfaithful to them when he (or she) is diagnosed as HIV positive. Parents discover that their son is homosexual. The burden of coping simultaneously with fear, bereavement and anger is very great. Many pastors tell stories of how parents have been enabled to overcome their shock of discovering that their child is homosexual, and even to welcome their son's lover into their circle of grief. But many also tell stories about when reconciliation proved impossible. The clergyperson or church member may often be able to mediate between those who are hurt and angry. Since they are seen to speak with some authority about God and God's message, they may be able to give reassurance about forgiveness.

Eucharist

The eucharist symbolizes with great power that we are one family fed from one source:

> 'Though we are many, we are one body, because we all share in one bread' (Alternative Service Book).

We gather as one family: sick and well, poor and rich, 'gay' and 'straight', and are united with one Lord. In the preaching of the word (if it is good preaching) we are assured that we are welcome, and we are prodded into welcoming others. In the eucharistic offering, our work is united with the offering of Christ, and our weaknesses are covered by his perfection. All that I have said previously about people with AIDS being united with the vicarious death and suffering and resurrection of Jesus is symbolically enacted in the eucharist, and therefore through the symbol made real. In the passing of the peace which has become common practice in many churches, our status as members of a family is confirmed. We may take the hand of, or even embrace, one another. For those who are HIV positive this is a powerful expression of being accepted. For those who are not HIV positive, hugging someone with HIV quickly confronts and dispels the residual fears which nag within. In all these very simple ways, just by doing what it does Sunday by Sunday, the local church has at its disposal a ceremony and a ritual which has very great resources for caring for a community in which there is AIDS.

Sadly, the eucharist may also symbolize the exclusion of those who are HIV positive. Different churches have different historical customs with regard to the common cup. Catholics commonly do not administer the wine to members of the congregation; many Protestants use small individual glasses. But for those who do use a common cup, the symbolism of bonding is strong. Yet drinking from a common cup also brings to the surface all of our fears about contracting AIDS. It has therefore become usual in some of those churches to encourage, or at least to permit, people to avoid the 'risk' of infection by the custom of intinction, dipping the bread into the wine so as not to have to touch the chalice or cup with one's lips (e.g. Synod of Bishops, Church of the Province of Southern Africa, March 1991). This has become common practice in the Anglican and Lutheran churches of Uganda and Tanzania, which previously used the common cup.

There is no theological objection to intinction, which is a custom well established in history, usually to avoid the danger of spilling the consecrated wine. But when a congregation has customarily received communion from the cup, and because of AIDS the custom changes, the effect on those who are HIV positive is to make them feel unclean and dangerous, and the effect on the rest of the congregation is to reinforce their irrational fears. Thus the church contributes towards the exclusion of people with AIDS.

If there were sound medical reason for the change, then we would have to accept it. However excluded people with AIDS might feel, it would be wrong to expose other persons to the risk of infection. But there is no such risk. A report presented to the International Anglican Liturgical Commission says that there is 'no evidence of possible HIV infection through contact with saliva'. We cannot catch the virus from the chalice, because the concentration of the HIV virus in saliva is far too low to cause infection and because in any case 'neither oral contact nor ingestion of saliva afford viable routes of infection'. Thus, in the opinion of the report, 'given the comprehensive data currently available, the common cup, primary modality of communion under the species of wine, poses no known threat of HIV infection' (Johnson et al., undated, see also Dixon 1990:96).

Marriage

Marriage has become another AIDS battlefield. In Uganda and Tanzania, and maybe elsewhere, too, some church authorities are now insisting that those presenting themselves for marriage must bring evidence from the medical authorities that they have been tested for the AIDS virus and are not infected. This is understandable. It is also probably wrong.

It is understandable, because in a society where AIDS is very common, people who know that they could have the virus should indeed come forward for testing lest they infect an HIV free person, and also lest they fall pregnant and bring an AIDS baby into the world. The church is right to encourage people to be tested. If one or both partners is found to be HIV positive, they need to consider very carefully whether they still wish to marry, and they certainly should take measures not to fall pregnant, since there is a one-in-three likelihood that the baby will die of AIDS.

It is probably wrong to insist on disclosure, because this is a breach of medical confidentiality. It is also wrong to refuse to marry them, because that is a decision which the couple need to make for themselves. Provided that condoms are used, the risk of the uninfected partner becoming infected is significantly reduced to a level which the couple may feel acceptable.

The parents of the couple, of course, might not find it acceptable, especially as such a marriage ought to be childless. In authoritarian societies parents may well feel that they have a right to know whether or not their prospective son- or daughter-in-law will be able to procreate the children which the extended family needs for its future prosperity. In societies where extended families are the norm, to take in a potentially sick person endangers the well-being of all the members of the family. Thus real issues are raised in the question of AIDS and confidentiality which the church has not had to consider seriously before. Who should have priority? the individual? the couple? or the extended family? Whose needs should be paramount? It is not easy to answer these questions. In his view of marriage Jesus seemed to say that the couple, not the extended family, is what matters.

'For this reason a man shall leave his father and mother and be joined to his wife (Matthew 19.5).

Church refusal to marry a couple is tantamount to announcing to the parents and indeed to the whole community that one or other of the couple is HIV positive. This could have very serious consequences indeed. In addition, to refuse to marry an HIV positive person is to condemn that person to lifelong celibacy or to promiscuity. In the latter case the church itself will have contributed to the spread of AIDS. Thus the Catholic bishops of Uganda have said to their priests:

'You have no right to demand the result of the test or to deny the sacrament of matrimony to a couple on the ground of the HIV test result' (*African Ecclesial Review* 1989:297).

Upholding community morals

It is part of the church's role to be prophetic and to warn people that certain kinds of behaviour have terrible consequences. Part of the church's role is to recall those who will listen to a renewed and reformed sexual ethic. Does not compassion for those with AIDS compromise this moral stand? If we welcome them into church fellowship without judgment or condemnation, are we not party to the permissiveness which has given rise to AIDS? How can a church be both prophetic and loving, uphold the laws of God and yet be caring towards those who offend against God's law? Not everyone who has AIDS has been involved in personal sexual sin, but should we not draw the line at welcoming those who have AIDS because of homosexuality or adultery, at least until they are repentant?

The law of Christ, though, also requires that we have concern for the weak and the oppressed: 'Bear one another's burdens and so fulfil the law of Christ' (Galatians 6.2), and Jesus himself welcomed and forgave before he knew whether the person was repentant. AIDS is a consequence not just of aberrant sex, but of aberrant human relationships generally. It is a consequence of poverty, inequality and injustice in which we all share, just as much as of homosexuality or promiscuity. As I have argued above (p. 43), disordered sexual relationships will not be eradicated while society itself is disordered. A church which seeks to promote sexual faithfulness will also try to develop better human relationships in every aspect. Responsible and caring sexuality cannot be imposed by force or legalism. We have all seen the kind of marriage where the sex is legal, in the sense that the couple are married, but where it is an expression of power and domination rather than love. A better sexual ethic involves encouraging the development of a society which is more caring in every way.

Caring for those who suffer, even as a consequence of their own foolishness and sin, is part of this. In a time of AIDS the role of the church is to be compassionate, to support as well as to warn, to care for as well as to criticize.

'The people of God should be the family that embraces and sustains those who are sick, caring for them as brothers and sisters without barriers, hostility or rejection' (The Catholic bishops of Uganda, in *Ecclesial Review* 1989:292).

This embracing without rejection needs to extend to its own members, including its own ministers and clergy.

Raymond was an unmarried English-born Anglican priest who was on the staff of a wealthy and conservative suburban congregation in an Episcopal parish in America. He was a lively preacher and a popular pastor. But he grew sick, and had to tell his Rector and his Vestry that he had AIDS. They correctly assumed that he was homosexual. They guessed the parish would make the same assumption. They asked him to resign, suggesting that he would do best to return to England to be cared for there.

There are quite a number of ministers, priests and members of religious orders, who are diagnosed as having AIDS. In some cases the virus has been contracted through blood transfusions, but to be honest and realistic, in most cases it is because they, too, have been involved in extramarital sex. If they are open about having AIDS, that is tantamount to admitting illicit sexual activity.

Here is a real test of whether the church acts as it preaches. If the minister is asked to resign on the basis that he is clearly unfit to be an example to the people of God, then we cannot expect other employers to be more merciful to their employees. But when clergy have been honest about their HIV status, and where bishops or congregations have worked through the issues with the minister, standing by him[10] and supporting him with forgiveness and compassion, there has often been real spiritual growth for both minister and people. Of course church authorities are in a difficult situation. The church should not give the impression that sexual sins are unimportant or irrelevant. But clergy may fall like anyone else, and are no less deserving of forgiveness and compassion. Weaknesses and failures do not cancel out other gifts and goodnesses. Often in the working through of the situation the congregation has been able to recognize gifts of love, courage and maturity in their pastor which might otherwise have remained buried. If the church is harsh with its own clergy, how can it urge society to love and care for people with AIDS?

For this reason the Catholic Aids Link is quite correct in opposing moves to have clergy or religious tested for HIV before ordination or profession (Catholic AIDS Link 1995). Understandably, churches and congregations wish to avoid the expense of training people who will be ill before they can use their training, and wish to avoid the scandal of employing someone whose life-style turns out to be inconsistent with the ideals of the church. Possibly, too, they wish to avoid the financial responsibility of someone dying of AIDS. However, to test for HIV before ordination or profession is impractical. It sets a poor example. It is also not in the best interests of the church. It is impractical, because a one-off test proves

[10]Or her, but I have not heard of a woman minister or religious who has AIDS.

nothing, since the person can contract the virus after the test. It sets a poor example to other employers because if all potential employers test for HIV positivity before they engage someone, then people with the virus will be unable to get employment, even though they may have ten years of reasonable health to look forward to and a family to support. It is not in the best interests of the church, because a priest or religious with AIDS is not necessarily a worse sinner than anyone else, and may well, through the pain and sickness, have great gifts of insight and courage to share.

The evangelizing church

As well as being a prophetic church recalling humans to live under the laws of God, the church is to be an evangelizing church bringing the news of God's love. This is why our message about AIDS must go beyond talking of punishment and due deserts. People with AIDS need to know that God loves them. Those who have sinned need to know that God forgives them.

Yet to talk about the love of God to people who are suffering and who face death raises again all the questions of theodicy, of why God allows such pain. Therefore talking about God's love can only take place in a context of showing God's love. The church needs to embody that love in its own care for people with AIDS. This care may sometimes be offered by the church as an organization; but individual Christians in their own care also show and make real the love of God which motivates their care.

> *Sister Maria is a nun who is also a psychologist and a worker with a major AIDS caring organization in Britain. Although she and many other workers in that organization are Christian, they care for people with AIDS regardless of their religious faith or affiliation. They do not necessarily talk about God, unless the person clearly wishes it, but, 'In our nursing of them,' she says, 'many of them find that God is there with them, whether or not they are Christian.'*

Evangelism means more than talking about the good news of God's love. It means making the good news come true. An evangelistic church which stands aside from AIDS is a contradiction of all that it claims. The gospel news is that God no longer sends messages from afar through prophets but has come amongst us in the Son, who entered into human life and human suffering. In those who continue to incarnate the presence of Christ in a world of darkness and suffering the gospel continues to be made true. In learning to care for those who suffer, we are, strangely, learning to care for Jesus himself who is now incarnated both in the caring church and in the person who needs care.

'[The church] should remember that every sufferer is Jesus in painful disguise, indeed is all of us in painful disguise' (Kirkpatrick 1988:4).

'Inasmuch as ye did it unto the least of these my brethren, ye did it unto me' (Matthew 25.40).

The liturgical church

The pain caused by AIDS, and the meaning within the pain, often need to be expressed in ways beyond the merely literal. In the liturgy and in the poetry, music, art and symbolism of the church, the pain, fear, bereavement, loss of dignity, as well as the defiant hope, may all find expression in a way that goes beyond words. The church needs to find space for all of this, using the liturgy and art which we already have and allowing new expressions through these media to emerge. It is not possible in this book to make specific suggestions, but merely preaching about AIDS is not enough, and local creative planning of symbolic and liturgical expressions of caring, of solidarity in pain, of being both dead and yet risen in Christ, will in many cases speak much more effectively than sermons alone.

The church as community

One thing that is implicit in all that I have said about the church is that it is, ideally, a community of mutual support and interdependence. In reality the church in the main-line denominations is far from being that. The vision of Ephesians remains, very often, merely a vision without much substance in reality.

'And his gifts were that some should be apostles, some prophets, some evangelists, some pastors and teachers, to equip the saints for the work of ministry, for building up the body of Christ until we all attain to the unity of the faith and of the knowledge of the Son of God, to mature manhood, to the measure of the stature of the fullness of Christ; so that we may no longer be children, tossed to and fro and carried about with every wind of doctrine, by the cunning of men, by their craftiness in deceitful wiles. Rather, speaking the truth in love, we are to grow up on every way into him who is the head, into Christ, from whom the whole body, joined and knit together by every joint with which it is supplied, when each part is working properly, makes bodily growth and upbuilds itself with love' (Ephesians 4.11–16).

I have quoted the text in full because there are several themes in it that are relevant to the church's task in the face of AIDS. In this vision, it is not only the apostolic or teaching ministry, the 'official' roles, which are important, though these have their place. The ministry is a 'whole body' ministry, every part having its role. There are different gifts which are all important. But they can only be harnessed by speaking to each other, 'speaking the truth in love'. The result of this interdependent, openly communicating body of people is that they all grow in maturity. They are no longer children, but can cope in a difficult and confusing world. Indeed, they grow into the stature of Christ who is their head.

As the church has grown from a Jewish sect into Christendom what has evolved is a concentration on only some of these gifts. It became a community which was passively dependent upon the clergy for guidance and for spiritual feeding in which lay persons were not expected to come to spiritual maturity but would always remain children. There was no expectation of two-way communication. The clergy told the lay persons how to live and what the Bible means, and the task of the laity was to obey. As the church grew larger, the individual contribution of lay persons was often lost in the weight of numbers. Except for a few chosen individuals, their only role was to provide finance. Despite theological differences about the priesthood of all believers, this is often still true of both Catholics and Protestants alike. It has been equally true of the church in the West and the church in newly evangelized countries. The advent of television and tele-evangelism has merely taken the passive role of the lay person as listener and payer even further.

Long before AIDS appeared on the scene, there have been moves to recreate a sense of community within the church, and to revive the contribution of ordinary lay membership. The Methodist class system was one such attempt. Most recently we have seen, in different contexts, the development of the house-church movement and the development of 'base ecclesial communities'. These latter are a product of liberation theology, growing out of a conviction that poor people understand the gospel better than others, since it is especially for them that the good news is intended, the 'preferential option for the poor'. The priest or bishop often comes from a well-educated and middle-class background. Rather than him telling the people what the gospel means in their situation, and how to respond in a Christian way to the demands of that situation, liberation theology believes that the people can best work this out for themselves. The priest may share in this search for the meaning of the gospel and make his own contribution from his background of theological training, but it will be the people who, through analysing their situation and seeking guidance from scripture and tradition, will discern together what God wills them to do. Their decisions may seem unorthodox but will be authentic responses guided by 'another Counsellor' (John 14.16). Segundo, for example, uses this passage to suggest that the conclusions to which the community comes may sometimes be different from the conclusions which, on the face of things, seem to be taught by the New Testament or church tradition. This is the idea of 'second learning' or 'deutero-learning'. The Holy Spirit, over the course of history, may lead us into new conclusions (Segundo 1976:108).

Thus base ecclesial communities are small gatherings of the local church in a particular village, sector of a township, or workplace, who will seek to analyse their situation and discern God's will for them in that situation. The will of God may be more clearly discerned through this process, but also, in the process of analysing and thinking through their situation, the community will be learning to take increasing responsibility for its own destiny, making its own history rather than having it made for its members by others. Thus they become the subjects rather than the objects of their society.

Base ecclesial communities have not always worked well in practice. Often the people have lacked the skills for social analysis; or their goals have remained regrettably short-term and materialistic; or they have exacerbated class divisions in the church. But the intention of empowering people to become a truly interdependent community taking shared responsibility for themselves is admirable. Indigenous churches in the Third World provide another example of this. These churches on the face of things often look very authoritarian, with a clearly defined leader in whom that authority is vested. But these churches are churches of the very poor. Their leaders therefore emerge from the ranks of the poor, with no resources from outside and no access to formal education. They will often earn their living through normal secular employment. Therefore they live in the same situation as the other members of the church. Their authority is not merely individual. Usually there is a well-defined hierarchy, and through the hierarchy many share in the decision-making process. Beneath the hierarchy, however, is a web of mutual interdependence and support. These churches, often very small, are communities where each individual has a place and a measure of power. Lacking access to First-World state benefits, the people help each other to cope with daily problems, assisting with sickness, with sharing food and money, with emotional support in bereavement or desertion or unemployment.

AIDS demands something of this vision in the church again. Of course there are clergy and members of religious orders who are HIV positive and who die of AIDS, but for those other ministers who are uninfected it is difficult really to understand the situation of a person with AIDS from within. A purely clergy-based ministry will not be enough. Only a shared ministry will have sufficient insight to offer real support.

People living in suburbs and cities have often lost a close sense of belonging. Very little sense of community survives in most Western towns and cities, where we hide behind our lace curtains and garden walls to shut out a hostile world, only inviting in our own particular friends, who in most cases have nothing to do with the local community. As urbanization becomes the norm in the Third World, the same tendency can be seen there too. Yet AIDS demands that the local community pull together to assist one another. The church, if it can rediscover a community life of its own, may have a contribution to make in helping rebuild local communities where they have broken down, or where they threaten to break down because of the burden which AIDS places upon them.

As the number of people with AIDS grows until, in many parts of Africa, few families are left untouched, it is quite impossible for a clergy-based ministry to meet the needs. Only a ministry which is shared with others can do so. Communities which have been hit hard by the virus are in a very similar situation to that of the Latin American poor for whom base ecclesial communities were envisioned. They need, as a community, to plan how they will cope with care of orphans, with people requiring home nursing, with the ever-increasing demands made upon the elderly as so many young people die. Without the social resourcefulness and co-responsibility that the base ecclesial communities were intended to provide, the people of the African village or township, waiting for official help and advice from a government which is stretched beyond its means to cope, will be helpless. Without the close sense of belonging together and working together that we find in indigenous independent churches, they will be isolated and friendless.

In Kamwokya outside Kampala, Uganda, the local Catholic church has developed a number of base ecclesial communities, called *bubondo*. These are complementary to, and not a replacement for, the large Sunday Mass congregation. They meet for prayer and spiritual reflection; but they also organize visits to sick people, acting as a link between them and the hospital, and they distribute gifts of food from the rest of the congregation.

'The small Christian communities in Kamwokya have enabled us to reach three to four times more people with AIDS than in neighbourhoods which don't have that kind of supportive, community-based organization' (Sr Dr Miriam Duggan, in Williams and Tamale 1991:10).

The church in a time of AIDS needs to be like the church described in Ephesians and elsewhere, the body of Christ in which each member plays a role and is supported by others. The church needs to become a close-knit community where the needs of individuals are the concern of all. The demands made upon the church, especially in the Third World, are so great that no other model will work.

The servant church

AIDS provides a wonderful opportunity for the church. The opportunity is not to increase its own numbers or authority, but to serve. 'I am among you as one who serves', said Jesus (Luke 22.27b). This should be our only motivation for involvement: to be of service. Some of those whom we serve will be Christians, some will not. Some may be persons of whose life-styles we profoundly disapprove: drug-users, sexually promiscuous people. Many will be poor people. All will be people who are hurting and in need, which is what gives them the right to expect that we should serve them. We may hope that those to whom we minister will come to be more firmly committed Christians, so that we may say that at the last they found peace with God. But that should not be why we serve them. We should serve them because in serving them we serve Christ.

However, our service is not only to those with AIDS but to their families, their spouses, their partners and their children. It is also very important that we seek to serve the carers. Doctors, nurses, health workers, visitors and others who care for those with AIDS are under great strain. There is so much death; there are so many bereavements. None of their patients, in the end, are cured. The pain may be alleviated, and death may be postponed, but in the end they die.

Aline is a doctor who works extensively with AIDS. At first, she says, it was very painful that people to whom she had got close died. She describes the case of a woman whose baby died of AIDS. 'We wept together', she says. She warned her patient not to fall pregnant again. But the woman came back to say she had so badly needed a baby that she was pregnant again. They wept again. Soon the woman died too. By now Aline was numb to pain, and blamed herself for feeling so little sadness. Then one day her pet dog died. Her grief, she says, was inappropriately extreme; it became clear to her that her pent-up grief for so much sadness had eventually broken through.

It is very hard for helpers to cope for long periods with the pain. In Africa and elsewhere where AIDS has so firm a grip, it is hard for church members, who may initially volunteer their service, to keep going when the needs are so great and so unrelenting. Some organizations working with people with AIDS have used a 'buddy' system, pairing up someone who has AIDS with a volunteer who will be a friend and supporter. The strain on the 'buddy' is very great, as also is the strain on those who care for people with AIDS in their own home. There is great danger of burn-out or emotional collapse. The church has a responsibility to care for, encourage and console them all. But in this case 'the church' is not someone outside ourselves, but simply means all of us having responsibilities to support one another through the pressure of the demands. The relevance of Luke, 'If any man would come after me, let him deny himself and take up his cross daily and follow me' (Luke 9.23), is clear.

A servant church is one in which power and authority are shared and are exercised for the common good. A strong church hierarchy may mean initially that the church responds quickly to AIDS if the hierarchy is well disposed. It also means that if the hierarchy is not well disposed or does not think AIDS is part of the church's business, very little will get off the ground. But as long as the hierarchy – bishops, clergy, even national church committees – insist on making all the decisions, the people whom they are meant to be serving remain passive and dependent. It is problematic that so many clergy keep power and decision-making in their own hands. Where the traditional culture is authoritarian anyway and closely tied in to chiefs or village elders, clergy authoritarianism feeds into and is itself fed by that culture.

This does not mean there is no place for the exercise of authority in the church. Often people do need help in knowing how to organize and how to make decisions. Churches are not necessarily governed best by a democracy where the majority have power through numbers. There is a place for *episkope* or oversight. Yet true *episkope* does not consist of merely telling other people what to do. It means helping the people of the church community to take increasing responsibility for themselves. It is committed to the development of the people's self-reliance.

Authority in the New Testament is often linked with the idea of pastoring. Elders are told to tend the flock, not in a domineering way but as examples to be followed (I Peter 5.1–4). Jesus is described as both bishop and shepherd, *episkopos* and *poimen*. A shepherd is one who is closely associated with the flock, living alongside the sheep, which is why John has Jesus describe himself as the good shepherd (John 10.11). In Mark's Gospel, although Jesus is clearly shown to have great spiritual authority, he also keeps a low profile, preferring not to emphasize his healing miracles, urging those he healed to tell nobody. He is indeed Lord, but his is a subtle, hidden Lordship. Matthew and Luke tell us that Jesus shared his authority. He sent out the Twelve (and in Luke subsequently the Seventy), telling them to go out and do the same works as he had done, to heal and to cast out demons (Matthew 10.1–15; Luke 9.1–6). Of course Jesus walked about doing good in the land, but he trained others to imitate him and follow him. He exercised a shared and participatory ministry.

In the face of the huge demands placed upon the church by AIDS, no group of clergy or medical experts or trained social workers on their own will be able to meet the needs. Their various skills need to be combined, and to be shared with others in the community so that everyone has responsibilities and abilities.

The church is the bride of Christ

In the face of the gloom cast by AIDS, it is also important to remember that the church, as well as being a crucified community, is meant to be a joyfully expectant community. The references to the church as the bride of Christ conjure up images of a bride waiting for her bridegroom filled with expectant and excited hope.

This hope is not easy to maintain where AIDS has run rampant. But the problem is not new. It was not easy to maintain hope when the evangelists first recorded the stories about Jesus as the bridegroom. Expectations of an early return of Jesus had waned. Ominous signs of persecution were beginning. Christian converts were asking why, if they had been promised new life in Christ, they were now discovering that all they really received was ostracism, threats of danger, and family tensions. The stories of the wise and foolish virgins (Matthew 25.1ff.), or the faithful and unfaithful stewards (Luke 12.42ff.), have as their point that we must cling on to hope when from a human point of view that hope seems groundless.

Without hope we cannot survive. The hope cannot be for a miracle cure for the illness, for in few cases is there any such cure. But there are different kinds of hope. We may hope that people who are HIV positive will be able to find joy and laughter in the years of life still left to them – perhaps more precious and more keenly appreciated because it is for a limited time. We may hope for finding joy in the meaningful service of others. We may hope for resurrection in its different forms. I have tried to deal with these ideas more extensively elsewhere in this book.

Sometimes those who care for people with AIDS, and those who mourn their dead, may feel that it is heartless to be joyful. But a church which is the bride of Christ has the right to be joyful even in suffering; because we must expect, in the suffering, to find God in Christ more fully present to us. Tears of sorrow and of joy are strangely close together.

Doctrinal orthodoxy

Even before we were aware of AIDS we already knew that there is a tension between the union of the church and the uniformity of doctrine. The days of monolithic, universally accepted systems of theology are over, if they ever really existed. Rahner reminds us that we live in a pluralistic age, surrounded by rival philosophies and rival disciplines of thought, and that the church can best respond to this by listening and learning, rather than trying to push our experience of God into a universal and uniform doctrinal system (Rahner 1972:52).

Yet at the same time, as Stephen Sykes has commented about Anglicanism (Sykes 1978:85), there must be some coherence of thought for our Christian identity to have any basis. No church can survive without some common vision. The Anglican church, that most doctrinally hospitable of denominations, is beginning to fall apart over liberal attitudes to homosexuality and women priests.

AIDS raises the tension between individual belief and official church doctrine. A person with a dread disease – one which is fairly soon a terminal disease – must find his or her own answer to that situation. Such people set off on a pilgrimage of faith, searching for life in the face of death. We need to encourage people who are HIV positive or who have AIDS to find their own authentic path on this pilgrimage. We may hope that they will find guidance and direction from the Christian tradition. People may draw from the experience of other Christians and from the riches of the Christian heritage and history, but they will also draw from the experience of people with AIDS who are not Christian. It would be inappropriate and false for the church to tell people what they should think or feel, unless we are in the same situation.

> 'If I'm going to listen to advice I want to be sure that the person giving it understands what I am feeling, and, with respect, if you've never tested positive then you don't. You can speculate, you can ask around, but at the end of the day I know that you can walk away from it. We, the diagnosed, can't' (*CARA News* 1995:11).

No one person's pilgrimage of faith will be exactly like another's. That does not mean we have no advice to offer. Our advice, though, should come from our own lived experience or the experience of others. Christian belief should not be guided by canons of orthodoxy so much as by canons of authenticity. We may hope that from reflection on our experience there may be pointers for others on their own journey of discovery. We may warn that some paths of action or of attitude have in our experience proved to be dead ends. But we may not try to make someone else's journey follow the same route as our own. If our AIDS ministry is to be authentic and credible, we cannot build it on ready-made answers.

Outside the church

Outside the church there is no salvation, said Cyprian, third century bishop of Carthage. Of course Cyprian was not talking about help with social problems. He did not mean that Christians cannot work together with non-Christians or with the secular state on social issues. Since he lived in the days when Christianity was not officially granted a right to exist, he did not have to face that question. Christians were still a closed body, looking after their own.

But now there can be no question of the church going it alone with regard to AIDS education or care. In Western countries the resources of the state are so much bigger that the church needs to work alongside secular health authorities, as well as alongside other religious groups, in order to tap into those resources for its own AIDS work. In Third World countries, by contrast, the resources of the state are often so minuscule that unless the church co-operates and shares its resources, in some places there will be no AIDS education or care for those who are not Christian. What is jargonistically known as a 'multi-sectoral approach' is in fact hiding two important theological truths: all human beings fall within God's love; and God's grace is not imprisoned within the institutional church. If churches fail to work alongside other churches, other religions and secular bodies, they will be fencing out part of what God is doing.

This raises difficulties for Christians who believe that salvation is found in Jesus and Jesus alone. Cyprian's views still hold for some Christians. There is still a temptation to 'go it alone', to discount AIDS programmes run by many secular agencies as being non-Christian or, worse, as anti-Christian. Some major Christian AIDS agencies see other agencies as being 'soft' on homosexuality and permissive in their views on sex. When people with AIDS turn to alternative medicines, such as diets, aromatherapy, ayurvedic medicine, acupuncture, some Christians are hostile to this, seeing it as dabbling in the occult. In Africa, where AIDS affects the Muslim community and those following traditional African religion just as badly as Christians, the temptation again is for each religion to run its own programmes in insolation. Fortunately, in some African countries the government has taken the initiative to co-ordinate what would otherwise be wasteful, but there is also a great deal to be learnt from how other religions deal with AIDS.

I have suggested above that there is much to be learned from the independent indigenous churches about healing in the church as a community. There is also much to be learned from traditional African religions and from alternative medicines in both East and West.

In many parts of Africa, traditional leaders have made available to people inexpensive herbal remedies for some of the side-effects of AIDS such as nausea, which would otherwise be beyond their means. They are also able to offer a ministry to people with AIDS in a cultural context which is more familiar and therefore more convincing to them than what seems like the strangeness of Western medicine.

All of us cope with disaster by trying to fit it into some pattern of meaning. Western doctors may explain that AIDS is the result of a virus, and it is likely that this explanation of AIDS is quite widely accepted in Third World countries. But there is still the unanswered question: why did I personally fall victim to the virus? A tree branch may fall on me and break my skull: at one level I can say that my head hurts because the tree hit it. But why the tree fell at the moment I passed beneath it is another matter. So with AIDS, the entrenched belief still persists in traditional African culture that misfortune is caused by some person wishing it upon another – perhaps an enemy who is casting a bewitchment upon me, perhaps the ancestors who are warning or punishing me. Western medicine has nothing to say to this belief system; it only explains the mechanical cause of illness. This, of course, is not unimportant, but traditional African healers, operating within the people's belief system, can offer what may be complementary and meaningful interpretations to the people involved.

Of course it is important that traditional healers in Africa do not make misleading claims that they can prevent or cure AIDS. It is important that people with AIDS do not deceive themselves with false hopes about what alternative medicines can achieve, or that they do not convince themselves that they will only contract AIDS if an enemy or ancestor wishes it upon them (Barnett and Blaikie 1992:44). But where these healers have been taken seriously by the churches and by the medical profession, it has usually been possible to bring them to a recognition of what they are able or not able to offer, and often they are in fact able to offer real help with some of the side-effects.

Alternative medicines which are becoming popular in Western culture remind us, like traditional African religion, that a predominantly mechanistic model of medicine is inadequate even in the

West, and point to more holistic models. It is ironic that we Christians, so afraid of syncretism if we permit alternative medical practices from other cultures, are unaware of how closely we have allied ourselves to the prevailing materialistic model of medicine that comes from modern science. Hans Küng observes:

'The concept of the doctor as a mechanic and a repairer of the biologico-psychological machine "man" has already produced disastrous consequences' (Küng 1984:189).

To a large extent the current medical model in the West is still a model which treats the individual rather than the individual-in-community; and it treats the individual with mechanistic, primarily drug-related, methods. Some of the side-effects of AIDS and its treatment are nausea, fungal infections and itching, skin lesions, tiredness, depression. Alternative medical approaches are likely to look at diet, at massage, at homeopathic remedies for skin irritation and nausea, at 'imaging', i.e. imagining ourselves in a happy place so as to exercise a degree of mind-conditioning. They may offer approaches to meditation. Traditional African medicines are likely to look at relationships, at healing the individual within the community, and at healing the attitude of the community to the ill individual. They may also provide herbal remedies which are effective for relief of irritation, and easily available at an affordable price. These are all elements which are often missing in the medical model to which modern Western Christianity unquestioningly allies itself.

This does not mean that the medico-materialist model does not have enormous power for healing. One day, probably, it will discover a vaccine against AIDS. Nor does it mean that we should accept unjustified claims from alternative medicine to be able to cure AIDS, for there is no evidence that this is true. What the alternative models can do is to provide help with some aspects of the body and the spirit and thus relieve the suffering, and possibly prolong life expectancy. We need to be able to use all of these models as appropriate. Medically there is everything to be said for a syncretistic approach.

The church needs to see that God is working in and through secular agencies and other religions. AIDS reminds us that

Christians are not alone in feeling pain nor in providing help. The AIDS crisis demands that we be able to work alongside others in the struggle against AIDS. It also demonstrates to us that people in other religions show the courage and love and self-sacrifice that we assume to be the fruit of God's spirit. Inevitably this raises the issue of Cyprian's view that salvation lies in Christ and his church alone.

AIDS forces us to realize that the image of God and the grace of the Holy Spirit are present in people of other religions. It also forces us to realize that Christians are just as likely to fall into sin as anyone else. Christians, even Christian clergy, have contracted AIDS in some cases through multiple sexual contacts, whether homo- or heterosexual. Thus we cannot say that Christians have more grace than persons in other religions, or deny the grace that is present in other religions. We will not enter here into how best to accommodate this obvious truth while still believing that Jesus is the way of salvation. What is clear from the AIDS pandemic is that people of all faiths are in need; people of all faiths are likely to be involved in the sort of sexual life-style which creates the risk of AIDS; and people of all faiths are capable of grace-filled courage in the face of death, and grace-filled love towards sufferers. In one way or another we have to construct a christology and an ecclesiology which takes account of this.

Since AIDS is a global epidemic, we must be involved in dialogue with other religions and people of no religion over how to deal with it. Hans Küng has said that there can be no world peace without religious dialogue.

> 'Constructive engagement with the other religions of this world for the sake of peace in the world is vitally important for the sake of survival' (Küng 1990:76).

There can also be no solution to AIDS without the same dialogue. In Africa, Christianity, Islam and African traditional religion are faced with a common crisis and need to work together to solve it. It is regrettably true that even within Christianity, Catholics and Protestants do not always work hand in hand but run their own separate programmes. It is even more true that Christians and Muslims find it hard to work together. Years of competition for converts are hard to put aside in co-operative ventures. Each side is equally convinced that they possess the whole and the only saving truth. The one thing they do agree on is that African traditional religion does not possess saving truth!

For practical reasons, since AIDS programmes often work best within small groups, there is some sense in having Catholic or Anglican or Lutheran or Muslim pastoral plans to cope with AIDS. But the people in the villages and townships do not live in such watertight compartments; AIDS cannot be dealt with except by dealing with the whole community. If religions persist in trying to go it alone, AIDS and the powers of evil will win.

AIDS, the church and the community

AIDS is not merely a medical problem requiring medical answers, but arises out of a network of complex shortcomings in the world-wide human community. Issues of poverty, of entitlement and access to land or employment to provide for daily needs, the unequal distribution of money and resources between individuals and between classes and nations, relationships between men and women, the willingness of governing authorities to get involved, are all part of what causes AIDS. AIDS exists because of inadequate economic, political, social, ethical and religious systems.

Since throughout its history the church has shown itself to be imprisoned within the same biases, blindnesses and divisions as the society in which it exists at any period, we may be sceptical about whether the church can make any contribution towards overcoming these social inadequacies. Yet there are particular contributions which the church is uniquely able to make. Its scriptures and tradition give a vision of an interdependent human community in which the needs of the most humble and vulnerable have first place in our priorities. The church has often been unable to give much practical expression to the vision, but that does not mean the vision has no credibility. Indeed it is arguable that many of the secular political visions which have been offered in this century, from socialism and Marxism to Nyerere's *ujama* or Kaunda's African socialism, have been derived from the biblical vision of the kingdom of God. The church is certainly not in itself the kingdom, but it can still point to the kingdom and keep the vision alive in a society which is now becoming sceptical about any social system which is not a kind of Darwinian capitalism of the survival of the fittest.

The church always needs to be self-critical. But there is no value in becoming so self-critical and discouraged that we cannot see the potential that lies within the church. In its ordinary routines of prayer groups, visiting teams, youth groups, young mothers' groups, women's groups, the church has an enviable network for an effective AIDS ministry already in place, and AIDS may provide us with an opportunity to become relevantly involved in the community.

'AIDS gives us a new and compelling opportunity to be the authentic church our Saviour Jesus Christ calls us to be' (Louw 1990:42).

We must be very careful how we express this. It would be crass to say that we welcome AIDS because through it the churches can become stronger. We may not say that God sent AIDS as a practical lesson for the church. But we may say that God is able to bring good out of great evil. People with AIDS can help the church learn how to be a caring community.

If this is to come about, the church will first need to eliminate fear of the AIDS virus. We cannot welcome people with AIDS into the renewed human community, or into the church community which is meant to be a sign and forerunner of that renewed community, as long as they are still seen as a threat to community health. Although it is medically well established that the virus cannot be passed on through normal social contact, there are still atavistic fears which make us wary of putting ourselves or, especially, our children at risk. Occasional stories about children contracting AIDS through nursery school play feed these fears.

It must be said that there is always some small degree of risk; it is always just possible that a minor abrasion or cut exposed to the bodily fluids of an HIV positive person may lead to infection. The risk is so small as to be negligible. In earlier centuries ministers of the church exposed themselves to much greater risk in caring for people with the plague than is the case with the AIDS virus. The church needs to provide adequate and accurate information to its members about how AIDS is or is not contracted. Church members need to be challenged to display some small degree of courage consistent with following Jesus and in breaking down barriers which prevent easy social mixing with people with AIDS. This is partly why pandering to the fears about a common cup discussed above is so regrettable.

Because AIDS is rarely spoken about in church, persons with AIDS have no way of knowing how acceptable they will be. There is a conspiracy of silence. People with AIDS only tell closest friends, for fear of ostracization. Even in countries where AIDS is common tragedy, the illness is only mentioned within the family. Neighbours, although they may draw their own conclusions, are not told.

If the church is to be relevant in this crisis it must be the one place where everyone knows that people with AIDS will be welcome. But that will only become common knowledge if AIDS is spoken about often and publicly and in a non-condemnatory way. 'Persons with AIDS or HIV infection should not, merely on account of this, be restricted from work, school, or living in community with others, travelling with them, or using the same equipment or facilities', say the Catholic bishops of Uganda (*African Ecclesial Review* 1989:229); but then the church must take vigorous steps to ensure that persons with AIDS are not in any way restricted from these things in the community life of the church.

AIDS requires that the whole community be involved in care. This is an ideal which is difficult to achieve in a busy and self-centred life where nobody knows of other people's concerns. Community involvement is especially important in Third World countries where there are few state social services and health resources are thinly stretched. Church-run clinics in many places already provide centres where people with AIDS can meet and find mutual support. People with AIDS need to be kept at the forefront of the community's awareness. It often takes a long time to die of AIDS as the person grows progressively weaker and less able to do things. Regular home visits help provide assurance and contact. Simple tasks like helping to buy food, helping with housework, tending the plot of land, or providing basic home care such as assistance with washing, do not require technical skills but only time and love. The church with its network of visitors and intercessors, its buildings and gathering places, is in a position to

make a quite unique contribution in initiating all of this. In doing so,
it may recover its lost sense of usefulness and identity and find new
confidence in its vocation.

AIDS, the church and human rights

AIDS raises many complex and new human rights issues. In
particular, the tension between individual human rights and community rights becomes very marked. Western human rights of the
kind enshrined in the *Universal Declaration of Human Rights* are
normally of an individualist kind, the rights of an individual to
freedom and protection under the law. With the advent of AIDS,
individual rights to choose one's own sexual behaviour, for example,
must be weighed against community rights to prevent the sort of
sexual activity which leads to AIDS. A document on the rights of
people with AIDS claims that '. . . information should not be
disclosed to a third party about a person's HIV status without that
person's consent' (*United Kingdom Declaration*). It also claims that
'people with HIV and AIDS have the right to marry and to found a
family'. These are typical first-generation human rights, and the
document points out that these rights are enshrined in various
international treaties. But individual rights to confidentiality about
one's health status are brought into conflict with the right of a
partner to know that he or she might have been infected, lest he or
she infect others in turn. Many people would think that the
authorities have a duty to contact and warn such partners. Parents in
Africa express the right to know whether the person whom their son
or daughter plans to marry is free of AIDS because, in their view,
they have a right to expect grandchildren. We have seen that some
churches demand the right to know whether persons seeking
marriage are HIV positive. Do people with HIV and AIDS really
have the right to have children when it is certain that the child will
have only one parent at best, and when there is at least a one in three
chance that their child will be born with AIDS and die painfully
within a few months or years?

These issues cannot successfully be dealt with by legislation. For
practical reasons it is usually unwise to seek to enforce what is good
for the community upon unwilling individuals except as a last resort.

Compulsory mass testing is impossible. It is necessary in most cases to rely on people coming forward voluntarily for testing where appropriate – perhaps because they know their life-style puts them at risk, perhaps because they feel ill. We do want people who think they may be HIV positive to come forward for testing, for their own sake perhaps (if care and treatment are available), but also so that they may be careful in their sexual relationships with others. But enforced disclosure of HIV test results to partners, community elders or employers not only puts the person with AIDS at risk of prejudice and isolation, but means that people who are feeling ill will resist testing. Enforced isolation of people with AIDS will lead to suppression of the illness. The right to confidentiality turns out to be necessary for practical reasons, even in Africa.

Whether people who have AIDS have a right to have children or not is problematical. There is a common belief in Africa that those who die without children to remember them will not be 'ancestors', but will be lost souls with no roots. A woman without children remains a mere child herself in the eyes of her fertile peers. When it is culturally necessary for people to have babies, they will do so despite the risk that the baby may die. So many babies die anyway from other causes in Africa that a one-in-three chance of infection may not seem too high a risk. But people with AIDS must surely also have the right not to have children who may die in infancy, and thus have the right to contraception and perhaps to abortion.

None of these things can be satisfactorily dealt with by law. It is not helpful to think in terms of legalities. What the church can do is to shift the debate from legality to one about persons voluntarily taking responsibility for other people as well as for themselves.

'It is clear that the only acceptable policy is one that must rely on voluntary efforts by informed, motivated persons' (Ruth Macklin in Hastings Centre 1991:77).

Inasmuch as we live in an individualistic, anti-communal age of putting the needs of self first, church commitment to the way of discipleship, to loving others as we love ourselves (Mark 12.31), to laying down our lives for our friends (John 15.13), is very important in creating a climate in which we and people with AIDS voluntarily choose to act in ways which are for the good of the community rather than just good for ourselves.

'Our society is currently gripped in an old and confusing struggle with how to balance individual rights and community responsibility. We wrestle with the larger questions of how to protect individuality without leading to excessive individualism, and how to foster community without imposing corporate coercion' (Ashby 1989:29).

The church is a servant church, serving God and serving God's people, especially the poor. But it has also become a relatively powerful national institution in many places, with important international links. It should not shy away from using this power constructively, challenging human rights abuses and government inactivity. In August 1995 the Zairean government commenced a compulsory repatriation of refugees from Rwanda. The consequences for the refugees would have been severe. African heads of state were noticeably silent. Archbishop Tutu, however, together with other international figures, protested and the repatriation process was halted. Church pressure can make a difference.

In some measure the structural adjustment programmes of the International Monetary Fund and the World Bank have helped create social conditions in which AIDS flourishes.

'Developing countries, especially poorer ones, were often forced to enter into structural adjustment programmes in order to obtain IMF or World Bank loans . . . applying them in a manner which gave developing countries little choice other than drastically to restructure their economies along the lines mandated by these programmes' (Lurie et al. 1995:540).

The programmes have social consequences, which contribute significantly to the creation of conditions in which HIV infection runs rampant.

'Four phenomena that may result from SAP [the Structural Adjustment Programmes] have conspired to undermine the social fabric of many developing countries, potentially promoting behaviours that place their citizens at increased risk for HIV infection: (1) declining sustainability of rural subsistence economy; (2) development of a transportation infrastructure; (3) migration and urbanization; and (4) reductions in spending on health and social services' (Lurie et al. 1995:541).

The international network of churches, and churches which have influence in countries where the IMF and World Bank find their funding, could well exercise that influence to modify these programmes. Countries could be encouraged to reduce spending on military and luxury commodities; long-distance truck drivers could have their work schedules changed to spend more time at home; large infrastructure projects could give way to smaller-scale, labour-intensive projects.

' . . . the kind of paternalistic "top-down" approach favoured by the IMF and World Bank must make way for a truly co-operative development policy in which the desires of developing country citizens can be heard' (Lurie et al. 1995:544).

In these and other ways the churches could bring pressure to bear to change some of the social circumstances which increase the risk of HIV epidemics.

'The urgent need at present is for the developed countries to donate significant resources to the developing world to facilitate education, condom distribution, the control of other STDs, the improvement of public health services and family planning initiatives.'

So says one medical report on AIDS in Africa (Garnett and Anderson 1993:21). The international church can play an important role in pressuring Western nations to take their responsibilities more seriously.

It is important that the church takes its social role very seriously. However much we may wish that individuals would change their behaviour to live in more responsible and caring ways, unless the social conditions in which they live are also changed, individual behaviour is likely to remain unaffected.

Slow and small beginnings are still beginnings

The kingdom of God grows slowly, said Jesus, from small beginnings like a plant which grows mixed with tall weeds. The enormity of the AIDS crisis appals us. What we can do seems so small and inadequate. But doing something small is better than doing nothing at all. And small plants do, in the end, grow into trees which give shade to the birds.

5

AIDS and Being Human

'What is man that thou art mindful of him, and the son of man that thou dost care for him?' (Psalm 8.4).

Why indeed should God be mindful of a human race that with AIDS has found yet another way to destroy itself, along with nuclear warfare, ecological destruction and all the other swords of Damocles that hang above us? AIDS could immediately be brought under control if humans would only live as our consciences tell us that God demands, in mutual faithfulness to one partner till death parts us.

Attempts to understand human nature as the second millennium draws to its close end up with confusing opposites. We are lonely individuals living in a closely bonded world community. We are foolish sinners who are capable of heroism and self sacrifice. We place our trust in technology, yet turn desperately to alternative spiritual therapies. We seek our destiny in the here-and-now, but are forced by the unfairness of life in this world to look for a life to come.

We are created to live as a family

Modern middle-class people live in their insulated suburban cocoons and isolate themselves from their immediate community. We barely know the family next door. Friends and extended family live far away, but motor cars and public transport make occasional visits possible, so we do not need contact with people living in our vicinity. The modern poor are often just as isolated from their immediate neighbours. They move from their rural villages with their networks of support into the crowded informal settlements fringing the towns where they hope to find work. In the competitive and crime-ridden worlds of these townships, doors must be securely barred at night and the cries of neighbours in trouble shut out.

Yet we instinctively feel ourselves to be part of one human family. The middle classes may live anonymously, knowing little of the needs of the family over the fence; but their television sets bring disturbing pictures of people from all parts of the world. We weep over pictures of abandoned children in Bosnia. Living in suburban isolation, we are part of a global village. The people in the new urban slums of Africa and India, especially the women, while they try to shut their doors and windows to the dangers outside, also begin to build new networks of self-help as they discover that mutual local support can give them more power to negotiate for their rights.

The Christian vision of humankind is that we are one family of God's children bonded with a common destiny, living in mutual interdependence, each individual loved by God as the shepherd loves each sheep in his flock, but each individual nevertheless finding his or her identity only as a member of a community. In the face of the disintegration of the family of mankind into tribes, languages, classes and nations, Christianity offers the vision of the church as the new family of mankind where race and class and gender no longer divide, where we are one body of differentiated but interdependent parts.

The truth, though, is that the church in reality is not often like that. Now, however, AIDS is forcing us back upon one another. Those who contract the virus in the townships return to the home villages to be cared for. Extended families come into their own once more to cope with orphans and widows. The virus reaches out and invades the insulation of middle-class privilege. Although fewer people in that class will contract the virus, they are not left untouched; and the economic and social well-being of us all is deeply affected. The pain of one becomes in some measure the pain of us all. We are thrust back into an older pattern of human relatedness, the pattern of the village and the larger family which Christianity has tried, but largely failed, to preserve.

But as AIDS bites deeper, those traditional networks also begin to collapse. People in the Third World will be forced to develop new networks of relationship beyond immediate kinsfolk and neighbours. The church will have a role to play in providing a basis for these new networks. Because the economic consequences of AIDS will be so devastating, people in the richer countries will have to find ways of sharing money and resources, not in a dictatorial or authoritarian way but in a genuine human partnership. The church already has a role to play in providing a framework for that international partnership. AIDS forces us back into being one human family.

We are both weak and strong

AIDS forces us to re-evaluate ourselves. Christianity has taught that human beings are made in the image of God, but also caught in original sin. We are destined for partnership with God, and yet there is a fatal flaw in our nature which prevents us from fulfilling our potential. In the last two centuries of the millennium humans have come to believe that they are masters of their own destiny. Better education, better housing, better technology were expected to eradicate social malfunctioning. Slums would be replaced by housing estates filled with contented families. Crime would diminish. Nations would live together in a united fellowship, and negotiation would replace war. Once people understood the social sciences, we believed, we would all behave rationally; and for those who did not, a small adjustment in their brain chemistry, through some mood-lifting drug, would put their attitude right.

But perversely those with better education and more social advantages act in unpredictable and self-destructive ways. Although everyone knows the dangers of drugs and alcohol, drug addiction and alcoholism are growing. The vision of a brave new world living under the banner of a United Nations with its ideals of international co-operation, world peace and human rights for all has dissolved like a mirage. East-West tensions after the Second World War, the wars in Vietnam, Cambodia or Laos, the endless disasters of Africa, the disintegration of Yugoslavia, the rise again of exclusive nationalisms and ethnicities, have destroyed our confidence that world peace can be attained.

AIDS is yet another sign that our human community is disintegrating. It reminds us of our lusts and selfishnesses; it is the consequence of a world where men use women and young girls for sexual gratification, where women and children are forced into prostitution. It is the consequence of economic exploitation. It is a symptom of that fatal flaw which we call original sin. Even when people know that casual sex leads to AIDS, they persist in risky behaviour. It appears that we are simply unable to control or direct our sexuality. For all our confidence in education and social restructuring, we are unable to change human behaviour or to alter the economic structures which keep two-thirds of the world in economic slavery.

G. B. Caird (1956), commenting on Paul's letter to the Romans, talks of four powers which hold us in their thrall. The powers are sin, flesh, law and the 'authorities'. We are unable to follow the dictates of our own conscience, says Paul. I can will what is right, but I cannot do it (Romans 7.18). I am in the grip of my lower nature, obeying the dictates of what Paul calls the flesh. Thus the law which God has given us itself becomes a tyrant, for it traps us into guilt and defiance against God. And the rulers of this world, spiritual and secular, put here by God to establish peace and righteousness, themselves become corrupt and oppressive.

AIDS reminds us that in important respects nothing has changed. We are often unable, corporately or individually, to do the things we should or to stop doing the things we should not. Not even the threat that our behaviour leads to our death makes a significant difference. We are under the domination of sin and death, and of social structures which we cannot understand or master. We are helpless and in need of a Saviour.

Paul is convinced that in Christ we have the Saviour who breaks that domination. Here we need to state our case carefully. There is no evidence that Christians have been less affected by AIDS than any other group, that Christians are more in control of their sexual desires, or that Christians have more clue than anyone else about how to transform the unjust economic structures that are such an important foundation for AIDS. We may have very good Christian theories about sex and economics, but we seem to be as unable as anyone else to live out those theories. Clergy, religious, ministers and sincere Christian laypersons are all amongst those who contract AIDS. How then can we claim that Christ has saved us?

Part of Paul's meaning, of course, is that we are saved from the 'wrath' of God. Our helplessness and sinfulness do not separate us from God, and physical death does not mean spiritual death; sinners are forgiven and justified in faith (Romans 5.1). That is an important message for a world with AIDS. Paul does seem, though, to have meant more than this. He seems to have thought that if we are in Christ we shall have put sin behind us.

'Thanks be to God, that you who were once slaves of sin have become obedient from the heart to the standard of teaching to which you were committed, and having been set free from sin have become the slaves of righteousness' (Romans 7.17–18).

We could say that those who contract AIDS because of their sexual behaviour are not true Christians, and that Paul's words remain true for true Christians. But I hope that earlier chapters have established that all of us share in the guilt of AIDS and are in part responsible for the pandemic. In so far as social injustice and prejudice, profit-taking and economic oppression, are as much part of the cause of AIDS as sexual promiscuity, there can be no finger pointing. In the sense that one way or another we all fall short of the mark (Romans 3.23), we are all, Christian or not, in the power, still, of sin.

But that is not the end of the story. AIDS also shows us that human beings are courageous and self-sacrificial. People with the virus who face their illness and death with courage and dignity point to an innate nobility within humans, Christian and not Christian. People who give so much of themselves, with sensitivity and insight – social workers, nuns, doctors, parents, lovers – point to an innate unselfishness in humans. We bear the mark of our creator. We see for ourselves that humans are indeed made in the image of God. There is something very wonderful about the human spirit, and also something perverse and uncontrollable. AIDS points us to the potential and to the disaster of the human condition. We are victims of our fallenness, and we are witnesses to our goodness. Individuals are often both of these things at the same time.

In this mixed condition we need one another. We have already commented that AIDS throws us back together in mutual co-dependence. Christians believe that though we are individuals beloved by God, we exist not just as individuals but as one people of God. AIDS reinforces this. We shall need to discover a renewed sense of community, and we shall also need to remember the importance of each individual. Jesus, we are told, was often surrounded by multitudes, over whom he sometimes wept, and to whom he often preached. But again and again he also noticed individual faces in the crowd: Zacchaeus hiding in the tree, the woman with the haemorrhage who touches his robe. Jesus lived out the prophetic belief that God cares for each individual. That is not always easy for those dealing with the AIDS epidemic. The numbers are so large, and keep growing, and the resources to cope are so small that individual needs can get lost in the crowd. That is why organizations like TASO in Uganda and elsewhere which provide counselling services for the individuals crowding the AIDS clinics are so important. It is also a significant ministry which Christians can offer. When experts and professionals are thin on the ground, we need to remember that people with AIDS and their families and dependents need someone just to talk to, someone who makes them know that they are noticed and cared for as individuals.

We are spiritual beings

AIDS recalls us from an over-spiritual pietism. Just as Jesus took the physical needs of people around him very seriously, feeding the hungry and healing sick bodies, the church in this time of AIDS is forced to help care for peoples' physical needs now. Yet AIDS reminds us that humans are not to be cared for on a physical level alone. We have placed our health in the hands of medical technologists who diagnose the faults in our bodies as a mechanic diagnoses the faults in a car engine, and by chemical or mechanical means, by medicine or surgery, seek to fix or to cut out the malfunctioning part. But we are spiritual beings as well as physical, psychosomatic unities of body and soul, and AIDS demands a holistic understanding of human nature. 'Is not life more than food, and the body more than clothing?', asks Jesus in Matthew's Gospel (Matthew 6.25).

While AIDS forces us to take present needs seriously and to minister to people in the reality of life here, it also raises for us even more acutely the question of our destiny beyond life on earth. We are reminded of our own mortality, that 'man that is born of woman hath but a short time to live and is full of trouble. He cometh up and is cut down like a flower' (Book of Common Prayer). Indeed, it is likely that AIDS has become a fashionable cause in the world of entertainment precisely because it turned upside down the view that life and youth will last for ever. Death had become the unmentionable. Suddenly, with AIDS, death became a constant reality for an age group who thought that they could postpone their mortality. We see once again the precariousness and preciousness of life. Like our forbears who had no option but to hope for heaven since their lives on earth were short and full of pain, our hopes are turned beyond this life. We ask again about the meaning of life and are not satisfied with purely worldly answers.

Psalm 8 answers its own question about what humanity is with the confident assertion 'Thou has made him little less than God and dost crown him with glory and honour' (Psalm 8.5), and the author of the letter to the Hebrews sees in Jesus the one who fulfils this confident vision, who shows us the glory of human nature triumphing over the paradox of suffering and death.

> *James is speaking at an HIV support group house church. 'I thank God for sending me AIDS', he says. 'I was never so close to my parents before I was tested positive and had to tell them I was gay. Now all that dishonesty is behind me, and I'm close to my father. I'm closer to God too. AIDS has brought me to God. I try to testify to my parents how important God is for me, but I don't think they listen much. But still I love them and they love me and they have even come to love Herb (his partner). So I'm a deeply happy man. I never was before.'*

We are dying

AIDS faces us with death. It may also face us with resurrection. Ron Russell-Coons, a Christian pastor, himself sick with AIDS, took as his text for a sermon about AIDS Paul's words from II Corinthians:

'Though outwardly we are wasting away, yet inwardly we are being renewed day by day. Our light and momentary troubles are

achieving for us an eternal glory that far outweighs them all'
(II Corinthians 4.16–17, Russell-Coons in Russell 1990:40).

Since it is made clear in a later chapter in the book that at the time of
the sermon Russell-Coons was seriously ill with AIDS, it is hard to
know how he can regard his troubles as 'light and momentary'. Yet
he is not alone in this conviction. Kevin Kelly quotes people with
AIDS who addressed a conference in Indonesia:

> 'On their own admission, the quality of their lives has deepened
> enormously. Wimol actually said to me, "AIDS is my gift", and
> Thaksin told the assembled theologians at our meeting, "To
> compare my life before HIV/AIDS and my life today is like
> comparing night and day"' (Kelly 1995:598).

How are we to take this? Does it show that if we have faith in Jesus,
and faith in the resurrection, then we can face death without fear,
because we know we are going to a better place? That is partly what
James meant. But not everyone with AIDS becomes a born-again
Christian, though some do, and not everyone with AIDS believes in
heaven. Russell-Coons is clearly not just talking about life after
physical death. He is saying, as Paul was saying, that he had found
new life, in the face of death, *before* death. The sheer courage of some
people with AIDS is a reminder to us that new life in the face of
death is possible.

People who are told they are HIV positive are, in effect, being
given notice of death. They face death themselves; and they face us
with the fact that we too face death, though for many of us the
prospect may not be so immediate. Apart from rare exceptions, there
is no hope for cure for HIV positive people; but then there is no cure
for the mortality of any of us. Although we try not to believe it, we are
all dying.

Death is not a subject high on our theological or pastoral agendas.
Where once upon a time preachers urging us to repentance would
warn us that we might die before the sun rose, and children were
taught to pray 'if I die before I wake I pray the Lord my soul to take',
now we talk about 'realized eschatology', about life in the
here-and-now rather than pie in the sky when you die. Modern
theologians are often skittish on the topic of personal resurrection.

Our emphasis is on making the most of the present. AIDS raises questions about that. AIDS forces us to realize that we all live in the face of death. We are faced with the question of what to believe about the life to come.

Death and hope

But dealing with AIDS is not only a matter of looking forward to peace with God when the suffering is over. Since someone who is HIV positive may still have ten years or more of productivity before the sickness comes – and because those of us who are not HIV positive may also have many years of health left – the challenge before us is to live joyfully and purposefully in the present moment even though we are dying. Eschatological living is not just about expectations of life after death, though this is important and we shall discuss it here in due course. Eschatological living is about living with hope now, living to the fullest degree that we are able in the present, even though we know that the present is coming to an end. The paradox is very difficult. We are all slowly dying; people with AIDS are mostly dying soon. We have no hope of escape. Yet in that dying we search for life.

> 'The spectre of AIDS catapults us into an accelerated spiritual growth – or toward early death – and it all depends on the model of eschatological living we choose to follow' (Cherry and Mitulski 1988:86).

From a pastoral point of view this is very important. Mother Teresa is quoted as saying:

> 'We want to create hope for the person with AIDS and acceptance in the hearts of the people. We must give hope, always hope, and remove the bitterness that harms them when they are avoided by everyone' (*Prayers and Reflections on AIDS*).

Without hope and purpose, the years between learning one is HIV positive and the coming of death would be unbearable. Viktor Frankl, examining how to help people survive the Nazi concentration camps, found that some people, albeit a few, were able to develop a power of defiance and resistance towards their terrible and hopeless situation. Partly it had to do with having some useful task. 'The mental vacuum of these people had to be fended off' (Frankl 1973:101). Indeed, the extraordinary way in which he was able, while a prisoner himself, to observe and learn from his situation, presumably had to do with his seeing this as a scientific task for which he was uniquely equipped.

But Frankl believed that mostly it had to do with whether or not a person possessed faith that his or her life had *meaning* (Frankl 1973:102). This meaning had to do with whether or not one mattered to somebody, made a difference to somebody's life. This is part of what Frankl means by his concept of 'logotherapy'. What drives people on is a sense that life must have some point to it. Frankl found that it did not matter if there was very little prospect of living long enough to accomplish the meaningful task or role, because in every case the person was aware of someone 'present' to them, even if that person had already died, someone to whom they mattered and who believed in them. For some people this person would be God; for others, a friend or family member.

Living with hope means believing that there is something we can do with our lives. Without that belief, we shrivel and die before our time (Steinke 1992:533). HIV positive people and those already ill with AIDS need to be enabled to find this kind of purpose, perhaps in being reconciled with family, perhaps in service to friends and community.

> *Bernard gave up his job in a cosmetic salon when he heard he was HIV positive. He wanted to use the time left to him in some constructive way to offer support to others with AIDS. He now serves as a lay visitor on a hospital chaplaincy team. He co-ordinates the local work of the National Episcopal AIDS Coalition.*

Many people with AIDS do in fact become involved in community service like Bernard, or with the family, like James featured at the start of this chapter. In this way they have found hope for the present moment.

This search for hope is not a search for a miracle cure which will prevent death. This would not be real hope, but rather a clinging to pretence. Russell-Coons in his sermon says that 'Healing is different from a cure' (Russell 1990:41). Healing is learning to live in hope and joy amidst death, to enter into the paradox, to embrace the chaos. It is because some people with AIDS have been able to find this hope that they become pioneers, experts on death and dying, for the rest of us who may be more slowly, but just as certainly, moving towards death (Countryman 1987:130).

Annette Jones expresses this in an unfortunate way, but we know what she means. People with AIDS, she says, are the 'living dead' among us, touched already with the awe-filledness of death, who serve as a reminder to each of us that every living thing will die (Jones 1989:214). We cannot be saved from dying. We can be helped to live in the face of death.

'We should be aware that we are being ministered to as we grow with these sufferers, and through them, in our Christian understanding of death and deathlessness' (Kirkpatrick 1988:5).

Because AIDS faces us with death, it faces us with ultimate spiritual questions. Is there a God? Is there a purpose to life other than one we defiantly place upon it in the face of existential absurdity? Is there any basis outside ourselves for hope? Is there meaning beneath the chaos? These questions are not new. Perhaps the apparent randomness and absurdity of life with AIDS drives us towards belief in a God who will ultimately make sense of it all. John Hick rejects the views of Cupitt and those like him who say that the only meaning in life is the meaning we impose upon it. Hick says that this is too stark, too pessimistic, to be helpful (Hick 1993:13). Many people with AIDS would agree, but not all. Discovering hope does not necessarily mean accepting Christian faith. People with AIDS do not all find the same answers.

Yet in that search for answers they need support. People with AIDS may be prophets to the church of the possibility of life before death, but it is hard for them to maintain that hope on their own. Often they have been faced with great loss, not only of health but of employment, security, money, even house and home. Family members will often have been badly hurt by the HIV diagnosis. Marital infidelity, homosexuality, things we have been able to keep hidden from outsiders, come out into the open. Often, therefore, the person with AIDS is filled with guilt at the hurt that has been caused. The person has lost self-esteem. He or she may be faced with bitter criticism from others and from themselves. They may stand quite alone. We can only have hope if we rediscover some sense of personal worth.

> *'We went together to tell his Mum and Dad that he had HIV, but first, the most difficult, to say that he is homosexual. Then we found ourselves propelled to the door ... ejected by the torrent of disgust and vindictiveness. Then we were backing down the neat, patterned tile path. His mother screaming, "The sooner you are dead the better," and his father, red-faced and eyes bulging, slammed the door shut on us.*
>
> *In the shocking silence I hear for the first time his urgent, despairing pleading which I realize he has been repeating throughout. "But I need you, I'm dying, I love you, I'm afraid."'* (Cara Trust 1995:111).

As we face death, we also face the whole meaning of life. Death raises questions for us about the purpose and value of our life up to that point, as well as questions about what is to follow. As each of us faces into lost opportunities that will not come again, relationships that we have harmed and now wish to restore, things that we regret that we now repent of, as well as sadness and bitterness about hopes which remain unfulfilled and unable to be fulfilled, we need caring, forgiveness, and restoration of a sense of self-worth.

People who are HIV positive may for understandable reasons become clinically depressed. A South African study suggests that depression itself may further shorten their life.

> ' . . . depression is the most important psychological variable that influences the longevity of those who are HIV positive, whether directly or indirectly. Learned helplessness also plays an important role in the etiology of depression' (*CSD Bulletin*, June 1995:17).

It is here that the role of the church is important. Those who offer care for the physical symptoms of AIDS, the hospitals and health services, may not be able to respond to the spiritual and existential questions which all of this raises. It is hard when you have lost so much to find renewed hope, and some people with AIDS are never able to do so. The church needs to inculcate the idea that we are all in this together and will support one another through the loss. People with AIDS need the community of faith, and if the church fails them – as often it will because the experience is so foreign and so frightening for those of us who have been protected from our own mortality – then they will and do turn elsewhere for a community to help them in their struggle to find and maintain hope. People with AIDS often need a faith community where they can search for a path to renewed life and be supported in that search.

Death and dogmatism

But precisely because they have so much to teach us about authentic faith and hope, the church also needs the people with AIDS. We are all dying. We need to support one another through the valley of death. Here is the difficulty. For many Christians, new hope is pinned exclusively to literal belief in the resurrection of Jesus ('If Christ has not been raised, our faith is vain': I Corinthians 15.14). Yet our support for persons with AIDS needs to be unconditional. People with AIDS need to make genuinely free, independent decisions, and choose a path for themselves even if that path may deviate from orthodoxy. We have to foster integrity, independence and self-acceptance as a basis for the new hope, or the hope will be ill-founded and will crumble. This is not easy for a church which is sure it has the answers and which is uncomfortable with, if not outrightly hostile to, answers which differ from its own. Yet until we too face the same issues that people with AIDS do, we have no right to say that our answers are the end of the matter.

'Most clergy have missed the complexity and nuances of AIDS and its diverse sufferers. AIDS is not only about dying, it is about living with an often brutal disease that may span many years of an individual's life. AIDS is about the "worried well" and the HIV-antibody positive. AIDS is about healing and support for people continuing to work and play as they live with AIDS . . . AIDS can be about disfigurement and dementia, about hunger and home-lessness, about depression and despair' (Doubleday and Ports 1992:282).

This means that our support for people with AIDS cannot be conditional upon their holding doctrines about risen bodies or everlasting souls which they do not in all honesty believe, nor may we force these or any doctrines upon them. Our ministry is not pointless if people with AIDS do not come to believe in the resurrection of the body and the life of the world to come.

However we may interpret resurrection, there can be no resurrection without death. Belief in resurrection should not make us underestimate the depths that people with AIDS have to plumb first. Russell-Coons may proclaim that compared with the weight of glory his troubles are 'light and momentary', but one can only make that claim after entering into and overcoming the bitterness and sadness which it is clear he has experienced. If we are to find new life before our body dies, then we must enter death before our body dies. We must experience the death of bitterness, of anger, of escapism, of trust in false saviours and false hopes.

Elisabeth Kübler-Ross has suggested in her well-known book the stages through which a person facing death must pass, although often in a muddled and overlapping way. We deny the approaching death with shock, and shut it out of our mind. We become angry, often at inappropriate people, and hit out in our rage at anyone nearby. We try to bargain with God or with fate: 'If only you will let me live,' we say, 'I will obey you for evermore.' We become depressed, withdrawn and quiet. But in the end we come not just to accept the death with resignation but to welcome it (Kübler-Ross 1970). For Kübler-Ross the fact that people facing death eventually come to accept it is a pointer to the hope for a life to come.

A person with AIDS must go through these stages. We must accept death before we accept resurrection. But so must the church; for what must also die are our set patterns of thought, our dogmatic beliefs in the face of inexorable evidence that they are false.

> '[AIDS] summons the institutional church to come forth from its sepulchre and to discover the content rather than the form of the resurrection in relation to life and death' (Pattison in Woodward 1990:12).

To believe in resurrection is to be willing in faith to explore the implications of how we are called to respond to AIDS. AIDS confronts us with new moral dilemmas and the need to respond to these with love. Resurrection means living in the discomfort of 'the dialectic of the Christian narrative and the narrative of HIV/AIDS in mutual abrasion and re-interpretation' (Dyson 1994:174). Facing the death of the world that we know, the death of our prejudices and preconceptions, we all go through just the same stages of denial, anger, bargaining and depression. Only then can we begin to discover new points of view.

By upsetting the way we perceive the world, AIDS may in fact enable new visions to be born in us. AIDS punctures the illusions of our denial phase and forces us onwards, at least into angry resistance against change, eventually perhaps into acceptance of that change.

'I've been forced to admit that forces other than rational and physical ones appear to be operative in my life. I've come to believe that it's not only permissible for me to admit that my sense of order has been arbitrary, it's necessary for me to admit that if I'm to be truthful' (Sabatino 1992:98).

Then and then only, having admitted and faced the truth, can we begin to find renewed faith.

'My final ability to admit my lack of control opened me to the possibility of prayer, of receiving spiritual energy and strength' (Sabatino 1992:98).

'[Praying] represented to me an admission of the limits of both my rational and physical dimensions. I was totally helpless. I had to admit my lack of control. For the first time in my adult life I admitted that I was a creature and that there must indeed be a God, someone who created life' (Sabatino 1992:97).

The writer, through his experience of AIDS, has obviously found his way into religious faith. While it would be both insensitive and immoral to use AIDS or any tragedy as a lever for conversion, it is true that AIDS or other misfortune may bring us to the point where we can no longer go on as we did before. We look beyond ourselves and our own inadequate resources.

It is important that those whose journey does lead them to search for help and strength from God should receive sensitive guidance. Yet how can those of us who are not HIV positive give guidance to one whose situation is so much more desperate than our own?

There are two responses to that question. One is that we need to recognize that in many cases people with AIDS are best ministered to by others with AIDS; that people with AIDS can and do form communities of self-support. In this way they may find precisely the hope and purpose which Victor Frankl said was necessary. But the other response is that all of us, in one way or another, face suffering, abandonment, despair and death. All of us are deeply vulnerable. If we wish to be of help to others, we need to have examined our responses to our own circumstances, and ask ourselves whether we have truly faced our own despair, truly accepted our own pain, and confessed our weakness and vulnerability. Perhaps we, too, are still in stages of denial, anger or bargaining. To be of service to people with AIDS, people in the church need to enter into their own pain and to die in Christ. 'Do you not know that all of us who have been baptized into Christ Jesus were baptized into his death?' (Romans 6.3).

Inevitably our motives are always mixed. Those of us who seek to help and to minister may do so because we derive a sense of power and authority in the relationship. We may be seeking a way of giving legitimate expression to our own hidden sexuality. We may be looking for a substitute for love and family. We may do it because we derive a sense of worth and purpose from helping others. There is nothing wrong with this, as long as we are aware of and honest about our own needs as far as we can be. But this kind of honesty requires humility. We surrender any sense of superiority over those whom we seek to help. We confess our own weakness and fallenness. This is painful, and often we prefer to hold on to our illusions of selflessness. We prefer to avoid the death of self. Unless we accept and endure the pain, and look squarely into our own needs in the relationship, the helping relationship becomes skewed and manipulative, harmful to both the helper and the one to whom help is offered. In ministry there is ultimately no strong partner and weak partner, no wise and foolish, though at appropriate times in the relationship one or other partner may be dominant. We are the blind leading the blind, the lame supporting the lame. There must be a death to puffed up illusions about our own strength. This death is one which individuals must pass through, but is also one which the church as a corporate entity needs to endure. On the whole this is what is still seriously lacking in the response of the corporate church to AIDS. Too often the response is a rather pompous one which dispenses advice and warnings to those enmeshed in the evils of foolish sex and drugs. As long as the church continues to see itself as a body which is free of sexual weakness, which is beyond reproach, which has all the wisdom and all the answers, which has no need to listen but need only give authoritative advice, it can offer little useful contribution to the struggle against AIDS.

But if we come as people who are also lost, guilty and weak, then of course it is appropriate for us to share with people with AIDS our own convictions about God, about the saving love of Jesus, about the underlying power of the Holy Spirit – and about our hope for life beyond the grave. In fact, unless we have something to offer from our own experience, corporate and personal, of these things, the church has no particular contribution to make that any other secular agency does not already offer.

Many modern theologians do not believe literally in a physical resurrection. Some do not believe in a personal life after death at all. The accumulated effect of biblical criticism, modern sceptical rationalism, and living in a Western world of agnosticism about that which cannot be encompassed within the methodology of the natural sciences has made it difficult to believe in the same way as Christians of earlier generations.

'There seems to be no way of rescuing a convincing account of "objective resurrection" from this heterogeneity of improbably historical, dogmatic and speculative interpretation in order to give confidence about living positively in the vulnerable movements of contingent nature and history' (Dyson 1994:166).

It is interesting that the author of this passage is writing about resurrection in the context of the AIDS crisis. Even though he writes about AIDS, he believes that however badly we may want to believe in what he calls 'objective resurrection', we cannot avoid the reality that there is, in his opinion, little reliable ground for doing so. For Dyson, the offer of resurrection to those with AIDS is the offer of an existential resurrection from falsehood, alienation or guilt.

But liberal theologians are challenged by the AIDS crisis to think again. Whatever may be said about helping people live positively in the years left to them, and however skilfully we redefine resurrection to mean some kind of present existential reality, the fact is that AIDS mostly cuts people off in the prime of their lives, often unfairly, often with little chance to develop personal character beyond youthful brashness and self-centredness. AIDS raises again for us the moral problem of premature death.

Belief in life after death became more general in early Judaism after the Maccabean wars, when young Jewish men died in the prime of their lives defending their faith. Justice seemed to demand that there was still a life to come, where life could be brought to fulfilment and completion. AIDS forces exactly this same injustice upon our consciousness. In fact, says Hans Küng, we all hope for another life to come, be it a secular utopia or a Christian heaven, because not to hope in something better than present injustice and unfairness and pain would be to surrender to despair.

It may not be as difficult now to believe in life after death as it once was, partly because of the collapse of scientific positivism, but even more because of the work of people like Raymond Moody and Eckhardt Wiesenhutter in exploring the experiences of those who come very near death and which suggest the possibility of a reality beyond the grave. But, since their subjects did not actually die, nothing, says Küng, is really proved beyond saying that the possibility of life after death remains at least an open possibility, and that dying may not be as painful as we fear, though even that is not certain (Küng 1984:37).

Küng, however, does believe in a resurrection, not so much on the basis of the Gospel records, which Küng concedes are problematical in their inconsistencies, but on the basis of Paul's testimony, for example in I Corinthians 15. The essential meaning of the resurrection does not depend on stories about an empty tomb. The essential meaning is that Jesus did not remain dead but is alive, and was experienced as alive by the first apostles. This fact, he says, is both a challenge and a hope to us (Küng 1984:138).

Even Paul's evidence, however, cannot be taken as proof. There are considerable philosophical problems with the concept of a resurrection or continuing life after death.

'We find ourselves baffled . . . by a set of conceptual issues that are demanding in the extreme' (Abraham 1985:202).

What can be asserted is that Paul, like other first-generation Christians, certainly believed that Jesus was still alive, and that belief was a centrepoint to their lives. At this distance of history there can be no question of proving more than that. Belief in resurrection is not inconsistent with near-death experiences; Küng has tried to show that belief in resurrection is not illogical or devoid of meaning. But such a belief is a matter of faith, not proof.

What Küng does is show us what sort of difference belief in resurrection makes to our view of life. If Paul's testimony is true, then God is able to call non being into being, death into life. Even in death, God is able to bring about something more, something new; death is not an end, for there is no end in God (Küng 1984:147). Death is an enemy which can be, and has been, overcome; not just physical death, but death in all its forms. Our view on life and death is radically changed. Without belief in resurrection, 'man must discover his total solitude, his fundamental isolation' (Küng 1984:281).

Küng is anxious to make clear that belief in resurrection is not only belief in life after death but also changes the way that we live now. We hope that life will be brought to fulfilment, that injustice will be overcome, that those who are cast down will be vindicated (Küng 1984:150). The hope of resurrection is thus a critique of a society in which the lords of death still reign. AIDS is one of the lords of death. Faith in resurrection means faith that even AIDS can be overcome and can be turned into an opportunity of triumph.

'In the fight against AIDS the choice is clear: giving in to old habits of fear and resistance, or accepting the challenge to turn these bleakest of circumstances into a triumph' (Grover 1989:259).

Resurrection, says Hans Küng, means that 'one day I shall be fully understood, fully accepted, able to be myself without fear' (Küng 1984:287). How desperately many homosexual men long for that time of full acceptance!

'A meaning is given to the inexorable evolution of the cosmos, only then will the conflicts and sufferings of nature be overcome and its longings fulfilled' (Küng 1984:288).

How desperately many people living with AIDS and all its attendant agonies, physical and emotional, long for that sense of meaning and purpose in the face of death! AIDS forces us to think again about the fact that it is difficult to make sense of the concept of living meaningfully without belief in resurrection.

'Then I saw a new heaven and a new earth . . . and I heard a loud voice from the throne saying, 'Behold, the dwelling of God is with men. He will dwell with them and they shall be his people, and God himself shall be with them; he will wipe away every tear from their eyes, and death shall be no more, neither shall there be mourning nor crying nor pain any more, for the former things have passed away' (Revelation 21.1–4).

The Ugandan Catholic bishops have said that the church's duty in a time of AIDS is to comfort the dying and the bereaved with the hope of life after death. This would certainly be a distinctive Christian contribution to AIDS ministry. We have to learn to counsel people to prepare for death. Hope of resurrection helps us to approach death with dignity, rather than clinging to life fearfully. Yet while Küng confidently places his faith in life after death, others say we must bravely accept that the 'consolation' of resurrection must be abandoned, even in the face of AIDS.

'The acute problem about resurrection as a dogmatic/biblical theme is how we deal with the theological sediment that accumulates in and around it through the centuries and in succeeding cultural milieux. It seems clear . . . that we must envisage ways which open up contemporary and often bitter experience which offers little or none of the "consolation" of resurrection that we have been led to believe is our portion and privilege' (Dyson 1994:174).

At the very least we are called to reopen the question of the meaning of resurrection for serious attention.

Even belief in a literal resurrection does not mean there is no pain in death. There is no 'cheap consolation' to be found (Küng 1984:285). We cannot take refuge in false religion which avoids the pain. That, says Küng, is why Jesus died.

'There is no depth of human existence, no guilt, no hardship, fear of death or forsakenness, that is not encompassed by a God who is always ahead of man, even in death' (Küng 1984:215).

We cannot claim aggressively that our own convictions are necessarily true and impose them upon others – whether those convictions are towards belief or towards non-belief in literal personal resurrection. What we can do is to face the pain and the chaos, look together at historical resources which the church has to offer, and support one another in responding in faith, whatever that may mean for different individuals. Perhaps, then, even for those who cannot believe in life after death, Küng is not right about being left in solitude and isolation; for it is up to us to share in their pain and stand with them in their struggle. Being with those dying of AIDS until the end is part of our calling in Christ.

6

AIDS and Women

An article in *The Tablet* suggests that AIDS makes us rethink three aspects of our theology.

> 'The pandemic of AIDS challenges us to face up to our need for a triple conversion. We must promote economic justice for all; we must throw off whatever contradicts the full and equal dignity of women and men; and we must formulate a more satisfactory person-respecting sexual ethic' (Kelly 1995:599).

We have discussed the first and last of these challenges already. In considering the second challenge, that of the full and equal dignity of women, it becomes clear that economic justice and a healthy sexual ethic is inextricably bound up with the freedom and dignity of women. I have suggested that economic injustice and unsatisfactory sexual ethics both help create conditions in which AIDS spreads. They also both contribute to the oppression of women, which in turn also contributes to the AIDS pandemic.

Churches have been ambivalent about the role of women. The question of the ordination of women still rankles. It may seem to stretch a point to say that those who oppose the ordination of women are contributing to the spread of AIDS, and indeed Kelly himself is not exactly saying this. What he does say is

> 'Maybe the Catholic church is not giving the priority it should to promoting the full and equal dignity of women and to combatting whatever violates this in the attitudes, structures and behaviour found in society and especially in the church itself' (Kelly 1995:599).

Whatever reasons churches may have for refusing to ordain women to the priesthood, the impression we give is that women are unfitted for spiritual leadership. Where we fail to promote the dignity of women, we make the spread of AIDS more likely. It is not only Catholics and Orthodox who restrict the authority of women. The ministry and institutional control of virtually all churches is still predominantly male. Many Christians, on the basis of Pauline teaching in Colossians 3.18 or Ephesians 5.22, believe that the head of the family, including the extended church family, must be the man and that wives must be subject to their husbands. It is true that the passages referred to, as well as urging women to obey, insist that men must love their wives as Christ loved the church. Nevertheless, the model upheld is that the ideal role of women is to be supportive and obedient. Although men are to protect and care for women, they do so under conditions which they determine. Men bear the responsibility of decision making, and lay down the grounds of the relationship, just as Christ lays down the grounds of the church's relationship with him.

Thus by its teaching and by its practice the church often endorses a world view in which men make the decisions and women live under them. The irony of an entirely male hierarchy – the College of Bishops – whose views are expressed by a male Pope, deciding on issues such as contraception and abortion which only affect them indirectly but are deeply important to women, has often been noted.

Where the power of women is already circumscribed by tradition and culture, Christianity often imposes a double burden. Bette Ekeya, a Kenyan woman theologian, speaks about the Itseso people, but what she says would also apply in many other parts of Africa. In their traditional culture, she says, the role of a woman was limited to domestic responsibilities. Her father decided whom she should marry, and her destiny after marriage was determined by her husband. But within the tradition she did have protection against maltreatment or desertion. She did have status and power, even religious power, on issues to do with domestic responsibilities like the care and protection of children. There were certain rituals that she would perform. She also had access to a religious authority in the person of the diviner, often a woman, who within her own interpretative system had psychological insight into the strains of family life from a woman's perspective. Thus in traditional life, though her role was circumscribed, a woman had some power and some sympathetic support.

With the coming of Christianity, the authority of the husband was further legitimated, but the protection of the traditional structures and the support of the diviner was removed as being pagan.

'Besides the cultural norms and taboos that bound her and held her in subjection, two other oppressive elements have been added to her world: the loaded interpretation of certain biblical passages, and the predominantly male church ministries and institutions' (Ekeya in King 1994:139).

All of this has considerable significance in creating a number of factors which affect the spread of AIDS and which increase the suffering experienced by women because of AIDS. In Europe and North America, the number of women who are HIV positive has risen, but the majority of those sick with AIDS are still men. By contrast, women in Third World countries in many ways endure the major impact of AIDS. More women than men get AIDS. They contract the virus younger than men. Those who do not have the virus must care for relatives who are ill with AIDS, and when the sick die, they must care for and support those left behind.

Because they have little control in their own lives or in their sexual relationships, they find it more difficult to protect themselves from AIDS. They are somewhat more likely to contract the virus in heterosexual sex than men because the skin lining the vagina tears more easily than that of the penis, especially if the man is inconsiderate or especially around the time of menstruation, when the uterine lining is exposed (Spohn 1988:96, also *New York Times*, 1 November 1994). In Africa, women often use herbal remedies to dry the vagina, thus increasing the risk of tears and HIV infection. Adolescent girls whose sexual parts are not fully mature and who are sexually inexperienced are also at particular risk. They are more likely to suffer vaginal tearing, and because they are sexually inexperienced they become a target for men who fear that older and experienced women are more likely to be HIV positive. Thus amongst younger people there are often more women than men who are affected. In South Africa 61% of people with AIDS between twenty and twenty-four years of age are women (*Epidemiological Comments* 1994:221).

Women are not only more vulnerable towards contracting the virus. Even if they remain uninfected, the consequences of the virus in their family are more serious for them. Since in most cultures men are the primary breadwinners, able to get jobs more easily and at a better rate of pay than women, women are dependent upon men for support, especially if they have chlidren. If a wife dies, the husband still has his job, and in traditional societies his mother will usually take the children. If her husband dies, a wife is in a worse situation than a man who loses his wife, since she will find it difficult to maintain herself and her children. The death of a breadwinner hits everybody hard, but women most especially, since often the only other way of earning money for food is prostitution.

Prostitution is a major factor in the spread of AIDS. Therefore prostitutes are often blamed for the illness, as if it is all their fault and the men who use them have no moral responsibility. An American television talk-show host Geraldo, in his television programme on American networks on 27 January 1995, interviewed a number of self-confessed prostitutes. It was clear that the assumptions behind his questioning were that most prostitutes have AIDS, are indifferent to the fact that they spread AIDS, and are thus a major health risk to society. Geraldo was reflecting a common attitude to prostitutes. They are seen as 'fallen women', greedy, drug-crazed, morally weak, who are responsible for the collapse of both public morality and community health. They are seen as a danger to the community. In fact, as women's rights groups point out, a street-wise prostitute who routinely uses condoms is at less risk for contracting the virus than a woman who has unprotected sex with her HIV positive husband or long-term partner (Pearlberg 1991:37). Prostitutes are not necessarily as much of a health risk to the community as the men who use them and go from woman to woman without using condoms.

But this is not how it is perceived. In church tradition it is Eve who initiates the disobedience to God and Eve who is in league with the tempter. Adam is only the victim of his wife's bad influence. In the same way, in the world today women are commonly seen as the ones who tempt men into evil sexual ways. It is believed that men cannot be blamed for falling for women – it is how men are made; whereas women, on the other hand, exploit this built-in male weakness and set out to seduce men for their own selfish ends. Men believe themselves to be the helpless victims of women's wiles. Brad Weiss reports how amongst the Haya people in North West Tanzania, women are blamed for the spread of AIDS. The men say that young women are greedy for new clothes; that the women turn to prostitution as an easy way to get money for the desired clothes. The money they receive as prostitutes makes them disregard the authority of their fathers or their boyfriends who would otherwise keep them under control (Weiss 1993:19ff.).

The reality, as Weiss points out, has nothing to do with clothes. Women in the Kagera district, as in many places in Africa, do not normally inherit land from their husband, nor can they pass on bequeathed land to their own children. They have no rights of inheritance unless they invoke Western law – that is, unless their husband wills the land to them. Otherwise the land passes on to a male relative. Therefore the only way they can get access to land on which to be buried themselves, and pass land on to their children, is to buy a piece of land; and since there is no industry in Kagera, the only way to earn the necessary money is through the sex trade. It is not greed for clothes but economic necessity that drives them to prostitution.

Prostitutes are the symptoms of the sin of all of us,

' . . . the victims of the sinful men who abuse them and of the widespread sinful attitude that regards women as inferior to men . . . They are also victims of the structural sin of an economic system which has destroyed the livelihood of the farming communities from which these women came' (Kelly 1995:597).

Migration trends towards urbanization have profound implications for the status of women. Male migrant workers leave sexual partners in the countryside, to whom they have at least some degree of responsibility, and take multiple casual partners in the city to whom they have none. The women remaining in the rural areas are dependent on the men to provide them with support, so are in no position to negotiate for safe sex when their husbands return on occasional visits.

Because of poverty, and because prostitution is the only way to earn money when agriculture has collapsed, families in many parts of the world send their daughters away from the village into the towns, often even into neighbouring countries, to serve as prostitutes and thus rescue the family from their poverty.

'Faced with a declining rural economy and a paucity of jobs for women in urban centres, 1 million Thai women have gravitated to the sex industry . . . Large scale migration of commercial sex workers from poorer to richer countries is also common and may spread HIV infection. Approximately 10,000 Thai commercial sex workers work in Japan, while women from Laos, Myanmar and southern China engage in commercial sex work in Thailand' (Lurie et al. 1995:543).

For economic reasons, developing countries hope to promote tourism. Because of the tourist trade in countries like Thailand or Kenya, and because men prefer young prostitutes who, they think, are less likely to carry the AIDS virus, there is great demand for young girls. So the demand for prostitutes grows. In parts of Africa, young girls will pay their school fees or get free transport to school by giving sexual favours to comparatively rich 'sugar daddies'. All of these girls are extremely likely to become HIV positive. They too are the victims of poverty.

Yet still the myth persists that it is all the girls' fault. The assumption is that men need sex because of their nature, and that they cannot be blamed for that. Therefore women must provide for that need. Thus women, especially girls and young women, are forced into prostitution, or persuaded and pressured by older men into providing sexual favours. They are exploited and victimized, but when the sexual activity leads to illness, then they are seen as the ones who are responsible. Promiscuity, it is believed, is all the fault of loose women who take advantage of a man's natural need for sex and tempt or seduce him. Sexually transmitted diseases are therefore seen to be the fault of unclean women.

The church in its own way has encouraged this way of thinking. Most women in Christian hagiography are either virgins or martyrs. Books of lives of the saints are full of stories of women whose families wish them to marry but who resist, eventually to enter a convent. If a virtuous woman marries, she has sexual intercourse with her husband since it is her duty to meet his needs, but she does not have sexual desires or needs herself. A married woman must obey her husband even if he is cruel, since by such obedience she may eventually convert him.

Yayon Matsui, a Japanese woman theologian, suggests that there are three factors which especially contribute towards the violence which women experience in Third World countries. They are also major factors in the spread of AIDS. These factors are development policies, militarism and culture (in King 1994).

The development policies imposed by the International Monetary Fund and the World Bank on poor countries, she suggests, create circumstances of extreme poverty. Most Third World countries have only two things to offer in any quantity on the world market: raw materials and cheap unskilled labour. These countries are therefore at the mercy of richer countries who can often depress the price of raw products merely by changing fashion, and which keep labour prices low in order to be competitive. Usually a condition of receiving international loans is that the country concerned allows the world market to set the price of seed, food and wages. Subsidies to help subsistence farmers are discouraged. Thus the flight to the cities continues, women and children are forced into very low wages if they are able to earn at all, and prostitution flourishes. The rapid urbanization of much of the Third World also contributes significantly to the breakdown of family structures and the rise of casual sex.

The wars which have been endemic in parts of Africa, the Middle East and Asia have created large numbers of soldiers; thus again a sex trade to service the soldiers grows and flourishes. The use by the United States military of countries like the Philippines for rest and recreation means large numbers of prostitutes there. Prostitution not only spreads AIDS but keeps women in continued subjection, since prostitutes have no rights over their customers.

Our theology must be one which, unfashionably, takes issue with the sacredness of stock market trends. It must emphasize the duty that richer countries have to share wealth and resources with poor countries. Our theology must also be one which seeks to promote peace rather than war, one which deglamourizes war. In short, our theology ought to be one which emphasizes all the things that the United Nations is meant to bring about and is unable to achieve. On the whole the modern church probably has quite a good record in these matters. The church of today is much less likely to legitimate capitalism and militaristic nationalism, though since we are imperfect our record will not be unblemished (for example, the Anglican bishops in Rwanda were widely, if as yet unprovenly, believed to have supported the genocidal regime of the Hutus; the Serbian Orthodox church has been a major factor in encouraging Serbian militancy).

But, says Matsui, the traditional culture of many Third World societies also contributes towards keeping women in subservience. On the matter of culture the church record is not so good. Guilty feelings about Western arrogance make it difficult for the modern church to criticize traditional African and Asian culture. Yet there are elements in Third World culture which encourage the spread of AIDS and which prevent women from taking any constructive role in combatting AIDS. The custom of polygamy is one. Where a man has several wives, should any one of the group become HIV positive the whole group is likely to contract the virus. Yet merely condemning polygamy is unlikely to be effective, since polygamists are not Christians anyway. The church needs to be able to work with polygamy, to keep an open mind about some of the possible social benefits of polygamy, in order to focus on the one factor essential for AIDS prevention, which is that the polygamous family needs to be faithful to each other.

The traditional custom whereby a brother of a dead man takes responsibility for the widow by making her his wife has become a particularly dangerous custom in a time of AIDS when the dead man possibly died of AIDS. What is needed is the promotion of the idea that a woman has the right to own property in her own right, and thus to inherit her husband's land and possessions.

But in truth polygamy and Levirate marriage are only very small factors in the spread of AIDS. What is really needed is a new sexual ethic in which people have the right to expect and demand faithfulness from their spouses and in which people who will not be celibate or faithful use condoms. It is here that both traditional culture and traditional Christianity have failed.

Maria has been married for ten years. She discusses with her friends a lecture they have been given at their workplace on using condoms if they fear they may be exposed to AIDS. She says, 'How can I tell my husband to use such things? He will want to know where I even heard about these matters. If I tell him I have heard it here he will say I must stop working if such things are discussed. I think he will give me this AIDS. I know he is having sex with young girls. But what must I do? If I cry to him he will bring one of those girls home in my place. Then what must I do? A woman must just bear these things. There is nothing I can do.'

In many of our cultures, white and black, women play a subordinate role in the sexual relationship. Where a woman depends upon the man for financial support – whether in the form of a one-time payment to a prostitute or ongoing support for a wife or mistress – she is not able to lay down conditions such as, you must be faithful to me; or you must use condoms. In many cultures it is regarded as unseemly for women even to know about condoms. As I have suggested, women are seen to be either sexless and innocent virgins or loose and immoral temptresses of innocent men. In order not to be thought of as the latter, a woman must know nothing of sex at all.

'Specific cultural and religious obstacles (for example prohibition against condom use or open discussion about sexuality) may also impede a woman's ability to practice "safer sex"' (Pearlberg 1991:41).

For women, the practice of 'safer sex' is thus no easy matter. A 'nice' woman does not feel free to raise the issue. To do so would be to show improper familiarity with sexual practices, and also to question the faithfulness of her partner. Thus she would risk losing his regard – and his financial support. Prostitutes on the other hand are expected to know about such things, but since they are being paid for their services they are not seen as deserving of any consideration. Men do not like wearing condoms, and prostitutes risk losing clients if they insist.

Traditional culture makes it difficult for women to insist on rights. Christianity compounds this difficulty. The Pauline view of marriage is that the man must be the one who ultimately makes decisions in the family. He is in authority, just as Christ is in authority in the church. Of course Paul also says that the man must love his wife. But in a culture which emphasizes male authority, partly now on biblical grounds, who is to determine what 'loving' means?

The reality of what happens is often more like the following scenario. The man does indeed 'love' his wife, in that he provides her with some protection and some money for accommodation or food. He also sees it as his duty to protect her from herself and from her 'weaker' nature. Thus any resentment or disobedience on her part should be punished. Also, since she is a woman and therefore has a nature easily tempted towards foolish attractions, he must watch out for and punish any signs that she is straying in her affections. Women do not need sexual release, and if she is attracted elsewhere it will be for frivolous reasons. Condom use might well indicate such straying. Since the man is quite sure that he himself carries no sexual illness, if a woman insists on a condom he assumes she is indicating that she fears she is infected by someone else.

He, on the other hand, since he is a man, must by nature and quite properly seek sexual release when he is away from home, or when she is pregnant or lactating. This is not his fault; it is how men are and, provided he continues to support and keep her, she has no grounds for complaint. If she suspects he has affairs with other women, it is not her business to ask about such things, since he is after all her superior and her guardian and he knows best.

It is not only men who believe this: women and their daughters are commonly brought up to share the same conviction, that their duty and fulfilment lie in providing for some man a home, food, sexual release, and a family. It is very difficult, if not impossible, for women in this situation to have any say over their sexual behaviour. Their duty is to meet the needs of their man. Unless some man finds her attractive and wishes to make her his partner, a woman has failed in her main purpose for living. A man who invites a woman to sleep with him is doing her a favour. He is reassuring her that she is attractive and can therefore respect herself as a woman. He is giving her the knowledge that she is desired and needed. For a woman to refuse a man sex is to risk that no one else will ever ask her. Girls therefore cannot easily refuse sex.

To this is added the further conviction that a woman, to be fulfilled, must have a child. A childless woman in many cultures has no point of contact with the majority of other women. The other women are all mothers, bound up with caring for their children. The childless woman is seen as being a failure and deeply unfortunate. This is not only because women are naturally maternal and long for children. It is because having a baby who depends on you, who gives you unconditional love, is an emotional necessity for many women who do not experience much tenderness in their married lives. Having a child, in a poor country, is often also the only insurance that in old age one will not be left destitute. A childless woman has no one to care for her needs once her husband and his brothers are dead.

Having a child also ensures life after death. In much traditional African religion, it is believed that parents live on as 'ancestors', still part of the family, still loved, remembered and obeyed. But this is only true if someone recalls them. In Zulu custom in South Africa, some time after a person has died, the extended family will gather for a feast. It is the duty of the head of the household to '*buyisa*' or call forth the newly dead person to rejoin the family circle. Without that call, without a family to belong to, the shade will wander as a restless spirit, rootless and unhappy, until it ceases to exist. The extent to which these beliefs persist for those who are Christian varies, but certainly for some, children are felt to be a necessity, since without children there is no eternal life.

Thus for personal affirmation of their worth as a person, and for all the various reasons that make having children so important, women in traditional societies are very dependent upon men. All of this is part of the reason why AIDS spreads so relentlessly in Third World countries, especially Africa. Women cannot easily refuse sex, or insist upon 'safer' sex, for this would

(i) offend the man who gives you your reason as a woman to be alive;

(ii) risk being rejected and being left without support;

(iii) deprive you of babies and children who for all these reasons are seen as essential.

What is therefore needed is to find ways of helping women value themselves independently of men, marriage and sex. Women need to know that they are important in their own right and not just as wives, mothers and lovers. But if women are to be enabled to change their view of themselves, then men also need to be helped to realize that their own virility and manhood does not depend upon regular sexual intercourse and impregnating women. Without these changes in how men and women see themselves and each other, it is most unlikely that sexual behaviour will change. It is unlikely that AIDS will diminish unless most women and most men have found quite different ways of thinking about themselves.

Christians who insist upon emphasizing the authority of men in the family, and Christians who insist that the main purpose of sex is still procreation, are making such re-education very difficult, and are thus helping to ensure that AIDS continues to take its toll. Christians will say that their intention is always to insist upon authority and procreation within Christian parameters of love and concern, and that they are opposed to the exploitation of women as much as anyone else. But a one-sided authority is always likely to be a misused authority. When Christianity adds legitimation for what are already oppressive features of a traditional culture, a situation is created where AIDS will flourish.

In all these ways AIDS highlights the need for women to be enabled to take some control over their own lives, to make decisions, to have equal access to jobs and salaries, to be equal in power with men. The theological question which is raised is, as Kelly says, whether in its teachings and its own life the church is really helping to set women free. A church whose scriptures are written by men and interpreted by men, in whom all authority is vested in men, whose imagery for God is almost all male, is a church which is really helping to keep women in a position of subservience and second-class citizenship. We cannot avoid the fact that in that case, unless we seriously try to challenge and change this, we are part of the problem of AIDS rather than part of the solution.

AIDS therefore forces us to take feminist theology seriously. One of our present difficulties is that although there are many feminist theologians, their debate still tends to be a closed one with other women and a few male supporters. For feminist theologians,

' . . . every theological doctrine and concept has to be examined anew in light of the growing awareness that women had been oppressed in the church at least as systematically as in other parts of society' (Young 1990:13).

The experience of women and the perspectives of women need to be part of the perspective of all of us. Women need to be empowered if AIDS is to be checked. After all, it is not stretching the point to see a link between AIDS and the refusal to consider ordaining women.

Christian feminists who urge us to look more carefully at the scriptures and the Christian tradition in order to balance out the oppressive texts with others more liberative for women are therefore entirely justified. There are all the Pauline texts about men and women being equal in Christ; there is the fact that from the start there were influential Christian women leaders in the church; there is the surprising truth that from the first, unlike the Jewish temple and synagogue, women were part of Christian worship and Christian congregations.

The AIDS crisis demands that feminism should be accepted as part of the mainstream of Christian theology, and that Third World theologies should embrace feminist liberation as enthusiastically as they have embraced race and class liberation.

The End

AIDS is not really the end. It is not the end of the human race. As with all epidemics, the disease will peak and lessen off. Eventually we may find a cure. Eventually AIDS education will at least reduce the numbers who are at risk.

AIDS is not the end for the church. I have tried to suggest ways in which I believe AIDS may change the way we think about God, about ourselves and about the church. AIDS may even be a new beginning for the church. If the church grasps the opportunity to serve God in humanity in the particular ways which it can do better than any other institution, it may earn new respect for its views and its teaching. Probably, as throughout history, the church's response will be partial and patchy.

AIDS will not be the end of human complacency, selfishness and sin. It ought to remind us of our fragile hold upon life and health. It ought to be the end of irresponsible and uncommitted sex. It probably will not be.

But for those of us – and we are a growing number – who are HIV positive, or who have AIDS, or who care for someone with AIDS, or who meet with people with AIDS, it will be an end to old assumptions, and to life as we knew it. AIDS will have brought an end – and a beginning. The end may have brought with it very great pain, especially for the bereaved. Beginnings are frightening, for we do not know the new country in which we find ourselves. But we are not in that new country alone, nor should we try to find our way alone. There are others around us who have also been brought to the new country. In and through those others, we may find God and God's Christ. All may seem to be chaos, 'darkness upon the face of the deep', without form and void. But the spirit of God moves over the chaos. God is in the beginning, and in the end, alpha and omega.

Within the chaos are the seeds of human love and support, and the undergirding divine presence.

'Lo I am with you always, to the close of the age' (Matthew 28.20).

Bibliography

William J. Abraham, *An Introduction to the Philosophy of Religion*, Englewood Cliffs, NJ: Prentice Hall.

ACET Newsletter, 1995, London: AIDS Care, Education and Training, February 1995.

Samuel K. Ada, 1994, *Ecumenical Letter on Evangelism*, Geneva: WCC.

Chris Adams, 1989, 'AIDS and changing realities', *Christianity and Crisis*, Vol. 49, 11 September 1989.

African Ecclesial Review, 1989, Vol. 31, no. 5, October 1989.

V. K. Agadzi, 1989, *AIDS: The African Perspective of the Killer Disease*, Accra: Ghana University Press.

Peter Aggleton, Peter Davies and Graham Hart, 1990, *Aids: Individual, Cultural and Policy Dimensions*, Basingstoke: Falmer Press.

Anna Maria Alonso and Maria Teresa Koreck, 1989, 'Silences: Hispanics, AIDS and Sexual Practices', *Differences*, Vol. 1, Winter 1989.

Gene Antonio, 1986, *The AIDS Cover-up: The Real and Alarming Facts about AIDS*, San Francisco: Ignatius Press.

Aristotle, 1980 revised ed., *The Nicomachean Ethics*, tr. David Ross, London: OUP.

Homer U. Ashby, 1989, 'How Shall the Congregation Respond?', *Church and Society*, January-February 1989, Vol. 79.

Tony Barnett and Piers Blaikie, 1992, *AIDS in Africa: Its Present and Future Impact*, London: Belhaven.

David Barrett (ed.), *World Christian Encyclopedia: A Comparative Study of Churches and Religions in the Modern World, AD 1900–2000*, Nairobi: OUP.

Roy W. Battenhouse (ed.), 1955, *A Companion to the Study of Augustine*, London: OUP.

Michael D. Biskop (ed.), 1992, *AIDS: Opposing Viewpoints*, San Diego: Greenhaven Press.

Charles E. Bouchard and James R. Pollock, 1989, 'Condoms and the Common Good', *Second Opinion*, Vol. 12, November 1989.

Walter Brueggeman, 1978, *The Prophetic Imagination*, Philadelphia: Fortress Press and London: SCM Press.

Alan Cadwallader, 1992, 'The Hermeneutics of Purity in Mark's Gospel: Considerations for the AIDS Debate', *Pacifica*, Vol. 5, no. 2, June 1992.

G. B. Caird, 1956, *Principalities and Powers*, London: OUP.

Edwin Cameron, 1993, 'Human Rights, Racism and AIDS: The New Discrimination', in *South African Journal on Human Rights*, Vol. 9, part 1, 1993.

Albert Camus, 1972, *The Plague*, New York: Vintage Books and Harmondsworth, Penguin Books.

The Cara Trust, 1995, *A Gift Wrapped in Thorns*, London: The Cara Trust.

CARA NEWS, Spring 1995.

Catechism of the Catholic Church, 1994, London: Geoffrey Chapman.

Catholic AIDS Link, 1995, *Positively Called – HIV, Priesthood and Religious Life*, Pastoral Aids Series no. 2, London: Catholic AIDS Link.

Catholic AIDS Link Newsletter, No. 16, November 1994.

Catholic Bishops of Uganda, 'Message', quoted *African Ecclesial Review*, Vol. 31, no. 5, October 1989.

Centers for Disease Control, 1995, *Births to Unmarried Mothers: United States 1990–1992*, CDC: Atlanta.

Henry Chadwick, 1986, *Augustine*, London: OUP.

Kittredge Cherry and James Mitulski, 1988, 'We are the Church Alive, The Church with AIDS', *Christian Century*, Vol. 105, 27 January 1988.

James F. Childress and John Macquarrie (eds.), 1967, *A New Dictionary of Christian Ethics*, London: SCM Press and Philadelphia: Westminster Press.

Michael J. Christensen, 1991, *The Samaritan's Imperative: Compassionate Ministry to People Living with AIDS*, Nashville: Abingdon Press.

J. Michael Clark, 1989, 'AIDS, Death and God: Gay Liberation Theology and the Problem of Suffering', *Journal of Pastoral Counselling*, Vol. 21, No. 1, Spring/Summer 1989.

Mary Clark (ed.), 1984, *Augustine of Hippo: Selected Writings*. London: SPCK.

John B. Cobb and David Ray Griffin, 1976, *Process Theology: An Introductory Exposition*, Philadelphia: Westminster Press.

Jon Cohen, 1994, 'Are Researchers Racing towards Success, or Crawling?', *Science*, Vol. 265, No. 5177, 2 September 1994.

L. William Countryman, 1987, 'The AIDS Crisis: Theological and Ethical Reflections', *Anglican Theological Review*, Vol. 69, April 1987.

Charles Cozec (ed.), 1991, *The AIDS Crisis*, San Diego: Current Controversies.

Created Design – Some Pastoral Guidelines for the Care of Lesbian and Gay People, 1994, London: Catholic Aids Link.

CSD Bulletin, Vol. 20, No. 5, June 1995.

Don Cupitt, 1980, *Taking Leave of God*, London: SCM Press.

Don Cupitt, 1989, *Radicals and the Future of the Church*, London: SCM Press.

Patrick Dixon, 1990, *The Truth about AIDS* (revised ed.), Eastbourne: Kingsway.

Jack Dominian, 1987, *Sexual Integrity: The Answer to AIDS*, London: Darton, Longman and Todd.

Fyodor Dostoevsky, 1990, *The Brothers Karamazov*, tr. Richard Pevear and Larissa Volokhonsky, San Francisco: North Point Press.

William A. Doubleday and Suki Terada Ports, 1992, 'Fighting AIDS and HIV Together', *Envisioning the New Community: A Reader on Urban Ministry*, Louisville, Kentucky: Westminster John Knox Press.

Anthony Dyson, 1994, 'The Body of Christ has AIDS', in Stephen Barton and Graham Stanton (eds.), *Resurrection: Essays in Honour of Leslie Houlden*, London: SPCK.

The Economist, Vol. 320, 21 September 1991.

Ecumenical Trends, Vol. 19, April 1990.

Liz Edman, 1992, 'Inner City AIDS: Survival, Advocacy and Pressure', *Christianity and Crisis*, Vol. 52, 21 September 1992.

Epidemiological Comments, Vol. 21 (10), October 1994, Department of Health: Republic of South Africa.

Ronald Eyre, 1977, *The Long Search: Zulu Zion*, BBC video film.

Austin M. Farrer, 1962, *Love Almighty and Ills Unlimited*, London: Collins.

Alan Fleming, Manuel Carballo, David W. Fitzsimons, Michael R. Bally and Jonathan Mann (eds.), 1988, *The Global Impact of AIDS*, New York: Alan R. Liss.

Ursula Fleming, 1988, *Meister Eckhart: The Man from God Hid Nothing*, London: Collins Fount.

Anthony Flew and Alisdair Macintyre (eds.), 1955, *New Essays in Philosophical Theology*, London: SCM Press.

Viktor E. Frankl, 1973, *Psychotherapy and Existentialism*, Harmondsworth: Pelican Books.

Michael F. Fumento, 1990, *The Myth of Heterosexual AIDS*, New York: Basic Books.

Robert D. Gamble, 1989, 'Introduction to a Frontier of Ministry', *Church and Society*, Vol. 79, January-February 1989.

William Gardner, Susan G. Millstein and Brian L. Wilcox, 1990, *Adolescents in the AIDS Epidemic*, San Francisco: Jossey-Bass.

Geoff P. Garnett and Ray M. Anderson, 1993, 'No Reason for Complacency about the Potential Demographic Impact of AIDS in Africa', *Transactions of the Royal Society of Tropical Medicine and Hygiene* 1993, 87, supplement 1.

Thomas Giles, 1992, 'Churches lack Guidance on AIDS', *Christianity Today*, vol. 26, 23 November 1992.

Cheryl Townsend Gilkes, 1991, 'To Sit and Die or to Stand and Live', *Journal of Religious Thought*, Vol. 47, Winter-Spring 1991.

Bonginjalo Goba, 1995, *The AIDS Pandemic in Uganda and Tanzania*, Cape Town: Centre for South-South Relations.

John Godges, 1986, 'Religious Groups meet the San Francisco AIDS Challenge', *Christian Century*, 10–17 September 1986.

The Grail, Vol. 5, no. 1, March 1989.

Deirdre Green, 1989, *Gold in the Crucible: Teresa of Avila and the Western Mystical Tradition*, Longmead, Dorset: Element Books.

Jesse Green, 1995, 'Prohibited: The Miracle AIDS Drug', *The Independent Magazine*, issue 344, 22 April 1995.

Jan Zita Grover, 1989, 'AIDS: Metaphors and Real Life', *Christianity and Crisis*, Vol. 49, 11 September 1989.

Colin E. Gunton, 1991, *The Promise of Trinitarian Theology*, Edinburgh: T.&T. Clark.

Julie Hamblin and Elizabeth Reid, 1994, 'Women and the HIV Epidemic', *WIN News*, Vol. 20, no. 1, Winter 1994.

Charles Hartshorne, 1953, *Reality as Social Process: Studies in Metaphysics and Religion*, Glencoe: Free Press.

Anthony E. Harvey, 1994, *Promise or Pretence? A Christian's Guide to Sexual Morals*, London: SCM Press.

The Hastings Centre (eds.), 1991, *Aids: An Epidemic of Ethical Puzzles*, Aldershot: Dartmouth.

Gilbert Herdt, 1987, 'Homosexuality', in M. Eliade (ed.), *The Encyclopedia of Religion*, New York: Macmillan.

John Hick, 1966, *Evil and the God of Love*, London: Macmillan.

John Hick, 1993, *Disputed Questions in Theology and the Philosophy of Religion*, London: Macmillan.

Leonard Hodgson, 1943, *The Doctrine of the Trinity*, London: James Nisbet.

J. L. Houlden, 1986, *Connections: The Integration of Theology and Faith*, London: SCM Press.

Basil Hume, 1995, 'A Note on the Teaching of the Catholic Church concerning Homosexual People', in *Catholic AIDS Link Newsletter*, No. 18, June 1995.

The Independent on Sunday, 11 June 1995.

William James, 1960, *The Varieties of Religious Experience*, London: Fontana.

Matthew R. S. Johnson, Ronald K. B. Pearce and Richard G. Matthews, undated, *Aids and the Common Cup*, London: International Anglican Liturgical Commission.

L. Annette Jones, 1989, 'AIDS: A Mission Opportunity for the Church', *International Review of Missions*, Vol. 78, April 1989.

Stephen C. Joseph, 1992, *Dragon within the Gates: The Once and Future AIDS*, New York: Carrol and Graf.

Kevin T. Kelly, 1990, 'Sexual Ethics: Experience, Growth, Challenge', *The Month*, September/October 1990.

Kevin T. Kelly, 1995, 'Living with HIV/AIDS', *The Tablet*, Vol. 249, No. 8075, 13 May 1995.

Søren Kierkegaard, 1941, *Concluding Unscientific Postscript*, tr. David F. Swenson, Princeton: Princeton University Press.

Ursula King (ed.), 1994, *Feminist Theology from the Third World*, London: SPCK.

Bill Kirkpatrick, 1988, *AIDS: Sharing the Pain*, London: DLT.

Mark R. Kowalewski, 1994, *All Things to All People: The Catholic Church Confronts the AIDS Crisis*, New York: State University of New York Press.

Elisabeth Kübler-Ross, 1970, *On Death and Dying*, London: Tavistock.

Elisabeth Kübler-Ross, 1987, *AIDS: The Ultimate Challenge*, New York: Macmillan.

Hans Küng, 1989, *Eternal Life: Life after Death as a Medical, Philosophical and Theological Problem*. London: SCM Press and New York: Crossroad Publishing Co.

Hans Küng, 1990, *Global Responsibility: In Search of a New World Ethic*, London: SCM Press and New York: Crossroad Publishing Co.

Judith Landau-Stanton and Colleen D. Clements, 1993, *AIDS, Health and Mental Health: A Primary Sourcebook*, New York: Brunner/Mazel.

Belden C. Lane, 1986, '*Hutzpa k'lapei Shamaya*: A Christian Response to the Jewish Tradition of Arguing with God', *Journal of Ecumenical Studies*, Vol. xxiii, No. 4, Fall 1986.

C. S. Lewis, 1960, *The Four Loves*, London: Geoffrey Bles.

Daniel Louw, 1990, 'Ministering and Counselling the Person with AIDS', *Journal of Theology for Southern Africa*, Vol. 71, June 1990.

Peter Lurie, Percy Hintzen and Robert A. Lowe, 1995, *AIDS* 1995, Vol. 9, No. 6.

Dennis P. McCann, 1981, *Christian Realism and Liberation Theology: Practical Theologies in Creative Conflict*, Maryknoll, NY: Orbis Books.

Robert B. Mellert, 1975, *What is Process Theology?*, New York: Paulist Press.

Paul Monette, 1988, *Borrowed Time: An Aids Memoir*, San Diego: Harcourt Brace Jovanovich.

William Morris, 1986, *The Logic of God Incarnate*, Ithaca, NY: Cornell University Press.

Itumeleng Mosala, 1989, *Biblical Hermeneutics and Black Theology in South Africa*, Grand Rapids: Eerdmans.

V. Chandra Mouli, 1992, *All against AIDS: The Copperbelt Health Education Project, Zambia*, London: Action Aid.

Ronald Nash (ed.), 1987, *Process Theology*, Grand Rapids: Baker Book House.

New York Times, 1 May 1994.

New York Times, 9 September 1994.

New York Times, 13 September 1994.

New York Times, 1 November 1994.

New York Times, 3 February 1995.

Maura O'Donahue, undated, *A General Overview of the HIV/AIDS Pandemic*, London: CAFOD.

Gerry Pearlberg, 1991, *Women, AIDS and Communities: A Guide for Action*, Metuchen, New York: Women's Action Alliance.

E. Allison Peers (tr.& ed.), 1946a, *The Complete Works of St Teresa of Jesus*, Vol. 1, London: Sheed and Ward.

E. Allison Peers (tr. & ed.), 1946b, *The Complete Works of St Teresa of Jesus*, Vol. 2, London: Sheed and Ward.

Jennifer Philips, 1988, 'The Future of AIDS: Parishes can Help', *Christian Century*, Vol. 105, 1 June 1988.

John Piper, 1987, 'Just Say No to Condoms', *Christianity Today*, Vol. 31, 4 September 1987.

Prayers and Reflections on AIDS, undated, London: CAFOD.

Karl Rahner, 1972, *Theological Investigations*, Vol. 9, London: Darton, Longman and Todd and New York: Crossroad Publishing Co.

Carl Raschke, 1982, *Deconstruction and Theology*, New York: Crossroad Publishing Co.

Robert S. Root-Bernstein, 1993, *Rethinking AIDS: The Tragic Cost of Premature Consensus*, New York: Free Press.

Richard Rothenberg, 1993, 'Chronicle of an Epidemic Foretold', *The Millbank Quarterly*, Vol. 71, No. 4, Winter 1993.

Richard L. Rubenstein, 1992, *After Auschwitz: History, Theology and Contemporary Judaism*, second ed., Baltimore: Johns Hopkins University Press.

Letty M. Russell (ed.), 1990, *The Church with AIDS: Renewal in the Midst of Crisis*, Louisville, Kentucky: Westminster Press.

Dennis Ryan, 1988, *The Tablet*, 17 December 1988.

Willem Saayman, 1991, 'Some Reflections on AIDS, Ethics and the Community in Southern and Central Africa', *Theologia Evangelica*, Vol. 24, no. 3, September 1991.

Willem Saayman and Jacques Kriel, 1992, *AIDS: The Leprosy of Our Time*, Johannesburg: Orion.

Frank Sabatino, 1992, 'AIDS as a Spiritual Journey', *Second Opinion*, Vol. 18, No. 1, July 1992.

St Louis Post Dispatch, 3 July 1994.

Matthew Schofeleers, 1989, 'A Pastoral Dilemma in Southern Africa', in Jerald D. Gort, Hendrik M. Vroom, Rein Fernhout and Anton Wessels (eds.), *Dialogue and Syncretism: An Interdisciplinary Approach*, Grand Rapids: Eerdmans.

B. D. Schoub, 1989, quoted in *Medical Chronicle*, January 1989.

Robin Scroggs, 1983, *The New Testament and Homosexuality: A Contextual Background for Contemporary Debate*, Philadelphia: Fortress.

J. L. Segundo, 1976, *The Liberation of Theology*, Maryknoll: Orbis Books.

Earl A. Shelp and Ronald H. Sunderland, 1987, *AIDS and the Church*, Philadelphia: Westminster Press.

Randy Shilts, 1987, *And the Band Played On*, New York: St Martin's Press.

Ronald Sider, 1988, 'AIDS: An Evangelical Perspective', *Christian Century*, Vol. 105, 6–13 January 1988.

Linda Singer, 1989, 'Bodies – Pleasures – Powers', *Differences*, Vol. 1, Winter 1989.

Joseph Wayne Smith, 1991, *AIDS, Philosophy and Beyond*, Aldershot: Avebury.

Something to Celebrate: Valuing Families in Church and Society, 1995, London: Church House Publishing.

Susan Sontag, 1989, *AIDS and its Metaphors*, New York: Farrar, Straus and Giroux.

Kenneth South, 1992, 'Churches and AIDS: Problems and Solutions', *Christianity and Crisis*, Vol. 52, 21 September 1992.

South African Catholic Bishops Conference, 1990, *Pastoral Statement on AIDS*.

William C. Spohn, 1988, 'The Moral Dimensions of AIDS', *Theological Studies*, Vol. 49, No. 1, March 1988.

Paul Steinke, 1992, 'Pastoral Notes on AIDS and Hope', *Christian Century*, Vol. 109, 20–27 May 1992.

Elizabeth Stuart, 1993, *Chosen: Gay Catholic Priests Tell Their Stories*, London: Geoffrey Chapman.

Richard Swinburne, 1979, *The Existence of God*, Oxford: OUP.

Kenneth Surin, 1986, *Theology and the Problem of Evil*, Oxford: Blackwell.

S. W. Sykes, 1978, *The Integrity of Anglicanism*, London, Mowbrays.

Adrian Thatcher, 1993, *Liberating Sex: A Christian Sexual Theology*, London: SPCK.

Adrian Thatcher, 1995, Review in *Theology*, Vol. xcviii, no. 782, March/April 1995.

Helmut Thielicke, 1964, *The Ethics of Sex* (tr. John Doberstein), London: 1964.

Dylan Thomas, 1971, *Collected Poems* (ed. Daniel Jones), London: Dent.

Ruth Morgan Thomas, 1992, 'HIV and the Sex Industry', in Judy Barry, Val Morrison and Sheena McLachlan (eds.), *Working with Women and AIDS*, London: Routledge.

The Times, 17 May 1995.

John Tuohey, 1990, 'Methodology and Ideology: The Condom and a Consistent Sexual Ethic', *Louvain Studies* Vol. 15(1), 1990.

Uganda AIDS Commission, 1994, *HIV/AIDS Situation Analysis*.

United Kingdom Declaration of the Rights of People with HIV and AIDS, Date and publisher not given.

Kenneth Vaux, 1989, 'Theological Ethics and AIDS: Law and Gospel', *Currents in Theology and Mission*, Vol. 16, No. 4, August 1989.

Abraham Verghese, 1994, *My Own Country*, New York: Simon and Schuster.

Wall Street Journal, 11 March 1994.

William E. Wallace, 1993, 'The Church in a Ditch: Points of Connection', *Christian Century*, Vol. 110, 7 April 1993.

Washington Post, 29 June 1994.

Simon Watney, 1989, 'Missionary Position: AIDS, "Africa" and race', *Differences*, Vol. 1, Winter 1989.

Robert Way (ed.), 1986, *The Cloud of Unknowing and the Letter of Private Direction*, Wheathampstead, Herts: Anthony Clarke.

Brad Weiss, 1993, 'Buying Her Grave: Money, Movement and AIDS in North-West Tanzania', *Africa*, Vol. 63, No. 1, Winter 1993.

John White, 1990, 'AIDS, Judgment and Blessing', *Themelios*, Vol. 15, No. 2, Jan/Feb. 1990.

Barry L. Whitney, 1985, *Evil and the Process of God*, New York: Edwin Mellen Press.

Glen Williams and Sunanda Ray, 1993, *Work Against AIDS: Workplace-Based AIDS Initiatives in Zimbabwe*, London: Action Aid.

Glen Williams and Nassali Tamale, 1991, *The Caring Community: Coping with AIDS in Urban Uganda*, London: Action Aid.

James Woodward (ed.), 1990, *Embracing the Chaos: Theological Responses to AIDS*, London: SPCK.

World Press Review, January 1994, Vol. 41, No. 1.

Michael Worsnip, 1994, unpublished report.

Ian Young, 1993, *The AIDS Dissidents: An Annotated Bibliography*, Metuchen, New Jersey: Scarecrow Press.

Pamela Dickey Young, 1990, *Feminist Theology/Christian Theology*, Minneapolis: Fortress Press.

'The Last Things'
in a Process Perspective

NORMAN PITTENGER

'The Last Things'
in a Process Perspective

London EPWORTH PRESS

Set in 11/12 pt Imprint
and printed in Great Britain
by W & J Mackay & Co Ltd
Chatham Kent
SBN *7162 0149 6*

Contents

Preface

The purpose of this book ought to be clear from its title. It is an attempt to sketch briefly, mostly by way of suggestion, what significance may be discovered, for men and women living today, in the traditional scheme of the 'last things'—death, judgement, heaven, and hell. It admits frankly that this scheme, as it has come down to us, is incredible, however valuable and helpful, not to say apparently 'true', it was for many who have gone before us in the path of Christian discipleship. But it tries to point out certain indispensable realities in human, above all in Christian, life which that outworn scheme somehow managed to present to those who accepted it.

I should like to emphasize that at best this is a 'sketch'; and that it is 'mostly by way of suggestion'. I should be the last to assume that I have said everything that might be or ought to be said on the subject, and I am very conscious of serious omissions as well as of many shortcomings. In extenuation, however, I plead that in the compass allowed me—for these chapters were originally lectures—nobody can say everything. What I have done is to select, according to my best judgement, what seemed of crucial importance and hence could not be omitted. And that is all that I *can* say, as an excuse for this book's inadequacy to the theme with which it attempts to deal.

It remains to thank the authorities of the several divinity schools in the United States which were kind enough to ask me to lecture in February 1970. The principals, deans, and other officials, as well as the theological students and others who heard the lectures, will know how deeply indebted I am to them all. The lectures, practically in their present form, were delivered at the Episcopal Theological School, Cambridge, and the Boston Theological Institute.

Two further chapters (on The Centrality of Love and After the 'Death of God') have been added, since they deal with related subjects. The second of these (Chapter Eight) originally appeared in *The Church Quarterly* for April 1969; I am indebted to the Editor for permission to reprint it here.

NORMAN PITTENGER

King's College
Cambridge

*To my students
in New York and
in Cambridge
1935–70*

ONE

The Traditional Scheme

It is frequently said, in criticisms or comments on the various
new movements in Christian theology these days, that the one
area to which they give little or no attention is the one that has
to do with what are called in text-books of doctrine 'the last
things'. For example, one of the charges against *Honest to God*,
almost as soon as it appeared, was that John Robinson had
said nothing in that book about 'future life'—although the
critic must have forgotten that not many years before the
bishop had written, while still a theological teacher, a treatise
entitled *In the End God* which is a considered and very interesting and suggestive discussion of exactly that subject as well
as of the related aspects of 'the last things'.

Although, in this particular instance, the charge was mis-
directed, it is true, I think, that the detailed and careful consideration of 'the last things' has been infrequent in the 'new
theology'. Much is said about the eschatological perspective,
much is written about the way in which the 'coming Kingdom'
impinges on the present world, and much is asserted about the
need to take the eschatology of the Bible seriously. Here,
however, eschatology does not signify what the theological
text-books include under that phrase. The term is used, perhaps more properly, to denote the special Jewish insistence on
'the end', 'the good time coming', the Kingdom either in its
final appearance (with some) or in its 'anticipated' or 'realized'
form (with others).

Whatever may be the case with the new theologians who are influenced by 'secularization', by 'the death of God', or the existentialist conceptuality provided by Heidegger—and here John Macquarrie is an exception, since his *Principles of Christian Theology* does include a consideration of the subject—not many theologians who prefer to approach the re-conception of Christian theology with the use of 'process thought' have published extended studies of 'the last things'; or, if they have, I have not come across them. Schubert Ogden is the notable exception, in what I regard as his excellent essay on 'The Hope of Faith', included in *The Reality of God*. By and large, though, the subject is not one that appeals to such thinkers.

I should wish to associate myself entirely with the process theologians. And it seems to me a useful enterprise to undertake in these chapters a consideration of 'the last things', although in short compass and in the light of my own obvious incompetence I can only open up the discussion and make what may be a few helpful suggestions. Certainly I do not claim that I shall do more than raise questions, suggest a few possible answers, and urge readers to pursue the matter for themselves. But of the importance of the subject I have not the slightest doubt; and as you will see, this is not because I wish to cling in some obscurantist way to something that has been traditionally sacred, but because I am convinced that death, judgement, heaven, and hell—'the four last things'—are subjects with which we *must* concern ourselves, however different from our ancestors may be the way in which we wish to understand what those terms denote.

So much, then, by way of preface to the lectures. I now turn to a fairly straightforward and, I hope, accurate sketch of what the tradition in Christian theology, found in those textbooks to which I have referred, does in fact have to say on these matters. Since I myself was taught this scheme, many years ago, I shall outline what I *was* taught, under the heading used in those days, of 'Christian Eschatology: Death, Judgement, the Intermediate State, Heaven, and Hell'. You will see that a fifth term has been added here—'the intermediate state'; this is because my own instruction was received in an Anglican theological school of tractarian background and of Anglo-Catholic sympathies. Hence the common Catholic and Orthodox view that 'something happens between' death for every man, and arrival in heaven, so to say, was included in the picture. Had I been educated, theologically, in a more Protestant divinity faculty that term would not have been found, of course. But 'the intermediate state' was certainly an element in the general picture for most Christians, indeed it still is and increasingly so among Protestants too; hence I shall include it in my outline-sketch.

What were the sources of this teaching? The present study is too brief to permit any proper analysis, but we may say that Christian eschatology, understood in this sense, is the product of a marriage of ideas found in Jewish thought, including the inter-testamental period, and the hellenistic soul-body portrayal of man. The story is exceedingly complicated; it would be a great service if some scholar or group of scholars would investigate it, in the light of our modern knowledge of Jewish and early Christian ideas, as well as with attention to the diversity of the thought about man found in the Graeco-Roman world.

Things are not quite so simple as an earlier generation of historians and theologians took them to be. There are questions like the possible development of a more 'spiritual' view of resurrection of the body, among Pharisaic thinkers in the period immediately before and contemporaneous with the beginning of the Christian era; the uncertainty about the supposed fate of the non-Jewish peoples when Judaism began to talk of God's Kingdom 'coming on earth', however transfigured the earth may be, and with this the nature of that Kingdom and the degree to which and the way in which it *was* coming; exactly how early Christian thinkers brought together the Jewish notion of resurrection and the hellenistic idea of immortality—for it is apparent that they resolved the obvious contradictions in a far from simple manner. But, generally speaking, we can say that the doctrine of the last things was gradually worked out from taking with utmost seriousness, and even with a stark literal understanding, much in the later Old Testament documents, as well as what the teaching of Jesus, then of St Paul and St John and the rest of the New Testament, was supposed to have said. Here was a disclosure, in so many words (and I would emphasize that it *was* thought to be 'in words', that is, in propositions stated in or deducible from that teaching), of man's destiny. Along with this, the philosophical notions about soul, about immortality, about a realm above and beyond the hurly-burly of this world, present in the tradition of Greek philosophy and variations on that philosophy in the early Christian era, had become so much part of the atmosphere of thought that inevitably these two affected Christian thinkers.

The marriage of this Jewish-Christian eschatological picture and the Greek philosophical view was not easily accomplished, nor was that marriage without its difficulties—it was hardly a quiet and successful relationship. But such as it was, it slowly matured; and the end-product was the sort of thing which finally was worked out in, say, St Thomas Aquinas and other medieval theologians, on the one hand, and in Calvin's *Institution of the Christian Religion*, on the other. And so far as the Bible had its unquestioned place in the enterprise, it was used as if the teaching found in it, especially in the gospels and the Johannine-Pauline literature, were a revelation in actual words of what death, judgement, heaven, and hell (and, where this was accepted, purgatory or paradise or the 'intermediate state') really were. As in so many places in Christian theology, the 'proof-texts' were found for what the Church wished to say, through its theologians.

It is a nice question, of course, whether a good deal of the teaching was based on these texts, or whether the texts were discovered, after careful searching, to bolster up ideas that had slowly gained acceptance. But this situation is not peculiar to 'the last things'; it has been found fairly generally in the whole

Christian theological enterprise. In any event, so far as the Bible was used, it was used in a way like that followed today by fundamentalists: the words were taken at their face-value, even if that 'face-value' seems a little odd and not always *obviously* what it is assumed to be. When there were contradictions in those materials, a reconciliation was effected, or at least attempted, through the use of the 'different levels of interpretation', where the historical meaning, the moral meaning, the theological meaning, and the highly mystical meaning could be distinguished and an appropriate distribution made in the discussion of this or that biblical text.

But what was the resulting teaching?

First of all, that human life in our span of years and so far as man's history is concerned is, like the created world itself, derivative from a realm of heavenly existence which abides eternal over against the transient, mortal, and uncertain span of our years. Of this fact, death stands as the great sign. Every man dies. This is the inescapable fact which no one can deny. But not *all* of him dies, for man himself is compounded of soul *and* body; and while the body dies, the soul cannot die. By its very nature it is immortal.

You must remember that I am not attempting here to make critical comments on the scheme; rather I am trying to present it as it was generally, and commonly, held and taught. If I were to make those critical comments, I should be obliged to say something at this point about the way in which this notion of the soul's immortality is very doubtfully found in the Scriptures and how it is an importation into Christian thinking from elsewhere. But that is not the point. For the generality of Christian theologians, the soul was taken to be immortal, so that when the human body came to die, the soul was 'released' from its bodily dwelling-place and enabled (shall we put it this way?) 'to go elsewhere'. The Book of Common Prayer, before recent revisions, talked in just this fashion; and, in doing so, it was typical of the common Christian teaching.

Death was the most important thing that happened to man

5

and all of his life before death was to be seen as a preparation for that event. The importance of death was not only in its being the end of this mortal life; it was also in its being the moment when, in a 'particular judgement', the future destiny of the one who died was fixed. There was no possibility of repentance *after* death; as we must note, there was either the definite sending to eternal damnation of the evil man or the preparation of the good man for a final heavenly state (in circles that did not accept some doctrine of an 'intermediate state', there was instead a sort of 'waiting' until the final consummation)—but the moment of death, with its judgement of this and that individual, was absolutely final in its determination of the direction that was thereafter to be taken.

But if the soul was immortal, and human destiny determined at that particular judgement by a God who, although he was indeed merciful, was also just and would treat each man according to that man's merits—whether simply his own merits or in the light of 'the merits of Christ' in which by repentance for sin he took refuge—what happened to the body? Obviously the body corrupted in the grave. Yet there was the teaching about the resurrection of the *body*, so somehow this must be included in the final destiny of each man. Hence it was taught that at a later time, when God began to wind things up as we might put it, there would be a resurrection of all bodies. Precisely how this could occur was not known, but in some appropriate fashion these bodies would be raised from their graves, reconstituted in some equally appropriate fashion, re-united with 'their' souls—and then there would be a final judgement, in which the soul-and-body together would face the Grand Assize, to receive the statement of the great Judge as to its eventual fate.

There was a good deal of puzzlement here. *How* would these bodies be raised? What would they be like? How, in some transformed condition, were they to be permitted to enter into heaven, to be in the presence of God for ever? What about the bodies of those whose destiny had been determined, at their death, to be not heaven but hell? This sort of question was much discussed—St Augustine, for example, was troubled about the bodies of the very young or the very old or those who had been maimed or crippled. The general picture is clear, however. Bodies would be raised, quite literally. Soul and body would be re-united, as the hymns put it and as art portrayed it. Graves would be opened, bodies would emerge in their re-constituted form, and man as the union of soul and body would face the judgement of God.

Some very few would be, so to say, exempted from at least part of this. In the Catholic theology in which I was brought up, the saints were somehow to be granted the *immediate* vision of God, at the point of their death. What happened to *their* bodies was not entirely clear, although in Roman Catholic circles it was believed (and in quite recent times it has been made an indisputable dogma) that the body of the Blessed Mother of our Lord had not in fact died at all but had been received into heaven, thus anticipating the general resurrection which was to be a part of the more general human lot. Those saints, already in heaven, were constantly interceding for men and women on earth. With God himself, they were in bliss; but because they had shared and hence knew our mortal lot, they could be trusted not to forget their human brethren and they continually prayed for those left behind.

On the other hand, the souls which were not thus in heaven already were in a state either of preparation for heaven (among Protestants, this of course was denied—but exactly 'where' those souls might be was left an open question, although some have described the 'state' as being a sort of 'cold freeze' until the day of final judgement), or, having completed their preparation, were now awaiting the day when they would be re-united with their bodies and so enabled to enjoy the heavenly bliss which was promised them. They could be helped by the prayers of their brethren who were still 'in the flesh', we were taught; or at least, *I* was. Prayers for the dead were an important part of Christian devotion, since through them those who were in the intermediate state would be furthered on their way towards the perfection which God intended for them.

It was, of course, a natural and very human thing to wish to remember, and indeed to demand the right to remember, those whom we 'have loved long since, and lost awhile'. But it was also an act of piety to do so. In Protestant communions, the practice of prayers for the dead had been given up, along with acceptance of the notion of an intermediate state of some sort. But even there, as recent liturgical forms show, the human desire sooner or later had to be satisfied; and in some fashion, perhaps by *comprecation* (that is, praying for the departed by associating them with prayers for ourselves), the realization of this 'communion' had to be made available. In Catholic circles, especially in the west, such prayers were taken to be a way in which somehow the purification or purgation of the departed soul might be accomplished more effectively, even if the idea of the intermediate state as 'punishment' was not held.

Furthermore the most solemn and sacred of all acts of Christian worship, the Eucharist, could be 'applied' to those who were dead. How often have I heard, and how often after ordination have I said: 'Of your charity, pray for the *soul* of X, that God may grant it a place of light and refreshment and peace.' Thus the 'intention' of the celebration could be *for* the departed, either one by one or, on All Souls' Day, for them all.

So far I have spoken of the way in which death and judgement were presented, with, perhaps, too extended a reference to the idea of the intermediate state. Now we come to heaven, the goal or end of those who in that state were being purified and prepared for heavenly joy. Heaven, of course, was said to be the vision of God, so far as 'immortal mortals' could see him; it was the place, in a spiritual sense of course, where the blessed dwelt in profound fellowship one with another in God himself. Responsible theological teachers did not take at their face value the pictures of heaven which were found in hymnody, nor did they regard the somewhat extraordinary set of images in Revelation as being an exact representation—indeed, these images, laden with Jewish eschatological conceptions of the nature of the Kingdom of God when there should be 'a new heaven and a new earth' were sometimes felt to be slightly embarrassing. But there was a reality behind *all* the pictures and images—and that reality was life in God, with all the saints, where suffering and pain would be no more and where all the anguish of this mortal life would be absent entirely, being replaced by sheer joy such as that of the angels themselves.

Some of the greatest theologians had been prepared to say that *one* of the joys possessed by the blessed in heaven would be to witness the suffering of the damned in hell. This unpleasant idea was refined in these responsible thinkers to mean that the blessed would rejoice to see God's justice vindicated, rather than delight in the actual sufferings of those who through their own choice had shown themselves utterly unworthy of heavenly bliss. But hell was a real possibility. In certain of the theologies the fires of hell were taken almost literally, but in most of them the everlasting pains endured there were summed up in phrases like 'deprivation of God'—and hence of abiding happiness—or the pain of recognizing the evil done in this life with its inevitable consequences. A few more recent writers had interpreted hell in a less terrible fashion; they had even turned it into a kind of purgatory in which the anguish was a necessary means of purification—for such thinkers hell was not everlasting or eternal (whichever you choose) but temporary; in the end God would win all men to himself. Such universalism was not regarded as orthodox, however, no matter how much more it might seem to be in accordance with the supposedly Christian conviction that God is love.

I quite realize that the sketch which I have just given can be faulted as being too brief and too selective; it can also be called an unfair parody of what was in fact taught. To this I can only reply that this *is* what I myself was taught, first, as part of instruction given in my parish as a child and later, with many refinements and qualifications, in lectures in theology as an ordinand—although I should add that my teacher was himself, quite obviously, very ill at ease about the scheme, left it to the very end of his course, and even then touched upon it gingerly. In fact he engaged in a process of gentle 'de-mythologizing', although that word had not been invented in that time. Certainly the two or three 'standard texts' which we were supposed to master *did* talk in that way, however, although at least one of them left it open to the reader to make his own interpretation of what the scheme, presented as *the* orthodox view, set forth in such precise detail.

It is hardly necessary to say that this scheme does not commend itself to most of us today. Obviously there are many who still accept it, or something like it; to deny that would be nonsense. But, by and large, it has been given up in that form or in any close approximation to that form. This has been for various reasons. A new approach to the Bible has been one of them. A view of revelation as found, not in propositions, but in events of history and their meaning has been another. A third has been a conviction that much in the scheme stands in stark contradiction to the belief in God as love—especially in the bits about hell and endless suffering. Still another has been the feeling that nobody could ever have the knowledge to enable him to draw so exact and precise a map of 'the future life', as it has been called. And a fifth reason is that the portrayal of 'the last things' in these terms, indeed the emphasis on some destiny for man out of this world which makes what goes on *in* this world merely preparatory for heaven or a way of avoiding hell, is thought by a great many people to entail a neglect of their duty here and now to live in Christian love and to find in that their deepest satisfaction, whatever may await them when this life is ended.

But however we may analyse the reaction, reaction there has been. Thus in a large number of sermons, in much religious instruction, and in the emphasis found in theological teaching, death, judgement, heaven, and hell have little if any place. I can recall, in recent years, only one sermon that I have heard on death, one on judgement, and none whatever on either heaven or hell. Nor do I think my experience very unusual, for it has included many parish churches, college chapels, and the chapels of theological schools. Furthermore, a glance through the syllabuses of a number of theological colleges has disclosed that they include but the briefest mention of the traditional scheme. And an admittedly hurried examination of several texts intended for use in courses of instruction before confirmation or in 'religious studies' in schools for adolescents has made it plain that this whole set of ideas is either entirely absent or is so 'muted' (to put it so) that it plays no really significant part in what children or confirmands learn as they are introduced to the Christian faith and its theological implications.

I do not wish to dwell on this, however; surely the change in atmosphere and attitude must be familiar to most of us. What I do wish to say is that we still find in our liturgical forms, even in some (if not all) of the revised ones, the relics of the traditional scheme, and that our hymns still suggest many if not every one of the ideas that I have so briefly, and some will think unfairly, sketched for you. Perhaps this is one reason why there is so often an air of unreality about our worship, when such liturgical forms and such hymns are used, as they must be. For these reflect, however dimly, a scheme which is no longer *taught*, as part of the faith, or in fact believed.

But what chiefly I wish to suggest is that while I for one welcome the disappearance or 'muting' of the traditional teaching about the last things, I also think that they did point to important truths about human life as well as about Christian faith. This does not mean that I desire a return to the former state of affairs; it does mean, on the other hand, that it may very well be incumbent upon us to attend to these matters, to see what 'values'—if I may use that not too happy word— the old scheme somehow preserved, and then to consider whether or not those values may be stated in some other fashion—that is, in a fashion which will not be quite so out-rageous as I, with many others, think the scheme I was taught really was.

In other words, I have the feeling that we have a job to do. This is why I very much regret that the so-called 'new theologians' have not written much, if anything, on the subject, for I believe that they could have helped us considerably and that their failure to do so has left us impoverished. There is a familiar saying about 'throwing out the baby with the bath-water'. In a way that saying applies here. We certainly do *not* want the old 'bath-water'; but maybe the 'baby' has something still to say to us. I apologize for this very strained image; but I am confident that you will take my point. What, then, did the older scheme have to say, in terms of enduring values or meaning, which we should *not* reject when quite rightly we reject the scheme itself?

In the remainder of the book I shall attempt this task, but in a very preliminary and suggestive way. First, however, I must indicate the particular approach which I shall take and the materials and method that I wish to use. That will occupy our attention in the next chapter. Then I shall say something about death, judgement, heaven, hell, and the so-called inter-mediate state. A later chapter will consider what may be said about the Christian hope in its relationship to 'personal existence' after death.

In closing the present chapter, let me say, very briefly, what seem to me some of the obvious values in that older scheme which most of us have by now given up. Such a statement will perhaps provide some preparation for the more detailed discussion in the following pages.

First, then, the fact that death was so stressed in the scheme made it very clear that this event in every human life is of enormous importance. That we shall die is the one inevitable thing to which we must adjust ourselves. But death is not simply the inescapable end of each man's life; it is also the plain demonstration of his mortality, a mortality which both conditions and characterizes everything that he is and does up to the moment when he is pronounced dead. Doubtless it is absurd to dwell on death as such; it is equally absurd to attempt to deny it, to cover it up, to pretend that it is not there —one thinks of the pathetic way in which contemporary funeral customs so often try to disguise what as a matter of obvious truth a funeral is all about. Such fashions are pathetic; they are also silly. So is the evasion of the use of the word itself, with the substitution of such phrases as 'passed on', 'has left us', 'has gone away'. People *die* and we should honestly and courageously accept that this happens. And as I have said, this dying stands as the sign over every bit of human life. We are mortal men, who during a certain relatively short period have responsibilities, know joy and sorrow, contribute to the race of which we are part. Anything else that we may wish to say about ourselves cannot be a denial of that mortality.

Again, the stress on judgement in the old scheme made apparent the place of decision in human life and at the same time the responsibility that comes with decision. It faced men with the one-way movement of history, in which what has happened has indeed happened; it cannot be *undone*, no matter what may be *done with it*. We are what our decisions have made us, even when we grant that the area in which those decisions were taken may have been restricted. Having made the decisions we have made and having become what we are in consequence of those decisions (although obviously other factors have entered in as well), we cannot evade or avoid appraisal in terms of them. *Who* appraises is not the issue here; but *that* there is appraisal is plain enough. The traditional scheme made it impossible to escape from this.

When the scheme included, as it did in my case at least, the intermediate state, this was by way of showing that nobody was good enough, loving enough, faithful enough, to be counted perfect, save (as the scheme claimed) for those few who were called 'saints' in a quite special sense of that word—not the New Testament sense, incidentally. Furthermore, in its own odd way it stressed the love of God, who provided opportunity for 'growth in his love and service', as a prayer puts it, and whose justice was therefore mitigated by his mercy. When this belief was coupled with the notion of a last judgement which would not occur until God 'had accomplished the number of his elect', in words from still another prayer, it said something about the corporate nature of human life, the equally corporate nature of whatever destiny men have, and the need for patient waiting until our fellowmen have found their capacity for fulfilment along with us. Prayers for the dead again indicated the social nature of human life, our belonging together, and our helping one another as we move on towards our goal, whatever that may be.

Heaven stood for the sheer joy which may be known when men are in such a relationship with God, in company with their fellows, as will mark their own realization or actualization, through the gracious influence of love at work in and even beyond this mortal life. At its best, it did not invite those who believed in it to a selfish satisfaction but spoke of 'social joys', in widest sharing, in and under and with God himself.

Hell is the difficult aspect of the scheme, for all too often it succeeded in introducing the element of terror or fear into human existence. 'The fear of the Lord' frequently became sheer terror in the face of possible unending pain. Hence there was always the danger, and often the horrible reality, of men and women trying 'to be good', as the phrase goes, lest they find themselves in 'the fires of hell'. That, certainly, was not only a poor way to persuade people to 'be good', but was also an invitation not to be good at all, in any genuine sense— only to be 'prudent' in the worst meaning of that word. And yet there was something else. That was the utter horror of lovelessness, the desperate state of life in which no response is made to God's solicitations and invitations. And there was the stark recognition that evil *is* evil. A good God might have ways of dealing with evil, but that it was evil could not be denied. So Thomas Hardy's words were seen to be true:

If way to the better there be
It exacts a full look at the worst.

The reality of death as a fact: the inescapable element of decision and the consequences in searching appraisal: the social or communal nature of human existence, coupled with the honest recognition that *no* man is in and of himself a perfect agent of the purpose of God and the love of God: the joy of fulfilment with one's brethren in the imperishable reality of God: and the terrible character of evil—these were values which the older scheme somehow affirmed and expressed.

This does not mean that we should attempt to resurrect that scheme. It is far too late in the day to do that, I should claim. Nor does it mean that the scheme as it stood was a very satisfactory or even worthy mode of expressing the values which I have noted. On the other hand, it suggests—if it does nothing more than that—a necessity on our part to find ways which will provide for an expression, an affirmation, of those values in our own terms and in our own way. If we can achieve something like that, we shall also have maintained a certain continuity with our fathers in the faith. I believe that this last is not unimportant for us; indeed I believe that it is of the highest importance. My reason for believing this is that true *radicalism* in theology, as elsewhere, consists in penetration *to the roots*; which is to say, in getting at what utterly unacceptable ideas, as we see them, were attempting to say. It may well be that then we shall feel obliged to reject that which they *were* trying to say; on the other hand it may be that we shall discover that this which they were trying to say is significant, perhaps even essential, in the total Christian stance of faith. In respect to the impossible and incredible scheme which I learned as a young man, I believe this to be the case. For God's sake, quite literally; for man's sake, quite surely, let us give up the *scheme*—but let us see to it that we do not lose altogether the insight or intuition which was behind it and which was expressed, sometimes in ghastly and ridiculous fashion, in its several elements.

TWO

An Approach to a New Perspective

In closing the last chapter I spoke of the values which had been represented in the outworn traditional scheme of the last things. I suggested that true radicalism in theology meant an effort to get to the roots, to see what was deeply intended in patterns, pictures, and propositions that to us are not credible. And I mentioned the importance of maintaining such continuity as is possible, in this and in other respects, with our ancestors in the Christian fellowship. In a word, I was urging a theological variation of Leonard Hodgson's by now well-known point about Biblical enquiry. What must the case really be, so far as we today can grasp it, if people who thought and wrote and naturally accepted such and such ideas put things in the way in which they did put them? Hodgson was suggesting that after all the preliminary scholarly work has been done, this is the question which the interpreter of Scripture must ask. And I am suggesting that after we have discovered, so far as may be, how this or that theological idea came to be, on what grounds and with what intention it was asserted, we have then to ask a similar question.

I realize that some of those who call themselves 'radical theologians' will regard such a procedure as quite absurd. They will disclaim any responsibility for maintaining continuity with the past of the Christian fellowship and will urge that we must start afresh, with no *impedimenta* from the past. It must be observed that such theologians usually do not fulfil that implied intention, for they still insist on their loyalty to Jesus, at least, even if their way of being loyal to Him is as various as, say, William Hamilton's talk about Jesus as being 'the place where we stand' or Paul van Buren's sense that somehow association with Jesus provides a 'contagious freedom'. What is more, when some of these thinkers say that they are 'giving up' God, it is to be noted that at the very same moment they seem anxious to preserve, in some fashion or other, what the faith in God meant and supplied to those who did, as a matter of fact, deeply believe in Him. Their presentation of that significant and presumably enduring 'reality' is not very impressive, in some instances anyway; but the intention is there.

Thus I would conclude that *in principle* what I have been urging is not so obscurantist, reactionary, or nostalgic as it might appear. But I wish also to remark that what such critics often imply is a very unhistorical notion of how any faith, and *a fortiori* Christian faith, does work as a matter of historical development. They are not really radicals at all, when they suggest the necessity of starting entirely fresh, and demand that there be no commitments of any kind to the religious traditions of the past. For religious faiths do not grow that way, nor do they come into being in that way in the first place. Such entirely revolutionary ideas rest upon a failure to see that the Jewish prophets, for example, were related to, and in many ways dependent upon, the tradition which they received, and were enormously affected by the fact of their participation in the life of the people of Israel. Jesus Himself, claimed by some of them as the great revolutionary, was first and last a *Jew*, thinking in Jewish terms, talking in Jewish ways, dependent for His teaching upon the Jewish tradition. He was *not* a revolutionary in the sense intended; He was a genuine radical in the sense that I have suggested. Nor is this process limited to Judaism and Christianity. It is the way in which religions and faiths of all types have historically developed.

Of course some complete revolutionary may propose his own esoteric religious ideas or proclaim his own peculiar faith.

The men I am criticizing evidently do not much like such ideas or faiths, which they are likely to denounce as 'mysticism' or as erratic affirmations of eccentric individuals. But even if they did take a more favourable attitude, the fact would remain that the positive religions, as they used to be called in studies of religious phenomenonology—that is, the faiths or religions which grasp large numbers of people, make an impact on the world, and show a capacity to persist in some community form —are social in nature; grow out of a past which is not entirely rejected even when the great prophets, teachers, reformers, and renovators come along; and always, or almost always, take towards their supposed origins and their historical development a respectful if (thank heaven) not an uncritical stance.

And the same is true in what used to be called 'secular' areas, although that word has now become so ambiguous in meaning that one hesitates to use it. In philosophical development, A. N. Whitehead said, all western thought is 'a series of footnotes' to Plato's dialogues. Something like that is indeed the case; and only a very ignorant person would be prepared to deny the continuities, with genuine differences and, one hopes, genuine advances, in the total philosophical enterprise. Similarly, in scientific thought, where once again we are indebted to Whitehead, among others, for making clear to us the way in which such thought, along with the procedures it uses and the attitudes it takes, represents a genuine process of development and not sheer novelty entirely unrelated to the past. In social theory and its implementation in social structures, of which Marxism may serve for an example, we may observe the same sort of movement. Karl Marx himself was keenly conscious of this, as a study of *Das Kapital* will show; and, what is even more significant, his doctrine of the dialectic in history is a clear illustration of what I have been urging. Novelty, yes; but continuity, too. The *talk* may be about 'revolution', about the 'qualitative leap', but what happens is a development of social, economic, and political ordering out of the past, while the 'qualitative leap', as Marx himself remarked, comes from the accumulation of a quite enormous number of quantitative changes. It is not *sheer* novelty, although it is new; it is not *unthinking* continuity, although it is related to the past and builds upon, while it also greatly modifies, that which the past has done.

By my references to 'process' in the preceding remarks I have indicated that I stand within a certain philosophical school. Thus I begin my admission or confession of the approach, the materials, and the methods which I believe to be necessary in the indispensable job of re-conceiving the last things, along with re-conceiving the totality of the Christian theological tradition. First, then, a processive view of the world and everything in it; and along with that, what might be styled, perhaps daringly, a processive view of what-it-is or who-it-is that the term *God* points towards.

It is hardly necessary to state here what process thought has to say; and, in any event, I can refer those who do not know about it to a recent small book of my own, entitled *Process Thought and Christian Faith* (Macmillan, New York, and Nisbet, London, 1968), in which I attempted to give a brief sketch of that conceptuality with special reference to its availability for the enterprise of Christian re-conception. Perhaps sufficient will have been said if I point out that process thought is based upon wide generalizations made from those experiences of fact, and those facts of experience, which demonstrate to us the dynamic, active, on-going 'creative advance' of the world; and which, in recognizing and accepting the patent reality of such a world, sees man as part of it sharing in that movement, and a principle of ordering and direction, which may properly be called *God*, explaining why and how the advance goes on as it does.

God, so understood, is not only the chief causative principle, although He is not by any means the *only* such principle (since there is freedom of decision throughout the world-order); He is also the supreme affective reality, because what happens in the world, by precisely such free decision and its results, makes a difference to and (if we may put it so) contributes to the divine principle in providing further opportunities for advance as well as in enriching the experience of the divine itself or himself.

The world is a processive order; it is also a social one, in which everything in it affects everything else, from the lowest structures and forces up to man himself—and, says process thought, to God too. There is a mutual prehension by one occasion of other occasions, to the remotest point in space and time. That prehension may be positive or negative—a grasping and being grasped that accepts or rejects what is offered and being offered. Since God, on such a view, is not the great 'exception to all metaphysical principles to save them from collapse', in Whitehead's by now famous declaration, but is 'their chief exemplification', He too is in a real sense processive. But He is *chief* exemplification, not simply another one of the same sort as all others known to us. He is in some genuine fashion *eminent*. He is, as Charles Hartshorne would put it, 'the supremely worshipful', who is unsurpassed by anything which is not Himself; yet in His own life He may surpass, in richness of experience and capacity for adaptation and provision of new opportunity for advance, that which He has been. Hence God is supremely temporal rather than eternal in the common acceptation of the word, which usually is taken to mean utterly 'time-less'.

God works in the world by providing 'initial aims' for each occasion or event or occurrence or 'entity' (which was Whitehead's word); His 'power' is in His persuasion, in His 'lure' (which is also Whitehead's word), not in coercive force. In a word, 'his nature and his name is love'. Both Whitehead himself and his distinguished American exponent (who also makes his own distinctive contribution to process thought) Charles Hartshorne are very clear about this. It is these two who have been the fathers of this conceptuality, so far as English-speaking countries are concerned, although many others have assisted, some of them (like Teilhard de Chardin) from a quite different starting-point.

Whitehead once wrote that Christianity, unlike Buddhism, is a faith—based on certain historical events taken to be, in his own term used elsewhere, 'important' or crucial or disclosing —seeking a metaphysic. The fact is the total impact of the person of Christ, in whom Christianity finds 'the disclosure in act of what Plato discerned in theory'. And what is this? It is, again in his own words, that 'the divine nature and agency in the world' are precisely such love, such persuasion, such tenderness. Nor was this asserted without regard for the patent presence of evil, both in man himself and in those recalcitrant, negative, retarding, occasions, with their consequences, which anybody with his eyes open must admit. Hence, in its wholeness, the availability of process thought for use in Christian thinking: Christ as the disclosure of 'what God is up to' in the world.

But I have used the term 'metaphysic' and this can provoke an instant reaction from those who think that the day of metaphysics or of ontological statement is over. Here I should respond that *it all depends*. If by metaphysics or ontology one means either the construction of grandiose schemes in which some super-terrestrial being is set up as controlling the world, having once got it going, reducing the world to irrelevance or meaninglessness in comparison to his subsistence as absolute or *esse a se subsistens*, in Aquinas's phrase; or some privileged knowledge of the *what* of things behind all appearances, such as gives us a precise acquaintance with Kant's *ding an sich*, the realm of the noumenal as above, beyond, and unrelated (save by logical connection) to the phenomenal—if either of these be what metaphysics means, then its day is indeed past.

On the other hand, if by metaphysics one means exactly what I suggested earlier—the making of wide generalizations on the basis of particular experiences, the constant reference back of those generalizations to further areas of experience, and the resultant 'vision' of how things 'are' and how 'they go'—

then metaphysics is by no means finished. Even those who denounce metaphysics in the former sense are eminently metaphysical in the latter. One has only to read such 'anti-metaphysical' writers as the earlier positivists, whether Comteian or in the Vienna Circle with its English disciples known as 'logical positivists', to see how true this is. They indeed do have a metaphysic, in my second sense; but, if I may venture to say so, it is a very *bad* metaphysic since it is not recognized as such and hence has not been exposed by these thinkers to severe and searching criticism. The same is the case with the 'anti-metaphysical' theologians. Harvey Cox's *The Secular City* simply reeks of metaphysics, in that second sense; so does R. Gregor Smith's *Secular Christianity*—and admittedly Thomas Altizer's books are highly metaphysical in statement and intention, while William Hamilton for all his eschewing of metaphysics presupposes throughout his 'death of God' writing exactly the same sort of thing.

Thus I am not ashamed of the metaphysical emphasis in process thought, once it is seen what kind of metaphysics the process philosophers are talking about. Here there is no setting-up of a super-terrestrial, sheerly supra-natural, being called 'God'; since, in Whitehead's words, 'God is in this world or he is nowhere'. Here there is no claim to privileged access to the *ding an sich*, for any such dichotomy between noumenal and phenomenal is absurd—*what a thing is* is known in, and consists of, *what a thing does*; or, in Christian terms, we know God in terms of His activity in the world, working towards communities or societies of shared good in spite of the recalcitrance, the back-waters, the negativities, or compendiously 'the evil', with which he has to deal. And when the Dutch philosopher C. A. van Peurson in his exciting article called 'Man and Reality' (*Student World*, LVI, 1963) and others who think like him contrast the *ontological* and the *functional* and insist that metaphysics *must* mean the former attitude, they do not see that there is a sense in which this need not be said at all. How things go—their functioning—may be, and I believe it is, *what they are.* Thus, again in Christian terms, God *is* love precisely because He *acts lovingly*; and any statement of a formally abstract sort, such as the one I have just made—'God *is* love', etc.—is precisely what I have now called it: a formally abstract statement made on the basis of what are taken to be concrete events or occasions, and with validity only insofar as it affirms exactly such an understanding of the functioning which is observed, experienced, and hence must be talked about.

But I have said enough about all this. My main point is simply that I find process thought, with its view of God, eminently available for Christian use. Particularly, I find the view of God both as providing the 'initial aim' and also as being the 'supreme affect' most suggestive and helpful. In respect to the deep significance seeking expression through the traditional teaching about the last things, I find this conceptuality so suggestive and so helpful that it will provide a framework within which I shall try to urge a way of securing for ourselves those meanings or values or existentially significant affirmations.

The mention of 'existentialism' here, while I intended it in a slightly different way, brings us to the second point which I wish to make. This has to do with the interpretation of Scripture. More especially, it has to do with the enterprise known as 'de-mythologization', in relation to what the father of that enterprise calls *existenzialinterpretation* of the biblical material and most importantly of the material that has to do with the *kerygma* or the Christian gospel to which faith is a response.

I think that the word '*de-*mythologizing', in its English form, does not do justice to what Bultmann really intends; and it is a puzzle to me why he has accepted this term as a satisfactory English description of the enterprise which in German is styled *entmythologisierung*. Admittedly the English term does translate the German, but at the same time the '*de-*' suggests to the English reader almost exactly the opposite of Bultmann's intention. For what he wishes to do is not to discard the mythological material—mistaken science, talk about the divine in this-world idiom, highly fanciful material about descent and ascent of a supernatural divine being who pre-existed this world, etc., etc.—but to get at what it is *really* saying. I think that the term *in*-mythologizing would serve better, since the whole programme is concerned to get 'inside' the myth and there discover the *kerygma* or gospel which the myth clothes and states in a form natural at one time but impossible, because incredible, today. It is not necessary for me to recount *why* Bultmann finds this incredibility in the form; suffice it to say that he is not committed to any particular scientific world-view, although Jaspers and others have charged him with this, but is simply stating that the contemporary man does not as a matter of fact think or talk in terms of such a form. Hence, if the gospel is to speak to him with its demand for decision, it must be freed from those thought-patterns so that its essential *drive* may be made clear to him, a drive or proclamation in action which the ancient forms today succeed in covering up or making absurd.

I ought here to admit that I should wish to go beyond Bultmann; I agree with Fritz Buri and his American exponent Schubert Ogden that we need also to *in-kerygmatize*, if I may put it so, the gospel proclamation itself. But this does not suggest that there *is* no gospel and that Jesus Christ is not central to Christian faith. What is involved here is exactly what the ancient 'Fathers', or some of them, affirmed when they spoke of the possibility of salvation for those who had never heard about and hence could not or did not respond to the specific historic event of Jesus Christ. The work of the Eternal Word of God, present in men spermatically, as Justin Martyr for example put it, offered this possibility of salvation, so that the historical accident of having lived *after* Jesus or having heard about Him was not the necessary condition of the salvation which God purposed for His human children. These 'Fathers' spoke of the specific activity of God in Jesus Christ as being indeed the fulfilment, completion, and adequate expression, *vis-à-vis* men, of the Eternal Word of God, but they did not regard salvation as available *only* through Jesus; even in the Fourth Gospel, it would seem to be the writer's intention to have the *Word* speak, rather than the historical Jesus in isolation from that Word 'who was in the beginning with God', 'by whom all things were made', 'who was the light of every man', and who in Jesus Christ was decisively 'made flesh and dwelt among us'.

In the sort of language which Bultmann and Buri would employ, the possibility of authentic existence before God, in which men live in faith and with love, is granted to every man by virtue of his being human. This Bultmann would deny; this Buri would affirm. I should agree with Buri and I should say that the point of the Christian gospel is to 're-present', as Ogden puts it, that possibility; to 're-present' it in starkly human terms, under human conditions, in Jesus as what I like to style 'the classic instance' of what God is always 'up to', rather than the totally other or the sheer anomaly, as so many (including Bultmann, presumably) would wish to regard him.

What is important for our present purposes in Bultmann's enterprise, however, is the insistence on getting at what the biblical material is saying without our being obliged at the same time to accept for ourselves the form in which it is said. It is exactly this method which I wish to employ as we continue in succeeding chapters to discuss the truth found in the last things. Or once again, in Leonard Hodgson's way of phrasing it, we are trying to find what the state of things really is, how things really go, in a fashion which makes sense to us, when we grant that men and women who lived at *that* time, under *those* conditions, with *those* presuppositions, spoke about the matter in *that* way.

Furthermore, this kind of approach will free us from supposing that because this or that particular description of man's destiny is found stated in this or that particular way in Holy Scripture, we are obliged to accept it as necessarily 'the case'. This applies, I should claim, not only to Old Testament material and the literature of the New Testament apart from the gospels. It also applies to Jesus' own teaching. He was a Jew, He thought and spoke like a Jew; this is part of His being 'very man', as Chalcedon said He was. Hence with His own statements, so far as they are His own, such a 'proportionate interpretation', in a fine phrase from Bishop Westcott, is required quite as much as it is required for other pieces of biblical teaching.

I also wish to stress the importance for us, in this enterprise, of the social and psychosomatic understanding of man which has been so wonderfully recovered in recent years. The biblical perspective in regard to 'corporate personality' is now restored in quite 'secular' circles; to be a person *means* to be intimately and essentially related with other men. 'No man is an island entire unto himself'; and to come to know our personal humanity is to see it in its rich relationship with other persons. Atomistic views of man will no longer serve, not because we dislike them but because they are not accurate statements of a truth which is known to us in our deepest human existence. And with this stress on 'the body corporate' goes also an emphasis on man's corporeal nature. We are not 'souls' inhabiting 'bodies'; we are psychosomatic organisms, more or less integrated entities in which bodily existence is characterized by the capacity to think, to feel, to will. Here again it is not because we prefer this view; it is because, so far as we can understand ourselves and what human existence is like, we see it to be true. We owe much here to the depth psychologists and equally to those who in medical work have shown the relationship of mental processes to bodily ones. Man is an organic unity, however adequately or inadequately this is actualized in a given person's experience.

Furthermore, we belong to and with our environment. The *mit-welt* of which Heidegger speaks is not confined to our fellow-men; it includes the realm of nature as well, since we are 'organic to nature', as Pringle-Pattison insisted many years ago. The evolutionary perspective makes this apparent; our

An Approach to a New Perspective

animal origin demonstrates it. This is why we cannot follow certain existentialist writers in speaking about human history as if it were being played out against a background of irrelevant natural recurrence. Nature itself, the whole world of stuff or matter, is *there* and we are somehow part of it. We ought not to attempt to separate human experience and history from nature, but rather to see that nature itself is historical—by which I mean that it is processive, with movement and change, even if on the macrocosmic scale this does not seem obvious to us. The sort of philosophical conceptuality which I urged upon you earlier is from one point of view merely an affirmation of exactly that kind of historical view of the whole world-process. But for our present purpose, it is enough to say that when we are thinking about the last things, our thought must include much more than human existence and human personality in its body-mind totality, even in its social relationships. The realm of nature itself must be in the picture.

I am not competent to speak about what may be contributed to us by the depth-psychologies which I have just mentioned. Harry Williams has written a useful little book on *The Last Things* in which he does just this; and I refer you to that book as well as to other essays, by him and by such writers as the late David Roberts, for some development of this theme. But insofar as this psychology talks of man's deep emotional drives, his purposive activity, his striving for realization of selfhood, his need to love and to be able to receive love, and with these the twistings and distortings which may be uncovered in him— insofar as it does this, it helps us see something of what true fulfilment is about and has much to say concerning such actualization of man, with man's consequent 'satisfaction' and the joy which it provides, about which in an entirely different idiom the heavenly city was a picture. At the same time, the horror of hell, as real deprivation on the part of those who were loveless, because they could not love nor accept love, finds its parallel in the state of lovelessness and hence of utter despair, concerning which this psychology has so much to say.

My final point has been implied in everything that has so far been advanced. This is the practical consequences in actual and concrete human living which may be found in coming to some awareness of what the last things were trying to say. God, as chief causative principle and as supreme affect, is 'in this world or he is nowhere'; biblical material, and in relation to it Christian liturgical and hymnological imagery, with the theological articulation of this, intend to make affirmations which are to be found *in* the pictures and forms and myths— and these we must seek to make meaningful and valid for ourselves in our present existence; man is an 'embodied' and a social occasion or series (or 'routing') of occasions, organic to the world of nature, and can only truly *live* as he lives in due recognition of these facts and sees them as integral to himself. Each of these points, which we have so far discussed, along with whatever of value is to be found in the psychological analysis to which I have just referred, speaks directly to us as and where and when we *are*.

In other words, the talk about the last things is not only, if it is at all, talk about something that happens in an imagined future state, once we have died the death which each man must die. It is talk about us as we now live, in this world and with this world's responsibilities as well as its privileges. From one point of view, it might be said that futuristic references are by way of being *aberglaube*—'over-beliefs' which may or may not be necessary consequences of what is said about the here-and-now as Christian faith interprets it.

I do not wish to deny those futuristic references, as I have called them. In a later chapter I shall have something to say about them, although I shall emphasize that they belong to the realm which our ancestors used to describe as 'a religious hope' rather than to the realm of verifiable experience or the realm of concrete Christian existence as we are called to share it. I do wish to stress, however, the reference to concrete and actual existence *now*.

Many years ago, when James Pike and I were commissioned

to prepare, for the Authors' Committee of the Division of Christian Education of the Episcopal Church, a book which would state in fairly simple fashion the 'faith of the Church' (so the book was entitled when finally it appeared, after much revision and re-writing), we talked with Bishop Angus Dun of Washington about the project. The two authors, with the whole membership of the committee charged with preparing the book, visited Bishop Dun and spent with him an entire day. We discussed the plan of the volume, the subjects to be included, and other such topics. I shall never forget Bishop Dun's repeated insistence that in approaching each topic, we must see to it that the main emphasis was always on what he called, as I remember it, 'what this means for living as a Christian today'. The particular topic upon which he first made this comment was the doctrine of creation; and he said that the only way in which this could properly be approached was by being as clear as we could about what it means to a man 'to be a creature, living in a created world' with all that this implies, entails, and suggests.

I do not wish to father on Bishop Dun what I am trying to suggest in these pages, but I think that the point which he made at that time is highly relevant to what we are attempting to do here. What did the last things *mean* to men and women who accepted the scheme quite literally or with this or that reservation or re-interpretation? What is the deepest *meaning* in that scheme, which because it is somehow integral to the Christian faith we must seek to guarantee and preserve in our re-conception and re-statement of that faith? What does this *mean* for you and for me, for any Christian? And finally what can it *be made to mean*, without cheating or falsification, for every man and woman who wants to come to that profound self-understanding which is the other side of (and utterly integral to) the understanding of God *vis-à-vis* man?

So in the next chapter we shall begin by thinking about death.

THREE

Death

Many years ago a visiting preacher at the General Theological
Seminary—I *think* it was Allan Whittemore, then superior of
the Order of the Holy Cross—began his sermon with some
words which startled the congregation into almost shocked
attention. The words were these, as I remember them:
'Everyone of you within sound of my voice will, within not
too many years, be a corpse'. The sermon which followed was
the one sermon about death and its meaning that I have ever
heard preached; I noted that one sermon earlier.

I confess that I have entirely forgotten what the preacher
said after his striking first sentence. But that sentence I have
never forgotten, nor can I; since it made me face, for the first
time and with utter seriousness, the absolutely inescapable fact
that *I* was going to die. Of course I had always known that *men*
died, and in a sense I was well aware of my own death as one of
those men. What that sentence did, however, was to make me
starkly conscious of the fact that not only do *men* die but that I,
in my concrete actual human existence, faced death too. In a
way, it was a realization of what Martin Luther meant when he
said that every man dies *alone*—in his particularity, in what
Whitehead called, in another connection, his 'solitariness'.
That is, it was I, Norman Pittenger, then a young man and a
somewhat eager theological student, looking forward to a long
and I hoped successful span of years, who was brought face to
face with the inevitability of my own entirely personal death.

Now the fact that each of us dies alone, in his 'solitariness', as this or that particular person, does not for a moment signify that we do not belong to the human race, exist in relationship with our fellowmen, and find the meaning of our lives not in isolation but in solidarity with others. Far from doing that, it emphasizes our belonging, relationship, and solidarity, since it makes plain that in this mortal existence of ours, before that 'moment of truth'—not the *only* such moment, but a determinative one in so many ways—which is our own death, we can find our deepest satisfactions and our best fulfilment only in companionship and in the giving-and-receiving which is love. Once we know that we are to die, each for himself and each by himself, we are brought to value all the more highly and treasure all the more carefully that companionship and that giving-and-receiving which is life in loving. Every moment of our existence before death is now coloured by the realization, however dim it may be at any given moment, that *now* is the time—'the accepted time', if I may use here St Paul's phrase in a very different context—when we must find ourselves in others and become what nowadays we have learned to style a man 'for others'.

Death is not simply a biological fact. Obviously it *is* that, since as a matter of human biology men do and must die. As Heidegger has said, death is indeed human life in its finality; and, in a very profound sense, all of our existence is 'towards death', precisely as a biological fact which we must accept. Yet it is not *this* sense, the straightforward biological reality, which gives to the fact of our dying both its high significance and its peculiar poignancy. What does that is the related and equally inescapable truth that death is also 'the finality of human life'. By this I mean that it is the qualifying of human life in such a way that we know ourselves to be mortal men who have no claim to anything else and who must honestly and bravely face the truth of their mortality. If they do not do so, they are less than men. Someone has said that a distinguishing factor, as between human life and animal life, is that while the animals die, as do we, they do not know that they are going to die, whereas we die, as do they, but we know that we are going to do so.

Not only does each man die, and because he is going to die recognize himself as mortal, but all men, each for himself and as himself, are also to die. Thus it is not only *I* who know myself to be mortal; every other man, and all men together constituting the human race, are able only to understand himself and themselves, when the mortality which I am stressing is accepted for what it is.

If we agree, as surely we must, that the one inescapable and inevitable fact about every man and about the whole race of men is this death, we should also agree that it is in no sense morbid to face up to it and endeavour to come to terms with it. On the contrary, it is the measure of our humanity that we live daily as those who know that they are going to die, and hence are mortal, and that we can, as it were, adjust ourselves to that stupendous fact.

Indeed, at no time in his history has man been content to consider death 'a mere incident', however much he has been tempted to do so and however many times he has sought to cover up the fact in one way or another. Or, if this statement seems too extreme, at least we can affirm confidently that those who have thought longest and deepest about human life have never been able to dismiss death in a cavalier manner. They have seen it, rather, as a tremendous event which is to be regarded seriously and respectfully, often fearfully; and, if they have been 'religious' in any sense, they would add that they must approach death and regard its importance faithfully, too. In recent years, more especially, we have learned to take death with high seriousness, not only because there has been so much of it through war and famine and other ills but also because our literature, whether in poetry or novel or drama, has been so conscious of the fact and so insistent on bringing it to our attention. In this there has been a return to the attitude of an earlier day, although with marked differences because of loss of faith or enfeebling of it. The easy dismissal of death, or the assertion that 'for those who believe, there is no death', is taken to be, what it often is, an easy evasion of the dread reality itself—escapism, childish refusal to face facts, and above all (in our special interest) unwillingness to accept our human mortality.

Death is *there*, then. The question is, how can we come to terms with it?

Death is not there alone; it is there, as I have argued, with a finality about it. For if it is true, on the one hand, that death is the end of human existence for each and every one of us, it is on the other equally true (to repeat the words I have already used) that death is human life in its finality. That is, it is the distinctive event which colours, conditions, and qualifies every moment of our existence. And as I have also said a few moments ago, man is the only animal, so far as we know, who is aware of his mortality and who may therefore meditate on the fact that he dies. He who has never pondered this truth, and, in this sense, if in no other, 'prepared for death', is by that token less than a true man. His life is less than authentic; it is properly to be described, by the phrase that Heidegger uses, 'inauthentic'—that is, false, based on wrong understanding, cheapened and superficial. Such a man is living under an illusion because he is out of touch with 'things as they are' in human existence.

One of the most familiar ways in which people seek to evade both death *as* finality and the finality *of* death is through the notion of the 'immortal soul' which 'survives' the fact of our biological death. The ideas associated with that notion are specifically Greek in origin, so far as our culture and our Christian theological development are concerned. We are well aware of this ancestry. The classical statement of the notion is to be found, of course, in the speeches which Plato records from Socrates, or which he has put into the mouth of Socrates, in the dialogues which tell of the last days and death of that great and noble man.

The rational principle in man is individuated; it inhabits a corporeal 'house' for this present time. But since it is one and simple it is indestructible. It participates, in some mode, in the eternal realm of forms, although it is not identified with that realm. When a man's body dies and suffers corruption, the soul is not affected by this occurrence; it 'escapes' from the body which is dying and returns to its true abode. Thus no matter what may happen to the body, man's soul is immortal and since it is *this* which constitutes his distinctive human quality, death is an important and tragic incident, certainly to those who loved and cared for the one who dies, but it is not a final incident—there is more to come, so to say.

The old American song,

> *John Brown's body lies a-mouldering in the grave,*
> *His* soul *goes marching on* . . .'

puts the idea succinctly and popularly.

A great many Christians have thought that this was the teaching of the Christian faith on the subject. They have confused 'immortality of the soul' with whatever may be intended by the biblical phrase 'resurrection of the body'; while theologians have attempted, as we have already observed, when I described the older scheme which comprised the last things, to bring the two conceptions together in a fashion which will retain each of them and yet relate them so that a consistent pattern may be provided. But of course the two conceptions cannot be brought together in that way; and the internal conflicts, the lack of balance, and the arbitrary way in which the two have been associated, demonstrate this plainly enough. We shall have something to say about 'the resurrection of the body' at a later point. For the present, my argument is simply that the talk about 'immortality of the soul' has served to provide for a great many Christian people what they wrongly took to be the right and proper Christian way of escaping the stark reality of total death.

Years ago, in my course in Apologetics in the General Seminary, I put what I take to be the truth of the matter in the

following words: 'We all die; and all of us dies.' Perhaps that
was too glib a phrase; and I know that, when my students
repeated it to their friends, and later in their ministry to their
parishioners, my intention was misunderstood by the auditors.
Yet I remain convinced that what I was seeking to say in that
phrase is the truth. And it is the truth which traditional talk
about the last things has served to emphasize, however uncomfortable it may be and however men may have sought to
evade it. All of us *do* die; that we know. And all *of us* does die—
that is the point which I am now making.

In the Old Testament we find that even the Jews could not
quite easily find their way to accept this. *Sheol* was certainly
not much of an existence; in that dim realm, 'the dead praise
not thee, O Lord', we read. And for a Jew a 'state' in which
God could not be praised was hardly a condition of genuine
life. But apart from the teaching about *sheol*, borrowed or
inherited from more primitive modes of religious thought, the
Jew at least was prepared to recognize the full reality of death.
Until the time of the Maccabees, Jewish faith was not dependent upon nor did it presuppose a kind of 'immortality' or
'resurrection', call it what you will, which alone made it possible to commit oneself wholly to Jahweh and to the doing of
his holy will. And I should say that this plain fact of Old Testament faith stands as a judgement upon any effort in more
recent times to insist that *unless* 'immortality' or 'resurrection'
—again call it what you will—is in the picture, there can be no
deep and genuine faith at all. Christians may wish to say something more, but they simply must not suppose that God, faith
in Him, commitment to Him, service of Him, *and* a denial of
the reality and inescapability of death go together. Above all,
they must not suppose that it is integral to faith in God, with
its consequences, to believe that all *of us* (in the special sense I
have given that phrase) does not die.

While this is the fact, the very reality of our mortality has
emphasized our responsibility for what we do and thus what
we are during the time which we have. 'We shall not pass this

way again'; yet while we are *in via*, as St Augustine puts it, we have both our duty to fulfil and our contribution, such as it may be, to make to the ongoing creative advance of the cosmos. That contribution may be very slight, to all appearances, but it is *ours* to make—and unless *we* make it, it will not be made. This statement introduces us to other ideas, about which something must be said in another context. Among these is the point that with the 'perishing of occasions', as Whitehead has described *one* side of the process, there is also the reception into God and hence both the preservation and use, of whatever good has been achieved within the process itself, to the end that the advance may continue, that further good may be actualized, and that the purpose of God (which is just that actualization of good, through love which is shared in the widest conceivable degree) may be realized in more places and times and in more ways. That is the *other* side of the 'perishing of occasions' which includes our own perishing through the inevitability of the death which awaits us.

In St Paul's letter to the Romans there is a celebrated and much discussed passage: I quote it in the version found in the New English Bible: 'It was through one man that sin entered the world, and through sin death, and thus death pervaded the whole human race, inasmuch as all men have sinned.' Or, in the Revised Standard Version: 'Therefore as sin came into the world through one man and death through sin, and so death spread to all men because all men sinned' (Romans 5:12). The meaning of this passage has been a matter of dispute among New Testament experts, although it is quite obvious that if it does nothing more it asserts that the Apostle believed that there was some connection between the fact of death and the reality of human sin. But whether he intended to tell his readers that death, as a biological fact, is the consequence of one man's sin (namely, Adam's) becoming contagious and hence affecting all men, is by no means entirely certain. Some think he intended to say just this; others seem to believe that St Paul is working up towards his plainly stated conviction that sin in itself *is* death—shall we say, death as loss of God whose service is not only, as the collect tells us, 'perfect freedom', but also true *life* as men are intended by God to live it.

If the latter be the correct interpretation, then 'the sting' in death, as a biological happening which all of us must experience, is to be found in man's sin which is his alienation or separation from God. It is not that because Adam, or anybody else, or the whole race of men, have sinned that they come to die; rather, it is that in facing death, as they must, they know themselves to be in a fashion *already* dead, because to live as 'the enemy of God' is really to be a dead man, however 'alive' one's physical body might be.

Whatever St Paul was trying to communicate about his own belief, there has been a strain in the Christian tradition which has taken the first of the two meanings and has talked as if death were the punishment inflicted on man for his failure to obey God's commands. Had Adam not sinned, it has been said, man would have been immortal, although what this might entail has not been worked out in any great detail. The second of the two possible meanings has been stressed by another strain in the Christian tradition, with more probability so far as our human experience can guide us. And it is this aspect which seems to me to be of significance for us as we see what the scheme which included death among the last things has to say to *us*.

At this point it would be desirable to spend considerable time in discussing the meaning of the word 'sin' itself, but we shall not do that. I take it that we shall agree that 'sin' does *not* denote the various particular acts of this or that man which in some ways contravene God's purpose—the sort of acts with which codes and commandments and sets of rules or laws concern themselves. These are manifestations of something more basic—and that more basic 'something' is what we are getting at when we speak about 'sin'. I should define this in two ways; or rather, in one definition with two aspects.

First, sin is a condition or state or situation in human

existence in which men find themselves impotent before the requirements which they see, however dimly, are laid upon them simply by virtue of their being men. It is a 'grace-less' state, as one might put it; because it is a state in which there is failure in harmonizing the ideal and the actual, failure in integration of the self—always, mind you, the self in its relation with others, for we know of no other human selfhood—and failure to move towards the actualization of the possibilities which are present as the 'initial aim' of our lives is made into the 'subjective aim' (in Whiteheadian language) whose realization constitutes our 'becoming' in manhood.

That is one aspect of the meaning of sin—it is the humanly understood side. The other aspect is introduced when we are aware, as we ought to be, that God's purpose for man, as Paul Lehmann has so admirably told us, is 'to make and keep us human'. That condition or state or situation in which we are *not* realizing our subjective aim and find ourselves impotent in the face of the requirements which it makes upon us may be summed up simply by saying that although we are made to become men, we do not actually get very far along the path, knowing ourselves to be both incompetent and impotent, however grand may be our projects and however optimistic may be our hopes. God's purpose for us, his will, is nothing other than that we should become ourselves as he initially aims us to become—and I have put it in this somewhat clumsy way because I wish to stress the *aim* which is integral to human nature.

Sin, the noun in the singular, is a religiously freighted term whose purpose is to point to *that* state: our failure to become what we are created to become and hence our failure to 'obey' God's command which is precisely that we shall become what we are created to become. With that definition in mind, we may (if we wish—and moral theologians *have* wished) go on to speak of the particular acts, in thought or word or deed, in which this situation manifests itself. But as every sensitive person ought to know and as every counsellor (and every priest who has 'heard confessions') does know, man's root problem is not in these particular acts. They are symptomatic of something much more serious and those who think that by dealing with symptoms they have cured a disease are only deluding themselves and harming the patient. The disease, if the word may be permitted, is the situation or state or condition which I have described and it is *that* which requires attention. One central element in the Christian gospel is the affirmation that in a very real way God deals with that situation—this is the meaning of what we call redemption or salvation or atonement.

For the moment, however, that is not our concern. Our concern is that the fact of human death, as an inescapable biological event which is also the qualification of our humanity as mortal, brings vividly before us something else. It makes us realize, with a startling clarity and with sometimes terrible anguish, that *at our best* we are mortal failures. I quite realize that this may seem an exaggerated, even an emotive, way of stating it; but I am quite sure that any honest man or woman, conscious of his mortality, is also conscious of the fact that he is not what he might have been, that he cannot shift the blame to somebody else's shoulders (however many extenuating circumstances he may feel justified in adducing), and that, in at least one sense, the sense I have indicated above, he *is* a mortal failure. 'I am an unprofitable servant, for I have done only what was commanded of me'—yes, but more than that, 'I am a *very* unprofitable servant, for I have not even done, nor been competent and willing to do, that which was commanded of me.'

This at once introduces us to the responsibility which is ours, as men, to become what we are intended to become. Such responsibility is not imposed upon us from without, by some alien agent or a *deus ex machina*; it is the law of our being or, in much better language, the law for our becoming. If it were thrust on us from outside, it might be only a threat with penalty attached. Because it is integral to our very 'routing', to ourselves as a series of occasions constituting our personality-in-the-making, it is a lure or an enticement or solicitation. But our failure involves penalties, none the less. The penalties are not imposed from outside, either, as if by an alien agent or a *deus ex machina*. They are the ineluctable working-out, in our own existence, of decisions which have been made by us in whatever freedom we possessed. And those decisions, as Robert Frost once wrote of 'The Road Not Taken', 'have made the difference'.

God is love: every Christian would agree with that Johannine affirmation, based as it is on the certainty that God *acts lovingly*: 'Herein is love, not that *we* loved God, but that he loved us, and sent his Son that we might live through him.' I wish to gather together what so far has been said and relate it to this basic Christian affirmation of God as love, 'pure unbounded love', and nothing but that sheer love-in-action.

We die, physically. All of us dies. Death, as giving our existence its specific quality, shows us to be mortal, along with all our fellow-men. This mortality includes the responsibility that we shall become what we were created to be, which is authentic or true men, fully and completely human. Our failure to become what is initially our aim, and subjectively our intentional aim as well, means that we are, in at least one sense, precisely *that*—viz., 'failures'—although God may, and Christians at least believe that He does, deal with that situation if we permit Him to do so. These things the fact of death makes clear.

This is what we have been saying so far in this chapter. But now, as I have said, we turn to what I might call, as I heard a young man put it, 'this love business which Christians talk about'. How, it must be asked, does *that* come into the picture? My own reply would be that it comes in at every point and in every way. Far from being an addition, it is the very heart of the matter. For as God *is* love, so that the affirmation of His love is no afterthought or addendum to a series of propositions about His omnipotence, omniscience, omnipresence, transcendence, etc.; in similar manner in respect to human nature and activity, to human becoming, to human existence as such,

love is no addendum, no afterthought, no extra, but the central
reality itself. This needs development, however. The mere
statement of it will not suffice.

Man is intended to be a lover. It is for this purpose that he
comes into existence and it is for this purpose that he lives.
This may seem to be sheer sentimentality; but it can only seem
so when we do not properly understand the nature of love. In
another place I have attempted to provide what might be
styled a phenomenology of love (*Love Looks Deep*, Mowbrays,
1969). In that book, written for the general public and not for
scholars, I suggested that love includes the following elements
or aspects: commitment, mutuality, fidelity, hopefulness,
union—and that its goal is fulfilment in and with another or
with others. It is obvious that none of us is a 'perfect lover', for
none of us achieves anything like perfection in these several
ways in which love *is* and in which love *expresses itself*. But the
question to be asked is not whether we are thus 'perfect'. The
answer to *that* question is plain enough. The question which
ought to be faced is whether we are *moving towards* fulfilment,
with our fellows, in the several ways which love includes in
itself. In other words, are we *becoming lovers?* Is our actualization of the potentialities within us in the direction of our
becoming more committed, more open to giving-and-receiving,
more faithful, more hopeful in relation with others, more in
union with them? And we have only this mortal span in which
to *become* in this way, for death always stands as the end, the
terminus, of our loving and of our mortal learning to love.

Our human responsibility is to become what we are intended
to become. Thus that responsibility is that we shall become the
lovers we were meant to be. Our tragic situation is that we fail,
at so many places, in so many times, and in so many ways. It is
not only that we are frustrated in this. The frustration may be
due to the concrete conditions in which our existence is set;
about that we can often do little or nothing. Nor is it found in
the fact that within the space of years which is ours we are
frustrated in another sense, the sense (namely) that we do not

have time, as we say, to bring to fruition that which we would wish to accomplish. The frustrations such as I have just mentioned, and other frustrations like them, are inhibiting factors but they are not the decisive factors. What is decisive is whether we are or are not open, within the imposed limits, to the loving, the receiving love, the life in love, which will make us into authentic men whose very authenticity is in their 'becoming in love'.

It is astounding to notice that popular songs, so often contemptuously dismissed by the sophisticated and so frequently condemned as cheap or vulgar or sentimental or lustful by those who think of themselves as 'religious', have got hold of the truth which I have been suggesting, while the sophisticated and the self-consciously 'religious' fail to see what this is all about. It is so easy to dismiss this sort of lyric because it is usually replete with sexual allusions. Yet this may be the importance of the popular song—and that for the reason that human sexuality and the capacity to love (in all the aspects which I have listed) are closely associated. Repression of sexuality can produce precisely the lovelessness which is man's chief trouble, while the expression of sexuality, under the control of love in its aim to be related in mutuality to another or to others, can be a way for realizing love—and realizing it both as a matter of consciously grasped experience and also as a concrete movement towards the fulfilment of self in association with others of our race.

I may refer here, perhaps immodestly, to the book which I just mentioned, where I have sought to show how this comes to be, while in still another book, *The Christian Understanding of Human Nature* (Westminster, Philadelphia, and Nisbet, London, 1964), I tried to relate the theme to Christian theology in a wider sense. Daniel Day Williams, too, in his *The Spirit and the Forms of Love* (Harper and Row, New York, and Nisbet, London, 1968) has worked on the same lines. With these books, and especially Dr Williams's, in mind, I shall not pursue this subject here.

I must make one further point, however. We are thinking about the traditional scheme of the last things and we are doing this as those who in some fashion would wish to confess ourselves as Christians. For us, then, the faith in God enters the picture in a special way. God *is* love, we have said; He has declared this love in His loving action in the total event of Jesus Christ. Let us not forget that this love, declared in action, went to the limit of identification with humanity. Not only is God present in and with men, through his activity in the man Jesus—and elsewhere too, in varying degree and mode. God is also participant in the death which every man must die. To put it mythologically, as nowadays many would phrase it, God in Christ experiences everything in human existence including the death which puts an end to it. 'He learned by the things which he suffered'—and the Greek of that text suggests that what is meant by 'suffered' is what we should call 'experienced' or 'underwent'.

So the love which was worked out in human terms in the life of the Man of Nazareth was a love which knew mortality in its fullness, of body and of soul. It knew the responsibility of becoming itself, completely authentic and therefore entirely free, under those conditions and in that fashion. It is our faith that in that Man it did not 'fail', not because it had peculiar privileges or unique divine prerogatives, but because it held fast to its 'initial aim', making that its own 'subjective aim' and thus through 'the travail' which mortal existence imposed upon it finding the 'satisfaction' or fulfilment which was its destiny. To participate in that love which is humanly worked out in Jesus is truly to live in authenticity. Christian life, I should urge upon you, is just that authentic life in love. Because it is 'life in love', shared with Jesus Christ as the One who did thus realize and actualize love-in-action, it is also 'life in Christ'. And since life in Christ, shared with His human brethren, is both the reflection of and participation in the life which is truly divine—*God's* life—such 'life in love' is 'life in God', for God *is* love.

But none of this is possible without our facing the reality of our dying, any more than it was possible for Him whom we call our Lord and Master. To put it figuratively, the triumph of Easter Day is achieved in and on the Cross of Good Friday—it is not some 'happy ending' which cancels out the suffering that preceded it. Easter triumph in love is God's writing his 'O.K. That's the way things are and that's the way I am'—writing it across the tree on which Jesus hung on that fateful day.

For us this means that we must undertake the responsibility of loving, for that and that only makes possible the authenticity of living. In some lines that W. H. Auden once wrote, in *Letters from Iceland*, there is a compelling statement of this responsibility as it reflects itself in the call, so well known to us today, to social action in the world where we live out our days.

> *And to the good, who know how wide the gulf, how deep*
> *Between ideal and real, who being good have felt*
> *The final temptation to withdraw, sit down, and weep,*
> *We pray the power to take upon themselves the guilt*
> *Of human action, though still as ready to confess*
> *The imperfection of what can and must be built—*
> *The wish and power to act, forgive, and bless.*

FOUR

Judgement

In speaking of the momentous significance of the fact of death, not only as the *finis* or clear terminus of earthly life for every man and for the whole race of men, but also as the event which qualifies and colours each life, we introduced in our conclusion the possibility and the necessity of love.

Man is made to become a lover, we said. In this mortal existence, known as such by reason of our dying, this 'becoming' is frustrated by factors which prevent its complete realization, but much more importantly for each of us the failure in loving is due to our own incompetence and our own impotence in accepting love, both as a giving and as a receiving of self in the mutuality which love is. For this we must somehow shoulder the responsibility, since we know deep within ourselves that we *are* indeed responsible. However difficult it may have been, however many obstacles circumstances set in its way, man senses that he *could* have loved more than he did. A mature man is prepared to accept the responsibility for his not having responded to the opportunities of loving which in various ways, some great and some small, were open to him. Death is there; and it makes it plain to each man that during his mortal span he has both the opportunity and the duty to love.

What on earth and sky can *judgement*, with which in this chapter we are concerned, have to do with *love*? Perhaps that is the first question which we may feel obliged to ask. My answer would be in the Pauline phrase, 'much every way'.

One of the reasons, if not the only one, that this question can be asked is that we are the victims of a sentimentalized notion of love and its manner of working. I have commended popular songs for their stress on love and I have said that one thing about them that I find valuable is their association of love and sexual desire. This is commonly regarded as what is wrong about them; on the contrary, in my view, this is what is right about them. The thing that I believe is often wrong is not their use of sexual images and their talk about sexual desire, but the tendency (in some of the songs at least) to sentimentalize love. By this I mean to make it seem soft, cosy, sweet, comforting, and nothing else.

But it is not in such songs that we discover the worst manifestations of this tendency. It is in the devaluation of the very word itself, which for so many of our contemporaries, and even in many Christian circles, has come to suggest a kind of sloppiness, a simple and quite uncritical acquiescence in anything and everything. In that common misunderstanding of love we discover exactly the softness, the cosiness, about which I have spoken. Thus love becomes niceness. It is taken to be sweet, which indeed it is, but it is not grasped as being 'bitter sweet', if I may use here the title of one of Noel Coward's songs, found in a musical play of the same name. It has not seen the truth in the Spanish folk proverb, that 'to make love is to declare one's sorrows'; nor has it noticed that the deepest expressions of love are not only painful to the one who loves but can also make inexorable demands on the one who is loved —demands which are not arbitrary and certainly not coercive in their manner of expression, but which are inexorable none the less, since they expect of the beloved the full and complete realization of all his possibilities as a lover.

The sort of love about which I was speaking in the last chapter is such love as was shown in Christ, who 'having loved his own that were in the world, loved them unto the end' . . . the end of death on their behalf, which demanded (again, let us recall, in no arbitrary and coercive way) the response from them of a returning love which would show itself in their loving one another. The discourses put in Jesus' mouth by the Fourth Evangelist and the remarkable summary found in the fourth chapter of the first Johannine epistle are very pointed here— love is seen both in its wonder of identification and its mutuality in giving and receiving *and* also in its strange inexorability.

Love *hurts*, too. The identification to which I have just referred is no easy affair; it implies and it involves such a total sharing that the pain experienced by the one who is loved is also the pain of the one who loves. And even more profoundly, the anguish in such identification is the more terrible when the lover knows deeply and inescapably, as in all honesty he must, the failures of the one who is loved. These too he shares; and the anguish is compounded when, knowing these failures— these defects and lacks, shall we say?—he *still* loves. As St Paul tells us in the most famous of all the bits of his epistles, 'there is nothing love cannot face; there is no limit to its faith, its hope, and its endurance'. And he adds (I am using in my quotation the New English Bible) that 'love will never come to an end'—it never fails, as we more usually quote the Pauline passage. Or, in our own idiom, 'love can and does *take it*'.

Once we have come to understand that love is like that, we shall never be guilty of sentimentalizing. We shall see that love is comfortable in the meaning of that word in Elizabethan times: it is strengthening and invigorating. It is thus comfortable precisely because it has 'gone through many waters' which have not defeated and cannot 'drown it'; it is 'terrible as an army with banners', not because like such an army it uses force, but because it is in itself the only really strong thing in the whole world and in human experience. It is strong *because* it is patient, not strong in spite of its requiring patience.

Now all of what I have been saying ought to be perfectly obvious to anybody who professes and calls himself a Christian and who has learned what love is from contemplation of the figure of his Lord and Master. God is love *like that*—indeed we ought to put it more forcefully and say that such human

love as we see in Jesus is the very reflection of the reality of
divine love on the stage of human affairs. That is the way the
world goes; the grain of the universe is exactly like that,
however the appearances of things may seem. I should say
that the basic affirmation of Christian faith is just there: the
commitment of self to a love like that as the disclosure of how
things go, most profoundly, and the 'life in scorn of consequence' (in Kirsopp Lake's grand words) which follows
when such commitment is undertaken.

But if that is 'the disclosure of God's nature', known through
his 'agency in the world', as Whitehead would put it, then it is
also true that each man is intended to actualize in his own
existence that love. He is to 'live in love' because to live so is
truly *to live*. The English recusant poet Robert Southwell
wrote lines that I delight in quoting: 'Not where I breathe, but
where I love, I live.' He spoke not for himself alone but for all
men—as all men, once they have been opened up to the understanding of themselves, may be brought to see. This is 'the life
which is life indeed'.

It is with this background in mind and in this context that
we can see why judgement is related to love. Although the
word 'judgement' is not a happy one, as we shall see, what it
intends to say is utterly integral to love. The relationship is no
incidental or accidental one; it is tied in with the very reality
of loving in itself. Indeed we might put it briefly by saying
that love always *is* judgement, in the meaning which I shall try
to give to that not too satisfactory word which traditionally has
been employed to denote what I am talking about.

But what *am* I talking about?

Simply, one could state it in these words: I am talking
about the honest recognition or facing of things as actually
they are, with the consequences they have had, exactly as those
consequences have been. I am talking about a brave and fear-
less *appraisal* both of the situation and of those who are in the
situation. So I shall use the word 'appraisal' in the remainder
of this chapter, rather than the word 'judgement'; the latter

fails seriously, for us today at any rate, because it is so tied up with notions of law-courts, assizes, and the other paraphernalia of 'justice' in the legal sense. *Such* notions have little or nothing to do with love; they are a matter of human justice which *may be* a mode of love's expression in certain situations but they are also very misleading because love is ultimately not concerned with 'justice' in the vulgar sense—it is *above* justice, whose interest is either retributive or distributive, for the interest of love is with *persons*, persons in society with their fellows, and the fulfilment of selves in the giving-and-receiving which is mutuality or union.

Furthermore—and this I wish to stress—the rewards and punishments motif is not part of the kind of appraisal that I think love entails. The only reward that love can offer is more opportunity to love; its only punishment can be failure on the part of the lover to continue in loving. If we import into our thinking ideas about rewards and punishments, as these are commonly understood, we turn God into 'the ruthless moralist' who, as Whitehead once remarked, is one of the false 'gods' that men have worshipped to their own frightful hurt. I say this with full recognition of the fact that in the gospels we find something of the rewards and punishments motif. But if one looks at what is said there, interpreting it in the light of what Jesus Himself *was*, as the community of Christian faith remembered Him and His impact upon them, we shall see that the reward promised to those who love God or do His will is really the presence of God and the joy of 'seeing him'; while the punishment is the alienation from His presence and that joy, the result of not loving which the victim has imposed upon himself. In any event, as we shall see when we discuss the meaning of the heavenly promise, as part of the scheme of the last things, it is not genuinely Christian to think that anybody can want God *and* something else. In having God, or better in being had by God, we have *all* that 'we can desire', as the collect puts it; it is not a matter of 'God and a lollypop', as I have heard it said. St Francis de Sales once commented that 'he who seeks God in order to have something more, does not know what he is seeking'. To seek God *is* to seek all good; and to live 'in God', which is to live 'in love', is in itself the *summum bonum*.

As mortal life in its finality, death introduces into our mortal existence the fact of appraisal. This is a concept which many have sought to remove from our thinking about human life. The reason for this is not only that it seems to give a somewhat unpleasant note to the portrayal of that life. Rather, as I see it, the reason is two-fold. First, the pictures of 'judgement' have been drawn so often from law-courts and the like that they bear little relation to the Christian insistence on God as love. Hence when that insistence is taken with the utmost seriousness, the whole idea is dismissed as mistaken—once again, to use the familiar aphorism, 'the baby is thrown out with the bath-water'. But second, the understanding of love itself has been sentimentalized, as I have said, and hence it has been thought that love has nothing to do with appraisal, evaluation, and the honest recognition of things as they are and persons as they are, however much we may love them.

Whether people like it or not, appraisal is a genuine and persisting factor in human existence. Appraisal means that each man is responsible for his life and for the decisions which he has made in the course of it; and it means also that each man must be prepared to give what traditional thinking describes as 'an account of his life'—in the face of whatever ultimately determines and assesses true values in the whole scheme of things. If that 'ultimate' is love, as Christians believe, the appraisal is all the more searching and it is all the more terrible to be aware that one must face it. 'It is a terrible thing to fall into the hands of the living God', we read in *Hebrews*. On which we may comment that it would indeed be 'terrible' to fall into the hands of one who is what Whitehead styled 'the ruthless moralist'; but it is even more 'terrible', in the most profound sense of that word, when one must look at the love which we have pierced by our own lovelessness, the cosmic Lover (as I like to put it) whose readiness to give love and to receive love is so devastatingly complete. The Love 'that moves the sun and the other stars', in Dante's final words in *La Commedia Divina*, cannot be faced with nonchalance or ease.

Appraisal, in the meaning I am giving to the word, is not necessarily 'final', if by this is suggested that it is not also *present*; indeed I would wish to say that it is essentially present, in this and in every moment. Every man, day by day, is appraised. The question which is being asked is insistent in all moments and in every moment of our existence: 'How do I "stack up" against the way things really "go"?' That question is asked, I have said. But by whom?

It is asked by each man of and for himself. That is the measure of our human responsibility and thus the determinant of our humanly moral earnestness, precisely as death is the measure of our humanity as mortal. And by 'moral earnestness' I do not mean the sort of moralism which centres itself in obedience to codes or laws or sets of commandments, whether they be ten or of any other number. These have their place, doubtless, in the living of human life; but it would be wrong, I think, to assume that 'moral earnestness' means only a meticulous 'keeping of the commandments' in as devoted a manner as possible. Christian, or even human, 'obedience' is not exhausted by anything like that. 'One thing you lack', Jesus is reported to have said to the 'rich young ruler' after that youth had said, doubtless in complete honesty and with entire accuracy, that he had kept the commandments all his life. What was lacking was genuine 'obedience', not to a set of moral requirements imposed from on high, but in a certain quality of spirit. And I think that the 'Follow me', in that *pericope*, is not simply a call to be a disciple in the obvious meaning of the word. It is a call to be *like Jesus*—which is nothing other than to be a lover, to become what one is intended to become, and thus to find oneself fulfilled as a man.

Thus our self-appraisal is in terms of our love. The question comes down to this: in what ways, to what degree, have I or have I not opened myself to love, to give love and to receive love, to commit myself in utter faithfulness, to live in real mutuality, to look at others with 'eager expectancy' (as Baron von Hügel defined 'hope'), and thus in the truest sense to have been *a man*? It is obvious that when this question is asked, by each of us for himself, the answer must be in terms of failure. Yet the *direction* which we have taken, the aim which has been ours, is the determinative factor. Is *that* the end which has been ours?

But none of us really knows himself completely. It is not to us that hearts are open, even our own; desires known, even our own; no secrets hid, even our own. Nor is it to our fellowmen, who also appraise. This is true, whether we are thinking of the contemporaries whom we know and who know us, of the wider society of which we are a part, or of history in its great sweep. By each of these we are evaluated; but none of these can know the complete truth about us. The appeal to the 'judgement of society', like the appeal to the 'judgement of history', is an appeal which is inescapable; whether we like it or not, that appeal is always being made. But because the society of our fellowmen, intimate or remote, is marked by the same mortality which is ours as persons, while the whole sweep of history as we experience and know it is also a mortal history—under the sign of death—any appraisal made in this way is also limited and partial.

The point is not that such appraisals are made 'in time' and not 'in eternity', as some would like to phrase it; I have already tried to make it clear that such a dualism will not serve us and that God himself is 'temporal' although in what we may style 'an eminent manner'. The point is that the human capacity to understand, in the most profound sense of the word, is so slight that nobody ought to venture to make what he can never in fact make, 'a final judgement' about anybody else, or even about himself. 'Judge not, that ye be not judged'; no man, no society of men, and no long historical sequence of men in society, knows enough or knows fully enough to make any appraisal that can claim to be entirely accurate and that can suppose itself to have seen everything that should enter into the making of such an appraisal.

But *God* is 'the fellow-sufferer who *understands*', as Whitehead says. *His* understanding is the supreme wisdom which knows things as they are; and it is unto him 'that all hearts are open, all desires known, and from whom no secrets are hid'. This is simply another way of phrasing the Christian faith itself—the faith which declares that God *is* love and that we are assured of this because he *acts* lovingly, above all has acted lovingly in the total event of Jesus Christ. People often smile when it is said that only love can really see another person as he is; we are inclined to think that love is 'blind', failing to see defects and always ready to discover values and virtues. This is indeed the case with human love, which is mortal and under the conditions of that mortality cannot be 'perfect', while at the same time it is under the 'condemnation' of failure. But the divine love, God himself as cosmic Lover, is in a different situation—or so a Christian must believe. That love *knows*; and knowing, that love *understands*.

I claim, therefore, that the only 'just' appraisal, the only 'judgement' which can take *all* the facts into account, is God's. And only He can make a 'final' judgement. His appraisal will be accurate, while at the same time it will be merciful. In stating it in this way, I am trying to indicate what seems to me the insight in the traditional view that God is just, not in the human sense of meting out, distributively or retributively, the proper rewards or punishments according to some prior set of laws or regulations, but in the divine sense (if I may say it this way) of complete understanding. Further, I am trying to indicate, by the word 'mercy', that God's appraisal is more than accurate, in terms of complete understanding; it is also characterized by God's *chesed*, his 'loving-kindness', his never-failing mercy, which always makes the best out of every situation and finds the best in every person. In saying this about 'the best', I do not intend the idea that this is read into the situation or the person. On the contrary, I suggest that precisely because God does know all desires, the secrets of human hearts, and the depths of each situation, He also knows there the 'initial aim' which in the first instance He gave, the entire condition of things which was there present, the possibilities which were offered, the efforts that were made, the failures that were experienced, and *everything else*. Knowing that, God's appraisal is 'charitable' appraisal in the true sense of that word—that is, it is *really* loving and thus can both see the best that is there and be prepared to use that best in the augmenting of good in the creative advance which is the cosmic process.

To speak in this way leads naturally to some further considerations in which (as I think) process philosophy can be of great assistance to us. In Whitehead's works there are two words which I wish to mention: one is 'decision'; the other is 'prehension', both negative and positive. I believe that these words, and the ideas that are associated with them, can be fruitfully used at this point of our discussion.

'Decision' means, of course, 'cutting off'. It should not necessarily imply conscious activity of the sort that we know in our own experience, when our 'decision' is or may be made with awareness of what is being done. If, as Whitehead claims and as process thought in general would assert, the element of 'decision' is found everywhere in the creative process, this should not be taken to mean that a quantum of energy, say, knowingly 'decides' for this or that among the relevant possibilities that are 'offered' to it. Similarly, the view which I share that 'subjective aim' is not only present at the level of conscious human movement towards the actualization of potentialities, in a dynamic process, but is also found at every level and at every point in that process, does not imply that such an 'aim' is consciously, knowingly, with full awareness such as we may assume is ours, 'subjectively' apprehended when the various occasions or occurrences or 'entities' in the order of creation move towards their own appropriate mode and degree of actualization.

For these reasons I think that Professor Hartshorne's use,

at one time, of the word 'panpsychism' was misleading, although I agree completely with what Professor Hartshorne was really concerned to assert. 'Panpsychism' (pan = all, psyche = soul) suggests some kind of *vitalistic* view, in which 'entelechies' (i.e. souls as opposed to bodies) are operative at all points and on all levels, after the fashion of the vitalistic biology of Hans Driesch and others. What I should claim, however, is that in a manner appropriate to the particular level and in a fashion suitable for the particular occasion, however 'large' or 'small', there is such 'decision' as entails a 'cutting off' of this or that possibility for actualization and an 'acceptance' of this or that other possibility. It is in this way that the creative advance goes on. Thus I think that human decision, in the self-conscious sense in which commonly we use the term, is related to and part of a general movement in which 'decision' is always a determinative factor. In this sense it is one of the 'metaphysical principles' which we require for our understanding of how things go in the world, even if in exactly that phrasing it is not part of a given categoreal scheme.

At the human level, with which we are concerned, such decision is made with some awareness of what is involved in it and certainly with a degree of self-consciousness in the making of it. This is part of what is intended when we speak of human responsibility. In any given situation, each human person brings with him from his past the totality of what has gone into making him what at that moment he is; this is his 'memory', in the most serious meaning of that word, including not only conscious and (as we might say) sub-conscious factors which might by the process of psychoanalysis be brought to the surface, but also the organic, physical, yes the physiological factors, which are 'viscerally' 'remembered'; including also the whole series of past prehensions—of graspings and being grasped—which have had their part and contributed their share in making him what he is *now*. Each human person too is *in* his relationships, contemporary with him although there is some slight span of time between their origination and their reception by him. And each human person is *towards his future*, as he moves in the direction of realizing or making actual the 'subjective aim' which is his on the basis of that 'initial aim' which has been provided for him in his beginnings.

Human decision is the way in which choice is made, among all possibilities offered at a given instant, so that actualization may occur. This happens constantly, since every occasion or occurrence is involved by necessity in the process of 'going on'. Most of the decisions may seem relatively insignificant or unimportant, but some of them are different—these are the decisions which respond to this or that possibility that may be strikingly determinative of the future direction to be taken. As such, they are responses to certain lures or solicitations of a peculiarly intensive sort. Every decision is a response to a lure or solicitation; that is how God effectively 'acts' in a creative process from which he is nowhere absent, by permitting things to 'make themselves' as decisions are undertaken that 'decide' the degree and kind of actualization that will occur. But *some* decisions are peculiarly significant; they are the response made to what is proposed as *important*, to use another Whiteheadian word. For a Christian, the event of Christ is important, in that sense, as providing a clue to 'the nature of God and his agency in the world'; the decision made for or against that clue is important, since it is determinative of whether or not life will be lived—that is, man will move towards becoming himself—in terms of the love which is there both manifested and released.

The decision may be negative or positive, because, in the process, prehensions, or graspings both of and by each occasion, may be either in terms of a 'yes' or a 'no'. A negative prehension means that the occasion rejects this or that which is offered to it, a rejection which may be made for a variety of reasons, the details of which we need not here investigate. A positive prehension means an accepting of what is offered, a receiving of it into the occasion which is presented with it as a possibility to be grasped, and this also may be made for a variety of reasons about which we shall not speak. But the *fact* of such rejections or choices is highly significant; and above all, to put it in a form of words, it is highly *important* that the *important* which is offered to each occasion as a possibility shall be decided for or against in an *important* way. Which is to say, in a decision that signifies commitment or determination against commitment.

What has been said in the last few pages may seem to some to be illicit metaphysical talk. But I would remind any who think this that it all depends on what one means by 'metaphysics'. I do not believe that what I have been saying is anything like the erection of some grandiose scheme in which super-terrestrial realities are being set up and the whole apparatus of a quasi-Hegelian metaphysic is proposed. On the contrary, I should claim, what I have been saying is metaphysical in the second sense of the word which I proposed in an earlier chapter; it is the making of wide generalizations on the basis of experience, with a reference back to verify or 'check' the generalizations, a reference which includes not only the specific experience from which it started but also other experiences, both human and more general, by which its validity may be tested—and the result is not some grand scheme which claims to encompass everything in its sweep, but a vision of reality which to the one who *sees* in this way appears a satisfactory, but by no means complete, picture of how things actually and concretely *go* in the world.

But to return to decision as an enduring factor in the world process. In men, that decision manifests itself in self-conscious choice. With choice goes the responsibility for what is chosen— granted that there are qualifying and conditioning factors, that human freedom is limited in many respects, and that what we deeply *desire* is much more significant than what we may perhaps have been able effectually to accomplish in consequence of our decision. In the perspective of Christian faith, what is suggested here is that in the appraisal which is part of human mortal existence, we ourselves can be at best but partial judges. History, as well as the society of our contemporaries, is in the same case—not enough is known of human 'depths', as the psychoanalysts put it, for any appraisal to be entirely accurate. But God, who *is* love, who is 'the fellow-sufferer who understands', and whose wisdom penetrates all that is actual and is aware of the relevant possibilities (but *as* possibilities, not in whatever may be made actual among them, for that is 'open' until it happens and God's omniscience cannot mean that He knows, hence must determine, what will occur *before* it occurs), can make an appraisal that is both accurate and merciful—that is 'just' and loving.

The appraisal that God makes is worked out in what He does—or, in words that describe the creative advance as we know it, the appraisal is worked out in terms of what is taken into, and what is rejected from, the 'consequent nature' of God, God as He is affected by what occurs in the world; and then, in what use is made of what has been thus taken or received in the furthering of the project or purpose of God, the implementation of good 'in widest commonalty shared'.

What did this particular life contribute to God's experience, we might then ask, as God receives into Himself what that life has been on the way to becoming and what it has achieved as it has proceeded on that way? In a similar manner, we might ask the question, What has the total life of the human race contributed to this ongoing process of good? At every moment, such an appraisal is being made, in the most serious sense— not as a juridical pronouncement, but as acceptance or non-acceptance. When death comes, appraisal must also be made in the same way, for the total pattern of a given human life, made up as it is of a particular 'routing' of occasions bound together in the fashion we indicated earlier, has also contributed, or failed to contribute, in its very totality, to the creative advance in good. Indeed the whole of the created order, as we style it, is also being appraised in the same way. Each man, each community, humanity as a whole, the range of historical development, the realm of nature . . . all are knit together in an organic totality; all have played, or failed to play, their part in the good which is being achieved by God. God, however, is not aloof from His creation; He is 'in the world or nowhere at all' and by virtue of this He is participant in, identified (but not identical) with, and enriched—or, maybe, impoverished—in His own life by what has gone on, does now go on, and will go on, yet remaining always unsurpassed by anything not Himself. He is the supremely worshipful because that is true of Him and of no other. He is also supremely worshipful because He is the love which is both the depth and the height in all occasions and the enticement or lure which leads those occasions, by their own free decision, to their satisfaction or fulfilment in the context of the wide social pattern which is the world.

God can and does 'make even the wrath of man to serve him'. That means that in every way and in every place, God makes the best of everything, including human lovelessness and the failure which it entails. But the evil is still evil, the wrong is still wrong, the lovelessness is still lovelessness; this is no case of 'partial evil, universal good', in the cheery phrase of Alexander Pope's. While evil is not radical, if by that is intended 'at the root of things'—for it *cannot* be, if God is love and is Himself 'at the root of things' through His creativity at work in them—it is most certainly not to be dismissed or minimized or talked away. Yet God in the creative advance can be trusted, says Christian faith, to use whatever is usable for His purpose of love; and some of us may be surprised to see how this is possible to do when the use is made of what may seem to us extremely unpromising material. But when we judge in that way, we are ourselves appraised for the unloving creatures we are.

Finally, the divine appraisal very likely has little to do with what we would think to be the 'religious' areas of experience. Those are necessary for us; so I should wish to insist, in opposition to the contemporary writers who regard *all* religion, in any sense, as necessarily bad. But God's appraisal, because He is what He is, disclosed in what He actively does, and precisely because the world is what it is, in terms of what happens in it, is an appraisal of real worth, wherever it may be found and however it may be expressed. By this I mean that since God lures, entices, invites, and solicits His creation towards the actualization of its 'initial aim' which becomes its 'subjective aim', in each of its occurrences or occasions, so also He appraises—takes into Himself and receives and uses, or must reject because it is un-usable—whatever is done, including the doing which is man's 'becoming', in a very great diversity of ways. Most of them, doubtless, are 'secular', not specifically 'religious'.

The lure of God is known in every channel and area of existence, not just in those that have a 'religious' tinge. And in those 'secular' channels or areas, God is working 'secularly', as Whitehead put it long before 'secular theologians' appeared on the scene. When He works in such a way, His 'incognito' is to be respected, not denied. But none the less it is *He* who is 'acting' there—and God always acts in love, to secure a freely given response from those who are made to be lovers too and the appraisal of whom is in terms of the degree of their contribution to love's purpose in the creative advance of the cosmos.

St John of the Cross, using the word 'judgement' where I prefer the word 'appraisal', put in one sentence what I have been trying to say: 'In the evening of our days, we shall be judged by our loving.'

FIVE

Heaven and Hell

Man dies and his death is both the end of his life, biologically speaking, and the qualifying characteristic of his life, marking him out as mortal, as aware of mortality, as responsible in that mortal existence, an existence during which he is intended to actualize himself as a lover, becoming what he is made and meant to be. He is under appraisal, both by himself and his fellows and by the God who has provided for him his 'initial aim' and who will either receive the good which his becoming has achieved or find necessary the rejection of that which does not contribute to the creative advance at which God Himself aims.

And each man, in every age and at every time, like the whole race of men, and indeed like the whole creation, is faced with two possible 'destinies', one or other of which will turn out to have been his, in terms of the direction he has taken in his mortal existence. Nor am I speaking of 'destiny' here in a merely futuristic sense, as if it were coming after a long time or at 'the end of the days'. It is in the *now* that these destinies are made present as possibilities. For just as the myth of the creation of the world is significant in its existential confrontation of man with his dependence and with the equal dependence of the world, so the talk about the last things is *essentially* a matter of *existential* import, if I may be permitted that odd combination of words.

The possibilities which are presented are blessedness which

61

comes from self-fulfilment and the acceptance by God of that self-fulfilment—all of this, of course, in relationship with others and not in any presumed human isolation of selfhood— or the disintegration or failure which comes from self-destruction or rejection by God because there is nothing to be received by God in His consequent nature for the furthering of His purpose of good in the course of the process of creative advance. If ever this double-presentation of possibilities has been portrayed in literature, it is to be found in Dostoevski's *Brothers Karamazov*. In that novel, the great Russian writer shows Ivan, Aloysha, and Dmitri as caught in this dilemma of choice; and they are appraised, in their personal quality, as *blessed* or *damned*, as we might put it, not by the arbitrary *fiat* of a *deus ex machina*, but by the ineluctable working out of what they have made of themselves, what they have become, as this is evaluated in terms of what in an earlier chapter we called whatever ultimately determines and assesses true values in the scheme of things.

Thus for each of us, the exacting and inescapable question, which must be faced and answered, is the question of our total mortal life as we are now living it, a question which arises from our mortality with the responsibility which that entails, which puts itself to us in the form of our measuring up to the possibility of becoming authentically ourselves, and which issues in our realization (not so much in thought as in deeply felt experience as *existing* men) of blessedness, as we know ourselves becoming what we truly are, *or* in destruction or damnation, as we know ourselves both frustrated men and failures in our human fulfilment. Heidegger in his own way has made this point about men—not about men in the 'mass' or 'lost in the crowd', but about each and every man—although he has made it in his own way. So also have others, many others. They have seen that each of us is a mortal project, so to say, responsible for our actions and for the character which both reflects them and which they reflect, and hence either 'blessed' or 'damned'.

The Christian faith speaks to men who are in this situation.

When it is true to itself it does not gloss over the facts, nor does it sentimentalize them. Above all it does not deny them. On the contrary, it is exactly at this point—in the context of such facts as we have been outlining and with full awareness of the concern, the uncertainty, and even the despair which can come to every man as he looks at himself with unblinking eyes and in utter honesty—that the Christian gospel has its special relevance and the faith which it awakens has its special significance. In the sequel we shall say more about this. At the moment it will be useful to speak of the presuppositions with which that faith starts in giving its account of men in such a situation.

I wish to notice three of these presuppositions, although I am aware of the fact that they are not exhaustive. The three which we shall consider are: (a) that man is indeed a 'sinner' but that he is also capable of 'redemption' and hence of 'glory'; (b) that history is not a senseless enterprise—someone has described it as 'meaningless meandering'—but a purposeful movement; and (c) that the natural world, in which history and each human life in community with other human lives have their setting, is not evil but good and also shares in 'redemption'.

As to our first presupposition, or (a), the truth of man's sin is surely given in our experience. Only a little observation and a little introspection are sufficient to bring us to see this. The associated traditional doctrines of 'the Fall' and 'Original Sin', with all their historical absurdity and however much we may wish to put in their place some better way of stating what they affirm, tell the truth about man. He is indeed a sinner, fallen from 'grace'; he is not 'able of himself to help himself'. This is *not* a statement of 'total depravity', at least as that idea has been commonly interpreted; what is at issue is the patent reality in every man's experience of something very seriously wrong with him. In the sort of language we have used in these pages, man knows that he should be on the road to love, but he finds himself frustrated on that road; while at the same time he knows very well (once he is honest with himself) that he has so decided, often against his better judgement and in contradiction to his deep desires and purpose, to reject the opportunities to love and to receive love, that he is a failure. Oddly enough, as it may seem, it is precisely those who to others appear most adequately to have realized in their lives (to have made actual) their possibility of love—it is precisely *those* who are most conscious of themselves as failures.

The truth about man is that while he is indeed created 'in the image of God', he is in a state of spiritual insufficiency so pervasive and so disturbing that he cannot live authentically as a man, much less as a 'son of God'. In the divine intention, he was made for the fulfilment of himself, with others, in free and open relationship to his Creator. In actual fact, he lacks that capacity for communion with God and his own fulfilment —which are the same thing, seen from different angles—and in his concrete humanity he is frustrated *and*, what is more important, he is responsibly aware of having made himself, by accumulated decisions, incapable of right relationships with his brethren. In this way he has succeeded in putting himself in the position where he is *privatus boni*, 'deprived of good', and *vulneratus in naturalibus* 'wounded in his natural human existence'. Of course he is never completely 'deprived' of the good which is God, nor is he destroyed in the 'wounding' of his human existence. But his situation is such that he feels this most intensely; and in consequence he finds himself possessed by a tendency which makes him rest content (save in moments of deep awareness) with the lesser 'goods', with the immediately obtainable goods, a tendency which perverts his best instincts, and which prevents him seeing things 'steadily and whole'.

But this is only one side of the Christian picture of man. As someone has put it, if the first volume of a study of man's existence is about his 'fall' the second volume is about his 'redemption'. Indeed the whole point of Christian faith is here, so far as human experience is concerned. Man can be redeemed; or rather, man has been redeemed. Man's possibilities are tremendous. He was indeed created 'in the image of God'; that

image has been damaged but it has not been destroyed. When St
Irenaeus wrote about this he took the text from Genesis: man as
created 'in the image and likeness of God'. He distinguished, in
bad exegesis, between 'image' and 'likeness'. The Reformers
corrected the exegesis but they did not see that despite his
exegetical mistake St Irenaeus had hold of a profound truth. For
he had said that the 'image' is not lost, but the 'likeness' *is*. In
traditional terms of Christian theology, what he was asserting
was that man still has the capacity, but he lacks the power, to be
'righteous'—that is, to be authentic. To say that the capacity is
lost would be to denigrate God's creation of man as *good*.

Thus when we have admitted all that we must admit
concerning man's helplessness in his concrete situation, we
must go on to affirm all that we can affirm concerning man's
possibility of perfection—which means, in this context, his
potentiality for becoming completely ('perfectly' or in full
actualization) the man who loves. Human mortality shows
plainly enough that this 'perfection' is not achieved in the span
of our mortal life and under our present circumstances; that is
true enough. But it remains *as* the possibility; what is more,
Christian faith declares that God already accepts those who
acknowledge their failure and commit themselves utterly to
Him—so that they are already, as we might put it in mythological language, 'in heaven' or in other words discover themselves to be 'blessed'. Hence no Christian can despair of any
man, even of himself; for each man is 'a sinner for whom
Christ died', each man is loved by God, each man can direct
his life in response to that love made manifest in diverse ways
but 're-presented' (in Schubert Ogden's word) in Jesus Christ.
Therefore each man can 'work out his salvation in fear and
trembling, for it is God that worketh in him both to will and
to do his good pleasure'.

A silly optimism about man, such as we knew 'between the
wars' and in the 'golden days' of the liberal era, is not Christian. Our contemporary theologians often appear to wish to
revive that optimism, perhaps in violent reaction from the

other extreme which appeared between the wars in certain of the dialectical or 'neo-orthodox' theologies. But they are lacking in realism. On the other hand, the total pessimism of much traditional Reformed theology, whether Calvinist or Lutheran, and its more recent revival, as well as the perverse denigration of humanity not stated but implied in Catholic penitential theology with its fear of human impulses and its dread of sexuality, is not Christian either. I think that one reason for this, on both sides, is that a look at man, as he is, may give us too much confidence when we are superficial in our looking or too much despair when we only regard man's condition as 'cabin'd, cribb'd, confined' and as failing so terribly in its accomplishment. If by 'heaven' we mean the possibility of blessedness, whatever else we may find it necessary to say on the matter, it might be asserted that if we do not believe in the possibility of heaven, we shall not believe in the possibility of good for man. But more about this will be suggested at a later point.

Our second presupposition, or (b), was that history is a purposeful movement. The origin of that presupposition is deep in the Jewish conviction that 'God is working his purpose out', despite everything that appears to deny or impede that activity. Once again, in reaction from a notion of 'progress' which was a secular substitute for this Christian conviction when Christian faith had become an absurdity to so many, recent theologians have 'given up' this belief to all intents and purposes. Not all of them, but some of them, have transferred 'the divine far-off event' to some realm outside history altogether. They, more than any other thinkers perhaps, have indeed 'emptied out the baby with the bath-water', to return to the image we have used earlier. But it ought to be clear that 'the increasing purpose' is neither automatic progress without relapse or defection, nor 'heaven' *in the sense of a completely non-historical state*. 'The hope of heaven', as I shall argue, need not mean this at all; I should say, *ought not* to mean this. Too often it is taken to do so. But the purposeful movement in history signifies that every moment *counts*, every moment makes its contribution of the divine life, and every moment is related to God who is intimately concerned with all the variety and content of history. Furthermore, it signifies that something is being accomplished in history, even if it is not always obvious to us.

Mother Julian of Norwich relates that in a 'shewing' she saw the entire creation as 'a little hazel-nut'. She asked how it could continue, since it was so tiny, so insignificant, in relation to the vastness of God. The answer came that it continued 'because God made it, because God loves it, because God keeps it'. In respect to history, then, we may say that God sustains its every event and is the chief (not only) causative principle behind all causation. God loves His world and everything in it; He is *there*, in the world, with cherishing care 'tending it' and bringing it on towards final good, while at the same time He redeems it from triviality and frustration. The movement of history is part of that care. Finally, God keeps His world— there is His purpose which sustains it and moves through it, towards 'the manifestation of the sons of God'. Whatever may be the remoter intention of God in the awe-inspiring stretch of space and time, it is all of a piece with what He is doing in the historical experience of men—in a way, that is what the *homo-ousion* of the Nicene Creed affirms. In the historical realm, as in the natural order (if the two may properly be distinguished in this way), God's activity is two-fold: first, to secure from each moment and each event the good which may be actualized there; and second, to work towards such a 'completion' of the process of creative advance that He may say of it, with a joy that includes but transcends all suffering, that it *is* good.

Thus the historical realm is characterized by a purpose which is nothing other than God's incredibly cherishing love, shared with His creatures and moving through their free decisions towards a great end. And when things go wrong, as they do, God is like the sculptor who can turn an artisan's mistaken and distorting chiselling into a lovely figure. His purpose can make history meaningful even when man has done his utmost to destroy its meaning.

The third presupposition, or (c), insists that the natural world is good and that it shares in redemption. Like the second presupposition, this has its origin in the Jewish insistence, found so clearly throughout most of the Old Testament, on a *positive* understanding of the creation. As against all Manichean or dualistic philosophies, as also against all those religions which offer escape from the world into an ethereal realm of pure spirit, Christianity has denied that the world of *things* is evil. It is good, because God created it; it is good, because He loves it; it is good, because He is in it and works through it—to repeat Mother Julian's 'shewing'. Nature is an instrument for the divine purpose, not something alien to that purpose and hence to be rejected or denied.

On this matter the theology of the Eastern Orthodox Church has much to teach the rest of us. For that theology, the whole cosmos is 'to be redeemed'; everything in it, from the very dirt under our feet to the loveliest configurations and harmonies, has its place in that redemption. There is no reason to fear or hate 'dirt', to sniff at 'matter' or material things. These may be misused and they can be abused; but in themselves 'dirt' and 'matter' and the whole world of nature, to which we as men in our history are organic, are 'good stuff' and must not be despised nor rejected.

It is interesting in this connection to compare the two greatest English poets of our time. T. S. Eliot seems never to have overcome his dislike of the material world—he was not like Aldous Huxley, who dismissed it all as illusory, but he hardly appears to have *included* it in his great vision. On the other hand, W. H. Auden, in his *Christmas Oratorio*, writes superbly and lovingly of the possibilities of the natural world and speaks tenderly of man as *there*. The conclusion of that work, with its use of a Whiteheadian theme, is magnificent witness to what I am urging here. Auden writes: 'At your marriage/All its occasions shall dance for joy.' It is the marriage of man with God, with his fellowmen, and with the world itself that he has in mind.

We cannot picture or describe or even imagine the way in which the whole creation serves as 'the body of God'. But to be afraid of that phrase is to be afraid of the deepest intention in what Christian faith has to say about creation and about redemption. The cosmos, as God receives it and uses it, is *what the world means to God*, in terms of what has been done in it and with it, in terms too of the response made in and by the cosmos. And although what I have been urging is based upon Christian faith, as I anyway understand it, and is immediately related to human experience (for it is from that experience, in its context, that anything we say must begin), the corollary is that the cosmos has value *in itself*, not just as a stage of man's existence and for man's redemptive possibility. Such a cosmic setting for, involvement in, and relationship to what we know by faith about ourselves gives the Christian faith a sweep and range that saves it from the charge of parochialism or mere anthropocentrism. As I have said in the second chapter, this is one of the ways in which a process conceptuality seems to me to be of enormous use in Christian thinking.

I hope that this long discussion of presuppositions has not seemed an unnecessary intrusion into the subject of this book. I do not think it is an intrusion, since it has provided for us some ground on which to stand as we return to the particular topic, heaven and hell, with which we are immediately concerned.

Some years ago a novel appeared with the title *All This and Heaven Too*. I have completely forgotten the novel but the title has stuck in my mind. When one hears a discussion of Christian faith as promising abundant life, giving meaning to present-day existence, and substituting for broken personality the authenticity of an integrated and forgiven, accepted and accepting personality, one thinks of that title. Can it be, one wonders, that the 'heaven too' has significance for us today? I think that it does have such significance. And perhaps I can get at what I mean by recalling a popular saying of some years ago. When young people who wished to convey the idea that something was superlatively good, splendid, and *real* ('That's *for real*', they also said—and it is a significant phrase), they would often use these words: 'It's out of this world'.

Now that *might* have meant that this good, splendid, and real experience or thing was quite literally 'out of' the concrete world and in a completely spiritual realm which made that world irrelevant and ridiculous. But such was not the intention with which the phrase was used by young people. What they intended by it was something like this: Here is an experience in which we have found a wonder and glory, a beauty and splendour, such that it seems to be *more than*, although most certainly not opposed to and in flight from, the day-by-day experiences which are so familiar. I do not wish to exaggerate, but it might be suggested that in the famous line, 'bright shoots of everlastingness', something of the same sort is being said. There is a suffusion of ordinary experience with a glory that is very much present, very much here and now, yet unexhausted by the here and now and in a strange fashion evocative of a certain reverence. I am convinced that this 'more' in man's mortal existence is known to people of every type and under every condition, although they do not quite know how to express it. At any rate, it is plainly the case that they do not experience it *or* express it, for the most part, in specifically 'religious' terms.

It is easy enough to interpret what I have been describing in 'other-worldly' fashion. It is easy to speak of it as if it had to do with 'pie-in-the-sky-when-you-die'. A good deal of Christianity has been vitiated by this very unbiblical way of interpreting human life; as one of the recent popes said, 'true life' or 'real life' is not here but 'beyond death'. I am paraphrasing here some words of Pope Leo XIII in his very this-worldly encyclical about social justice, *De Rerum Novarum*; in his writing about that demand and necessity for social justice he could not emancipate himself from this false 'other-worldliness'. Nor is he alone in this, for it has been very much a part of traditional Christianity as commonly taught, preached, and understood. Yet it constitutes what Professor Bethune-Baker once described as the greatest 'apostasy' in Christian thought, for it made it possible to think that we could put off to 'another world' what it was our duty to do in *this* one. But if it is easy to fall into that sort of escapist 'other-worldliness', it is also easy to exhaust the significance of the experience to which I refer by entirely 'humanizing' or 'mundanizing' (if I may coin the word) what it delivers to us. Above all, it is possible to exhaust what the gospel has to say by talking about and working for the immediacies, assuming that there is in that gospel nothing more than an imperative for better relations among men, classes, races, and nations, with the building in the not too distant future of a society in which opportunity of fulfilment will be guaranteed to everybody.

I do not wish for a moment to decry the stress on the 'secular' import of the gospel nor to seem ungrateful for all that men like Harvey Cox and Gibson Winter, to name but two, have been teaching us. Nor do I wish to reject the truth of Bonhoeffer's insight about the gospel being concerned with *life*, right here and right now, rather than with some 'future life' which is promised to those who are 'saved'. To put it vulgarly, I am *all for* this recognition of the 'secular' import of the gospel in its impact on a society that is becoming more and more 'secularized'. And I agree that this relative autonomy of the 'secular' is a consequence of the whole development of the Jewish-Christian understanding of God and of history and of the world.

At the same time, I believe that precisely *in* the 'secular' as we live it in a 'secularized' society, there is something 'heavenly'—if I may phrase it so. But I must explain what I am trying to say, lest I be completely misunderstood and my meaning misinterpreted. Perhaps I can best do this by commenting on a passage from one of St Augustine's sermons (Sermon 256, section 3). He used these words:

'O the happy alleluias there . . . There, praise to God; and here, praise to God. But here, by those who are filled with anxious care; there, by those who are freed from care. Here, by those whose lot is to die; there, by those who live eternally. Here, on the way; there, in our fatherland. Now, therefore, my brethren, let us sing—not for our delight as we rest, but to cheer us on in our labour. As wayfarers are accustomed to sing, so let us sing and let us keep on marching. For if you are going forward, you are *indeed* marching; and to go on marching is a good thing, if we go on in true faith and in right living. So, brethren, sing, and march on.'

That is a beautiful passage, as we shall all agree. But what is wrong with it? I should say that what is wrong with it is that it seems to urge that the 'there' is *after* this existence and *only so*. But we need not to read it in just that way, although doubtless that was the way St Augustine intended it. We can just as well read it as speaking of the double nature of human experience as men exist in 'true faith' and as they seek after 'right living'. In the very *here* of our existence there may be the *there* of blessedness; and if perhaps something is added about what happens *after* that, it is no contradiction of what happens *now*, *here*, in this *present* moment of our Christian belonging. There is more in man and in man's experience, there is more in history, and there is more in the natural order than meets the eye. There is 'the whole creation groaning and travailing in pain', as it is being 'delivered from the bondage of corruption into the glorious liberty of the children of God'. *All* things, as St Paul says in another place, are somehow of God, for God, to God, 'whether they be things in earth or things in heaven'; and the 'heaven' need not be seen as a 'beyond' which is not also in the world in its travail, moving as it is in creative advance under and in God who is love.

Exegetes may say that St Paul did not 'mean' what I have been saying, any more than St Augustine meant what I have said is a possible way of using his words. Very well, I admit this. But just here I recall to you what I have urged earlier about the need for 'in-mythologizing', in the attempt to make clear to ourselves, what the case actually is as we can see it, if men like that, in their time, under their conditions, with their patterns of thought, spoke as they did. At the very least, I should claim, what I have been saying is a *possible* interpretation, for ourselves, of what they were driving at in their own way and in their own terms. So far as I can see, this is the only way in which we can be delivered from a literalism of the text which so often prevents us grasping what might be styled 'the deep intentionality' which is there. What is at stake, in my own conviction, is the seeing that it is not so much *beyond*, as it is *in and through*, 'the flaming ramparts of space and time' that redemption, re-integration, and the fulfilment of the divine purpose of love takes place. It is in *this* way that I should wish to understand the point of that eschatological motif which is so much a part of the biblical picture.

Christian faith affirms that man's action and character in this world have a determining quality in respect to himself, history, the world, and God—or so I am convinced. This confronts us again with those two 'destinies', those two 'ultimate possibilities', for man.

The first possibility which we shall consider is that he shall so terribly and persistently fail, in his ignorance and impotence and in his own decisions, that he must suffer a continuing rejection. That is hell; by definition, it is the absence of God. Hell is always a real and live possibility, although I shall wish to qualify this later and to say something on behalf of 'universalism'. None of the Church's theologies, however it may have been with this or that particular Christian writer, has consigned any single person to that fate. But the possibility of wilful alienation from God, and persistence in that alienation by free decision, is there. And since God cannot, by His own nature, coerce any man, but must win that man by His love, there is always the possibility that the offer of acceptance may be declined. Notice that I have said, throughout, 'the *possibility*'.

The other possibility is enjoyment of God, in which God accepts and receives into Himself the man who, in his ignorance and impotence and by his free decisions, has yet b een possessed of the kind of 'becoming' which makes him thus acceptable and able to be received by God. Everything that was said in the last chapter is relevant here, in respect to these two possibilities or possible destinies. We are not talking about some state 'after this life'; we are talking about the negative and positive pre-hensions by God of what is going on *in* this existence. That granted, the traditional scheme was *right* in speaking of 'heaven' as it did, with the 'beatific vision' and the bliss or happiness which is granted through that vision. Furthermore, popular hymnody was *right*, however unfortunate its images, in picturing this in terms of full satisfaction; it took the *best* moments of contemporary experience and used them in an eminent fashion to describe what this would mean. Homely fields in *Green Pastures*, the 'heavenly city', 'being with those I love', 'gardens and stately walks' in the Elizabethan lyric—all these were symbolic and suggestive of fulfilment. 'When I wake up after his likeness, I shall be satisfied', says the Psalm-ist. Such pictures need be misleading only if they are taken to be purely futuristic in reference, as if what was meant by 'heaven' was only compensation for the pains of earth. But we have already rejected any such way of understanding the deepest intention here.

The assertion of hell and heaven in the out-worn scheme of the last things confronted men with these two destinies or possibilities. But what about that other, found in Orthodox and Catholic theologies—'the intermediate state'? I believe that this too says something important and meaningful. I should put it in this fashion. *If* any occasion or 'entity' is accepted by God, for His own enrichment and for His use in the development of further good in the process, it is accepted with and in its obvious imperfections and its partial but real failures. It requires 'purification'; which is to say, it requires the negation of those elements or aspects or factors which are *not* acceptable and which would not enrich God nor provide material for His employment in the creative advance towards further and fuller good. To say it figuratively, those who might be prehended in an entirely negative way are those who have in them *nothing*—but are there any such?—which is enriching and useful. Those who are acceptable, precisely because there *is* a good which is enriching and useful, are not however *perfectly* 'good', as they themselves would willingly and honestly admit in the light of the appraisal with which our last chapter was concerned. Yet they can be accepted and received, they can be enriching for God Himself, and they can be employed in His purpose—but only if and when, in a phrase of Rupert Brooke's (in a different context but not entirely unrelated), 'all evil' is 'done away'. That 'evil' is *negatively* prehended; but the occasion as it is constituted, because it has such 'good' in it, is *positively* prehended. Nor do I think that such an interpretation is fanciful; indeed, I believe that it is precisely in this manner that the creative advance does go on, under God and with God participant in it, with God Himself 'in process' (if I may again use here the title of a book of my own which sought to say this in a relatively popular manner).

The very natural and very human desire to 'pray for the departed' might also be fitted into this pattern. Such prayers need to be cleansed from the medieval superstitions about them, to be sure. But if they are genuinely 'remembrance before God' of those whom we have loved, they are by way of adding our strong desire for such use of accomplished good as may be possible by the great cosmic Desire-for-Good which is God Himself, for such reception to God's enrichment, and for the 'communion' of those who have prayed with that same God, so that they too may have their share in that movement of love which is what God is up to in His world.

Finally, we must speak of the imagery of the 'resurrection' and of the 'consummation'. This rich imagery, found especially in I Corinthians 15, cannot readily be transposed into the language of prose, yet if it is taken literally it seems to most of us impossible and absurd. Traditional theologians attempted to put what the images portrayed into a system of concepts that hardly fit together and that for us today are as absurd as the literal pictorial presentation. Yet *something* is being said here, something which is integral to the Christian faith.

I suggest that the important thing that is being said is that the love which God manifested in the life, death, and victory of Jesus Christ is indefeasible. What is even more important, in the way in which the picture is presented to us, is that this love is indeed victorious—the story of Christ, we may recall Whitehead's saying, is told 'with the authority of supreme victory'. Love, 'the love of God which was in Christ Jesus our Lord', *reigns*—but reigns as love can only reign, not in the grandeur of some oriental Sultan's court nor with the coercive omnipotence of a dictator, nor as a 'ruthless moralist' who imposes his righteous will, but in the sheer fact of loving faithfully and unceasingly, through all anguish that His creatures know and that He shares. The 'joy of heaven' incorporates and transmutes but it does not deny that anguish.

Second, I suggest that the talk about 'resurrection of the body' is an assertion that the totality of the material world and of human history, as well as of every man in that history who, with his brethren, has achieved good in his existence in the world, is usable by God who through it has been enriched in His own experience without changing in His supremely worshipful deity—the God unsurpassable by anything not Himself, but open to enrichment in being what He is and in terms of what He does.

Thirdly, I suggest that the 'body' which is 'raised' is *Christ's* body. I do not mean here the chemicals, the biology, of the flesh which walked in Palestine two thousand years ago. I *do* mean the wholeness of that which Christ was, taken into, received by, enriching to, and usable for, 'the glory of God the Father'. Those who have shared in the life of Christ as the diffusion of His love in the world are by that very fact 'members incorporate in his mystical body', as the Prayer Book phrases it. Which is to say, they live in *his* love and they are a part of *his* life. The resurrection is for them a sharing in Christ's being taken into, received by, enriching to, and usable for God the Father. Thus the resurrection is not something that will take place in the distant future, when the 'scroll' is opened and a grand assize held. It is a present reality in the faith of the Christian. The 'Christian hope', grounded in the Christian faith, is a present experience; indeed, that hope, like the love which is participant in Christ, *is* in that faith. The living in Christ—by which I mean, as I have indicated, living 'in love' as a human possibility which has been 're-presented' for us in the Man Jesus—as Christ lives in those who respond and hence know what love is: this *is*, at this very moment, 'our hope of glory'.

What this comes to in practical experience needs to be said, as we close this chapter. It means courageous trust in the God who 'raised Jesus from the dead' and has given us confidence and hope. It means profound concern for and dedicated action in the world, yet with a certain 'detachment' which gives us perspective on what we undertake. It means the adoration of God as our 'refuge and strength', with the implementation of that adoration in daily experience, so that the faithful man becomes 'an other Christ' in this mortal existence, a personal channel through whom the 'Love that moves the sun and the other stars' is an almost tangible reality in the affairs of life. It means a life which, in New Testament idiom, is 'in the heavenly places' even while it is lived here; for belief, worship, and action are seen as worthwhile, since they can never ultimately be frustrated or useless—*God* receives them, enjoys them, employs them, to 'his greater glory', which is nothing other than His continuing loving action in the advance of the creative process towards the good. He is indeed the supreme affect, as well as the giver of all initiating aims.

SIX

Question and Hope

At several points in these chapters I have spoken of God as 'supreme affect'. This term I have borrowed from Schubert Ogden, who uses it in his fine book *The Reality of God*, a book to which I acknowledge my debt in the preparation of these chapters. At the same time I acknowledge him as the author of this phrase. In Ogden's book there is a chapter called 'The Promise of Faith' and I should like to commend it to you, for it seems to me that with a rather different approach, yet much more adequately, Ogden says in it much that I have been trying to suggest in what I have been putting before you.

Ogden's essay concludes with an honest statement that he does not, at the time of writing, see that such a portrayal of 'the promise of faith' as he has drawn—and I remind you that since he and I have said much the same thing, this would be true of my own presentation—necessarily entails what he calls 'subjective immortality', the persistence beyond death of the conscious self. Yet the portrayal still holds good, he claims; and he goes on to say that it is precisely because he is trying to think and write as a responsible Christian theologian that he feels obliged to affirm that such personal persistence is not in and of itself, by necessity, utterly integral to Christian faith. And I agree with him.

But the very reality of 'the promise of faith' raises the question of such personal persistence beyond death—raises it *as a question* which should be discussed. And it does not exclude the possibility that such persistence, in some mode, may be a legitimate consequence of the indispensable 'promise', even if it is not absolutely entailed by it. Interestingly enough, the fact that in so many prayers used in the Christian fellowship and in so many books dealing with Christian theology, this is actually spoken of *as* 'the Christian hope', or 'a reasonable, holy, and religious hope' (in one familiar prayer), may have its lesson to teach us. At least it warns us against the wrong kind of confidence on the matter, and it prevents us from succumbing too easily to that odd variety of self-centredness, in the worst sense, which demands 'immortality' because it is determined to play 'dog in the manger' in God's universe.

In this chapter I plan to discuss the *question* and to say something about the 'hope', although I know that I cannot provide an adequate answer to the former and I am in no position to speak with certainty about the latter.

In his recent study of process theology, Peter Hamilton has noted that he has found among the young people with whom he has worked as a chaplain and teacher of divinity a willingness to consider very seriously the reality of God but a feeling that talk about 'personal immortality' makes no sense. That book, *The Living God and Modern World*, is the most important British study of process theology; and it should be read. Furthermore, Mr Hamilton's remarks on this particular subject should be considered with care, for he represents, I think, in his comment about his own students what is also a prevalent attitude in other circles as well. I mention this for what it is worth, realizing quite well that what people think is no indication of what is true; realizing also that Christian faith is not to be 'cut' to the measure of popular opinion. None the less, if it should turn out that one *can* be a Christian without holding firmly to personal persistence beyond death, this is significant; and since, as I have just been saying, I think that such is indeed the case, I believe that nobody ought to *require* acceptance of some variety of personal persistence as a pre-requisite for a welcome into the Christian community which is grounded on that faith in God in Jesus Christ which the community exists to make available to men and women in every age.

But this may be beside the point. Let us proceed to the question and to the possible 'hope' and see what may be said about them.

First of all I should like to set side by side a negative and a positive consideration, each of them relevant to our question. The negative consideration has to do with that kind of selfishness to which I have already alluded. The positive one has to do with the intrinsic value of personal human existence.

I think that there can be little doubt that a good deal that is said in support of personal persistence after death is based upon a strong individualistic stress on the self. One can have no sympathy with the variety of humility which turns itself into a doormat and invites others to walk on one, in a manner which becomes a strange sort of self-pity masking as humility. Nobody is asked to be Uriah Heep! But it is also possible to be assertive about the self in a less obvious and equally unpleasant fashion. *I* am what matters; *my* destiny is the important thing; if God does not preserve *me*, the universe is a mess and nothing is worth while. 'Glory for me', the old gospel-hymn is supposed to have sung—but the very words show that the hymn is not about *the gospel*, for the gospel speaks of 'Glory to God', in whose 'glory' all good is contained.

There *is* a concern about the self which is healthy and, as a matter of fact and observation, essential to each of us; but there is also a concern about the self which is vicious and unlovely—and also, I should say, destructive of the very thing it seeks to assert. In the Christian tradition, *that* sort of concern about the self, 'the glory for me' variety, serves as part of the picture of hell. I introduce here, both for a little 'light relief' and because it makes my point so accurately, a poem by Rolfe Humphries which he entitled *Hell*. It may be found in his *Forbid Thy Ravens*, published some years ago by Scribners (New York):

Hell is a place of solitude enforced
On the great host, cut off by sorrow, going
Under a wind intolerably cold,
A wind from no direction, always blowing.

Hell is a place of everlasting noise,
Where voices, plaintive and obnoxious cry
Over and over again their favourite word
In constant iteration: I, I, I.

Hell is a place where mirrors are black water,
And rivers salt, and atmosphere like lead,
Where suffering is all the rage and fashion,
And everything is dead except the dead.

Hell is all right to visit, if we have to,
And hard enough to miss, in any case;
But, I insist, I would not like to live there,
Not if you gave me all the God-damned place.

It is the 'I, I, I' that I find significant in that poem. We all
'visit' hell, as Humphries has it, from time to time; it is indeed
'hard enough to miss', as the possible destiny to which I have
referred. But the horror of it, the death in it, and the 'solitude'
known there, are all summed up in those words 'in constant
iteration: I, I, I'. That is why hell is a 'God-damned place'.
William Morris was right in calling fellowship heaven, and
lack of fellowship hell. Sometimes I incline to think that those
who selfishly seek for personal persistence, for their own sake,
and in the demand that they shall not 'lose themselves' in the
'love and service of God', are really asking for hell—and if that is
what they are asking for, the *kind* of person who does ask in this
way has already obtained what he sought. He is already in hell.

The positive consideration which I should set alongside
this negative one has to do with what I have styled the intrinsic
value of personal human existence. This is not a matter of
concern for *my*self; it is basically a concern for the value known
and the love seen in others. John Baillie has written eloquently

about this in his *And the Life Everlasting*, where he speaks movingly of the incredibility to him of the thought that this or that friend, whose love has been shown towards him, shall not be accepted as being indeed a lover, with a worth that nothing can destroy. It is for his friend, for the one he loves, that Baillie asks personal persistence beyond death, not for his own self such as it is.

However we phrase this, there is a point here. And I think that within the systematic statement of process theology, a place has to be made for that profound feeling. If, as we shall be arguing in a moment, we may be sure of 'objective immortality', the taking into God's life of every good that has been achieved in the creative process; and if, as that understanding of the world order implies, *one* of the goods is the agency by which these given goods have been achieved, including at this point the human agent as a peculiarly significant focus—may it not be the case that not only the good which has been achieved but the agent who has achieved it (himself good, despite defect and the instances of his failure in this mortal existence) will be preserved beyond the 'perishing of occasions'? If value is never lost, as Whitehead claimed in his Ingersoll lecture on *Immortality*; and if value is always associated, in the process, with fact—may it not be that exactly in receiving all that has been done which is valuable, the doer of the valuable is also to be received? May not something like the 'communion of saints', in the divine life and usable by the divine agency, be a possibility? After all, 'personality' *is* in relationships.

I put these two considerations side by side, for what they are worth. At least they help us to see what the *question* is asking. Now I wish to make three statements which seem to me to be plainly true, either from a serious acceptance of the conceptuality which I have been assuming or from the deliverances of the Christian faith itself. These will help us to get the question in even more accurate focus.

My first statement is simply a repetition of what I have just said about 'objective immortality'. That each and every occasion or occurrence, each 'entity', makes its contribution, negatively or positively, to the creative advance is clear enough. The *way* in which this is done is by the good which has been accomplished being taken into God's 'consequent nature'— God as concretely he is, not abstracted from the world but in unfailing relationship with it. Everything that can thus be received *is* received; we might say that God is a good husbandman who wastes nothing. Anything not received, anything that is negatively prehended, is utterly use-*less*; it is 'cast as rubbish to the void', in Tennyson's words, because it can make no contribution to the abiding good and its implementation in the creative advance.

Is there anything that is like that? Obviously we do not know. Equally obviously the horror of evil, in all its forms, is not to be denied. But again with equal obviousness, God's capacity to transmute and transform what is most certainly evil into an opportunity for good cannot be denied by any Christian who has contemplated what we say God did with Calvary. Love such as God is, demonstrated in what God does in *that* instance, is able to 'work wonders' with the very worst of events and (may we not believe this?) with the very worst that men can do and even, I dare to say, with the very worst that men can be. 'Nothing is lost that can be saved'—is there anything or anybody who *cannot* be saved? Not against its or his free decision, that is to say; for in that case it would be coercion and hence literally nothing worth doing would be accomplished. But love can solicit, invite, lure, entice, in so many different ways and through so many different channels, 'secular' and 'religious', that one need not be hopeless about the matter. I have said that the only *really* strong thing is love; and I now add that the divine persuasion, working tenderly yet indefatigably, may very well be able, in the long run, to win free consent. That free consent would be to *God*, yes; it would also be the realization or actualization or fulfilment of creaturely potentiality.

My second statement has also been intimated at an earlier point. The 'resurrection of the body of Christ', in the sense in which I have presented it, is an assurance of faith. I do not need to develop this further, since I have already discussed it at some length.

And my third statement is simply a reference to what I have borrowed from Schubert Ogden, about God as 'supreme affect'. To him, into him, all good is a contribution. He knows, as such affect, the sting of anguish; he also knows the reality of joy. He takes them all, accepts them all, uses them all, in so far as there is any usability about them. And he does this *now*, not in some remote future. Mortal men strive and struggle, labour to do their best (and fail), move in the direction of fulfilment through the decisions they make. They die . . . 'and with God be the rest', as Browning puts it. To be able to say that, in complete confidence, *is* Christian faith; and 'the promise of faith' is the assurance that this *is so*. Thus the theocentrism so basic to the biblical witness is reaffirmed. As from God all initiating aims were derived, so to God all fulfilment must go as its 'final rest'.

Having made those three statements, I must confess that for me personally this is *enough*. But I have left it still as a 'question', not as a complete answer—the question, namely, whether or not there can be and is *personal* (*viz.*, conscious) persistence after the death which is the terminus of our mortal pilgrimage. Yet there is what I have called 'the hope'. I must say something about it.

John Baillie, in the book to which I have referred, places the grounds for this 'hope' in two Christian convictions. The first is that God is good—that He is 'pure unbounded love'. The second is the resurrection of Christ. For him it is inconceivable that a genuinely good and loving God would permit the annihilation of those persons whom He has created, whom He has so lovingly sustained, and upon whom He has showered such superabundant grace. And it is inconceivable to him that the communion with the 'risen Lord', which the fact of resurrection has made possible, should ever be brought to an end—a communion like that, in which love is shared so richly, has about it the quality of everlastingness, even (as Baillie would doubtless say) of eternity. Nothing, certainly not the moment of mortal death, can destroy it.

I believe that Baillie has singled out the two *big* matters, thus reducing any other 'arguments' to triviality. In effect, he says that if God does permit the annihilation of human personality, in its self-conscious awareness as recipient of God's love, there is something oddly selfish about God Himself. Now I should wish to say that it seems to me that this is a very strong point. If God is truly love, and if love is relationship, and if relationship means sharing, then it would be more like God as He relates Himself to the creative process to wish to 'share' with others that which is good, that which is being done towards good, and that which leads to enjoyment in good. Whether this means also something like the 'communion of saints', where the divine love is indeed 'in widest commonalty shared', I do not know. But I may be permitted to *hope* that it does.

As to the resurrection of Christ, I have already spoken about what this means, at least so far as I can understand its meaning. It is life 'in Christ', triumphantly victorious over everything evil—which is to say that it is life 'in love', of a type that does indeed have about it the quality of everlastingness and even, maybe, of eternity, although I dislike that word because of its suggestion that temporality is a lesser good or perhaps an evil. If one should seem to be thinking only of those who have 'encountered' the historical Jesus, then there would be a kind of unlovely and unlovelike selectivity which would make such talk seem a little absurd. But if one is thinking of life 'in love' as an authentic possibility for every man, wherever and whenever he has happened to live out his mortal existence, then I must say that I both understand and find strength in the argument.

As so often, a human analogy helps; and although some

contemporary theologians have been chary of using such analogies, one can be encouraged by the dominical employment of them and continue to find them useful. When I think of the love that I know so well between a particular person and myself—and I am in fact thinking of one particular person with whom I am so bound in love that it remains for me a source of wonder and joy—I am aware, in a fashion that words cannot adequately express, that there is something so *enduringly* real in our mutuality in giving and receiving, in our commitment one to the other, and in our hopefulness one about the other, that the thought of its having a terminus cannot enter my mind. 'This thing is bigger than either of us or than both of us', lovers often say in one form of words or another. The *thing* that is 'bigger' in such love is the activity of God Himself, I should dare to affirm. Yes, but the two lovers *share* in that; and by their sharing, they seem also—at least to themselves, each for the other—to share in the sort of endurance through all vicissitude which is characteristic of God who is never-failing love.

I do not know whether this also means conscious and personal persistence beyond the death of either partner or of both of them. But I may be permitted to *hope* that it does. And quite seriously I must add, 'with God be the rest'. Which, by the way, is exactly what Browning was prepared to say for himself and for his Elizabeth.

We have seen the question, in all its depth. And we have heard about the 'hope', with its poignancy and longing desire. It is almost time to end, but I wish to say one or two things more as I bring these chapters to a close. Since I have just used the word 'desire', I want to speak of it for a moment—or rather, to speak of what it is pointing towards. Then I want to return to that grand 'shewing' of Mother Julian of Norwich which I quoted earlier.

Desire . . . how much that word has been abused and how much derided! Yet it points towards something that might almost be taken as a definition of what it really means to be a man, even of what it means to speak about God. To say this may seem ridiculous; to many it will seem the sheerest sentimentality. But I wonder if it is either ridiculous or sentimental. In fact I do not really wonder; I flatly deny both charges.

For consider what desire is, as we know it in ourselves, in all our own 'desiring'. Often desire is used to signify sexual impulses, which are thought to be evil or at the best not very worthy. I have already indicated my rejection of such a view and my conviction that all love, so far as we know it humanly, has a physiological sexual aspect. The only question, in respect to sexual desire, is how it should best be expressed, both for the fulfilment of each person and for the best shared life of the community. Thus sexual desire is a good enough place to start when we think of what desire comes to, in our experience. To say briefly what I believe that to be, let me put it this way: desire is the yearning, affective, deeply-felt urge for fulfilment. It is how love works, when it is not a chilly matter of 'rational approval' or a Kantian affair of willing the good—both of which, in my judgement, are so absurdly inadequate that they need no further comment.

If this be what desire in man comes to, what about desire in God? Here I wish to contradict the thesis of Anders Nygren's great work *Agape and Eros*. As you will recall, Nygren insists that in God there is no *eros* (the Greek word, by the way, for what I have been calling 'desire', which significantly also in Greek means 'love'); in God there is only *agape*, which Nygren interprets to mean the love which gives without regard either to the value of the recipient or the urgency on the part of the giver to receive a returning love. I believe that this notion is biblically unsound, in view of much that is said about bride-and-bridegroom, husband-and-wife, lover-and-beloved as symbolic of God's relation to the world. I know that it is psychologically untrue; I am sure that it is existentially nonsensical. Theologically, it is disastrous. God *is* love; and in His loving He both gives and receives. He shares; He opens up and delights in mutuality. Unless this be the case, the

Christian faith is sheer absurdity and should be rejected out-of-hand, for the God about whom it is talking cannot be the God Nygren presents. In fact, as somebody has pointed out, Nygren's God of sheer *agape*, in the meaning he gives that word, is a moral reflection of the untouched, unmoved, self-sufficient deity as *ens realissimum*—note the neuter gender—which Christian theologians have tried to join with the living, loving, caring God of the Hebrew-Christian scriptures—and have failed.

God as *desire*, or as I have put it earlier as the great Desire-for-good, is the yearning God, seeking to fulfil others in relationship with them, and by that very token seeking their returning love, which because it is given to Him freely is also His own fulfilment, His own enrichment. A view of God as one who can receive nothing because He already has or is everything is a pagan conception; it is an idol which no Christian should pretend to worship. Nor does he, since worship can be given only to the lovable, the perfectly lovable. Cringing fear is appropriate in the presence of such an 'absolute' as sometimes has been named God and only humiliating cringing is appropriate in the presence of a deity conceived after the analogy of the worst type of man we know—namely, the one who is so self-contained and unrelated that he wants and needs and welcomes nothing, since he is entirely self-sufficient. Aristotle's so-called 'magnanimous man', in the *Nichomachean Ethics*, seems to me a ghastly model for God, with that man's 're-markable condescension' but with his incapacity genuinely to *share*.

Furthermore, as G. K. Chesterton once acutely remarked, the Buddhist image of Gautama is a squatting man, with eyes closed, absorbed in inner thought, and possessed of the kind of peace which is had through rejecting all desire. On the other hand, the Christian symbol is a Man hanging on a Cross, with His eyes wide open, embracing in passionate yearning the whole of the world. So George Tyrrell wrote. The contrast is significant. Certainly the one God is at work in Buddhism, but it must be *in spite of* that image of Gautama. Yet the Buddha was right in saying that desire is the cause of the world's suffering. It is, because to love with desire *is* to suffer. He forgot to say that it is also the cause of the world's joy, since to love with desire is the only way to abiding happiness, in the true meaning of that much mis-used word. God both suffers and rejoices—and the picture of Him as experiencing both is the unique thing about the Christian affirmation of Him.

Now I must say something more about that quotation from Mother Julian: that the world continues because 'God made it, God loves it, God keeps it.' It seems to me that we have here the basic grasp of 'how things go' which enabled Mother Julian also to see that 'all shall be well, all shall be well, all manner of things shall be well'. The two together give us the ground for the ultimate optimism which in Christian faith conquers all provisional pessimism. She knew that 'the world is in God's hands', as the negro spiritual says—God made it, God loves it, God keeps it. Everything is safe that is worth saving. So no Christian need fear. Hence, as I have quoted Kirsopp Lake as saying, faith is not 'belief in spite of evidence', although the evidence from time to time may be very powerful and disturbing to us; it is 'life in scorn of consequence' and it is an adventure and a risk and a challenge.

Faith is an invitation to become lovers. That is what it works out as, in practical experience, when its significance is rightly apprehended. It points to God as cosmic love and cosmic lover, who gives to everything its beginning by providing its 'initial aim'. It points to God as active lover as it sees Him supremely active in the Man Jesus and in all who participate in His Spirit. It points to God as the lover who not only gives but receives and cherishes what He receives, as it sees Him to be 'the supreme affect', in whom all good finds its home. It points to Him as love faithfully and everlastingly at work, as it recognizes that He will use whatever good He receives, along with His own urgent desire for good, in furthering the expression of love in the creative advance which is the world.

89

The traditional scheme of the last things will no longer serve us, I have said; yet that scheme did confront men with the Christian faith and it did make them face 'reality' with honesty and humility. The purpose of this book has been to suggest ways in which what that traditional scheme did for our ancestors may still be vital for us today. That is all I tried to do; and I hope that with all their inadequacies and imperfections, these chapters have brought to your attention some, but not of course all, of those consequences of the faith which we share.

Let the conclusion be, not mine, but Robert Browning's, from *A Death in the Desert*:

> *For life*
> *With all it yields of joy and woe*
> *And hope and fear . . .*
> *Is just our chance o' the prize of learning love,*
> *How love might be, hath been indeed, and is.*

28 29 30 31 - - - 25 26 27

1973 DECE

MON | TUES | W

SEVEN

The Centrality of Love

Almost a quarter of a century ago Professor Dorothy Emmet wrote these words in her *The Nature of Metaphysical Thinking*: 'In the great positive religions, and pre-eminently in Christianity, the life of the founder is directly relevant. The religion does not simply grow from developing the content of the founder's teaching; the life of the founder is held to be one of the crucial moments, perhaps the crucial moment, of history, in which some new relation to the transcendent has been established. The historic religion seeks continually to re-affirm and express this relation; in rite, celebration, meditation, way of life; and its theology makes it the key to an interpretation of the world' (*op. cit.* pp. 155–56).

I believe that what Miss Emmet said is of enormous importance; and I wish to apply her words to the contemporary theological situation, especially in regard to the various 'radical' movements of our day.

The first point is that in all significant groups working towards the re-conception of Christianity today, Jesus Christ is taken to be 'directly relevant'. If there is any one fact universally present in today's Christian thinking, in all quarters, that fact is its 'christo-centric' character. All too often, it seems to me, the christo-centrism is exaggerated, so that Jesus stands in complete isolation from everything else; He is often regarded as being, not the central or definitive fact, but the *only* one which needs to be considered. This is a great mistake, for it removes Him effectively from His context, de-historicizes Him, and hence reduces (perhaps even negates) that 'direct relevance' to which Professor Emmet refers. None the less, Jesus *is* taken with utmost seriousness.

Furthermore, thanks to the work of a hundred years of biblical study, we no longer regard Christianity as simply 'developing the content of the founder's teaching.' It is His *life*— the whole reality of what nowadays it is fashionable to call the 'Christ-event'—which is seen to be 'crucial'. So we are delivered from the 'imitation of Jesus' type of theology and from that kind of reductionist thinking which interpreted Christianity as 'following a great prophet' and nothing more.

All this is on the positive side. But I think that a considerable number of 'radical theologians' are not prepared to go along with Miss Emmet when she says (rightly, I am convinced) that the 'life of the founder', in this instance Jesus, must in authentic Christianity be seen as both establishing 'some new relation to the transcendent' and making that life 'the key to an interpretation of the world'. It is not only that some of the anti-metaphysical theologians, not to speak of the American 'death of God' writers (theologians I will not call them, for to do so is to engage in a contradiction in terms), reject any reference to 'the transcendent' and hence can hardly talk meaningfully of a 'new relation' to it. What I have particularly in mind is that while there is much talk about taking Jesus as a key to the interpretation of *human* nature, as it is often phrased, or to the meaning of *human* life, or to the point of *man's* existential situation, there is a lamentable tendency to stop there and not to go on to talk about 'the world'—by which Miss Emmet meant, I assume, the totality of things including physical nature; in other words the cosmos in its basic structure and its chief dynamic energy.

Existentialist theologians, for example, seem to forget entirely that human existence, about which they talk so much, has a location in time and space and in a given part of the natural order. As I have put it elsewhere, all history has a geography. I find that many others, too, appear to be content to see Jesus as relevant to human affairs but hesitate to draw any conclusions about His relationship to the cosmic situation in which such affairs take place.

One of the reasons that some of us have been attracted to process-thought is its emphatic insistence on the cosmic structures and the cosmic dynamic. Process-thinkers have seen that man is a product of the evolutionary movement, just as much as anything else. If that is true, as obviously it is, the natural order must be interpreted in such a fashion that it permits us to account for human life—and if we do that, we must account also for the fact that in human history there has appeared the Man Jesus, with whom also we must come to terms. Or arguing in the other direction, if we take Jesus as significant for human life and history, He must also be seen as having some relationship to the setting of that life and history— the natural order—and hence be as much a 'disclosure' of that as He is of *man's* existence.

Historically the Christian tradition has spoken of Jesus as the incarnation of God, the manifestation of the divine reality 'in the flesh'. It has not presumed to think that we can get to that divine reality by some escape from the human situation; nor has it taken the view of a friend of mine who once said, to my astonishment, 'Let's look at this as God Himself sees it'. We cannot do anything of the sort; we are men and our knowing of anything whatsoever is as men and in terms of human experience. As Aquinas said, all knowledge is *ad modum recipientis*, and the 'mode' of our human receiving is the human mode, which is tautological but none the less true and never to be forgotten. This truth of our human situation is met, in Christian faith, by the claim that God 'has come in the flesh'. Hence, in St Augustine's words, 'we do not need to climb up to heaven to find him (we could not do that, in any event), since he has come to us where we are'.

But it is *God* who has come to us where we are, not just the truth about human life in supposed isolation from 'the transcendent' and from 'the world'. I am convinced that until and unless the modern theologians who are calling for a 'radical' reconstruction of Christianity recognize this, they will fail us utterly in our need to see Christian faith afresh. The *way* in which this was done in an earlier day certainly cannot be ours in this time; but the vision, insight, intuition, conviction—call it what you will—that Jesus Christ establishes with the transcendent a 'new relation' into which 'in rite, celebration, meditation, way of life' (to use Miss Emmet's phrases) we are permitted to enter and to have it made our own—notice I did not say 'make our own', which would deny the divine priority in this event—*is* Christianity. And the consequence is a 'key to the interpretation of the world' which includes *everything* and not simply human life in a presumed separation from that 'everything'.

Somewhere in *Appearance and Reality* the English idealist philosopher F. H. Bradley remarked that 'the man who, transported by his passion, feels and knows that only love gives the secret of the universe', is not engaging in proper metaphysical discourse. That is rubbish, in my view. I do not think that a Christian can for a moment accept Bradley's pejorative judgement. Precisely *that kind of man*, 'transported by his passion'—in this case his being caught up into a relationship with God in Christ, although it may very well be true in other ways as well, since to be 'transported' by passion is to enter upon the most profound experience possible to human beings —precisely such a man does feel and know what is nothing other than 'the secret of the universe'. The secret is that *God is love*; and it carries with it the corollary that God who is love 'works in all respects for a good end to those who love *him*', in the natural order as well as in history.

Of course this does not mean that everything becomes sweet and cosy; the fact that Love incarnate suffered crucifixion negates any such sentimentality. The 'good' towards which God works 'in all respects' is not comfort; nor is the Christian religion 'a research after comfort' (Whitehead properly denounced such a conception). None the less it *is* a 'good': it is, indeed, the Kingdom of God which is the sovereign rule of love into which those who respond to God's love are admitted—and in being admitted given the task of conforming this world of human affairs to the pattern of the Love 'which moves the sun and the other stars'.

Thus I am obliged to say, with H. H. Price, that theism, at least in a Christian sense, is 'a metaphysics of love'; and with this, I am obliged to affirm that 'the world', including nature in its farthest stretches as well as in the intimacy of human existence, is given its proper 'interpretation' only when 'the key' to it is found in Jesus Christ. That, essentially, is what Christian faith is all about—it has a cosmic sweep and is not to be accepted as an affair of human importance only. Its message, accepted on the grounds of faith and in the continuing activity of utter self-commitment to that which is spoken forth in the event of Christ, is precisely that 'love is all and more than all', in E. E. Cummings' telling phrase.

The tragedy of Christian theology is that this faith, this message, has not been given the central place which it not only deserves but demands. For far too many of the great theologies of the Christian tradition, the recognition of love has been a peripheral rather than the central concern. This manifests itself not only in the way in which Aristotelian notions of the 'unmoved mover' or neo-Platonic ideas of 'being-subsisting-from-itself' have been taken to be the proper definition of what is meant when we speak of 'God', but also in liturgical language where all too often the basic concept implied or (as most often seems to be the case) affirmed is the utter immutability of deity, along with the rigidly legalistic moralism which it is suggested should mark those who claim to 'obey' the divine mandates. Of course I have exaggerated here. There are plenty of instances, in the traditional liturgies, of emphasis on the sheer love of God, His being affected by human attitudes and responses, and the tender relationship which He intends between Him and His children. Yet I think that I do not exaggerate when I say that the chief impression received by an observer is precisely the divine impassibility, the intransigence of the divine demand, and the requirement from men of a servile obedience rather than life in 'the glorious liberty of the children of God'.

At the same time that Christian theology has so emphatically insisted on the divine absoluteness (taken in the sense which I have indicated), there have always been elements in that theology which have suggested another idea. In some of the greatest of the Church's teachers there has been a strange ambiguity. In St Augustine, for example, the personal relationship of man with God, as well as the deepest nature of God Himself, has been interpreted in terms of a love which the theological structure would seem to render almost absurd. St Thomas Aquinas was also a 'double-man', in that while he accepted and sought to develop a Christian interpretation of Aristotelian ideas in which Aristotle's 'unmoved mover' was given priority over the relational view of God, at the same time in his own sermons, prayers, and occasionally throughout his writings there is the stress on exactly that relational view. This kind of internal contradiction seems to run through much traditional theology; it finds explicit expression in Luther's dichotomy between the terrible God, who put him not only in awe but in utter terror, and the tender and loving God whom he knew in Jesus Christ as the saviour, the loving friend, and the gracious Father of men.

The real question is whether we are to make absolutely central in our thinking the 'love of God which was in Christ Jesus our Lord' or in one way or another regard that love as so adjectival to the divine substance that it appears to be irrelevant. Indeed, to talk of 'substance' here is in itself misleading; for the use of that term, despite all the protests of the neo-Thomists and others, is certain to bring us to think of God in terms of unchanging and unchangeable inert *stuff*—and to do that is to deny, *ab initio*, the possibility of a God who responds in complete faithfulness and with the utter integrity of His own nature, yet with deepest awareness and sympathy. In other words, we find it difficult if not impossible to move from the model of deity as primarily substantial being, existing in and of itself, to the model of deity as genuinely participant and really affected by what goes on in His world.

It is the purpose of this chapter to argue, from many different sides, that another way is required. This is the way which is provided if we adopt, not the so-called 'classical' view of God, but the 'neo-classical' view—a view which stresses the relational aspects as being much more than *merely* aspects—as being, in fact the basic reality of God Himself. Unquestionably this will present very difficult problems for Christian theology and especially for the sort of theology which has been conventional during most of Christian history. Yet there is nothing sacred about that theology as such; for what is abiding in Christian faith is not this or that theological formulation, however widely accepted, but exactly what Professor Emmet has said: 'the life of the founder', the 'new relationship to the transcendent' which that life has disclosed, and hence the total impact of Jesus Christ on men, in all its richness and depth. If *this* is the abiding Christian 'thing', then theologies may be subject to change, as we come to understand more and more adequately what is being disclosed to us in the person of Jesus Christ. And what is being disclosed, I repeat, is the utter centrality of love.

We need not *blame* our fathers in the Christian tradition for what they did, although we may regret much of it and wonder how ever they could have said what so often they did say. What is required is to understand how, under the particular circumstances which were naturally theirs, they took the positions they did. But this does not entail *our* taking those same positions, especially in respect to such a central point as this one. The requirement from us is to do for our time, in the light of a deeper apprehension of the centrality of love, what in their own way they sought to do in their time. This will mean, I am certain, that we shall be obliged to give up that model of deity which, with the best intentions, they accepted from the general philosophy of the time. But it will not mean that the true 'intentionality' (as I may phrase it) which was theirs will be forgotten.

If we have available a philosophical conceptuality which is more congruous with Christian love, we shall be prepared to use that conceptuality in the task of theological re-construction. Yet in doing so, we must have the wit and wisdom to discern that in their insistence on the divine changelessness and even on the divine impassibility, they had hold of something important. We cannot phrase it as they did; but we can see that what they were talking about was the utter reliability of God, His faithfulness to His purpose, His inexhaustibility, His never ceasing to be and to act in accordance with His undeviating purpose of love. If *they* felt themselves forced to express this 'intentionality' in terms of a philosophical concept which for us is incredible, this must not suggest that the 'intentionality' in and of itself was wrong. There is a difference between the deepest instinct and desire which was theirs and the particular language (and with that language, the philosophical notions which it entailed) which they employed in stating that instinct and desire.

In any event, the point of this chapter, intended to prepare the way for further discussion of what I have styled 'another' (and I am convinced a *better*) theological approach, is simply to insist that we can only be loyal to our ancestors in the Christian tradition, but above all loyal to the chief stress in the faith which that tradition has conveyed to us, if and when and as we are ready to put stress on love's centrality—and to use *that* as our key to the whole theological enterprise.

Now almost all Christians would agree that Wesley was correct in writing of God that 'his nature and his name is love'. It would seem obvious to them that this is the Christian claim and many of them would say, if they heard us stress the absolute centrality of this assertion, 'Of course, that is taken for granted'. Right there, I think, is the problem. We simply cannot 'take it for granted' that 'God is love' and let matters rest there. Failure to go further, failure to see the shattering nature of that assertion, is the reason for an enormous amount of misunderstanding and the occasion for an even larger amount of misinterpretation of the Christian doctrine of God.

This was brought home to me not long ago when, after a lecture on the subject of 'process-theology', in which I had stressed the Johannine text, a member of my audience rose to put the following question: 'Of course it is the Christian faith that God is love. But unless God's love is backed by His power, what guarantee have we that it will triumph in the end and that Mother Julian's conviction that "all shall be well" will be vindicated?'

The short answer to the question would have been that my questioner obviously did not himself believe that God's love is very important. *If* love, in order to be truly effective, must be associated with coercive force—as he indicated was to him essential—then it is apparent that love is *not* recognized as supreme. What *is* supreme is power. He was saying that love is a very fine thing, that there ought to be more of it, that in some way or other God does care, but that in the long run the really effective instrument in God's control of the world is His capacity to coerce. It is as if someone offered us, with his left hand, the gift of love; and then, with his right hand, made a fist at us and said, 'If you won't accept love, I'll knock you down'. In other words, in such talk love is *not* the basic dynamic in the world; it is *not* the deepest and highest reality; it is *not* the essential definition of God. And so all the verbal assertions that 'God is love' really amount to nothing; they are *only* verbal assertions, with no genuine grounding in the structure of things and in how things go in the world. In my judgement, this is a denial of the central insight of Christian faith; it is the ultimate treachery.

Part of the problem, of course, lies in the meaning of *power*. If by power we intend to signify, as most often *is* intended, the use of coercive measures whether these be overt or subtle and hidden, then it would seem that to ascribe such a quality to God as His chief characteristic—as in fact, if not in word, is suggested when people talk as did my questioner—is a denial of the point of Christ's disclosure of God. Yet there is a sense in which love itself is powerful. By this I mean that although love will not use coercive measures, driving people to do what they will not do otherwise, *making them* (as the phrase has it) act in contradiction to their own freely chosen decision, love is the *most* powerful of all agencies in the world. This is because love can win response when nothing else can do so; it can lure, elicit, attract, incite—and in this way it can accomplish its ends.

Yet at the same time the ends which love would accomplish are not the selfish sort which would imply that the lover is seeking his own fulfilment without regard for the loved one. On the contrary, the ends which love seeks to accomplish and which only love can accomplish are always ends which are mutually shared and in which the loved one finds his fulfilment too. In other words, when love is central to the picture, we see *ends* and *means* to be 'of a piece'—the end is loved shared, the means is the sharing of love.

I believe that considerations of this sort are of quite enormous significance today. It might be said that the history of the past half-century is the story of human attempts to secure world-community, the triumph of righteousness and justice, the establishment of understanding among the peoples of the earth, but always through the exercise of some variety of coercion. The result has been anything but what was initially desired. The utter bankruptcy of power, in the coercive meaning of the word, is apparent.

This, I take it, explains the revulsion of so many young people—to take but one obvious example—from the political game, their contempt for warmongers and their unwillingness (as in the United States) to participate in a conflict which they feel will accomplish nothing save further suffering. Hence there is a surprising rediscovery of love among modern youth as the only means to the end, and at the same time an insistence that love is *also* the end to be sought. We may dismiss these young people as 'idealistic', even when at the same time they are criticized for being too 'realistic' in (say) their approach to human relations, especially in sexual matters. We may dismiss youth as being unwilling to be, as we think older folk are, starkly 'realistic' about the fact of power and its necessity in national, international, social, economic, industrial, and other areas of human society. But such criticisms, either of the 'idealism' of youth or of their 'unrealistic' appraisal of the situation, come very ill from people like ourselves. It is precisely *our* settling for the use of power, *our* unwillingness to 'try love', and *our* cynical distrust of the possibilities in love as means towards love as an end, which has brought us to the state we are in.

That force must sometimes be employed is not to be denied —very likely there was no other way in which Nazism, for example, could have been defeated in the short run; I am not advocating complete pacifism in every situation. But I am insisting that for Christians at least their religious conviction should be clear and the consequences of that conviction in their list of priorities as to means should be equally clear. If we *must* use coercion, then let us know that we are doing so; let us admit honestly that insofar as this is done we are not obeying the perfect divine will; let us recognize that at best the use of such force is a *pis-aller*, not the entirely right thing. And if and when force is used, let us not hallow it by thinking of *God* as essentially such coercive power. Above all, let us be repentant of the use we make of force and let us act, once force *has* been used, in such a manner that its evil sting is (if not removed then) drawn and the poison which it injects into the life of men is drained out by the renewed employment of loving action, concern, caring, and self-giving. Only so can we in any sense justify the force which we may have felt impelled to use in this or that given circumstance—we can never *glory* in coercion.

But I must return to the main point of this chapter, which is that we must decide, once and for all, whether we are to give priority in our thinking about God to the concept of love or to the concept of power. Yet that is not quite the right way to put it, since we are not dealing with concepts (which are abstract ideas) but with what nowadays would be called 'models'. What *model*, then, is to be chosen? If we chose power for our model, thinking of God in terms of a person known to us who exemplifies this quality (we must think in this fashion, however anthropomorphic it may appear, although we must carefully 'qualify' our model), it will follow that love will be adjectival and in a secondary place. On the other hand, if we decide for the model of love, thinking of God as more like a human lover (but with defects, imperfections, frustrations, distortions removed), it will follow that whatever power *is* exercised by Him will be loving in its essential quality.

This theological decision has consequences in practically every area—I should venture, even, to say in *every* area—of faith. An obvious instance has to do with the relation of grace and freedom. For centuries, men have worried about this problem: *if* God's grace is indeed His activity, coming before and present in every good human act, how *can* such acts be truly free and responsible acts on the part of the human agent? If God acts, then man's response is not truly his own. If a human act is genuinely free, then where does God come into it? So the problem has been posed. But surely that way of stating it presupposes that God's grace is coercive power. The model which has been assumed, before the problem is discussed, makes possible only the absolutely over-riding quality of God's action, man being only a puppet in God's hands. Or, from the other side, it is human agency which is in control and God can 'enter in' only as a sort of extra.

If the model of God is taken from the realm of loving relationships, however, things are seen very differently. In that case, God does not force His human children, nor do they act in entire independence of God's concern. The divine love is prevenient to, active in, and unfailingly related to everything that is done by men; but the way in which love works is through the luring, attraction, solicitation, invitation, to which we have referred. God's action is first, since He always loves men and surrounds them with His loving action—but it is genuinely loving action and hence not pressure of a coercive type. On the other hand, man too is active, but his activity is also in love; he responds freely to the love which is given him and in that response he knows that he is truly 'being himself', for he was intended by his creation to be a responding lover and in no sense a marionette pulled by strings manipulated by God—certainly not the victim of the divine coercion.

One could go through the catalogue of Christian doctrines and discover how in each of them a radical alteration will follow once we have decided that love, not power, is the decisive fact in God's 'ways with men'. It is obvious that a corollary is the recognition that love is always a *relationship*; and a relationship involves two who are in it—God to man, man to God—in which each of them is not only acting in a causal manner but also being acted upon in an affective manner. How different would be our thinking about the Atonement in such a context—to take but one other example. To take still a third, the understanding of the Incarnation would no longer fall into the dangerous trap of *either* 'God-made-man' or 'only' a very good Man who knows and serves God in a unique fashion.

Thus we can see that many, if not all, the most difficult questions in theological discussion have been vitiated by a peculiar variety of what Gilbert Ryle has taught us to call the 'category-mistake'. We have taken a set of ideas from one category—the force category—and have applied them almost without qualification to another category—the God-man relationship. What we should have done is to see that in the 'Galilean vision', as Whitehead called it, we have the clue to the proper category for use in the God-man relationship; the category is 'love in action', the divine Lover acting and the human intentional lover acting too. And then we should have found that the situation was very different from what it seemed to be when power was used as the interpretative key. Once accept the disclosure of God in Christ (and in all that is christ-like in human experience, for we ought not to be exclusively christo-centric in the narrower sense); once take that disclosure with utmost seriousness—and then God as 'pure unbounded love' becomes central in our thinking. It makes *all* the difference—and in my judgement, this difference is what Christian faith *is about*.

To take that key with such utmost seriousness and to use it with equal seriousness in the re-framing of Christian theology, will obviously require some very drastic changes in our ways of envisaging what the theological enterprise is all about. We may fear such changes; there is a tendency on the part of theologians to like things to continue as they have been. Yet risk is an element in life and it is also an element in all faith that is worth anybody's having. But on the other hand there would be a wonderful release of energy in thus accepting love's centrality, since love *is* a releasing (as well as a demanding and dangerous) matter.

Let me close with a little story—one which happens to be true in essence, even if there is a bit of embroidery in the way in which it was told to me many years ago. Perhaps it will illustrate my point about love and at the same time show that this emphasis is not entirely new in Christian thought.

In the reign of Charles I there was in Scotland a covenanting minister Samuel Rutherford, who was minister of Anworth in Galloway. One Saturday evening he was catechizing his children and servants. There was a knock at the door. He went to it, and the stormy wind blew in so that the tall tallow candles flickered and he could hardly see a venerable old man who stood muffled up in the rain. 'May I come in?' said the old man, 'And wouldst thou give me shelter for the night?' Rutherford at once said, 'Yes, right gladly. Come in and we will give thee porridge, but not before we finish our catechism.' 'I thank thee', said the stranger, 'and I shall be glad to take my share in the catechism with the others, if thou wilt.' So Rutherford went on asking questions around the family circle. It so chanced that when he came to the stranger, the question was, 'How many commandments be there?' 'Eleven', answered the stranger. 'Alas, sir', said Rutherford, 'I had thought that one so wise and venerable of aspect would have given a better answer. There be but ten.' 'Nay, kind host', replied the stranger, 'in truth there be eleven commandments.' Said Rutherford, 'But that cannot be; there are but ten.' The stranger then went on, 'Hast thou forgotten? There was One who said, "Behold, I give you a new commandment, that ye love one another."' Rutherford sprang to his feet. 'Who art thou?' he gasped. 'I am James Ussher', said the stranger, 'and I have come hither in private that I might have speech with thee.' It was the famous Archbishop Ussher, Primate of Ireland and one of the most eminent scholars of that day. 'Welcome indeed thou art', said Rutherford, 'thou wilt remain here, but tomorrow thou wilt preach in my church.' 'Yes, gladly', said the Archbishop; his eyes twinkled as he added, 'I think I have chosen my text already. Shall it not be from St John's Gospel, Chapter 13, verse 14?'

The text which Archbishop Ussher proposed runs like this: 'If I, then, your Lord and Master, have washed your feet; ye also ought to wash one another's feet.' It is found in that place where the Fourth Evangelist gives the account of the foot-washing in the Upper Room and where he cites the words of Jesus about the 'new commandment'. It is based on, indeed made possible by, the earlier words which the Evangelist writes as he begins this account: 'Jesus, knowing that the Father had given all things into his hands, and that he came from God and was going to God . . .' And *that* sentence assumes the truth of the even earlier words in the gospel narrative: 'Jesus . . . having loved his own which were in the world, he loved them unto the end . . .'

The Lord came from God precisely in order to love, in order to be the humanly visible instrument of the divine Charity. Christian theology, in my conviction, is nothing other than the explication and application of what that statement *means*.

EIGHT

After the 'Death of God'

The furore over the 'death of God' theology seems to have died down in the United States, but to continue undiminished in Britain. Perhaps this is because the publication in Britain of the writings of the advocates of this position was rather delayed; hence the impact which they make is very much a present reality. In the States, William Hamilton, among the first who talked and wrote in this vein, has said that the 'death of God' emphasis belongs to the past—the recent past, surely—and that today we must go beyond it. Whatever may have been the contribution it made, the contribution *has been* made; what comes next?

I do not myself subscribe to the view that theology works in the fashion which Hamilton's remark suggests—a sort of drunkard's progress, with no real direction and without obvious continuities. But I agree on three points: first, that the 'death of God' literature has made a contribution to theology, even if it is not the contribution which its spokesmen might think; secondly, that the movement is just as dead as its leaders said that 'God' was dead; and thirdly, that we must go forward to a doing of theology, in the Christian mode, which will take account of what that particular literature had to say. I wish to speak about these three points.

The talk about the 'death of God', I believe, was an extraordinarily misleading, even if highly provocative, way of saying something important. For what was really involved in the talk was the death of certain concepts of God, rather than a supposed death of God himself. One realizes that this interpretation has been denied by Thomas Altizer and other advocates of the view; they insist that they are talking about a genuine death of God as an historical occurrence. But even they show that the contrary is the case, as Altizer himself demonstrates when he claims that he is talking about the absolute immanence or 'presence-in-this-world' of the Word or Spirit, in consequence of the radical *kenosis* or self-emptying of the transcendent deity usually denoted by the word 'God'. That Word or Spirit most certainly is *not* dead; and Altizer's 'gospel' is precisely the reality in human experience and in the world-order of that Word or Spirit with whom men must reckon whether they wish to do so or not.

I am convinced that what has died, that whose death has been announced, is a series of models, images, pictures, or concepts of deity which for a very long time have been taken by considerable numbers of people to be the Christian way of understanding God. It is important in this connexion to note that each of the three leading advocates of the position is in reaction against a notion of God that represents just such a series of models. Paul van Buren was a disciple of Karl Barth, under whom he wrote his excellent doctoral dissertation on Calvin's teaching about Christ as the true life of men; Hamilton was an opponent of natural theology in all its forms, even if he studied at St Andrews under Donald Baillie—but it was the so-called 'neo-orthodox' line which had attracted him, theologically; Altizer is a slightly different case. He worked under Paul Tillich and with Mircea Eliade, but his reaction has been *against* the aspects of Tillich's thought which stressed 'being-itself' in God and *for* those aspects which emphasized the need for radical re-conception of Christian thought.

Whitehead, to whom I shall return, wrote in *Process and Reality* many years ago that the Christian theological tradition has tended to conceive of God in three ways, each of them mistaken: as 'the ruling Caesar, or the ruthless moralist, or the unmoved mover'. It has failed to give central place to what he styled 'the Galilean vision', in which God is shown as persuasion or love. Hence, in his striking phrase, 'the Church gave unto God the attributes which belonged exclusively to Caesar', seeing him 'in the image of an imperial ruler', 'in the image of a personification of moral energy', or 'in the image of an ultimate philosophical principle'. With certain qualifications I should say that Whitehead stated the facts here.

In various combinations and with differing emphases, the concept of God with which many Christian thinkers have tended to work has been composed of exactly those ingredients; absolute power, stark moral demand, and unconditioned (essentially unrelated, in the sense of a two-way movement) 'being-itself' as the ultimate cause of everything not-God, but not in any way affected by that which was not itself —and the neuter here is highly significant, *ens realissimum*. Great theologians, like Augustine and Aquinas (to name but two), have worked in this fashion; but they were also strangely discontented in doing so, since their *real* faith was in the biblical God of unfailing love-in-action, effecting his purpose of love in nature and history, and most profoundly open to and receptive of what went on in the world. Hence the ambiguity which (as I think) one can see running through so many of the great theologies.

But it was the stress on power, on 'ruthless moralism', and on transcendence in the sense of non-relationship, which many took to be demanded when one talked of God, although one might also add, as a kind of afterthought, 'Oh yes, he is also loving'. I do not parody here, for I myself have found often enough that when I have tried to present a theological point of view which made the reality of love absolutely central, and put the other so-called divine attributes in a place secondary to that love, I have been met with the response, 'Of course God is loving, but we have to begin with His omnipotence, or His transcendence, or His aseity (self-contained and self-existence), or His absolute righteousness with its consequent demands on men'.

This procedure seems to me to be entirely wrong, however traditional it may be. What we ought to do is to start with God self-disclosed in human affairs as love-in-action. Then, and only then, can we use (adverbially, as it were) the other so-called attributes. God as love-in-action is more than any particular expression of His love (hence He is transcendent); God as love-in-action is always available (hence He is omnipresent); God as love-in-action is able to envisage every situation in its deepest and truest reality and accommodate Himself to it, so that He can indeed achieve His loving ends (hence He is omniscient and omnipotent); God as love-in-action is unswerving in His love, unfailing in its expression, unyielding in His desire to confront men with the demands of love (hence He is righteous). If we had worked in that way, we should have been saved from many of our supposedly insoluble theological problems, most of which are based on taking the other, and as I think wrong, approach.

However this may be, the fact is plain that for contemporary men and women, not only of a sophisticated sort but also of quite ordinary attainments, the notion of God as absolute power, as unyielding moral dictator, and as metaphysical first cause never Himself affected, has gone dead. There are many reasons why this has happened; this is no place to discuss them, but among others we may mention scientific constructions, psychological discoveries, awareness of sociological conditions, and all that Bonhoeffer summed up in saying that man has 'come of age' (by which he did *not* mean that man is an entirely mature and adult creature who now can take the place of God, in a fashion not unlike the claim made by the Provost of King's in his recent utterances; but he *did* mean that we now know our own responsibility and that God treats us, not like slaves nor like little children, but like sons to whom He entrusts such responsibility). This 'going dead' of the notions I have mentioned is stated plainly for us in the writers who speak of 'the death of God'.

So much for my first point. My second is that the movement

called by that name is now itself a matter of the past; it has made its contribution and that is that. It has taught us something, and by now we ought to have learned what it had to teach us. Of course the learning has not been done simultaneously in all parts of the Christian world or anywhere else. Hence for some of us, it might be said, the situation is still *pre*-'death of God'; and, for those who are in this situation, the lesson is still to be learned. But for those who have got an inkling of what this is all about, who have learned the lesson, the situation is *post*-'death of God'; we must now go on to the constructive task.

I shall not spend time in showing how and why we are in that 'post' era. I only call in witness the remarks of Hamilton which I have already cited. He at least feels that the 'calling in question', the denials, the stark affirmation of the 'end of sheer transcendence, sheer moralism, sheer power' (as I like to put it), has been accomplished. So the problem for us, as for him, may be phrased in a typically American way: 'Where do we go from here?' And it is with that question that the remainder of this chapter will concern itself. But the one thing that is quite clear is that we do *not* 'go back', as if we could return to the older ideas and concepts, quite unchanged by what has happened during the past few decades. If we cannot retreat, rest content in the denials, the 'calling in question', and the like, neither can we into one of the theologies of the past. If I may say so, this is what I find troublesome in the writing of Dr Mascall on the subject. He is usually very sound in his criticisms of the 'death of God' school and, indeed, of the whole 'radical theology' which in one way or another is associated with it. But because of his failure to understand *why* such a theology in its various forms has appeared, he is unable to see any other solution than a 'return'. Leonard Hodgson, in his review in *Theology* of *The Secularization of Christianity*, made this point about Mascall; and he made it with such clarity and precision that I need only mention it here.

In going forward, then, with Christian theology *after* 'the death of God', we have several options. Let me mention some of them, assuming that we cannot work with Thomism (either 'classical' or 'revised'), nor with that peculiar Anglican affair known as 'liberal Catholicism' in the style of *Essays Catholic and Critical* or the writings of Charles Gore, nor with 'liberalism' in its reductionist form as found in Harnack or Harnack *redivivus*, nor in sheer biblicism in its fundamentalist dress. So I mention the following possibilities, getting some of them from an excellent little book of lectures given in Chicago a couple of years ago, *Philosophical Resources for Christian Faith*: (1) existentialism in some mode; (2) phenomenological (and in that sense non-metaphysical) enquiry; (3) analytical philosophy and its talk about *bliks* and various 'language games'; (4) process thought in its several forms. To these four I should add the so-styled 'secular theology' often advocated today, with a side-glance at revived and restated 'biblical theology'. Here are six possibilities.

Of some of them I must speak very briefly. For example, the kind of 'biblical theology' sometimes advocated assumes that we should go forward by taking with utmost seriousness the biblical images or motifs—not the literal, textual stuff of Scripture, which would involve us in a kind of new 'fundamentalism', but the main-line of biblical images. I am very much in sympathy with this approach, so far as it goes. For Christians the biblical images and patterns are of *first* importance, since it is from them that the Christian picture of God takes its rise. But it must be pointed out that these images and patterns are most diverse; further, they belong, in their explicit shape, to ages in which we do not ourselves live. Hence what is required is just what Leonard Hodgson has so often, and rightly, demanded: we must ask ourselves what the case *really is*, so far as we can grasp it today, if people who thought and wrote *like that*, phrased it in the way they did. Otherwise we shall be using the Scriptures in a very wooden and unimaginative fashion, even if we do not succumb to literalism in its obvious sense. Furthermore, if we wish to communicate the deepest meaning of those images and patterns, we dare not rest content with them as they stand. That would be to resemble the Chinese who, when shipwrecked on a desert island, made their living by taking in each other's laundry. We must translate if we wish to communicate.

Again, the use of analytical philosophy will help us enormously in the way in which we use words. It will enable us to clarify our language, to avoid contradiction, to stop talking sheer nonsense, to look for some kind of referent which will give the necessary verification to what we are saying as Christians. All this is of great importance, lest we fall into the temptation to use high-sounding words for the evasion of difficulties. It has been said that whenever some older theologians got to a hard place they simply quoted a few lines of Wordsworth or Tennyson, thinking that ended the matter; or they made a few biblical citations as if that were the complete answer; or (at worst), when the attack was most fierce, they used the word 'mystery' as a kind of 'escape-hatch'. But analytical philosophy is a neutral discipline—for which we may be grateful—and it gives us no working conceptuality for the statement of the theological implications of Christian faith with the claims that faith makes about 'how things really go in the world'.

The kind of phenomenological method which is often advocated is of a non-metaphysical type; that is, it is interested in description, in terms of how living religion, as a matter of deepest intuitive observation, effectively operates in human experience in the world where men live. This seems to me to be most valuable; a van der Leeuw, an Eliade, and others like these, can help us a great deal. How does faith function, what embodiments does it have, what attitudes does it demand? These are questions which ought to be answered. But I cannot think that their answer will provide the general conceptuality which we require if Christian faith is to be grounded in the stuff of reality and if the case for it is to be made in a manner which speaks meaningfully to the men and women for whom it exists and to whom it is supposed to address itself.

We are left with three possibilities: 'secular theology', an existentialist theology, and a process theology. I shall say something about each of them—and, as my ordering indicates, I shall come down in favour of the last of the three, as offering us the best conceptuality available today as we go forward from 'the death of God'.

The phrase 'secular theology' may be taken to mean one of two things: either a theology *of* the secular or a theology which *confines itself to* the secular realm. Since I have spoken critically of Dr Mascall I am glad to say here that I believe that he has written admirably about this distinction in the last part of his recent *Theology and the Future*. He has pointed out that a theology which is strictly *confined* to the world of 'here and now' cannot take account of the ultimate questions which men must ask, whereas every sound Christian theology is required indeed to speak of that 'here and now', but to relate it to God as a creative principle and to see God at work in the immediacies of human existence in the whole range of what we style 'secular existence'. In other words, I agree that Christian faith must see God *in the world* but that it cannot remain content with 'the world' as if it exhausted all there is of God. Whitehead once said that 'God is in this world or he is nowhere'; that is entirely sound. But Whitehead also said that the world and God are not identical; and I should interpret this utterance, along with others by him, to mean that there is in the divine life an exhaustibility which makes possible the wonderful novelty which the created order manifests, disclosing what Gerard Manley Hopkins named 'the dearest freshness deep down things'.

In any event, if a 'secular' approach to theology thinks that it avoids all metaphysical conceptions, it is profoundly mistaken. Of course one can mean what one wants by the word 'metaphysical'. If one intends to speak of a grandiose construction in terms of supernatural entities, with a schematic ordering of everything according to some superimposed pattern, metaphysics may very well be denied. It seems to me that the present-day attack on metaphysics is nothing more than an attack on idealistic constructions of this type, after the fashion (say) of Hegel or Bradley. But metaphysics can also mean—and process thinkers would say that it ought to mean— the inevitable human enterprise of generalizations widely applied, on the basis of a particular point or event or experience taken as 'important', to the rest of our experience of the world and the world which we surely experience. It can mean, then, the development of those principles which most adequately express what we experience and know, in the full range of our human encounters; and the result is a 'vision' which can be tested by reference back to experience and to the world experienced. Metaphysics in this mode is not some highly speculative system imposed on the world. It is an induction from what is known of the world. Everybody engages in this, usually in a very naïve manner; the 'philosopher', so styled, is only one who in a more sophisticated and critical manner engages in this attempt at making sense of things, including human experience.

But the self-styled 'secular theologian' is doing exactly that. You have only to read Gregor Smith, whose untimely death we all lament, to observe this. Both in *The New Man* and in *Secular Christianity* Gregor Smith is actively setting forth *this* kind of metaphysics, taking as his 'important' moment or event the historical encounters of men, specifically with Jesus, and from these developing a view of the generalized situation of man-in-the-world which, in my sense of the word, is inescapably metaphysical, even if he himself rejects the word and thinks that he is also rejecting the enterprise. What he is rejecting, it turns out, is only that 'supernaturalistic' species of metaphysics which idealistic philosophers have set forth in a pretentious claim to encompass in their thought all things in earth and heaven.

Thus, as I see it, the options which remain are in fact two: either an existentialist approach or a 'process thought' approach, since the 'secular' theology in itself does nothing more than deny a particular kind of metaphysic and leaves us open to the possibility of interpreting the secular world, and everything else in human experience, in some appropriate manner.

The existentialist approach in contemporary English-written theology has been associated with two names: one is Paul Tillich, the other John Macquarrie. I cannot mention the name of Tillich without reverence, for that great and good man was a dear friend of mine and I respect, honour, and love him, though he has now gone from us. His theology was an attempt to combine an existentialist analysis of the human situation with a Christian faith interpreted along the lines of German idealistic thought; he himself confessed that Schelling had been his great master. His method of correlation is, I believe, very suggestive and helpful; his masterly analysis of what it is like to be human is almost beyond criticism. But his final 'system', as he used to call it, seems to me to be too abstract in its statement to convey the Christian gospel, although in his preaching he was anything but abstract. I think that Professor Macquarrie's efforts, especially in *Principles of Christian Theology*, offer a much more 'available' approach for most of us. His insistence that every existential analysis presupposes and includes ontological affirmations seems to me right and sound; his way of using Heideggerian thought is instructive. He takes the biblical images with utmost seriousness and employs them effectively as being determinative of the total picture of God–world–man in the light of Jesus Christ.

If I were to make any criticisms of this existentialist mode of theologizing it would be to say that it is not sufficiently regardful of nature, in the strict sense of the physical world and the material stuff of things. And I should add that it lacks something of the dynamism which I believe is required of any Christian theology, not only because of the dynamic quality of biblical thought itself but also (and more significantly) because of the evolutionary way of things which men like

Teilhard de Chardin have so insistently pressed upon us. But I confess that *if* I did not find process theology more appealing I should opt for Macquarrie's approach. At the same time I must say that if those two criticisms of mine were met sufficiently, there would not be too much (I think) to differentiate *his* way from the one to which I now turn in conclusion.

It is not necessary for me to outline my reasons for preferring process thought; I have already indicated these in my book *Process Thought and Christian Faith*. It will suffice if I note that process thought regards the world as a dynamic process of inter-related (and hence social) organisms or entities, whose intentional movement is towards shared good in widest and most inclusive expression; and that it interprets deity along *those* lines. God is no unmoved mover, dictatorial Caesar, nor 'ruthless moralist'; He is the cosmic lover, both causative and affected, 'first cause and final affect' as Schubert Ogden has so well phrased it. He is always *related*, hence always *relational*; He is eminently *temporal*, sharing in the ongoing which *is* time. His transcendence is in His sheer faithfulness to Himself as love, in His inexhaustibility as lover, and in His capacity for endless adaptation to circumstances in which His love may be active. He does not coerce; He lures and attracts and solicits and invites. He waits for free response from the creaturely agent, using such response (which He has incited by His providing 'initial aims') to secure the decisions which enable the agent to make actual his own (the agent's) 'subjective aim'. In the historical realm and in human life He discloses Himself, precisely as love-in-action, in the total event which we name Jesus Christ. Since His love-in-operation is His essential nature—He *is* love, which is His 'root-attribute', not *aseity*, as the older theology claimed—the other things said about Him (transcendence, immanence, omnipotence, omniscience, omni-presence, righteousness, etc.) are to be understood, as I have already argued earlier, as adverbially descriptive of His *mode of being love* rather than set up as separate or even as distinct attributions.

We live in a 'becoming' world, not in a static machine-like world. And God Himself is 'on the move'. Although He is never surpassed by anything in the creation, He can increase in the richness of His own experience and in the relationships which He has with that creation. He is the *living* God; in that sense, we may say (as the title of a recent book of mine dares to do) that God is 'in process'. In other words, the basic point of the biblical images of God as the living, active, loving, personalizing agent is guaranteed.

But above all, since He is no dictator after the model of Caesar, no self contained being after the model of the worst sort of man we know, no moralist after the model of the puritanical and negative code-maker, He is truly to be worshipped. Worship means 'ascribing worth'; and this we can do only to a lovable because loving One. We cringe before power expressed coercively and arbitrarily; we tremble in the presence of rigid moralism, when we do not react against it in wild and desperate efforts to be ourselves; we can only be puzzled by the kind of absolute essence which is without affects from what goes on around and about it. But we can worship, truly 'ascribe worth', to the perfection or excellence which is love in its eminent and supreme form. God is that; hence He is adorable.

What is more, He is imitable. And with that affirmation I must end. We are to imitate God; both Aristotle and Plato said so, whilst Jesus gave it content by saying that we were to be 'like our Father in heaven'. Known as love-in-action, disclosed as that love by the event in which Jesus is central, caught up into life 'in love' (which, if 1 John 4 is right, *is* life 'in God'), we are enabled to become what God intends us to be, created lovers. That is why we are here; that is our destiny—or else Christianity is a fraud.